Sense and Nonsense about Crime and Drugs

A Policy Guide

Fifth Edition

Samuel Walker

University of Nebraska at Omaha

WADSWORTH

THOMSON LEARNING ™

Australia • Canada • Mexico • Singapore • Spain • United Kingdom • United States

WADSWORTH

THOMSON LEARNING™

Executive Editor, Criminal Justice: Sabra Horne
Development Editor: Terri Edwards
Assistant Editor: Ann Tsai
Editorial Assistant: Cortney Bruggink
Marketing Manager: Jennifer Somerville
Project Editor: Jennie Redwitz
Print Buyer: Mary Noel

Permissions Editor: Joohee Lee
Production Service: Matrix Productions
Copy Editor: Vicki Nelson
Illustrator: Asterisk Group
Cover Designer: Sandy Drooker
Cover Printer: Malloy Lithographing, Inc.
Compositor: TBH Typecast, Inc.
Printer: Malloy Lithographing, Inc.

For permission to use material from this text, contact us by **Web:**
http://www.thomsonrights.com
Fax: 1-800-730-2215 **Phone:** 1-800-730-2214

Library of Congress Cataloging-in-Publication Data
Walker, Samuel, [date]
    Sense and nonsense about crime and drugs : a policy guide / Samuel Walker.—5th ed.
        p. cm
    Includes bibliographical references and index.
    ISBN 0-534-55436-9 (alk. paper)
        1. Criminal justice, Administration of—United States.   2. Crime Prevention—United States.
    3. Drug abuse and crime—United States.
    4. Narcotics, Control of—United States.   I. Title.
    HV9950.W35 2000
    364.4'056'0973—dc21
                                    00-039889

Wadsworth/Thomson Learning
10 Davis Drive
Belmont, CA 94002-3098
USA

For more information about our products, contact us:
Thomson Learning Academic Resource Center
1-800-423-0563
http://www.wadsworth.com

International Headquarters
Thomson Learning
International Division
290 Harbor Drive, 2nd Floor
Stamford, CT 06902-7477
USA

UK/Europe/Middle East/South Africa
Thomson Learning
Berkshire House
168-173 High Holborn
London WC1V 7AA
United Kingdom

Asia
Thomson Learning
60 Albert Street, #15-01
Albert Complex
Singapore 189969

Canada
Nelson Thomson Learning
1120 Birchmount Road
Toronto, Ontario M1K 5G4
Canada

Contents

Propositions

1. Most current crime control proposals are nonsense.
2. Waging "war" is the wrong way to fight crime.
3. Both liberals and conservatives are guilty of peddling nonsense about crime.
4. Most crime control ideas rest on faith rather than facts.
5. Most crime control proposals are based on false assumptions about how the criminal justice system works.
6. Simply adding more police officers will not reduce crime.
7. Carefully planned problem-oriented policing strategies, directed toward limited geographic areas and involving non-criminal justice resource, can be successful in reducing crime and disorder.
8. Faster response time will not produce more arrests or lower the crime rate.
9. More detectives, or other changes in detective work, will not raise clearance rates or lower the crime rate.
10. Repeal or modification of the exclusionary rule will not help the police reduce serious crime.
11. Repeal or modification of the *Miranda* warning will not result in more convictions.
12. The death penalty does not deter crime.
13. Enforcement crackdowns do not deter crime over the long term.

14. Deterrence oriented policies that rely exclusively on criminal law enforcement do not enhance the inherent deterrent effect of the criminal justice system.
15. Preventive detention will not reduce serious crime.
16. Speedy trials can reduce pretrial crime while preserving constitutional rights.
17. Selective incapacitation is not a realistic strategy for reducing serious crime.
18. Gross incapacitation is not a realistic policy for reducing serious crime.
19. Mandatory sentencing is not an effective strategy for reducing serious crime.
20. Three strikes and you're out laws are a terrible crime policy.
21. Career criminal prosecution programs do not produce either higher conviction rates or lower crime rates.
22. Abolishing or limiting the insanity defense will have no impact on serious crime.
23. Abolishing plea bargaining will not reduce serious crime.
24. Limiting habeas corpus appeals of criminal convictions will have no effect on serious crime.
25. With the possible exception of domestic violence shelters, social service programs for crime victims will not reduce serious crime.
26. Victim recontact programs will not reduce crime.
27. Victim compensation programs may help crime victims, but they will not reduce serious crime.
28. Victim impact statements will not reduce crime.
29. Policies intended to get tough on crime will not reduce crime, not help crime victims, and may instead damage the criminal justice system.
30. Attempts to ban hand guns, or certain kinds of guns, or bullets, are not likely to reduce serious crime.
31. Attempts to deny ownership of handguns to certain categories of "bad" people are not likely to reduce serious crime.
32. Focused, proactive enforcement strategies may be effective in reducing crime-related crime in targeted areas.
33. Trying to "get tough" on gun crimes, specially through mandatory prison sentences, will not reduce gun-related crime.
34. Diversion programs do not reduce serious crimes.
35. Probation is an appropriate sentence for many offenders, but there is not evidence that one kind of probation treatment is more effective in reducing crime than other kinds.
36. Abolishing parole will not reduce crime.
37. Boot camps do not reduce crime.
38. Intensive supervision, with either probation or parole, will not reduce serious crime.
39. Home confinement and electronic monitoring will not reduce crime.
40. The promise of restorative justice remains unproven in reducing serious crime.

41. Reducing discrimination, and the perception of injustice, may help to reduce serious crime.
42. With the possible exception of drugs (to be discussed in the next chapter), decriminalization will not reduce serious crime.
43. Police crackdowns will not reduce illegal drug use or serious crime associated with drugs.
44. Drug interdiction and eradication efforts are doomed to fail.
45. Tougher sentencing is not likely to reduce illegal drug use or serious crime associated with drugs.
46. There is no evidence that DARE or other drug education programs reduce illegal drug use.
47. Drug treatment can help individuals who have made a commitment to end their drug use. But there is no evidence that any treatment program consistently reduces drug use for all persons enrolled in the program.
48. The impact of legalizing drugs on serious crime is not known at this time.

✦

Foreword

Shortly after its initial publication, Samuel Walker's *Sense and Nonsense About Crime and Drugs: A Policy Guide* was recognized as an important new book, a substantial contribution to the literature on crime and justice. Over the years, as he has reworked its themes and developed its arguments in four new editions (in the third edition updating the title to reflect an expanded discussion of drugs and drug policy), the field's appreciation of this book has only gotten better. Today, it is a mainstay text in the study of crime and justice; some would call it a nascent classic work in the field. It is a respected argument about our knowledge base for crime and justice and it is one of those rare books that is deeply respected by scholars and policy makers alike.

It is, therefore, with extraordinary pleasure that I welcome this, the Fifth Edition, to the Wadsworth Contemporary Issues in Crime and Justice Series. The series is devoted to giving detailed and effective exposure to important or emerging issues and problems that ordinarily receive insufficient attention in traditional textbooks. The series also publishes books meant to provoke thought and change perspectives by challenging us to become more sophisticated consumers of crime and justice knowledge. If you are looking for a book that will make you an informed student of crime and justice policy and practice, you could not find a better book than the one you are now holding in your hand.

Why is this book so important? There are two reasons. First, so much of what is commonly believed about crime—and so much of what shapes public policy on crime—is nonsense. Second, Walker's book was the first, and still the most effective, book written to point that out. This book provides a masterful critique of the American penchant for short-sighted, metaphorical strategies about crime (boot camps are a good example) or feel-good rhetoric about crime priorities (end poverty, end crime) that have, over the years, not gotten us very far in our pursuit of a safer society. Today, we are enjoying a welcome, sustained, national drop in crime rates. But this drop still leaves us with higher rates of crime than we want and (perhaps more to the point) the source of the drop in crime is more of a mystery to us than a lesson in crime prevention policy.

The contribution of this book—what makes this book special—is its even-handed willingness to show how favorite strategies of diverse political agendas have, as their foundation, some degree of "nonsense." If there is a lesson this book brings to us repeatedly, it is that cherished images of crime and justice are flawed, inaccurate, doomed to fail for particular reasons of (more or less) well-known facts that we so often want to ignore in order to sustain our favorite ideologies. This book challenges us where we need to be challenged: in our willingness to ignore reality in order to nurture our too-frequently inadvisable pet ideas about crime and crime-fighting.

You want your police to be tough, chase dangerous criminals, make life-saving arrests? Well, Professor Walker points out that you have to contend with the fact that police spend very little of their time taking these actions and even when they do act that way, not much in the way of crime controls seems to result. You want your judges to lock 'em up and throw away the key? Walker shows all the ways that this belief is expensive and ineffective, even counter-productive. You think we need to save money through closer surveillance of the people convicted of crime? Make our lives safer by treating juveniles as though they were adults? End drug abuse through an all-out war on drugs? Here again, the book sheds cool light on hot emotions, showing how such strategies can backfire.

This book is not, however, just about nonsense in crime and justice. "Perhaps nonsense gets the majority of the attention, because so much of what we do is based on faulty thinking." Walker is willing to tell us about what makes "sense" as well. Big proposals lack much support and politically popular proposals may be downright silly. But there are small, less ambitious ways we can contribute to a safer society and we can do so without suspending our constitutional rights or giving up our public freedoms. By the time Professor Walker completes his analysis, what emerges is a powerfully dispassionate analysis of today's crime and justice policy. He gives us a carefully crafted challenge to start "making sense" in the way we talk about crime and the way we develop policies to cope with it.

If you are getting ready to read this book, chances are you are contemplating a career in the field of criminal justice. At the very least, you have an informed citizen's interest in the problems of crime and justice. In either case, you have come to the right place to become more intelligent in your pursuits. After you read this book, you will join a large number of its alumni, dedicated to crime policies that make sense. I commend you.

Todd R. Clear, Series Editor

❖

Preface

ompleting the Fifth Edition of this book is an occasion to reflect on what has changed and what has not changed in the world of criminal justice since the First edition was published in 1985.

In that year, the drug crack had only just begun to appear on the streets of America. Community policing was still a new and untested idea. Boot camps were also just a new idea. Crime rates were high, and the juvenile homicide rate was about to soar even higher. I doubt that any knowledgeable professionals in the criminal justice field would have predicted that the then–already high American prison population would soar to its current level.

Much has changed since 1985. Indeed, there have been significant changes since 1991–92. Most importantly the crime rate has been dropping steadily for eight straight years. It now seems clear that this is neither a temporary dip nor a statistical artifact. The decline in serious crime has occurred in most (although not all) major cities. The number of murders in New York, San Diego, and some other cities has fallen to levels not seen since the 1960s.

Something very positive is happening in this country, and not just in the area of crime. Teenage pregnancies have also fallen. Unemployment is at record low levels. New AIDS cases are down. Across the board, social indicators have been moving in a positive direction.

This situation presents us with a serious paradox. The basic argument of this book, from the First Edition to the present one, is that crime control ideas that are popular with the public and criminal justice professionals do not work.

As the title of this book expresses it, they are nonsense. This is true for putting more police on the street, locking up more offenders, and implementing drug treatment and education programs. The point of this book, from the first edition to the present one, has been to present in an accessible form the evidence on these various policies. But if these policies do not work, how do we explain the reduction in crime? This is a serious question that demands an answer.

The First Edition was written primarily as a response to the conservative crime control agenda that dominated public policy at the time. This conservative agenda stressed crime control through tougher law enforcement policies, including exciting new policy initiatives using the concepts of incapacitation, deterrence, and programs targeting career criminals. The book examined these proposals in light of what was then known about the administration of criminal justice. In the interests of fairness, I subjected liberal crime control policies to the same critical scrutiny. I found them equally lacking in empirical support.

By the time of the Third Edition, the wheel of the policy debate had changed in one significant respect. The conservative/liberal dichotomy that provided the framework for the first two editions was no longer as clearly defined as it was originally. Basically, the liberal perspective had collapsed, and most politicians who defined themselves as liberals had adopted most of the traditional conservative policy agenda: more police, more imprisonment, and so on. Meanwhile, some prominent conservatives had embraced the idea of legalizing drugs, a traditional liberal proposal. In short, the world of criminal justice policy has become more complex than it was when the first edition of this book appeared.

Finally, the state of knowledge about crime and criminal justice continues to advance. We know far more about what works and what does not than we did eighteen years ago when this book was originally conceived. I have attempted to incorporate this new knowledge with each edition. One consequence of the advancing state of knowledge is that many issues that once seemed simple are now ambiguous. With the advent of problem-oriented policing and community policing, for example, it is no longer possible to say that police efforts have no effect on the communities they serve. The exact nature of those effects and their durability over time are matters of controversy, but we cannot simply declare that nothing works. Similarly, it is not necessarily true that all forms of mandatory sentencing are evaded by courtroom work groups. It appears that some mandatory provisions are not fully implemented, but many are.

The administration of justice is extremely complex. In this book I have attempted to capture some of this complexity while at the same time providing students with a clear sense of the general patterns of the administration of justice.

ACKNOWLEDGMENTS

This fifth edition represents a substantial revision of my understanding of crime and the administration of justice. I would like to give special acknowledgment to my colleagues in the Department of Criminal Justice at the University of Nebraska at Omaha for the atmosphere of collegiality that we have maintained. Whenever I have a question on a particular issue, I can always walk down the hall, engage someone in a conversation, and come away with a new insight or at least some useful suggestions on where I should look for the information I need.

I would also like to thank Steve Kline for his cartoons giving this edition a fresh look. For their help with various aspects of revising the manuscript and preparing it for publication, I would like to thank my graduate research assistants Carol Archbold and Leigh Herbst.

Samuel Walker

PART I

❖

Thinking Clearly
about Crime

1

Crime and Policy:
A Complex Problem

THE MIRACLE OF FALLING CRIME RATES

Crime in America is down. For almost seven years now, beginning in the early 1990s, serious crime has been dropping dramatically. The FBI reports that the crime rate dropped 22 percent between 1991 and 1998 (and dropped another 10 percent in the first six months of 1999). The National Criminal Victimization Survey (NCVS), meanwhile, reports that "every major type of crime . . . decreased significantly between 1993 and 1998." Violent crime was down 27 percent and property crimes down 34 percent.[1]

The reduction has been particularly dramatic in certain cities. As Figure 1-1 indicates, both the murder and robbery rates in San Diego in 1999 were one-third the levels in 1991. A similar decline has occurred in New York City, where the number of murders in 1998 fell to levels not seen since the mid-1960s. In Boston, the number of homicides dropped from 152 in 1990 to 43 in 1997; among persons age 24 and under, they fell from 62 to 15, while firearms homicides among juveniles age 16 and under fell from 10 to none in 1996 (with one in 1997).[2]

Coming after three decades of high crime rates, the drop in serious crime seems like a miracle to many Americans. For the first time in a generation, there is good news. Something seems to be working. Since crime rates began to soar around 1962 and 1963, crime has ripped the social fabric of American society. In addition to the very real harm of particular crimes—the terrible

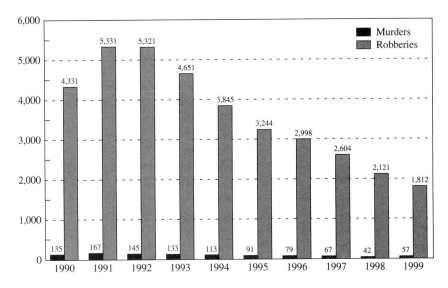

FIGURE 1-1 Murders and robberies, San Diego, 1990–1999.

SOURCE: San Diego Police Department.

human suffering of murder and rape, and the financial losses of burglary and theft—crime has generated massive fear in ordinary Americans and damaged the quality of life in our neighborhoods. Moreover, as a political issue, "crime" has been intertwined with the race issue and has contributed to the racial polarization of American society.

The current decline in serious crime is particularly surprising because only a few years ago some criminologists were predicting just the opposite. In 1996, for example, James Alan Fox warned of a "ticking time bomb" of violent crime in the near future because of the projected increase in the number of teenagers. But in fact, the homicide trends moved in exactly the opposite direction.[3]

Is It for Real?

Many skeptics ask whether the current decline in crime is real. Is it genuine or the result of a statistical artifact, or manipulated crime data, or simply a temporary drop? All of the evidence indicates that it is genuine. First, both of the two sets of government crime data, the Uniform Crime Reports (UCR) and the National Crime Victimization Survey (NCVS), confirm the trend. In the past, they have often reported different trends. Now, however, these two reports take the nation's temperature with different thermometers and get the same readings. It might be possible for one city to manipulate its crime data to make itself look good, but it is not possible that both the UCR and NCVS could be manipulated to this extent. Second, the decline in crime has continued now for about seven years and does not appear to be a temporary blip.

One of the reasons for this conclusion is that so many other social indicators—unemployment, births to teenage girls, and others—are moving in a positive direction and began moving at about the same time. We will have more to say about the trends in other social indicators shortly.

The Great American Paternity Fight

There is an old adage that failure is an orphan but success has many parents. So it is with the reduction in crime; everyone wants to claim responsibility for it. New York City officials claim that it is the result of the NYPD's "zero-tolerance" policy.[4] The White House claims it is the result of the 100,000 new police officers funded by the 1994 Violent Crime Control Act. Other policy makers believe it is the result of tough new sentencing laws that have incapacitated a large number of serious offenders. Some criminologists believe that the reduction is associated with a decline in the use of crack cocaine. Still others believe that it is one of several positive consequences of an extremely healthy economy.[5]

Where does the truth lie? Most leading criminologists are still reluctant to provide any definitive answers. Criminologist Lawrence W. Sherman says that "it is very hard to say with any certainty" what caused this change. Michael Smith of the Vera Institute believes that it is may be a broader "cultural trend which is difficult to define."[6]

THE PURPOSE OF THIS BOOK

This book attempts to answer these questions. It is a book about crime policy, a search for sensible answers to the basic question: *What works?* What policies are effective in reducing serious crime? Our agenda here is to review some of the major crime control proposals and evaluate their effectiveness in light of what we know about crime and justice. Previous editions of this book have sought to determine what *might* work. Now, in the face of steadily falling crime rates, we have to turn the question around: What *did* work? Did certain crime policies contribute to this phenomenon? If so, which ones? What is the evidence? For all practical purposes, the analysis in this book is the same. We want to determine the impact of particular policies, if any, on serious crime.

One of the major obstacles to finding sensible crime policies is that there are so many *bad* ideas. In the face of high crime rates, people have grasped desperately at any idea that seemed to offer a quick solution. Politicians readily obliged them, offering simplistic solutions that promised quick and dramatic results. One of the most recent examples is the so-called "three strikes" law, providing mandatory life prison sentences to persons convicted of a third felony, enacted by 15 states between 1993 and 1994 alone.[7]

We will frame our discussion in terms of a series of propositions. Our first proposition is this:

PROPOSITION 1:
Most current crime control proposals are nonsense.

UNDERSTANDING THE CRIME PROBLEM

Crime in the United States is surrounded by myths. Public fear and concern about crime has been high for over 30 years. Gallup polls in 1994, 1995, and 1996 consistently found that despite falling crime rates, people regarded crime as "the most important problem facing the country."[8]

America's Two Crime Problems

Your risk of being a crime victim depends a lot on who you are. The victimization rate for robbery in 1994 was 4.8 per 1,000 for white Americans and 14.0 for African Americans. The burglary rate was 78.6 per 1,000 for the poorest Americans (annual income of less than $7,500), compared with 40.9 for the wealthiest (income of $75,000 or more).[9] Data on homicides provide especially dramatic evidence of the racial disparity in victimization. The number of murders reached an all-time high of 26,250 in 1992. While the overall murder rate that year was 10 per 100,000, it was 9.1 for white males and 67.5 for African-American males. For white females it was only 2.8 but 13.1 for African-American women.[10]

In short, many analysts believe that the United States has *two* crime problems: one that affects most white, middle-class Americans and another that affects people of color, the poor, and young people of color in particular.

Very poor neighborhoods have been overwhelmed by crime and drugs. For their residents, whom some analysts call the *underclass,* the quality of daily life worsened significantly in the 1980s.[11] In many neighborhoods the drug trade almost completely took over the streets, with open drug use and selling.

Percentage of Household Population

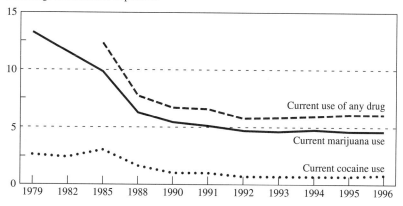

FIGURE 1-2 Drug use trends, 1979–1996: Percentage of households reporting illegal drug use, last thirty days.

SOURCE: Office of National Drug Control Policy, *Data Snapshot: Drug Use in America, 1998* (Washington, DC: Government Printing Office, 1998), plate 35.

One block in Brooklyn was described as an open "drug bazaar," where drugs occupied "the entire life of [the] neighborhood." Despite a steady stream of arrests, one police officer conceded that "the whole neighborhood is into it."[12]

Elliott Currie, meanwhile, citing the evidence from two different surveys of drug use, argues that we have two drug problems: one involving the majority of the population and the other concentrated in the inner cities.[13] The National Household Survey (NHS) indicates that despite public hysteria about drugs, use of illicit drugs dropped substantially between 1979 and 1996. As Figure 1-2 indicates, the number of current users of cocaine in 1996 was one-third the level reached in 1985. Current marijuana use is less than half the 1979–1982 levels.[14] The methodology of the NHS, however, probably undercounts many people who are most at risk for serious drug abuse: low-income adults who do not have stable employment or residence. The Drug Abuse Warning Network (DAWN) surveys hospital emergency room admissions in urban areas (489 hospitals in 1995). "Drug-related episodes" rose by 65 percent between 1978 and 1995. Cocaine-related episodes quadrupled between 1985 and 1989, declined for one year, then increased significantly from 1991 to 1995. Heroin-related episodes have also increased.[15] These data suggest a worsening drug problem for one segment of the population at the same time that the NHS data indicate a significant decline in drug use for the general population.

The American crime problem is actually a problem of *violent* crime—murder and robbery, in particular. In a careful review of comparative crime rates, James Lynch points out that property crime rates in other industrialized countries are similar to, and in some cases higher than, those in the United States. The types of robbery also differ. Far more American robberies involve the use of a firearm than in other countries. In this respect, they instill more fear in their victims.[16]

As we search for sensible crime policies, we need to keep in mind which crime problem and which drug problem we are talking about. Many proposed policies are unrelated to the most serious parts of the crime problem. Some policies are justified in the name of serious crime but in practice affect less serious crimes. The National Criminal Justice Commission, a private group that includes many leading criminologists, argues that the war on crime has been a case of "bait and switch."[17] (The term comes from the area of consumer fraud, where a retailer advertises a low-priced item and then claims that it is sold out and tries to sell a higher-priced item). According to the commission, the war on crime has promised to attack *violent* crime but has mainly resulted in the imprisonment of more *nonviolent* offenders. In California, for example, 73 percent of the increase in the prison population between 1980 and 1993 involved persons convicted of nonviolent crimes. As we examine different crime policies in the chapters ahead, we want to make sure that they have an impact on their intended target.

WAGING WAR ON CRIME

For over thirty years, we have waged a "war on crime." President Lyndon Johnson first declared war on crime in 1965. President Richard Nixon then announced his own war in 1969, and President George Bush declared war on drugs on September 5, 1989.[18] Other politicians and policy makers have followed their lead and used the rhetoric of "war" to characterize our crime policy.

The consequences of the war on crime and drugs have been enormous. The number of prisoners increased six-fold from 196,429 in 1970 to 1.9 million by the end of 1998. United States has been on an imprisonment orgy, and as Figure 1-3 indicates, the last twenty-five years represent a radical break with the past. The incarceration rate rose from 96 per 100,000 in 1970 to 452 per 100,000 in 1998 (state and federal prisoners). This compares with incarceration rates of 111 per 100,000 in Canada, 79 in Australia, and 42 in Japan.[19]

The prisons are only part of the story. The national jail population more than doubled between 1979 and 1998, rising from 153,394 to 592,462 inmates. The number of people on probation grew from 1,079,258 adults in 1976 to 3,417,613 by the end of 1998, and the number of adults on parole soared from 156,194 to 704,904 in the same period. Thus, the total number of people "under correctional supervision" by the late 1990s was about 5 million!

The imprisonment boom is the product of several forces. Public attitudes about crime and criminals became increasingly punitive, particularly with respect to drugs. These attitudes have been translated into laws producing more and longer prison sentences, particularly for drug offenses. The Clark Foundation report *Americans Behind Bars* concludes that "much of the growth

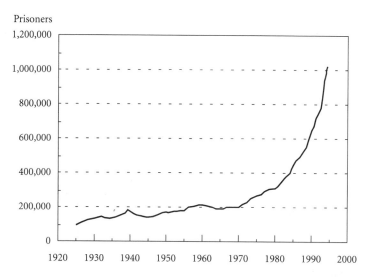

FIGURE 1-3 Sentenced prisoners in state and federal institutions on December 31, 1995.

SOURCE: Bureau of Justice Statistics, *Sourcebook of Criminal Justice Statistics—1995* (Washington, DC: Government Printing Office, 1996), p. 554.

in prison population has resulted from a doubling of the number of arrests for drug law violations and a tripling of the rate of incarceration for arrested drug offenders." [20]

The impact of the war on crime is one of the main themes of this book. Is it responsible for the recent decline in crime? Has it contributed to the recent reduction in crime rates? Or has it made things worse, increasing the alienation of African American young men in particular?

Conservatives such as John J. DiIulio and the Council on Crime in America argue that a punitive policy is necessary, morally justified, and if used properly, effective. As the council puts it, prison is "socially beneficial and cost-effective." They believe that the recent decline in the crime rate is proof that punishment works.[21]

Race and the War on Crime

Elliott Currie, Jerome Miller, the Sentencing Project, the Clark Foundation, and the National Criminal Justice Commission believe that the war on crime has made things worse: that it has not deterred crime, that it is racially biased, and that it has contributed to the destruction of inner-city communities, and as a consequence it has increased the likelihood of juvenile violence.

Currie and others argue that the war on drugs has been waged primarily against young black men. The Sentencing Project found that (Figure 1-4). African Americans represent 13 percent of the population, 15 percent of all illicit drug users (according to the National Household survey), but 35 percent

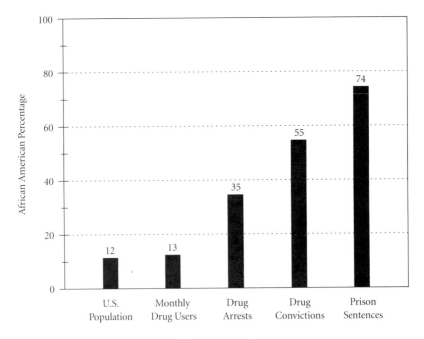

FIGURE 1-4 African Americans and drug possession.

SOURCE: Marc Mauer and Tracy Huling, *Young Black Americans and the Criminal Justice System: Five Years Later* (Washington, DC: The Sentencing Project, 1995), p. 12.

of all people arrested for drug offenses, 55 percent of those convicted, and 74 percent of those sentenced to prison for drug offenses.[22]

Jerome Miller characterizes the war on crime as a case of "search and destroy" directed at young African American men.[23] The National Center on Institutions and Alternatives estimates that on any given day, 42 percent of the young black men (ages 18 to 35) in Washington, D.C., are under the control of the justice system: either in prison or jail or on probation or parole. The figure for Baltimore was 56 percent. About 75 percent of the Washington black men were likely to be arrested before they reach age 35.[24] A study by the California legislature painted a similar picture: one-sixth of the African American men over the age of 16 are arrested every year. Many of these arrests are for drug offenses. Yet the same study found that 92 percent of African American men arrested for drugs were subsequently released for lack of evidence.[25] In short, a huge number of African-American men are acquiring arrest records as a result of the war on drugs. By 1990, more black men were in prison than in college.

The disparate impact of the war on crime has had a profound impact on attitudes toward the justice system. One survey found that 80 percent of whites believed that O. J. Simpson was guilty of murdering his ex-wife Nicole Brown Simpson and her friend Ronald Goldman. But 80 percent of African Americans thought he was innocent.[26] The war on crime has contributed to deep distrust of the justice system among minorities.

Discrimination and the *sense* of unfairness contributes to the crime problem. Social psychologists in the field of procedural justice argue that people are more inclined to obey the law if they feel that the law and legal institutions are fair and treat them with respect. The sense of unfairness and alienation from the justice system, meanwhile, leads to disrespect for the law and a greater likelihood of law breaking.[27]

The War on Crime and the Criminal Justice System

The war on crime has also overloaded the criminal justice system so that in some instances it cannot perform some of its basic functions. In Philadelphia, the police commissioner described the criminal courts as being "on the verge of collapse" in 1990. The massive increase in arrests created a backlog of 12,129 cases, with the result many more defendants failed to make their scheduled court dates. The number of defendants who did not appear soared from 13,807 in January 1987 to a whopping 32,880 by July 1990. The system was incapable of tracking them down and bringing them into court. Law professor Gerald Caplan described it as "a kind of amnesty for some criminals."[28]

"Getting tough" has actually backfired in many states. As prisons become overcrowded, correctional officials are forced to release many offenders earlier than they normally would just to make room for the new arrivals. The percentage of sentences served in Texas dropped from about 30 to 35 percent during 1977–1980 to approximately 20 percent in 1990.[29] This process undermines the original intent of the tough sentencing law—to reduce crime through deterrence and incapacitation.

A very basic lesson is apparent here: The justice system can only handle so much business. It does not "collapse" like a building. It keeps on going, but only through adjustments that are often undesirable. We will discuss these adjustments in more detail in Chapter 3.

Finally, the enormous cost of the war on crime has drained tax dollars from other social needs, such as education, public health, and the economic infrastructure of roads and bridges. In California, for example, state expenditures for corrections were only half the amount spent on higher education in the early 1980s; by 1994, they were equal, at $3.8 billion. Prison budgets had risen dramatically, whereas the state colleges and universities had suffered drastic cuts.[30] If education has historically been an investment in the future of society, then the cuts in education to finance prison represent a *dis*investment in the future.

The Futility of Waging "War" on Crime

"War" is the wrong metaphor to use for reducing crime for several reasons. It raises unrealistic expectations, promising a "victory." The effective control of crime, however, will not come quickly or easily. A final victory in the military sense will never be achieved; there will always be some crime. A sensible goal is to get it down to some tolerable level.[31]

The war metaphor is also wrong because it suggests that we are fighting a foreign enemy. The "us versus them" attitude encourages police officers to think that suspects do not have the rights of American citizens. Community policing, which emphasizes close working relations between police and citizens, is a far more appropriate approach for a democratic society. Finally, as we have already seen, the current war on crime has had a terrible effect on American society, particularly on racial and ethnic minority communities.

These facts lead us to the following proposition:

PROPOSITION 2
Waging "war" is the wrong way to fight crime.

The truth is, we do not face a foreign enemy. We are up against ourselves. We need to deal with our own social institutions, our own values, our own habits, and our own crime control policies. The weight loss problem offers a more useful comparison. The solution does not lie in a miracle cure; instead, it involves difficult long-term changes in one's own behavior: eating less, eating less fattening food, and exercising more. By the same token, we will reduce crime when we make basic changes in all of our social policies that affect families, employment, and neighborhoods. There is no quick easy "miracle" cure for crime.

Crime Policy: A Plague of Nonsense

Americans have trouble thinking clearly about crime. The result is a lot of crime control proposals that are nonsense. Why?

The main reason is that we have been overwhelmed by violent crime. Despite the substantial decline in recent years, we still have far more violent crime than any other industrialized country. We murder each other eight to twelve times as often as do people in Europe or Japan. In 1990, the American murder rate was 9.4 per 100,000, compared with only 1.3 for England and Wales. The American robbery rate was 257 per 100,000 but only 55 in West Germany and 47 in Ireland.[32]

Fear of crime still pervades our daily lives like a plague, affecting the way we think, the way we act, the way we respond to one another. It has a corrosive effect on interpersonal relations, making us wary of small acts of friendliness toward strangers. It also distorts the political process, with politicians offering quick-fix solutions that offer no realistic hope of reducing crime. Fear and frustration about crime produce irrational thinking. Almost every year some new proposal promises to reduce crime by 30 percent or 50 percent.

Even some of the most informed experts on criminal justice are overwhelmed by the problem. When Jerome Miller first sent the manuscript of his book *Search and Destroy* to the publisher, his editor wrote back that it was "too pessimistic," with no optimistic recommendations on how to solve the crime problem. Miller admitted that his editor was right; he did not "have many suggestions—and those I do have, aren't likely to be taken."[33] Many other people have had the same problem: an inability to formulate sensible, realistic proposals for reducing crime.

Our response to the crime problem also resembles the way many people deal with being overweight—by "binging." Just as people go on crash diets, lose weight, put it all back on, and then take up another diet fad a year later, so we tend to "binge" on crime control fads. Yesterday it was "selective incapacitation." Today it is "three strikes." And so it goes. Typically, everyone forgets yesterday's fad without examining whether it really worked.

We need to make an important distinction regarding the goals of different reform proposals. Many sensible proposals involve reducing the *harm* done by the criminal justice system. The Sentencing Project, the Edna McConnell Clark Foundation, and the National Criminal Justice Commission have all made proposals for reducing the harm done by our current sentencing practices. In *Malign Neglect,* Michael Tonry offers a specific proposal for reducing racial disparities in sentencing.[34] Reducing the harm done by the criminal justice system is an important and laudable goal, but our focus here is on policies that will reduce *crime,* particularly serious crime.

THE GROUND RULES

The goal of this book is to identify sensible and effective crime policies. Let us begin by establishing the ground rules for our inquiry. First, we will focus on crime control. We are concerned with policies that will reduce the level of serious crime. We will consider questions of justice and fairness as a basic constraint on crime policy. Effectiveness—defined as reduction in crime—is not the only criterion for a sensible crime control policy. We have limits to what we can do. A democratic society respects the rule of law and standards of justice and fairness, unlike totalitarian societies that are based on the principle of unlimited government power. It might reduce crime if we just shot all robbers and drug dealers on sight. When an Islamic rebel group took power in Kabul, the capital of Afghanistan, in 1996, the group restored punishments such as stoning to death people guilty of adultery and cutting off the hands of thieves. One criminal was driven through the streets on a truck with an amputated hand and heavy weights holding his jaw open. Such practices, however, violate our standards of decency and due process.

Second, we will focus primarily on the crimes of robbery and burglary. This limited focus helps impose discipline on our thinking. Too many people evade the hard questions about crime by changing the subject. Liberals often find it difficult to talk about robbery and burglary, changing the subject to victimless crimes such as gambling, marijuana use, and unconventional sexual behavior. Conservatives focus on celebrated cases (particularly mass murders or extremely vicious crimes) that have little to do with the routine felonies of robbery and burglary. We will discuss the celebrated case phenomenon in Chapter 2.

At several points along the way, we will consider other crimes to illustrate certain points. An entire section is devoted to drunk driving because this subject provides very useful insights into such issues as police crackdowns, sentencing reform, and deterrence. Domestic violence also illustrates some issues related to deterrence. Chapter 13 covers drugs because it is impossible to talk about crime policy today without addressing the drug issue.

Third, this book concentrates on crimes committed by adults. Juvenile crime and delinquency are serious problems that warrant attention, but the world of juvenile justice is a special realm that deserves a separate critical inquiry.[35]

Thinking Clearly about Crime Prevention

As the 1997 University of Maryland report on *Preventing Crime* argues, many people are confused about the term *crime prevention*. The report points out that "the national debate over crime often treats "prevention" and "punishment" as mutually exclusive concepts, polar opposites on a continuum of 'soft' versus 'tough' responses to crime. . . ."[36] As we explain shortly, this dichotomy generally defines conservatives as the advocates of "tough" policies and liberals as the advocates of "soft" policies.

The Maryland report persuasively argues that this is a false dichotomy. Regardless of their label, all crime policies are designed to prevent crime. Particular polices are simply different means to that end. An allegedly "soft" treatment program (e.g., out-patient drug abuse counseling) is intended to prevent crime no less than is an allegedly "tough" sentencing policy (e.g., a "three strikes" law). From the standpoint of effective crime prevention, the real issue is not one of intentions or methods but consequences. Which policies reduce crime?

The Question of Reasonable Goals. Our search for sensible and effective crime policies raises a difficult question of criteria. What do we mean by *effective*? Let us say we find a policy that would reduce crime by 5 percent without doing any serious harm. Is that a goal worth pursuing? A 5 percent reduction is not much, given the size of our crime problem. We would still be swamped by murder, robbery, rape, and drug abuse. It would be easy to dismiss that policy as hardly worth the effort.

The issue here is one of reasonable goals. In his discussion of gun crimes, Gary Kleck makes a persuasive case in favor of modest goals. We should not expect quick and dramatic changes. Unreasonable expectations lead to disappointment and frustration. Kleck advises thinking in terms of modest goals that can be achieved.[37] In the long run, a sensible approach to crime will probably include a series of different policies, each one focusing on a different aspect of the larger problem and each one producing a modest reduction in crime.

Reducing Crime: The New Community Focus

The most comprehensive survey of the effectiveness of crime policies is the 1997 University of Maryland report *Preventing Crime*. One of the report's most important conclusions involves the *interdependency* of different policies and the context in which policies operate. "Crime prevention policies are not delivered in a vacuum."[38] A particular program may be effective in an economically healthy community but ineffective in one with a very high unemployment rate. One potentially effective program may need to be supported by other programs in order to fulfill its potential. The report suggests that "it may be necessary to mount programs in several institutional settings simultaneously—such as labor markets, families, and police—in order to find programs in any one institution to be effective."

The interrelatedness of crime policies, other policies, and the external environment may seem self-evident. Unfortunately, it has not been self-evident to most criminal justice researchers. Most evaluations of programs focus very narrowly on the programs themselves. To a certain extent, this limited scope is dictated by the canons of social science research, which call for controlling for the relevant variables. Thus, for example, an evaluation of a new sentencing law will control for variables related to sentenced offenders, judges, and, if it is a cross-jurisdictional study, different court systems. Such evaluations do not, however, control for the community environments into which offenders eventually return, either through probation or parole. A study of a police "crackdown" on crime typically does not control for changes in the local labor market or the nature of and changes in sentencing or correctional programs that affect the area being policed. This narrow focus is also the result of practical considerations: Given the limits of time and money, it is simply not possible to investigate all of these other factors.

The Maryland report represents a major conceptual breakthrough in thinking about effective crime reduction. The report identifies seven "institutional settings" in which crime policies are delivered: communities, families, schools, labor markets, "places" (e.g., crime hot spots), policing, and other criminal justice system institutions. One of the important aspects of this framework is that it reduces the criminal justice system—the major focus of most analyses of crime policy—to the humble status of merely one of seven institutional settings (although policing is designated as a separate institution, perhaps because that is the speciality of the report's principal author, Lawrence W. Sherman). The report suggests, again persuasively, that **"the effectiveness of crime prevention in each of the seven institutional settings depends heavily on local conditions in the other settings"** [boldface in the original].[39]

In Chapter 5, we will look at some new problem-oriented policing projects that move beyond a narrow police-only approach and attack crime by combining police efforts with noncriminal justice agencies and resources. In Chapter 6, we will discuss how a significant long-term reduction in traffic fatalities is not the result of enforcement "crackdowns" but rather of a variety of changes that are not enforcement oriented. And in Chapter 11, we will examine how the effectiveness of boot camps depends heavily on the aftercare provided to offenders in the community settings they return to after release from boot camp.

The Larger Context: Recent Social Trends

The importance of the larger social and economic context of crime is highlighted by recent trends in a number of social indicators. Not only is crime down, but a number of other indicators of the well-being of American society have also been moving in a positive direction. Unemployment in the late 1990s was the lowest since the 1960s. Welfare caseloads dropped significantly in the 1990s, and had begun dropping even before enactment of the 1994 Welfare Reform Law. New AIDS cases were also down. As Figure 1-5 indicates, births to teenage women declined sharply between 1992 and 1998.[40]

What is particularly striking is that all of these social trends closely parallel the trends in the crime rate. Not only are they moving in the same direction, but in several cases they turned in a positive direction at *almost exactly the same*

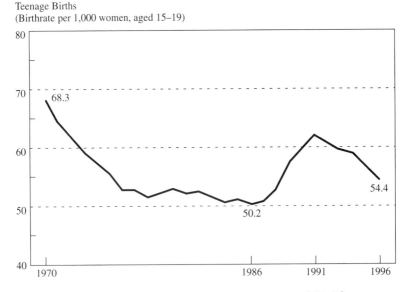

Teenage Births
(Birthrate per 1,000 women, aged 15–19)

FIGURE 1-5 Teenage births (birthrate per 1,000 women, aged 15–19).

SOURCE: National Center for Health Statistics.

time—in the early 1990s. This points in the direction of an important hypothesis: Crime is down because of the general social and economic health of the country, not because of any particular crime policy or policies.

GUILTY: LIBERALS AND CONSERVATIVES

Nonsense about crime is politically nonpartisan. Over the years, both liberals and conservatives have been guilty of making extravagant promises about crime reduction. In 1967, the President's Crime Commission, representing a liberal perspective, promised "a significant reduction in crime" if its recommendations were "vigorously pursued."[41] In 1975, the conservative James Q. Wilson offered a program that he claimed would reduce serious crime by 30 percent.[42] Neither of these promises, or many others like them, were realistic. Consequently, our third proposition is as follows:

PROPOSITION 3
Both liberals and conservatives are guilty of peddling nonsense about crime.

Crime policies are guided by certain underlying assumptions. Liberals and conservatives begin with different assumptions about crime, the administration of justice, and human nature. To make sense of different crime control proposals, it is helpful to analyze the underlying assumptions of each side.

CRIME CONTROL THEOLOGY

A serious problem with the debate over crime policy is that faith usually triumphs over facts. Both liberals and conservatives begin with certain assumptions that are almost like religious beliefs. Too often, these assumptions are not supported by empirical evidence. We call this phenomenon *crime control theology.*[43]

Most conservatives, for example, believe that the death penalty deters crime. This view persists despite the fact that no evidence conclusively supports it. Most liberals, meanwhile, believe that "treatment" works as a cure for crime and drug abuse, despite considerable evidence on the limited effectiveness of treatment programs.

In *Point Blank,* Gary Kleck points out how people switch sides on the deterrence question to suit their beliefs. Conservatives believe that the death penalty deters crime but then argue that the exclusionary rule will not deter police misconduct. Liberals switch sides in the opposite direction, arguing that the death penalty does not deter crime but that the exclusionary rule does work.[44] This leads us to the following proposition.

PROPOSITION 4
Most crime control ideas rest on faith rather than facts.

Conservative Theology

Crime control theologies represent idealized worlds that express people's highest hopes and deepest fears. Conservative crime control theology envisions a world of discipline and self-control in which people exercise self-restraint and subordinate their personal passions to the common good. It is a world of limits and clear rules about human behavior.

The problem, according to conservatives, is that criminals lack self-control. They succumb to their passions and break the rules. They kill because they cannot control their anger. They steal because they want something now and are unable to defer gratification. For conservatives, poverty is no excuse for crime. People remain poor because they lack the self-discipline to get an education, find a job, and steadily try to improve themselves.

Free will, rational choice, and moral responsibility reign supreme in conservative crime control theology. People are responsible for their own fate; they *choose* to commit crime. James Q. Wilson and Richard J. Herrnstein argue: "At any given moment, a person can choose between committing a crime and not committing it."[45] A good example of a policy based on rational choice theory is the "Just say no!" antidrug campaign. It assumes that all we have to do is persuade people to make the decision not to use drugs.

Rational choice theory holds that people weigh the relative risks and rewards of committing crime. If the risk of punishment is low or the punishments are relatively light, more people will tend to commit crime. If the chance of being caught and punished is high and the punishments are relatively severe, fewer people will choose to commit crime. Thus, the certainty and severity of punishment directly affects the crime rate.[46]

In conservative crime control theology, punishment has both a moral and a practical element. Because criminals choose to offend, they deserve punishment. They are morally responsible for their actions. Rules are the basis of a civil society, and rule breaking should be punished. This is called *retribution* or *desert*. James Q. Wilson summed it up in a frequently quoted statement: "Wicked people exist. Nothing avails except to set them apart from innocent people."[47] Conservatives also believe that punishment shapes future behavior through the process of *deterrence*. Specific deterrence is directed at the individual offender, teaching him or her that bad actions have unpleasant consequences. General deterrence is directed at the general population, teaching by example.

Conservatives are deeply ambivalent about the role of government in controlling crime. William J. Bennett, John J. DiIulio, Jr., and John P. Walters argue that the "root cause" of crime is "moral poverty" (as opposed to material poverty). Too many children grow up not learning right from wrong. Moral health, they argue, is nurtured primarily by strong, two-parent families, religious training, and social institutions that reinforce the right values. "Can government supply manner and morals?" they ask. "Of course it cannot," they answer. People are socialized into law-abiding behavior primarily by private institutions, beginning with the family. But, these conservatives argue, government does have an important role to play in providing effective examples of holding people responsible for their behavior. Thus, the swift, certain punishment of offenders helps breed moral health. Moral poverty is fostered by the failure of the criminal justice system to punish criminals. Thus, while government cannot do everything, it can do something.[48]

Underlying conservative crime control theology is an idealized image of the patriarchal family. Punishment resembles parental discipline. Minor misbehavior is greeted with a gentle warning, a second misstep earns a sterner reprimand, and serious wrongdoing receives a severe punishment. The point is to teach the wisdom of correct behavior by handing out progressively harsher sanctions and threatening even more unpleasant punishment if the behavior continues.

The real world of crime and justice, unfortunately, does not work like the family. It is filled with some very incorrigible children. Some are so deeply alienated from society that they do not respect the overall structure of authority. Punishment, in fact, may only distance them further. Some observers believe, for example, that arrest and imprisonment are such common experiences in some poor minority neighborhoods that they have lost whatever deterrent threat they might have once had.[49]

John Braithwaite's provocative book *Crime, Shame, and Reintegration* offers a useful perspective on this problem. Braithwaite describes the process of "reintegrative shaming" as being very much like the way a family handles someone who breaks the rules. But his theory also clearly indicates that informal sanctions work when close social bonds link the sanctioner and the sanctioned, and where no great differences in values exist in the community—that is, when the relationship more closely resembles a family.[50]

This is the heart of the problem. The family analogy breaks down in the real world because we have a highly fragmented society, characterized by great differences in wealth, race, religion, and lifestyles. Our society is anything but a tight-knit community with shared values. Braithwaite's theory, in fact, is a good explanation of why informal, family-style sanctions do not work in our society. His description of the conditions under which a system of reintegrative shaming can work is actually a very accurate description of a seventeenth-century New England village, where that approach to crime control was used very effectively.[51]

The limits of reintegrative shaming lend further support to the importance of a community orientation and the interdependency of institutions and policies emphasized by the Maryland *Preventing Crime* report. Effective reintegration requires a reasonably healthy community. Achieving a healthy community, in turn, probably requires a series of crime prevention programs directed toward a number of different institutions: families, schools, the local labor market, and so on.

Conservatives explain the failure of punishment to work by focusing on problems in the criminal justice system. Punishment, they say, is not certain or severe enough. Too many loopholes allow criminals to beat the system: the exclusionary rule, the Miranda warning, the insanity defense, plea bargaining, and so on. The idea that many criminals "beat the system" and "get off easy" is an article of faith in conservative crime control theology. Close these loopholes, ensure certainty of punishment, and we can reduce crime. Longer prison terms and the death penalty, meanwhile, will increase the deterrent effect and reduce crime. We will take a close look at this idea in several of the chapters ahead.

Liberal Theology

Liberal crime control theology views crime in a social context. According to liberals, criminal behavior is largely the result of social influences such as the family, the peer group, the neighborhood, economic opportunities, and discrimination.

Liberal crime policy seeks to alter these influences. Rehabilitation programs, for example, are designed to provide a structured set of influences that will shape the offender's behavior in a positive direction. Liberals favor community-based alternatives to imprisonment because they represent a healthier environment than prison. Supervised probation and parole are designed to provide positive external influences. Basic education and vocational training programs, meanwhile, are designed to equip the offender for success in life.

Liberals are as guilty of wishful thinking as are conservatives. A fundamental article of faith in liberal crime control theology is the belief that people's behavior can be reshaped through some kind of formal treatment program. The history of prison and correctional reform is the story of a continuing search for the Holy Grail of rehabilitation: a program that will truly reform offenders. The people who invented the prison in the nineteenth century thought that institution would do the job.[52] When it had obviously failed, reformers invented parole and the indeterminate sentence, advertising them as the magic keys to rehabilitation. When these measures did not solve the problem of crime, reformers came up with new variations (group counseling, intensive supervision, and so forth). None of these programs has demonstrated consistent effectiveness.

If conservatives refuse to face the facts about the failure of punishment, liberals refuse to look at the sad history of the failure of rehabilitation. Faith continues to survive in the face of repeated failure.

It is also an article of faith among liberals that the United States is the most punitive country in the world. We do, in fact, lock up more people than any other country. Our current incarceration rate of 452 per 100,000 leads the world. James Lynch's research offers a valuable comparative perspective on this figure. Using arrests as a baseline, he notes that the probabilities of an offender's going to prison are only slightly different in the United States, Canada, England, and West Germany. In this regard, we are no more punitive than most other countries. We do, however, give much longer prison sentences. Our incarceration rate is greater primarily because we have more serious crime than these other countries.[53]

If conservatives believe that most of our problems are the result of loopholes that let too many people off easy, liberals are guilty of blaming everything on overly harsh punishments.

Liberals are ambivalent on the question of individual responsibility. Although they emphasize the importance of social conditions in causing crime and reject the conservative preoccupation with individual responsibility, they cannot completely ignore the role of individual choice. Rehabilitation programs, in fact, are designed to influence individuals to make different (and better) choices. In the realm of the public policy debate, however, liberals tend to downplay the element of individual responsibility.

A Word about Rules

One way to distinguish between conservatives and liberals with respect to crime policy is their attitude toward *rules.* Everyone believes in rules and their application in a consistent fashion. This is what people mean when they refer to the "rule of law."

Conservatives and liberals mainly disagree over which set of rules to emphasize. In criminal justice, we have two basic sets: criminal law and criminal procedure. The substantive *criminal law* is a set of rules governing everyone's behavior. It defines certain behavior as criminal and specifies the penalty for breaking the rules. *Criminal procedure,* on the other hand, is a set of rules governing criminal justice officials. It tells them what they may not do (conduct unreasonable searches and seizures) and what they must do (bring the suspect before a magistrate without unnecessary delay).[54]

Conservatives emphasize the rules of the criminal law. Harming a person or taking someone else's property violates the basic standards of a decent society. Anyone who violates these rules should be punished. Liberals tend to emphasize the rules of criminal procedure. A free society is one that strictly limits the potentially awesome power of government officials.

One way to understand the difference between liberal and conservative attitudes toward rules is to recognize what each side sees as its worst nightmare. For conservatives, unchecked criminality leads to anarchy and the death of freedom. For liberals, unchecked government power leads to tyranny and the death of freedom. The difference is really a question of what represents the greatest threat to freedom.

Both sides are ambivalent about rule breaking. Conservatives tend to be willing to excuse violations of the rules of procedure to control crime. They will overlook the unreasonable search if it helps convict a criminal. Liberals, on the other hand, are more concerned about official rule breaking. They are willing to see a criminal suspect go free if a police officer or some other official has made a serious mistake. These differences are not absolute, of course. They are really matters of emphasis. Conservatives do not endorse gross abuses by the police, and liberals do not endorse crime.

The classic statement of the difference between conservatives and liberals on this issue is Herbert Packer's essay on the "two models of the criminal process."[55] Conservatives embrace the *crime control model*, which puts a high priority on the effective control of crime. To this end, they are willing to grant officials considerable leeway, not restricting them with a lot of rules. Liberals prefer the *due process model*, in which the highest priorities are fair treatment and the presumption of innocence. Formal rules (due process guarantees) are designed to achieve these goals.

Ideological Confusion: Switching Sides

The conservative/liberal dichotomy is a useful way to think about crime policy. It helps identify the basic assumptions that underlie different policies. In the last few years, however, this dichotomy is not quite as sharp as it was a few years ago. Strange things have been happening. Some conservatives have adopted traditional liberal policies, and many liberals have embraced traditional conservative ideas. Understanding the crime debate today requires sorting our way through this ideological confusion.

One major change involves the issue of legalizing drugs. Decriminalization has traditionally been a liberal proposal. They have argued that we should not criminalize behavior that does not harm others. Moreover, criminalizing a lot of behavior often tends to make things worse, by overloading the criminal justice system, encouraging corruption, and failing to respond effectively to what are really social and medical problems.

Surprisingly, many prominent conservatives endorse legalizing drugs. The most prominent is the writer and television talk show host William F. Buckley. We will examine the arguments in favor of drug legalization in Chapter 13. For the moment, it is important to note that some conservatives have switched sides and adopted a traditional liberal position.

Meanwhile, many liberals have adopted some conservative crime control proposals. The best example is President Bill Clinton. The 1994 Violent Crime Control Act, which he supported, calls for more police and longer prison sentences. In the 1996 presidential election campaign, political observers said that Clinton had moved to the right and embraced the traditional Republican position on crime.

In short, the ideological lineup on crime control policies has become very muddled. Nonetheless, it is still possible to identify a set of crime policies that, because of their underlying assumptions, can be classified as conservative and another set that can be classified as liberal. These categories will help us analyze the different policies we will consider in this book.

CONCLUSION

Crime is a serious problem in the United States. The recent dramatic reductions in the crime rate still leave a problem of violent crime that is far higher than other industrialized countries. Unfortunately, we do not have many good ideas about how to solve the crime problem. In this initial chapter, we have tried to sketch out some of the complexity of the U.S. crime problem. We have also indicated briefly why so many crime control policies are worthless. In the chapters that follow, we will develop these themes in more detail. The next two chapters take a closer look at how the criminal justice system actually works. Then we will turn our attention to specific crime control proposals. As we already indicated, our basic goal is to find some crime control policies that make sense and that are supported by persuasive evidence.

NOTES

1. Bureau of Justice Statistics, *Criminal Victimization 1998: Changes 1997–98 with Trends 1993–98* (Washington DC: Government Printing Office, 1999). Federal Bureau of Investigation, *1999 Preliminary Estimate* (11 November 1999).

2. Boston Police Department and Partners, *The Boston Strategy to Prevent Youth Violence* (Boston: Boston Police Department, 1998).

3. James Alan Fox, *Trends in Juvenile Violence* (Washington, DC: Government Printing Office, 1996). Philip J. Cook and John H. Laub, "The Unprecedented Epidemic in Youth Violence," in Michael Tonry and Mark H. Moore, eds., *Youth Violence* (Chicago: University of Chicago Press, 1998), pp. 27–64.

4. William Bratton and Peter Knoblach, *Turnaround* (New York: Random House, 1998).

5. A variety of explanations by prominent criminologists are offered in the symposium, "Crime's Decline—Why," *National Institute of Justice Journal* (October 1998), pp. 7–20.

6. Quotes from Clifford Krauss, "Murder Rate Plunges in New York City," *New York Times,* 8 July 1995: 1, 16.

7. Michael G. Turner, Jody L. Sundt, Brandon K. Applegate, and Francis T. Cullen, "'Three Strikes and You're Out' Legislation: A National Assessment," *Federal Probation* 59 (September 1995): 16–35.

8. Bureau of Justice Statistics, *Sourcebook of Criminal Justice Statistics–1995* (Washington, DC: Government Printing Office, 1996), p. 128.

9. Bureau of Justice Statistics, *Criminal Victimization 1994* (Washington, DC: Government Printing Office, 1996).

10. Bureau of the Census, *Statistical Abstract of the United States, 1995* (Washington, DC: Government Printing Office, 1995), p. 202.

11. Elliott Currie, *Reckoning: Drugs, The Cities, and the American Future* (New York: Hill & Wang, 1992).

12. Mary B. Tabor, "The World of a Drug Bazaar," *New York Times,* 1 October 1992: 1, 20; Mary B. Tabor, "Neighborhood Ruled by Drug Culture," *New York Times,* 2 October 1992: 18.

13. Currie, *Reckoning.*

14. The data are summarized in Office of National Drug Control Policy, *Data Snapshot: Drug Abuse in America, 1998* (Washington, DC: Government Printing Office, 1998). Department of Health and Human Services, *Preliminary Estimates From the 1995 National Household Survey on Drug Abuse,* Advance Report 18 (Washington, DC: Government Printing Office, 1996).

15. Office of National Drug Control Policy, *Data Snapshot: Drug Abuse in America, 1998,* plate 76.

16. James Lynch, "Crime In International Perspective," in James Q. Wilson and Joan Petersilia, eds. *Crime* (San Francisco: ICS Press, 1995), pp. 11–38.

17. Steven R. Donziger, ed., *The Real War on Crime: The Report of The National Criminal Justice Commission* (New York: HarperCollins, 1996), pp. 18–19.

18. On the history of "wars" on crime, see Samuel Walker, *Popular Justice: A History of American Criminal Justice,* 2nd ed. (New York: Oxford University Press, 1998).

19. Marc Mauer, *Americans Behind Bars: One Year Later* (Washington, DC: The Sentencing Project, 1992).

20. Edna McConnell Clark Foundation, *Americans Behind Bars* (New York: Edna McConnell Clark Foundation, 1994), p. 8.

21. Council on Crime in America, *The State of Violent Crime in America* (Washington, DC: Council on Crime in America, 1996). William J. Bennett, John J. Diulio, Jr., and John P. Walters, *Body Count* (New York: Simon & Schuster, 1996).

22. Mauer, *Americans Behind Bars: One Year Later.*

23. Jerome G. Miller, *Search and Destroy: African American Males in the Criminal Justice System* (New York: Cambridge University Press, 1996).

24. National Center on Institutions and Alternatives, *Hobbling a Generation: African American Males in the District of Columbia's Criminal Justice System* (Alexandria, VA: National Center on Institutions and Alternatives, 1992); Miller, *Search and Destroy,* p. 7.

25. Miller, *Search and Destroy,* p. 8.

26. Donziger, ed., *The Real War on Crime,* pp. 169–70.

27. Tom R. Tyler, *Why People Obey the Law* (New Haven: Yale University Press, 1990).

28. Michael de Courcy Hinds, "Philadelphia Justice System Overwhelmed," *New York Times,* 15 August 1990: 1, 13.

29. Sheldon Ekland-Olson, "Crime and Incarceration: Some Comparative Findings From the 1980s," *Crime and Delinquency* 38 (July 1992): 392–16.

30. Edna McConnell Clark Foundation, *Americans Behind Bars.*

31. Egon Bittner, "The Police and the 'War on Crime,'" in *The Functions of the Police in Modern Society* (Washington, DC: Government Printing Office, 1970), pp. 48–51.

32. Ineke Haen Marshall, "How Exceptional Is the United States? Crime Trends in Europe and the US," *European Journal on Criminal Policy and Research* 4(2): 7–35.

33. Miller, *Search and Destroy,* p. 235

34. Michael Tonry, *Malign Neglect* (New York: Oxford University Press, 1995).

35. Mark H. Moore and Stewart Wakeling, "Juvenile Justice: Shoring Up the Foundations," in Michael Tonry, ed., *Crime and Justice: A Review of Research,* vol. 22 (Chicago: University of Chicago Press, 1997), pp. 253–301.

36. University of Maryland, *Preventing Crime: What Works, What Doesn't, What's Promising* (Washington, DC: Government Printing Office, 1997), pp. 2-2.

37. Gary Kleck, *Point Blank: Guns and Violence in America* (New York: Aldine de Gruyter, 1991), pp. 432–33.

38. University of Maryland, *Preventing Crime,* pp. 2–4.

39. *Ibid.,* pp. 2–5.

40. A particularly valuable source is Marc Miningoff and Marque-Luisa Miringoff, *The Social Health of the Nation* (New York: Oxford University Press, 1999).

41. President's Commission on Law Enforcement and Administration of Justice, *The Challenge of Crime in a Free Society* (Washington, DC: Government Printing Office, 1967), p. vi.

42. James Q. Wilson, *Thinking About Crime* (New York: Basic Books, 1975).

43. George C. Thomas and David Edelman, "An Evaluation of Conservative Crime Control Theology," *Notre Dame Law Review* 63(2) (1988): 123–60.

44. Kleck, *Point Blank,* pp. 7, 13.

45. James Q. Wilson and Richard J. Herrnstein, *Crime and Human Nature: The Definitive Study of the Causes of Crime* (New York: Simon & Schuster, 1985), p. 44.

46. But everyone should read the article Wilson coauthored: James Q. Wilson and Allen Abrahamse, "Does Crime Pay?" *Justice Quarterly* 9 (September 1992): 359–77.

47. Wilson, *Thinking About Crime* [1975 ed.], p. 209.

48. William J. Bennett, John J. DiIulio, Jr., and John P. Walters, *Body Count* (New York: Simon & Schuster, 1996), p. 205.

49. See the discussion of this point in Daniel S. Nagin, "Criminal Deterrence Research at the Outset of the Twenty-First Century," in Michael Tonry, ed., *Crime and Justice: A Review of Research,* vol.

23 (Chicago: University of Chicago Press, 1998), pp. 4–5.

50. John Braithwaite, *Crime, Shame, and Reintegration* (New York: Cambridge University Press, 1989). John Braithwaite, "Restorative Justice: Assessing Optimistic and Pessimistic Accounts," in Michael Tonry, ed., *Crime and Justice: A Review of Research,* vol. 25 (Chicago: University of Chicago Press, 1999), pp. 1–127.

51. Lawrence M. Friedman, *Crime and Punishment in American History* (New York: Basic Books, 1993); Walker, *Popular Justice,* chap. 1.

52. David Rothman, *The Discovery of the Asylum* (Boston: Little, Brown, 1971).

53. Lynch, "Crime in International Perspective."

54. On the subject of rules and discretion, see Samuel Walker, *Taming the System: The Control of Discretion in American Criminal Justice, 1950–1990* (New York: Oxford University Press, 1993).

55. Herbert L. Packer, "Two Models of the Criminal Process," in *The Limits of the Criminal Sanction* (Stanford, CA: Stanford University Press, 1968), chap. 8.

2

Models of Criminal Justice

The triumph of faith over facts requires a willful disregard of the realities of crime and criminal justice. Many people believe what they want to believe about how the justice system works, disregarding any and all evidence to the contrary. This problem partly results from the fact the American criminal justice system is so complex. We actually have fifty-one separate criminal justice systems (fifty states plus the federal system), which include 18,769 separate state and local law enforcement agencies.[1] To get a sense of the bewildering variety of only the formal structure of different court systems, take a look at the Bureau of Justice Statistics (BJS) report *State Court Organization* (1980).[2] In addition, the criminal codes and the rules of criminal procedure vary in all of these systems.

The day-to-day administration of justice is even more complex than the formal machinery of the justice system. To the casual observer, things often seem chaotic. Many important decisions are made in informal, "low-visibility" settings, such as the hushed conference in front of the judge and the negotiated plea of guilty. Even many experts are mystified by some of the important features of our criminal justice system. We now have a general sense of what occurs in the hidden realms of police discretion and plea bargaining, but many other important decisions have not been researched. In this context, misunderstanding and myth prevail. Consequently, our next proposition is as follows:

> ## PROPOSITION 5
> Most crime control ideas are based on false assumptions about how the criminal justice system works.

Two attitudes dominate thinking about the administration of criminal justice: the Old Idealism and the New Cynicism. Neither is very helpful in explaining how the system works.

The Old Idealism is the civics-book picture of justice. This view holds that diligent and hardworking officials enforce the law as it is written in the statutes; a person who commits a crime is duly arrested and prosecuted for that offense; if convicted, he or she receives the prescribed punishment. It is an adversarial system of justice that determines the truth of guilt or innocence through a public contest between prosecution and defense, overseen by an impartial judge. Although inspiring, this version of the criminal process does not describe the reality of our justice system.

The New Cynicism is a mirror image of the Old Idealism. It portrays a chaotic criminal justice system where there is neither law, order, nor justice. Police discretion is completely out of control, with officers arresting whomever they want. Prosecutors plea bargain wildly. Some guilty people get off, while others are railroaded into prison. Defense attorneys are in league with prosecutors, cutting deals to suit each other's needs.[3] Sentencing is arbitrary and biased. Parole boards grant or deny release without rational or scientific basis for their decisions. Many people believe the entire criminal justice system is filled with race discrimination.[4]

The New Cynicism comes in two versions. Conservative cynics see irrational decision making undermining effective crime control. Criminals are not punished for their crimes: Either they are not arrested, they get their charges dropped, or they obtain early parole release. Crafty defense lawyers manipulate the rules of criminal procedure to beat the system. Liberal cynics, on the other hand, believe that the apparent chaos of the system produces systematic discrimination. The poor are punished while "respectable" offenders get off easy; African Americans and Hispanic Americans are the victims of systematic discrimination.

A major part of the challenge facing us is to find the truth about the justice system. It is undeniable that much criminal justice decision making *is* irrational. Many offenders *do* escape punishment: The risk of even being arrested for drunk driving, for example, is extremely low. There *is* racial discrimination in the system: The African American who murders a white person is far more likely to be sentenced to death than the white person who murders an African American.

But neither version of the New Cynicism adequately explains how the justice system handles routine cases on a day-to-day basis. This chapter argues that the system operates in a fairly consistent and predictable manner. Donald Black found predictable patterns in police arrest discretion.[5] A major study of plea bargaining found that about 80 percent of the outcomes were predictable with knowledge of the offense and the defendant's prior record.[6]

Despite a high degree of predictability, the justice system is filled with paradoxes and inconsistencies. There is much truth in the comment that "the problem is not that our system is too lenient, or too severe; sadly, it is both."[7] Norval Morris and Michael Tonry point out that we simultaneously send too many people to prison and give others meaningless forms of probation with little supervision: "We are both too lenient and too severe."[8]

Policing offers a concrete example of the inconsistencies in the administration of justice. In the same city, in the same precinct, on the same night, within the space of an hour, a pair of police officers will both *over*enforce and *under*enforce the law: They will be overly aggressive toward some young African-American men on a street corner and then not make an arrest in a domestic violence incident a few blocks away, denying the victim the protection of the law.[9]

THE CRIME COMMISSION'S MODEL

To help understand the administration of justice, social scientists have constructed models of the system. The first and most famous model (Figure 2-1) was developed thirty-five years ago by the President's Crime Commission (officially the President's Commission on Law Enforcement and Administration of Justice).[10] This commission introduced the "systems" approach to the administration of criminal justice, which has shaped thinking about the subject since it first appeared. Until it appeared, people thought in terms of separate justice agencies that had little relationship to each other.

The Crime Commission's model was a great leap forward in our understanding of criminal justice. It accomplished exactly what models are designed to do: provide a conceptual framework, or paradigm, that helps identify general patterns, define problems, and focus research and policy planning. The systems model focuses attention on the flow of cases among agencies, the interrelationships among agencies (or "components"), and the pervasiveness of discretionary decision making in controlling the flow of cases.[11] It focuses attention on discretion and the factors that influence decision making. It also emphasizes the dynamic relationship among components of the system and how decisions at one point (say, the prosecutor) affect decisions "upstream" (the police) and "downstream" (the judge).

The Crime Commission's model has its limitations, however. Based on the growing body of criminal justice research, we offer an alternative model.

THE CRIMINAL JUSTICE WEDDING CAKE

The major shortcoming of the Crime Commission's model is that it portrays a single justice system that handles all cases alike. Our alternative model is a four-layer wedding cake that focuses attention of important variations in how cases are handled (Figure 2-2). The wedding cake model was first developed by Lawrence Friedman and Robert V. Percival in *The Roots of Justice,* a history of criminal justice in Alameda County, California, between 1870 and 1910.[12] Additional support, based on contemporary evidence, is found in Michael and Don Gottfredson's *Decision Making in Criminal Justice.*[13]

The wedding cake model emphasizes two points. First, there are significant differences *between* types of cases, based on seriousness and other factors. Second, there are fairly consistent patterns of disposition *within* each category.

Celebrated Cases: The Top Layer

At the top of the wedding cake is a very small layer of "celebrated cases." These include exceptional and highly publicized crimes or controversies. The O. J. Simpson trial is, without a doubt, the all-time celebrated case. Because of Simpson's fame as an athlete and movie star, the viciousness of the crime, the money involved and high-powered legal defense team, and the volatile mix of race and sex, probably no other case like this has appeared in American history.[14]

Celebrated cases are different from other cases in several respects. First, they usually involve the full criminal process, including that rare event, the criminal trial. We get to see fundamental issues contested in public view: the sanity of the defendant; the admissibility of the evidence; the credibility of the witnesses; and the competence of prosecutor, defense attorney, and judge. Trials are dramatic events, filled with suspense about the outcome.

Second, celebrated cases receive an enormous amount of publicity, usually because of the nature of the crime itself (typically something ghastly) or the fame of the people involved (as either victim or defendant). A few cases become celebrated because they result in landmark Supreme Court rulings. The *Miranda* case is an excellent example.

Because of all the publicity, celebrated cases have an enormous impact on public perceptions about criminal justice. People mistakenly assume that they are typical of all cases. This fosters the belief that people like Ernesto Miranda (whose case gave us the *Miranda* warning) are "beating the system" every day through "technicalities."

The O. J. Simpson trial offers an excellent example of how celebrated cases distort public perception. Simpson's acquittal led many people to conclude that spouse murderers "beat the system" all the time. Even worse, it led many whites to believe that African-American jurors will not convict an African-American defendant. Both of these perceptions are grossly wrong.

In response to the Simpson trial outcome, the Bureau of Justice Statistics analyzed its data on spouse murders from the 75 largest counties in the country for 1988. This included a total of 540 cases.[15] As Figure 2-3 indicates, very

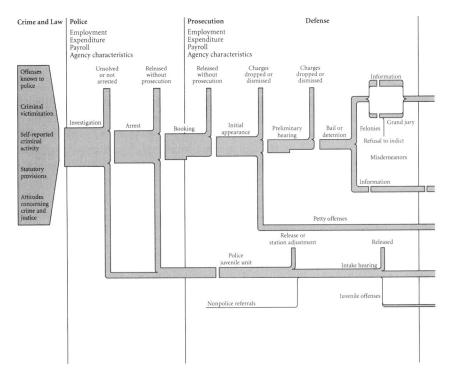

FIGURE 2-1 The Crime Commission's model of the criminal justice system.

SOURCE: President's Commission on Law Enforcement and Administration of Justice, *Task Force Report: Science and Technology* (Washington, DC: Government Printing Office, 1967), pp. 58–59.

few accused murderers beat the system. In fact, only 2 percent of the husbands were acquitted. Wives were more likely to win acquittal (14 percent) because there were more likely to be mitigating circumstances, such as killing in self-defense. The system was tough on spouse murder defendants at every stage. Only 13 percent were not prosecuted. And of those who were convicted, 71 percent were sentenced to prison (81 percent of the husbands and 57 percent of the wives).

Unfortunately, the BJS data set does not include the racial composition of juries. Because the data come from the seventy-five largest urban counties in the country, however, it is a safe assumption that racial minorities were well represented. Thus, there is probably no truth to the idea that minority jurors refuse to convict minority defendants. These data, in fact, indicate no difference in the conviction rates between whites and blacks: 81 percent of whites and 79 percent of blacks were convicted.

The great value of the BJS data set is that it reflects the routine, day-in, day-out administration of justice. It gives us a far more accurate picture of how the system operates than celebrated cases such as the O. J. Simpson trial.

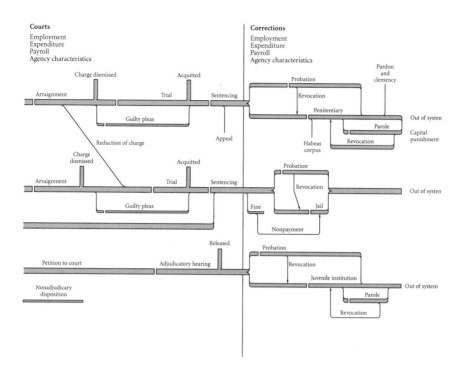

To understand how routine robberies and burglaries are handled, we need to turn our attention to the second and third layers of the wedding cake.

Serious Felonies: The Second and Third Layers

In their original version of the wedding cake, Friedman and Percival put all felony cases in one layer. The Gottfredsons made an extremely important refinement by dividing felonies into two categories based on perceived seriousness.[16] In our wedding cake, the more serious felonies go into the second layer and the less serious felonies go into the third.

A large body of research supports the view that criminal justice officials consistently classify cases on the basis of three factors related to seriousness: (1) the nature of the crime, (2) the suspect's prior record, and (3) the relationship between the victim and the offender. In a study of violent felony cases in Detroit, Spohn and Cederblom identified five different factors that distinguish the more serious from the less serious cases: (1) the seriousness of the charge, (2) the defendant's prior record, (3) whether the victim and the offender were

FIGURE 2-2 The criminal justice wedding cake.

strangers, (4) whether the victim was injured, and (5) whether the offender used a gun.[17] Jeffrey T. Ulmer's study of sentencing under the Pennsylvania sentencing guidelines found that while the guidelines were designed to limit sentencing discretion, there were some departures from prescribed sentences and that considerations of seriousness (prior record, offense type, severity) accounted for most of those departures.[18]

This classification process is informal; there is no actual checklist of factors (although some prosecutors' offices have formal limits on plea-bargaining certain kinds of cases, such as those that involve drugs, weapons, or rape).[19] Essentially, officials ask themselves, "How much is this case worth?"[20] The everyday language of police and prosecutors refer to "heavy" cases and "real" crimes as opposed to the "garbage" or "bullshit" cases.[21] A study of California probation officers found that they used the same definitions of "heavy-duty" and "lightweight" cases that judges and prosecutors used.[22]

These judgments about seriousness are shared by all the members of the courtroom work group. In brief, criminal justice officials work together day in and day out. To get their work done efficiently, they develop shared under-

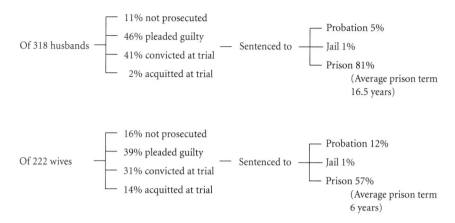

FIGURE 2-3 Spouse murder defendants.

SOURCE: Bureau of Justice Statistics, *Spouse Murder Defendants in Large Urban Counties* (Washington, DC: Government Printing Office, 1995).

standings about how to handle routine cases. This approach has two important consequences. First, it means that individual discretion is controlled *informally*, through understandings and expectations (as opposed to formal rules). Second, it produces a high degree of consistency *within* each layer of the wedding cake.

The shared definition of seriousness facilitates rapid disposition of a high volume of cases. Prosecutors and defense attorneys do not spend a lot of time arguing over particular cases. (We will discuss this effect in more detail in Chapter 8.) Actually, the idea of plea "bargaining" is misleading. The criminal court is not like a Middle Eastern bazaar, where people haggle the price of each item. Instead, as Malcolm Feeley argues, it resembles a modern supermarket, with set prices and high volume.[23] The "fixed prices" reflect the shared assumptions about how much cases are "worth."

Ulmer's study of sentencing in three Pennsylvania counties, however, found that the degree of shared understandings can vary. One county court system had a high degree of stability among its members (prosecution, defense, judges), and as a consequence their relations were characterized by a high degree of collegiality and agreement. A large urban county, on the other hand, had a high degree of turnover in the district attorney's office, which resulted in conflict between prosecution and defense and a high degree of collegiality and understanding between defense attorneys and judges.[24] In short, while *most* court systems operate under a system of shared understandings, there are important *variations* depending on the composition and culture of the local court room work group. We will discuss the work group in more detail in Chapter 3.

Robbery illustrates how officials distribute cases between the second and third layers. Because robbery is generally considered a very serious crime, most such cases end up in the second layer. About one-third of all robberies, however, are between acquaintances. These are often private disputes: a disagreement over borrowed money or tools where the "offender" takes back his or her

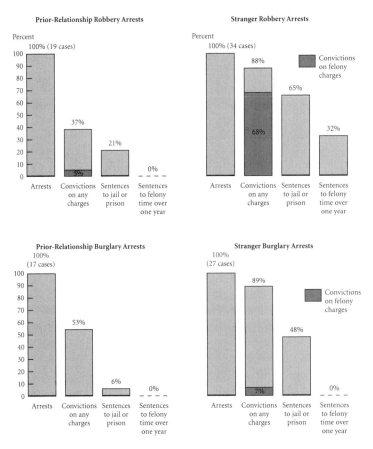

FIGURE 2-4 Outcomes of stranger and nonstranger robberies and burglaries, New York City.

SOURCE: Vera Institute, *Felony Arrests*, rev. ed. (New York: Longman, 1981), pp. 68, 86. Reprinted by permission.

property by force.[25] These robbery cases tend to end up in the third layer because they are not considered as serious as robberies by strangers. If, however, the offender has a long prior record of arrests and convictions, the case might remain in the second layer.

The Vera Institute's study of felony arrests in New York City illustrates the tremendous impact of the relationship between the offender and the victim.[26] Figure 2-4 indicates that 88 percent of the stranger robberies resulted in conviction. Moreover, prosecutors were not lenient in plea bargaining: 77 percent of those convictions (68 percent of the original arrests) were on felony charges. Nearly three–quarters (74 percent) of those convicted were incarcerated, and half of them did time of a year or more. This is hardly the picture of a system "soft" on crime.

The prior-relationship robberies are a completely different story. Only about a third (37 percent) of the suspects were convicted, and only 13 percent of them (5 percent of the number originally arrested) were convicted on felony charges. Slightly more than half (56 percent) of those convicted were incarcerated, but none did a year or more.

The powerful effect of prior relationships is also evident in rape cases. About half of the sexual assaults in the Vera Institute study were committed by men who knew the victim. Sixty percent of these cases were dismissed; another 20 percent ended in a guilty plea with only minor punishment. All of the stranger-rape cases, however, went to trial. Three-quarters of these resulted in conviction and imprisonment, and two-thirds of the prison terms exceeded 25 years.[27]

The most important point that emerges from this analysis is that the criminal justice system is very tough on second-layer felonies. Offenders who have committed a serious crime, committed it against a stranger, and have a long prior record are very likely to be (1) prosecuted on the top charge, (2) convicted, and (3) given a relatively severe sentence (usually prison). As Spohn and Cederblom found, the use of a weapon and/or injury to the victim, factors that raise the seriousness of the offense, increase the severity of the disposition.

The third layer is a different story altogether. The less serious cases are regularly dismissed; defendants are often allowed to plead guilty to lesser offenses; and, if convicted, defendants are placed on probation. Outcomes are less predictable in the third layer because less consensus prevails about seriousness and the appropriate response than in the second layer.

In their classic study of the jury, Harry Kalven and Hans Zeisel explain this lack of consensus in terms of a "liberation" hypothesis. Under certain circumstances, they argue, jurors are "liberated" from normal constraints.[28] Applying this hypothesis to the wedding cake, we can say that in the third layer the lack of consensus about the seriousness of the crime or the offender's prior record liberates prosecutors and judges from the conventional shared understandings of seriousness. This allows them to base their decision on other factors. In some instances, the defendant's race or other personal attribute becomes a factor.

Spohn and Cederblom explored the liberation hypothesis in a study of 4,655 violent felony cases in Detroit from 1976 to 1978.[29] They found that African Americans were more likely to be incarcerated than whites. But this was true only in the less serious crimes: in assaults rather than more serious felonies, in acquaintance crimes, and in cases in which there were no prior violent felony convictions or no gun was involved. The outcomes in the more serious crimes (that is, the second-layer cases) were more consistent, with whites and African Americans treated equally harshly. In the less serious (e.g., third-layer) cases, there was less consensus about how much these cases were "worth," and this allowed extralegal factors such as race to come into play.

We might note that crime *victims* make the same distinctions about seriousness as do criminal justice officials. The National Criminal Victimization Survey (NCVS) consistently finds that victims report the more serious crimes at a higher rate than less serious ones. In 1994, victims reported 55.4 percent of all robberies but only 26.8 percent of all thefts. Moreover, they reported 64.4 percent of completed robberies but only 41.1 percent of attempted robberies. The higher the value of the stolen property, the greater the likelihood that victims report crimes. In 1994, victims reported 57.9 percent of thefts where the value of the stolen property was $250 or more but only 13 percent of those in which the value was less than $50.[30]

Prior Relationship: A Policy Dilemma

The role of the prior relationship between victim and offender presents a major policy dilemma. At issue is whether it is legitimate to use this role as a factor in decision making.

In the area of domestic violence, research has found that police traditionally have taken into account the nature of the relationship. The more intimate the relationship, the less likely the police are to make an arrest.[31] Thus, they are less likely to arrest the abusive husband than the abusive boyfriend or lover. In response to protests from women's groups, many police departments have adopted mandatory arrest or arrest-preferred policies that either require an arrest in a felonious domestic assault or advise officers that arrest is the preferred disposition. The intent is to ensure equal enforcement of the law and to eliminate discrimination based on marital status.

Along the same lines, Susan Estrich argues that all sexual assaults should be prosecuted with equal vigor. Rapes between acquaintances should not be treated less seriously than stranger rapes. Estrich describes her conversation with a local prosecutor who explained that he used the prior-relationship criterion in *all* criminal cases, not just rape. He was accurately describing how officials generally handle criminal cases.[32]

What would happen if we did eliminate prior relationship as a decision-making factor in all criminal cases? At the arrest stage, it would produce more domestic violence arrests. (In fact, some evidence suggests that the police have been making more domestic violence arrests in recent years. The FBI's arrest data indicate that aggravated assault arrests have been increasing since the 1970s, compared with other felony arrests.[33]) At the prosecution stage, it would move a large number of cases from the third to the second layer of the wedding cake. This would, in turn, result in more offenders being sentenced to prison.

This outcome presents us with a policy dilemma. Eliminating prior relationship as a decision-making factor would produce greater equality in the administration of justice—a desirable outcome. At the same time, however, it would increase the overall punitiveness of the justice system. Is that a desirable result?

A general lesson can be learned here. Significant changes in criminal justice policy often involve major tradeoffs. The gains on one side of the equation need to be considered in light of the consequences on the other side.

Hard or Soft on Crime? Unraveling the Paradox

Is the criminal justice system hard or soft on crime? Our wedding cake illuminates the paradox noted by Zimring, Morris, and Tonry: The system is simultaneously harsh and lenient. A great deal depends on the seriousness of the case. The system is very hard on second-layer cases, such as robberies committed by people with long prior records. But it is relatively soft on assaults by offenders with no prior records. It is hard on stranger rapes but more lenient on acquaintance assaults.

Additional support for the distinction between the second and third layers of the wedding cake is found in some career criminal prosecution programs. We will look at these in detail in Chapter 8. These programs are designed to concentrate prosecutorial resources on a special class of cases involving career criminals to make sure they are convicted and sentenced to prison. The San Diego Major Violator Unit succeeded in convicting 91.5 percent of the career criminals it handled. But 89.5 percent of the career criminals were being convicted before the program began. Under the program, 100 percent of the convicted career criminals were incarcerated, but the rate was 95.3 percent beforehand.[34] In short, criminals deemed "serious" by commonsense criteria were already being taken very seriously. As Diana Gordon, former director of the National Council on Crime and Delinquency, puts it, "Being tough doesn't work because being lenient is not the source of the problem."[35]

The idea that our criminal justice system is already fairly tough on serious crime comes as a surprise to many people, partly because the usual aggregation of crime statistics into gross categories obscures the important distinctions we have identified. Aggregate data give the *appearance* of softness because relatively few cases end up in the second layer. Violent crimes represent only 10 percent of all felonies reported to the police. Larceny, the least serious felony, accounts for 54 percent of the total.[36] The wedding cake model allows us to focus on how the system responds to the most serious crimes, those in the second layer.

The Lower Depths: The Fourth Layer

The fourth layer of the wedding cake is a world unto itself. The lower criminal courts handle all of the misdemeanors in most jurisdictions. The volume of cases is staggering, far outnumbering felonies. The eight Part I index crimes account for only 17 percent of the 14.5 million arrests in 1998. About half of the Part II arrests involve "public order" offenses: disorderly conduct, breach of the peace, drunkenness, and so on. In fact, the largest arrest category in 1998 was "All other offenses (except traffic)," with a total of 3.8 million.[37]

Under the criterion of seriousness, these cases are not considered to be "worth" much at all. Few of the defendants are regarded as real threats to public safety.

Because of the huge volume of cases and their relative lack of seriousness, relatively little concern is shown for the formalities of the felony process. In an excellent study of the lower courts of New Haven, Connecticut, Malcolm Feeley concludes that these institutions remain virtually untouched by the due process revolution.[38] To enter these courts is to step back in time eighty years. None of the defendants in the 1,640 cases he examined insisted on a jury trial.

Half never had an attorney. Even for those that did, the lawyer's contribution was minimal. Even more shocking, by our standards of due process, defendants were arraigned en masse, in assembly-line fashion. Sentences were extremely light. Half of the defendants received a fine of $50 or less, and only 4.9 percent were sentenced to jail.

Feeley concludes that the "process is the punishment": simply being brought into the lower courts is the real punishment, quite apart from the eventual outcome of the case. Insisting on your "rights" only increases the "punishment." A private attorney, for example, would charge $200 to handle a case (about $800 at today's rates). This is four times the fine if you simply copped a plea at the earliest possible moment. Moreover, because most defendants in the lower courts are hourly wage earners rather than salaried professionals, the lost wages involved in fighting a case would generally exceed the potential fine. (Each case in Feeley's study averaged three court appearances. Fighting the case would only increase the number and length of court dates.)

The closer we look, however, the more complicated the picture becomes. A study of the Philadelphia lower courts offers a different view and illustrates the hazards of generalizing about American criminal justice. Stephen J. Schulhofer found that in Philadelphia's two lower courts—Municipal Court and the Court of Common Pleas—about half (48 percent) of all cases went to trial, virtually all defendants had legal counsel, and the punishments meted out to the guilty were relatively significant. Nearly a quarter (22 percent) of the convicted offenders received a jail sentence, and 17.4 percent received fines (which ranged as high as several hundred dollars). Schulhofer argues that Feeley overstated the "process" costs of contesting a case in the lower courts. The price of the likely penalty, at least in Philadelphia, makes the case worth fighting. The main reason appears to be that penalties are significantly stiffer in Philadelphia than in New Haven.[39]

We do not need to resolve the differences between Feeley's and Schulhofer's findings here. The basic points are that (1) the lower courts are very different from the upper courts, and (2) there are significant differences between courts in different jurisdictions.

CONCLUSION

Our wedding cake model of the criminal justice system is designed to help us make sense of the administration of justice in action. As we go along, the most important thing to keep in mind is that we should not be distracted by celebrated cases. They make great stories for the tabloids, but they interfere with our understanding of routine operations in criminal justice. In particular, we want to be very skeptical of any policies that are based on celebrated cases. And because we are primarily concerned with the control of serious crime—robbery and burglary in particular—we need to keep our eyes focused on the second layer of the wedding cake.

NOTES

1. Bureau of Justice Statistics, *Census of State and Local Law Enforcement Agencies, 1996* (Washington, D.C.: Government Printing Office, 1998).

2. Bureau of Justice Statistics, *State Court Organization 1980* (Washington, D.C.: Government Printing Office, 1982).

3. This interpretation is vividly captured in "The Practice of Law as a Confidence Game," in Abraham Blumberg, *Criminal Justice*, 2d ed. (New York: New Viewpoints, 1979), pp. 242–43.

4. Samuel Walker, Cassia Spohn, and Miriam DeLone, *The Color of Justice: Race, Ethnicity, and Crime in America*, 2nd ed. (Belmont, CA: Wadsworth, 2000).

5. Donald Black, *The Manners and Customs of the Police* (New York: Academic Press, 1980).

6. Peter F. Nardulli, James Eisenstein, and Roy B. Flemming, *The Tenor of Justice: Criminal Courts and the Guilty Plea Process* (Urbana: University of Illinois Press, 1988).

7. Franklin Zimring, Shelia O'Malley, and Joel Eigen, "Punishing Homicide in Philadelphia: Perspectives on the Death Penalty," *University of Chicago Law Review* 43 (Winter 1976): 252.

8. Norval Morris and Michael H. Tonry, *Between Prison and Probation: Intermediate Punishments in a Rational Sentencing System* (New York: Oxford University Press, 1990), p. 3.

9. Walker et al., *The Color of Justice*, chap. 4.

10. President's Commission on Law Enforcement and Administration of Justice, *Task Force Report: Science and Technology* (Washington, D.C.: Government Printing Office, 1967), pp. 58–59.

11. On the origins of the systems perspective, see Samuel Walker, "Origins of the Contemporary Criminal Justice Paradigm: The American Bar Foundation Survey, 1953–1969," *Justice Quarterly* 9 (March 1992): 201–29.

12. Lawrence M. Friedman and Robert V. Percival, *The Roots of Justice: Crime and Punishment in Alameda County, California, 1870–1910* (Chapel Hill: University of North Carolina Press, 1981).

13. Michael R. Gottfredson and Don M. Gottfredson, *Decision Making in Criminal Justice: Toward the Rational Exercise of Discretion,* 2d ed. (New York: Plenum, 1988).

14. Jeffrey Toobin, *The Run of His Life: The People vs. O.J. Simpson* (New York: Random House, 1996).

15. Bureau of Justice Statistics, *Spouse Murder Defendants in Large Urban Counties* (Washington, D.C.: Government Printing Office, 1995).

16. Gottfredson and Gottfredson, *Decision Making in Criminal Justice.*

17. Cassia Spohn and Jerry Cederblom, "Race Disparities in Sentencing: A Test of the Liberation Hypothesis," *Justice Quarterly* 8 (September 1991): 306.

18. Jeffrey T. Ulmer, *Social Worlds of Sentencing* (Albany: State University of New York Press, 1997), pp. 60–62.

19. William F. McDonald, *Plea Bargaining: Critical Issues and Common Practices* (Washington, D.C.: Government Printing Office, 1985).

20. Lynn Mather, "Some Determinants of the Method of Case Disposition: Decision Making by Public Defenders in Los Angeles," *Law and Society Review* 8 (Winter 1974): 187–216.

21. David Sudnow, "Normal Crimes: Sociological Features of the Penal Code in a Public Defender Office," *Social Problems* 12 (Winter 1965): 255–76.

22. John Rosecrance, "Maintaining the Myth of Individualized Justice: Probation Presentence Reports," *Justice Quarterly* 5 (June 1988): 235–56.

23. Malcolm M. Feeley, "Perspectives on Plea Bargaining," *Law and Society Review* 13 (Winter 1979): 199.

24. Jeffrey T. Ulmer, *Social Worlds of Sentencing* (Albany: State University of New York Press, 1997).

25. Donald Black, *Toward a General Theory of Social Control,* vol. 2 (Orlando, FL: Academic Press, 1984), pp. 1–28.

26. Vera Institute, *Felony Arrests,* rev. ed. (New York: Longman, 1981).

27. Ibid., pp. 42–43.

28. Harry Kalven, Jr., and Hans Zeisel, *The American Jury* (Boston: Little, Brown, 1966), pp. 164–166.

29. Spohn and Cederblom, "Race and Disparities in Sentencing."

30. Bureau of Justice Statistics, *Criminal Victimization in the United States, 1994* (Washington, D.C.: Government Printing Office, 1997), p. 84.

31. Black, *The Manners and Customs of the Police.*

32. Susan Estrich, *Real Rape* (Cambridge, MA: Harvard University Press, 1987).

33. See the arrest trends in Bureau of Justice Statistics, *Sourcebook of Criminal Justice Statistics–1998* (Washington, D.C.: Government Printing Office, 1999), p. 329–30, and previous editions for earlier arrest data.

34. Eleanor Chelimsky and Judith Dahmann, *National Evaluation of the Career Criminal Program: Final Report* (MacLean, VA: MITRE, 1979).

35. Diana R. Gordon, *Towards Realistic Reform: A Commentary on Proposals for Change in New York City's Criminal Justice System* (Hackensack, NJ: National Council on Crime and Delinquency, 1981), p. 16.

36. Federal Bureau of Investigation, *Crime in the United States, 1994* (Washington, D.C.: Government Printing Office, 1995).

37. Federal Bureau of Investigation, *Crime in the United States, 1998* (Washington, DC: Government Printing Office, 1999).

38. Malcolm M. Feeley, *The Process Is the Punishment* (New York: Russell Sage Foundation, 1979).

39. Stephen J. Schulhofer, "No Job Too Small: Justice Without Bargaining in the Lower Criminal Courts," *American Bar Foundation Research Journal* (Summer 1985): 519–98.

3

The Going Rate

EVALUATING THE SYSTEM

We now turn our attention to the question of how the criminal justice system works on a day-to-day basis. How effectively does it control crime? How successful is it in catching, prosecuting, and punishing dangerous criminals? Is the system fair? Is there a pattern of racial discrimination?

Great controversy surrounds these questions. In a book subtitled *The Collapse of Criminal Justice,* Judge Harold Rothwax bluntly declares, "The long arm of the law is somewhat fractured these days."[1] Rothwax describes case after case of criminals who committed serious crimes not being punished because of some loophole in the system. Other experts see a different problem. Jerome G. Miller argues in *Search and Destroy* that the system is "highly influenced by race," that there is systematic discrimination against African Americans, and that the criminal process "is an alienating and socially destabilizing exercise that usually creates more problems than it solves."[2]

Where does the truth lie? Is the system too weak or too harsh? Evaluating the performance of our criminal justice system is a difficult task. On some questions we do not have good data. Even where reasonably good data are available, experts disagree over what they mean. Is a three-year prison sentence for burglary "tough" or "lenient"? Is there systematic racial discrimination in sentencing? Some experts say yes, others say no.[3]

The debate is complicated by the fact that we have fifty-one separate criminal justice systems. Each one has its own distinct local legal culture, with slightly different traditions about how cases are handled. The Bureau of Justice Statistics (BJS) report *The Prosecution of Felony Arrests, 1988* illustrates these differences. In Los Angeles, 36 percent of all arrests are rejected by the prosecutor, compared with only 18 percent in Washington, D.C. In Portland, Oregon, 10 percent of all cases go to trial, compared with a national average of 3 percent. In Rhode Island, 43 percent of the cases that go to trial result in acquittal, compared with only 15 percent in Seattle.[4] Offenders convicted of a violent felony serve an average of 34 months in jail and prison in Illinois but 59 months in Pennsylvania; the national average is 54 months.[5]

Despite the local variations, we can identify some general features of the criminal process in this country. In virtually every local jurisdiction, there is a *going rate* for crime.[6] Some scholars argue that if you know the offense and the defendant's prior criminal record, you can probably predict the outcome of about 80 percent of all cases. Plea "bargaining" actually has very little impact on case outcomes.[7]

The going rate can change, however. Change can be the result of two factors. The first is a conscious change in *policy*. The new "three strikes" laws,

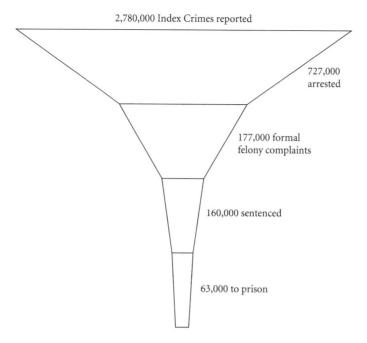

2,780,000 Index Crimes reported

727,000
arrested

177,000 formal
felony complaints

160,000 sentenced

63,000 to prison

FIGURE 3-1 The funneling effect of the criminal justice system.

SOURCE: President's Commission on Law Enforcement and Administration of Justice, *Task Force Report: Science and Technology* (Washington, DC: Government Printing Office), p. 61.

which dramatically increase the penalties for certain repeat offenders, is a good example.[8] A second kind of change is the result of *unplanned* developments. The impact of the post–World War II baby boom on crime was not planned by anyone. A significant increase in the workload of the justice system, meanwhile, produces adaptations. Arrests for "public order" offenses, for example, declined significantly between the 1960s and 1990s.[9] Some analysts believe that as serious crime increased, police simply shifted their priorities and gave less attention to relatively minor crimes.

THE FUNNEL

To understand the going rate, a good place to begin is the President's Crime Commission's analysis of the flow of cases through the system (Figure 3-1). These data are from the 1960s, but they are still relevant in terms of some general patterns in the administration of justice. The Crime Commission concluded that only 1 percent of all criminals go to prison. Only 63,000 offenders were sentenced to prison despite about 6 million reported and unreported crimes. Many people cite this 1 percent figure as evidence of the weakness of the system.

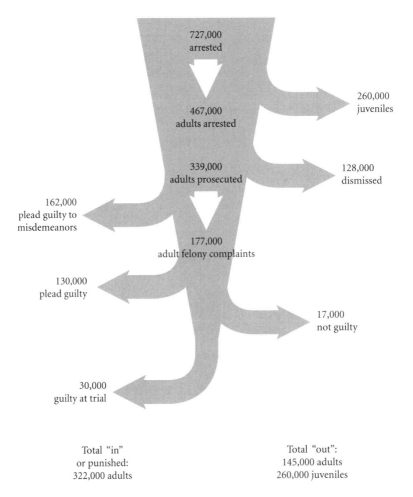

727,000
arrested

467,000
adults arrested

260,000
juveniles

339,000
adults prosecuted

128,000
dismissed

162,000
plead guilty to
misdemeanors

177,000
adult felony complaints

130,000
plead guilty

17,000
not guilty

30,000
guilty at trial

Total "in"
or punished:
322,000 adults

Total "out":
145,000 adults
260,000 juveniles

FIGURE 3-2 Silberman's recalculation of the Criminal Commission's funnel.

SOURCE: Charles Silberman, *Criminal Violence, Criminal Justice* (New York: Random House, 1978), pp. 257–261.

Charles Silberman, however, argues that the Crime Commission's analysis is "grossly misleading."[9] Reanalyzing the same data (Figure 3-2), he points out that about 260,000 (35.7 percent) of the original 727,000 arrests involve juveniles whose cases are transferred to juvenile court. What happens to those juveniles is, of course, extremely important but not our concern here. To remain consistent with our ground rules we will concentrate on the adults.[10]

Subtracting the juveniles leaves 467,000 adult arrests. Silberman argues that this is the proper baseline for assessing the performance of the adult criminal justice system. About 27 percent of these arrests (128,000) are dismissed, leaving 339,000 prosecuted adults. A prosecution rate of 73 percent is hardly a sign of softness on crime. Then, about half (48 percent) of these defendants plead

Table 3-1 Felony defendants, 1996

Offense	Percent of all arrests resulting in a felony conviction	Percent of defendants convicted of a felony sentenced to prison
Murder	71	92
Robbery	40	73
Aggravated assault	16	42
Burglary	41	45
Drug trafficking	66	39

SOURCE: Bureau of Justice Statistics, *Felony Sentences in State Courts, 1996* (Washington, DC: Government Printing Office, 1999).

guilty to a misdemeanor. These cases are not "lost"; the defendants are convicted and acquire a criminal record. We might disagree about severity of punishment, but the fact is that they are convicted.

Subtracting these convictions leaves 177,000 adult felony complaints. Of these, 90 percent are convicted: 130,000 by a guilty plea and 30,000 by trial. This is an extremely impressive conviction rate. When we combine the 177,000 felony convictions with the 162,000 misdemeanor convictions, we have a total of 332,000 adults convicted. This represents 69 percent of the adults arrested and 95 percent of those prosecuted. This is a picture of a fairly tough criminal justice system.

The Crime Commission and Silberman both used 1960s data. Have things changed in the past 30 years? The BJS report on *Felony Sentences in State Courts, 1996* (Table 3-1) indicates that 40 percent of all robbery arrests lead to a felony conviction, compared with 71 percent of all murder arrests, 41 percent of all burglary arrests, but only 16 percent of aggravated assault arrests. Those not resulting in conviction are rejected, dismissed, diverted, or referred. Of those cases that do result in a conviction, 90 percent are the result of a guilty plea. Finally, 69 percent of those convicted of a felony are sentenced to some form of incarceration (38 percent to prison; 31 percent to jail).[11]

The general going rate changed in complex ways between the 1980s and 1990s. In one important respect the system got tougher on criminals. The percentage of arrests for murder resulting in a felony conviction increased from 48 percent in 1988 to 71 percent in 1996; for robbery arrests, the increase was from 32 percent to 40 percent (see Table 3-1). At the same time, however, the percentage of convicted felons sentenced to prison fell, from 44 percent in 1988 to 38 percent in 1996. This drop was offset by an increase in jail sentences, with the result that the percentage sentenced to some form of incarceration remained stable at 69 percent. For those sentenced to prison, the average amount of time actually served increased significantly: from 38 months for robbers in 1988 to 48 months in 1996, and from 79 months to 128 months for convicted murderers.[12] In short, the system has gotten slowly but steadily tougher on crime, with important consequences for the justice system.

The wedding cake model helps us refine this analysis even further. Serious crimes are treated far more harshly than less serious crimes. In 1996, 71 percent of all murder arrests resulted in a felony conviction, with 92 percent of them receiving a prison sentence. Only 16 percent of aggravated assault arrests resulted in a felony conviction, however, and only 42 percent of those convictions resulted in a prison sentence. These data confirm the point we made in Chapter 2: The seriousness of the offense is a major factor in the disposition of felony cases, and the more serious crimes are treated more harshly.

Rejections and Dismissals: Loophole?

The high percentage of arrests that do not result in conviction is an important issue for further analysis. Is this case attrition the result of defects in the system (e.g., "loopholes") that can be corrected by new law or policy, or is it the result of factors that are inherent in the nature of criminal cases and the administration of justice?

Cases drop out of the system after arrest in one of three different ways. First, some arrests are dismissed by the police themselves. A police officer makes an arrest, but a supervisor refuses to sign off on it because of insufficient evidence or some other factor, and the suspect is released. Joan Petersilia found that about 11 percent of all arrests in California were dropped by the police.[13] The Police Foundation, meanwhile, found that many of these arrests are not officially recorded by police departments.[14] Second, prosecutors reject or refuse to accept some cases. Typically, they conclude that there is not sufficient evidence to prosecute the suspect. Third, some cases are dismissed later by the prosecutor or a judge.

Table 3-2 presents the BJS data on the reasons for rejections and dismissals in New York and San Diego. Evidence problems—either insufficient evidence or lack of any evidence—account for most of the rejections by prosecutors: 61 percent in New York and 51 percent in San Diego. Witness problems are the second most important reason: 18 percent of the rejections in New York and 19 percent in San Diego. For most crimes against persons (robbery, rape, assault), the testimony of the victim or a witness is the primary evidence. These data indicate that evidence and witness problems account for about 70 to 80 percent of all rejections (These data are from the 1988 BJS report; subsequent reports on prosecution and sentencing do not include the reasons for case attrition.)

Evidence and witness problems are also important factors in the dismissal of cases, accounting for 33 percent of the dismissals in New York City and 20 percent in San Diego. The lack of evidence or witnesses is a legitimate reason for dropping a case. A prosecutor cannot win a case without them. Dismissing cases for these reasons does not mean that the system is soft on crime. Officials are simply doing what circumstances force them to do. In short, rejections and dismissals are not a "loophole."

A closer look reveals that the term *dismissal* is misleading. Many of these cases are not really "lost." In San Diego, for example, almost half of the "dismissals" were diverted (11 percent), referred for other prosecution (27 percent), or covered by another case (10 percent). In other words, the defendant experienced some kind of sanction at the hands of the criminal justice system, through either prosecution on a lesser charge or involuntary treatment in a diversion program.

The BJS data clearly indicate that due process problems—illegal searches or coerced confessions—are not a major cause of rejections and dismissals. They accounted for only 15 percent of the rejections and none of the dismissals in San Diego. Equally important, due process problems arose primarily in drug and weapons cases. They accounted for only 1 percent of the rejections of robbery cases and 8 percent of the burglary rejections. In short, thousands of criminals are not "beating the system" in the early stages of prosecution because of legal "technicalities." Judge Harold Rothwax's attack on the rights of criminal suspects in his book *Guilty* is an excellent example of using only "celebrated cases" and ignoring the general patterns in the administration of justice.[15]

One unresolved question remains, however. The BJS data indicate that many cases are dismissed in the "interest of justice." What exactly does this mean? It may mean that the offense was not that serious, or that the victim and offender know each other, or that some form of private settlement has been worked out. Until more detailed research is done on this question, we do not know whether these dismissals are appropriate or whether they represent a covert pattern of bias in the system.

The decision to reject or dismiss a case is a highly discretionary one. Most of these decisions are made very quietly, and the prosecutor does not really have to account to anyone for them. An important question is whether a pattern of racial and ethnic bias is apparent in these decisions. Cassie Spohn and her colleagues found that women and white defendants were more likely to have their cases rejected than males and minorities. The racial and ethnic disparities were strongest at the rejection stage only. This may result from the fact that the decision to reject is much less visible than the decision to dismiss. Once a case has been accepted for prosecution, it becomes known to a wider range of people, and this visibility may act as a constraint on prosecutors and judges.[16]

Joan Petersilia's analysis of racial disparities found that black defendants were more likely to have their cases rejected and dismissed than whites. This apparent favored treatment, however, may be a result of discrimination at the arrest stage. Some research suggests that police arrest African Americans on weaker evidence than whites. When these weak evidence cases reach the prosecutor, they are more likely to be dismissed or rejected. In short, discrimination takes place, but at an earlier point than that identified by Spohn and her colleagues.[17]

Table 3-2 Why felony arrests are declined for prosecution

Manhattan, New York 1988

Most serious charge			Arrests declined due to:					
	Diversion	Other prosecution	Evidence	Witness	Due process	Interest of justice	Covered by other case	Other
Percentage of declinations	0%	3%	61%	18%	2%	10%	0%	6%
Murder and manslaughter	0	0	75	25	0	0	0	0
Rape	0	0	30	40	0	30	0	0
Robbery	0	8	63	22	0	3	0	4
Aggravated assault	0	3	33	40	0	13	0	11
Burglary	0	0	79	21	0	0	0	0

San Diego, California 1988

Most serious charge			Arrests declined due to:					
	Diversion	Other prosecution	Evidence	Witness	Due process	Interest of justice	Covered by other case	Other
Percentage of declinations	0%	0%	51%	19%	13%	11%	3%	4%
Murder and manslaughter	0	0	50	3	0	30	0	17
Rape	0	0	30	60	0	8	1	2
Robbery	0	0	49	36	1	6	0	7
Aggravated assault	0	0	39	46	2	9	1	3
Burglary	0	0	59	15	8	8	5	5

Table 3-2 continued Why cases are dismissed after filing or indictment

Manhattan, New York 1988

Most serious charge	Diversion	Other prosecution	Cases dismissed due to:					
			Evidence	Witness	Due process	Interest of justice	Covered by other case	Other
Percentage of declinations	0%	0%	19%	14%	0%	10%	6%	51%
Murder and manslaughter	11	1	17	15	0	2	14	39
Rape	0	0	13	33	0	4	3	47
Robbery	0	0	18	21	0	4	4	53
Aggravated assault	1	0	10	26	0	13	3	48
Burglary	0	0	15	11	0	13	6	54

San Diego, California 1988

Most serious charge	Diversion	Other prosecution	Cases dismissed due to:					
			Evidence	Witness	Due process	Interest of justice	Covered by other case	Other
Percentage of declinations	11%	27%	14%	6%	0%	7%	10%	25%
Murder and manslaughter	0	20	20	0	0	30	0	30
Rape	0	4	22	22	0	31	4	18
Robbery	0	17	27	27	1	4	3	22
Aggravated assault	2	26	21	17	0	5	5	23
Burglary	2	25	12	10	0	6	13	32

SOURCE: Bureau of Justice Statistics, *The Prosecution of Felony Arrests, 1988* (Washington, DC: Government Printing Office, 1992).

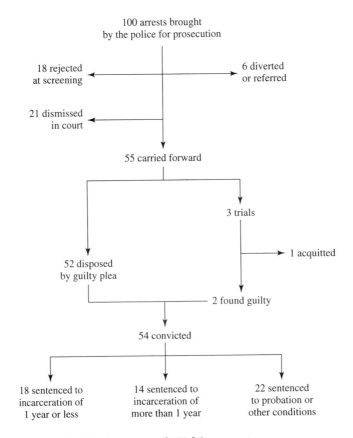

FIGURE 3-3 Typical outcome of 100 felony arrests brought by the police for prosecution.

SOURCE: Bureau of Justice Statistics, *The Prosecution of Felony Arrests, 1988* (Washington, DC: Government Printing Office, 1992).

From Indictment to Punishment

Once the weak cases have been weeded out, the criminal justice system becomes extremely punitive. Almost all of those offenders indicted are convicted, and the majority of those convicted are incarcerated, in either prison or jail. Persons convicted of violent crimes are even more likely to be incarcerated: 70 percent for all violent crimes, 82 percent of those convicted of robbery, and 87 percent of those convicted of rape.[18]

It is important to note that the term *incarcerated* includes people sent to prison and jail. Many people conclude that the system is soft on crime because they look only at the data on felons sent to prison. In practice, however, there are many "split sentences," involving a jail term followed by probation. In 1996, only 31 percent of convicted felons got probation; 38 percent were sentenced to prison and 31 percent went to jail.[19]

The category of *time served* is also important in trying to assess the going rate. The sentence pronounced by the judge does represent how much time the offender will serve. Most offenders sentenced to prison are released early as a result of good-time reductions and parole. The percentage of nominal sentences actually served increased from 32 to 45 percent between 1988 and 1996. The estimated time served by robbers increased from 38 to 48 months in that time period, while burglars served an average of three additional months (25 versus 22 months).

An International Perspective on the Going Rate

How does the going rate for crime in the United States compare with its counterpart in other countries? One of the standard liberal criticisms is that our criminal justice system is far more punitive than that of any other country. Conservatives, meanwhile, argue that we are too lenient and fail to punish criminals. James Lynch's careful analysis of comparative data suggests that both liberals and conservatives are clinging to their favorite myths on this question.[20]

On one hand, we do lock up a lot of people. We already have the highest incarceration rate in the world (350 per 100,000), and current sentencing trends suggest that this will continue.[21] And as our previous discussion indicates, we are fairly tough on those offenders we manage to arrest. From this perspective, it is hard to say that we are soft on crime.

At the same time, however, our high incarceration rate is mainly the result of our high rates of violent crime. The American murder rate was then four times higher than Canada's and ten times higher than England's and West Germany's. Our robbery rate was five times higher than those of England and West Germany. Violent crimes, moreover, were more likely to result in prison sentences. Furthermore, armed robbery was even more likely to result in a prison sentence than unarmed robbery. Lynch points out that a far higher proportion of robberies in the United States are armed than in other countries. In other words, we have a high incarceration rate in large part because we have such high rates of those crimes that typically send an offender to prison.[22]

The relevant question becomes: Is the going rate for particular crimes significantly higher in the United States than it is in other countries? Lynch estimated the chances of going to prison for a person arrested for murder, robbery, burglary, and larceny/theft in the United States, England, Canada, and West Germany. He found that a robber's chance of going to prison was 36 percent in the United States, 41 percent in Canada, and 39 percent in the United Kingdom. The odds were lower only in West Germany.

The odds of going to prison were also roughly the same for murder, burglary, and larceny in the three English-speaking countries. In terms of the tendency to send convicted offenders to prison, then, the United States is not that much more punitive than other countries.[23]

In terms of time served, however, the United States is significantly more punitive, especially for property crimes. Lynch found that average number of months served in prison for murder in the United States (50.5) was slightly higher than in England and Wales (43) but lower than in Canada (57). (Because of different methodologies, these estimates for the United States vary slightly from the ones cited earlier in this section.) Average time served for robbery was somewhat higher in the United States and substantially higher for both burglary and theft. Burglars in the United States, for example, serve an average of 16.06 months, compared with 5.23 in Canada and 6.72 in England and Wales. The gap was even greater for theft. Convicted thieves in America serve an average of 12 months, compared with only 2 in Canada and 4.65 in England and Wales.

A separate BJS report comparing crime and punishment in the United States and England and Wales between 1981 and 1996 found that the United States and England incarcerated an equally high percentage of convicted murderers, robbers, and rapists, but that the United States imprisons a far higher percentage of burglars, assaulters, and auto thieves. The BJS data also indicate that American incarceration rates have been stable, and in some cases rising, and that there is no truth to the claim that the American criminal justice system is "collapsing."[24]

Lynch's comparative research highlights the fact that the going rate consists of two components. The first is the tendency to imprison serious offenders. On this point, the American going rate is very similar to other industrialized countries. The second is the amount of prison time actually served. Here, the United States is more punitive—but primarily for property, not violent crimes. Lynch did not study drug offenses, but the United States is likely comparatively very punitive, in terms of both incarceration and length of sentences.

THE COURTROOM WORK GROUP

The going rate is established and maintained by the people who operate the criminal justice system. It is important to remember that "the system" is not an impersonal entity but a process carried out by people making a series of discretionary decisions.[25] A police officer decides to make an arrest; a prosecutor rejects a case; a judge sentences an offender to prison, and so on. To understand how the system works, we need to examine how these people work together.

Prosecutors, defense attorneys, judges, and to some extent police officers comprise the *courtroom work group.* In perhaps the best study of this phenomenon, Nardulli, Eisenstein, and Flemming characterize local courthouses as "communities." "After spending an enormous number of hours in various county courts," they observe, "we became convinced that the concept of a courthouse community can be an immensely useful tool in trying to understand them."[26] In this context, "community" means that a group of people work together and have a mutual interest in getting the job done as efficiently as possible.

The bureaucratic setting of the justice system heavily influences the decisions of individual officials. Even though a police officer has enormous discretion to make an arrest, that decision will be reviewed by others: a supervisor who signs off on it; a prosecutor who reviews the case and accepts it for prosecution; a defense attorney who might challenge the legality of the search; and a judge who will rule on a number of issues. All of these actions serve to constrain the police officer's actions.

Working together every day, members of the courtroom work group reach a general consensus about how different kinds of cases should be handled. This involves a shared understanding about how much cases are "worth." There are "heavy" cases (that is, serious violent crimes) and "garbage" cases (relatively minor theft). This valuation allows them to move cases along quickly.

Conflict between prosecution and defense is the exception rather than the rule. Although in theory we have an *adversarial* process, in which truth is to be determined through conflict between prosecution and defense, the reality is that an *administrative* system is in effect, with a high degree of consensus and cooperation. Experts on plea bargaining describe the process as a "supermarket": set prices and a high volume of business.[27] (We will discuss this phenomenon in more detail in Chapter 8.)

Frederic Suffett's study of bail setting offers an excellent illustration of consensus and cooperation in the courtroom work group. Only 3 percent of the cases he examined involve any conflict over the bail decision; some disagreement arose in another 9 percent.[28] Over the years, the members of this work group had developed a shared understanding about how much bail to set for different kinds of cases—in other words, how much each case was worth. In her study of plea bargaining, Alissa Pollitz Worden found a high degree of judicial agreement with prosecutorial sentence recommendations. She speculates that going rates "may be so predictable that a prosecutor need not make a formal recommendation in order to ensure that a sentence bargain will be honored by the court."[29]

Another example is John Rosecrance's study of presentence investigation (PSI) reports by probation officers. In theory, the PSI is an independent evaluation of a convicted offender's social history, taking into account criminal record, employment history, family status, and so on. Yet Rosecrance found that probation officers (POs) classified offenders very quickly on the basis of their offense and prior record. Even more important, they based their recommendations on what they thought judges and prosecutors wanted. The California POs he studied were in regular contact with prosecutors and discussed their cases with them. They rarely challenged plea agreements, which often included an understanding about the sentence. As one PO put it, "It's stupid to try and bust a deal. . . . Who needs the hassle? . . . Everyone, including the defendant, has already agreed."[30]

Nardulli, Eisenstein, and Flemming add the important point that courtroom work groups vary from jurisdiction to jurisdiction. Each "community" has its own "distinctive character." Typically, one person plays "a dominant role," "by virtue of personality, professional skills (or reputation), political power, longevity, or some other attribute."[31] Ulmer's study of three Pennsylvania courts found important differences related to the stability of the membership in local work groups. In the wealthy suburban court system ("Rich County") there was a high degree of membership stability and a culture of understanding and collegiality. In the large urban court ("Metro County"), on the other hand, there was considerable turnover in the prosecutor's office, which resulted in conflict between prosecutors and defense attorneys and close relations between the defense attorneys and judges. The Metro County example illustrates the extent to which other members of a courtroom work group adjust to some kind of disruption arising from one member of the group.[32]

The Limits of Reform

The courtroom work group has enormous power to limit, frustrate, or even block reforms in the administration of justice. A state legislature might pass a new law, or the Supreme Court might issue a "landmark" ruling, but that does not guarantee that anything will really change. A few examples illustrate the point.

The Supreme Court ruled in 1967 that defendants in juvenile court have a constitutional right to an attorney (*In re Gault*). Barry Feld, however, found that only half (47.7 percent) of the kids in Minnesota juvenile courts in 1984 actually had legal counsel. State officials simply did not comply with the law.[33]

Congress passed a "speedy trial" law in 1974, and several states enacted similar laws. Malcolm Feeley, however, found that these laws had almost no effect on the flow of cases. All members of the courtroom work group—judges, prosecutors, and defense attorneys—had their own reasons for delaying cases. The laws permit exceptions to the requirement and officials take advantage of them. As one judge explained, "Our court has figured out ways to deal with the [speedy trial] act that don't cause us to change our practices at all."[34]

A study of the new "three strikes" laws found that with the exception of California, prosecutors in most states were simply not using the law. Wisconsin had used it only once in a year and a half, whereas five other states had not used it at all. And in California, the law was frequently used by prosecutors in Los Angeles but hardly at all in San Francisco.[35] Prosecutors in San Francisco and most other states, in short, used their discretion essentially to nullify the law.

We should not be completely cynical about the prospects for change. Some reforms are implemented. A few examples illustrate the point.

- The "defense of life" rule was designed to reduce police use of deadly force. As a result, the number of persons shot and killed by the police fell from 559 in 1975 to 300 in 1987.[36]

- The Minnesota Sentencing Guidelines enacted in 1980 had the explicit goal of limiting the use of imprisonment. To a great extent this strategy has worked, and Minnesota has maintained the lowest incarceration rate of any state (with the possible exception of South Dakota).[37]

- The federal sentencing guidelines were explicitly designed to increase punishment for serious crimes. They have achieved this goal, and the number of federal prisoners increased from 32,695 in 1985 to 99,466 by 1995.[38]

The Dynamics of Reform

Which reforms work and which ones fail? A great deal depends on the nature of the reform itself. Some experts believe that modest reforms, which require only slight changes in how the courtroom work group operates, are more likely to succeed than sweeping changes. Raymond T. Nimmer argues that "the probability of system change is inversely related to the degree of change sought by a reform."[39] Eisenstein, Flemming, and Nardulli agree, concluding that "the more radical a proposed change the less likely is its adoption."[40] The "three strikes" laws represent radical disruptions of established going rates and probably for that reason have been ignored in most jurisdictions.

In their study of rape law reform, on the other hand, Cassia Spohn and Julie Horney found significant changes in only one of six jurisdictions. They speculate that the new Michigan rape law was so comprehensive that it forced changes in the attitudes and behavior of courtroom work group officials, whereas the minor reforms in the other five jurisdictions had little impact.[41]

In the conclusion of their study of courts and their communities, Eisenstein, Flemming, and Nardulli offer some other sobering conclusions about the possibilities for reform. On one hand, changes mandated from *outside* the courtroom work groups face serious obstacles. They agree with Feeley that work groups have enormous ability to resist change. At the same time, however, change initiated from *within,* by the work group itself, also faces major obstacles. Efforts by judges to speed up trials may be blocked by prosecution and defense attorneys.[42]

In short, *some* things work. We should not assume that "nothing works" or that "everything works." The important point here is that the power of the courtroom work group to frustrate reform is extremely relevant to our search for sensible and effective crime policies. Even if we found a good policy, officials could not implement it.

Criminal Justice Thermodynamics

The systems perspective on the administration of justice helps us see how changes in one part of the system affect decisions in other parts. Malcolm Feeley suggests that a major change may set off a "chain reaction throughout the entire system," forcing other officials to adapt and in some cases creating new and unanticipated problems.[43] We explain this chain reaction effect in terms of "criminal justice thermodynamics." You may remember from a physics class that the law of thermodynamics says that every action has an equal and opposite reaction. The justice system works in much the same way: actions produce reactions.

Our law of criminal justice thermodynamics states:

An increase in the severity of the penalty will result in less frequent application of that penalty.

Our law has an important corollary:

The less often a severe penalty is applied, the more arbitrary will be the occasions when it is applied.

The death penalty is an excellent example of the law of thermodynamics. Because it is the ultimate penalty, it exerts enormous pressure on the courtroom work group. Many devices are used to evade its application (plea bargaining to a second-degree murder charge, demanding a jury trial, using the insanity defense, appealing on every potential issue, requesting pardon or commutation, and so forth). Thus, the action of the prosecutor in filing first-degree murder charges (making the case eligible for the death penalty) causes a reaction by the defense.

Because the death penalty is rarely used, its application is very arbitrary. In the landmark case of *Furman v. Georgia* (1972), the Supreme Court characterized the application of the death penalty as being so rare that it is "freakish" and akin to being "struck by lightning."[44]

And as we have already noted, "three strikes" laws dramatically increase the severity of the punishment—typically, life in prison for conviction on a third felony (or in some states, third violent felony)—with the result that they are ignored in most jurisdictions.[45] Use of the law in California illustrates the "billiard ball effect" of a radical change on the rest of the criminal justice system. More defendants were refusing to plead guilty and demanding trials. The backlog of defendants awaiting jury trials immediately increased from 480 to 700 in the first ten months. This backlog produced overcrowding in county jails, with additional costs to taxpayers. The county auditor in Los Angeles reported that the law had cost the county $169 million in extra costs in less than two years. And as a result of overcrowding, more convicted offenders were being released to make room for those awaiting trials.[46]

Pamala L. Griset's study of correctional practices in New York illustrates how an increase in severity can produce adaptations that, in many respects, undermine the original intent of getting tougher with criminals. New York adopted a series of mandatory sentencing laws in 1973 and 1978, followed by several early release programs in 1987 and 1989. The result was an odd mix of indeterminate and mandatory sentencing policies. The prison population began to increase, but because of financial constraints, the state did not build all of the planned new prisons.[47]

The three new early release programs—shock incarceration, "earned eligibility" for parole, and CASAT (Comprehensive Alcohol and Substance Abuse

Treatment)—gave correctional officials enormous discretion over offenders' eligibility for early release. They began using these programs to reduce prison populations. Under earned eligibility, inmates gained a "presumption of release" for merely participating in a treatment, educational, or work program. Thus, they received a reward for what in the past had been considered minimal good conduct. The net effect was to release them early and to undercut the intent of mandatory minimum sentencing laws. Meanwhile, many offenders released under work release programs were allowed to live at home and report in twice a week. Over one-third of the participants in this "day reporting" program had been convicted of violent crimes. Here, also, correctional officials gained a vast amount of hidden discretion and used it to undercut the supposedly "tough" sentencing laws.

How Many Mistakes?

The fact that the administration of justice is a human process introduces the possibility of human error. How often does the courtroom work group make a mistake and convict an innocent person? Every year, a few spectacular examples come to light. A study conducted by an investigative team of Northwestern University journalism faculty and students resulted in the release of 13 people from death row because they were falsely convicted. In Illinois, in fact, one death-sentenced offender has been exonerated for every one actually executed.[48]

The relevant question is: How often do such mistakes happen? What is the error rate? Are there just a few "celebrated cases," or do miscarriages of justice happen all the time?

C. Ronald Huff and his colleagues undertook an ingenious effort to estimate the number of wrongful convictions. They surveyed 229 Ohio criminal justice officials (judges, prosecutors, public defenders, police), along with attorneys general from all states, and asked for *their* estimate of the frequency of wrongful convictions. After eliminating the extremely high and low estimates, they concluded that errors occur in slightly less than 1 percent of all felony cases.[49]

What are we to make of this estimate? From one perspective, an error rate of less than 1 percent is very good. We should all be so successful in whatever we do. It compares very favorably with the false positive and false negative rates we will encounter with the prediction problem in Chapter 4. But Huff and his associates projected this error rate to the national level and estimated 5,729 wrongful convictions in 1981 (one-half of 1 percent of the total of 1,145,780 convictions). Six thousand innocent people convicted of a felony every year is a shocking fact to contemplate.

As for the death penalty, Hugo Bedeau and Michael Radelet estimated that for every twenty persons executed in this country since 1900, at least one innocent person was convicted of a capital crime. They found a total of 343 persons mistakenly convicted of capital crimes; 25 were actually executed, while many of the others served prison terms of up to 25 years.[50]

BOX 3-1

Now let us say we wanted to improve the overall crime control effectiveness of the criminal justice system. Where is the best place to start?

The following list provides an overview of the administration of justice, including reported and unreported crime. Let us begin with 1,000 actual felonies. The NCVS tells us that only 360 will be reported to the police. The FBI tells us that only 21 percent of those cases, or 76, will be cleared by arrest. The BJS data tell us that 45 percent (34) of those cases will not be prosecuted. That leaves 42 adult felony indictments. Almost all of them will be convicted, and most will serve some time in prison or jail.

1,000	Actual felonies
360	Reported to police (36 percent reporting rate)
76	Arrests (21 percent clearance rate)
42	Felony indictments (55 percent prosecution rate)
41	Convicted
23	Incarcerated

It is obvious that the weakest point in the system is the failure of victims to report crimes. Some people might assume that if more crimes were reported, there would be more arrests (assuming a stable clearance rate of 21 percent), more convictions, and so on. This analysis might suggest that raising the reporting rate would increase the overall effectiveness of the system.

But would it? We need to consider the impact "downstream" of a higher reporting rate. First, the police would have more work, which would leave them with less time for other responsibilities. Second, it is not necessarily true that the clearance rate would remain the same. The rate might fall if it happened that people were reporting more crimes where there were no good leads (as in larcenies where there was no witness). Third, if the number of arrests did increase substantially, the jails would be more crowded, prosecutors and defense attorneys would have much heavier caseloads, court dockets might become more backlogged, and so on.

In short, an increase in the reporting rate might create more problems than it solved. The justice system might become less rather than more efficient, and the result would not necessarily be more offenders convicted and sentenced to prison. This exercise offers another illustration of the thermodynamics of the criminal justice system and the billiard ball effect of a major change "upstream."

CONCLUSION

A going rate for crime exists in the United States. If you are convicted of a certain crime and have a certain prior record, it is possible to predict the outcome of your case with a high degree of accuracy. The going rate does vary between jurisdictions but is fairly stable within each one. It is established and maintained by the members of the courtroom work group, the members of which work together daily.

The concept of the going rate is extremely important for our search for sensible and effective crime policies for two reasons. First, many proposed policies are based on mistaken assumptions about how the system works. They do not take into account the fact that the administration of justice is very stable, consistent, and predictable and that it is relatively tough on those offenders who are caught and prosecuted. Second, many proposed reforms would have trouble being implemented. The going rate is determined by the courtroom work group, which has tremendous power to adapt and either ignore or evade the intent of a new law or policy. Simply passing a new law does not necessarily mean that the intended changes will occur.

NOTES

1. Judge Harold J. Rothwax, *Guilty: The Collapse of Criminal Justice* (New York: Random House, 1996), p. 25.

2. Jerome G. Miller, *Search and Destroy: African-American Males in the Criminal Justice System* (Cambridge: Cambridge University Press, 1996), p. xii.

3. Samuel Walker, Cassia Spohn, and Miriam DeLone, *The Color of Justice: Race, Ethnicity, and Crime in America,* 2nd ed. (Belmont, CA: Wadsworth, 2000).

4. Bureau of Justice Statistics, *The Prosecution of Felony Arrests, 1988* (Washington, DC: Government Printing Office, 1992), Table 2.

5. Bureau of Justice Statistics, *Violent Offenders in State Prison: Sentences and Time Served* (Washington, DC: Government Printing Office, 1995).

6. An excellent discussion of the going rate is in James Eisenstein, Roy B. Flemming, and Peter F. Nardulli, *The Contours of Justice: Communities and Their Courts* (Boston: Little, Brown, 1988), and Peter F. Nardulli, Roy B. Flemming, and James Eisenstein, *The Tenor of Justice* (Urbana: University of Illinois Press, 1988). Also see Jeffrey T. Ulmer, *Social Worlds of Sentencing* (Albany: State University of New York Press, 1997).

7. Nardulli et al., *The Tenor of Justice,* p. 246.

8. Federal Bureau of Investigation, *Crime in the United States* (Washington, DC: Government Printing Office, annual).

9. Charles Silberman, *Criminal Violence, Criminal Justice* (New York: Random House, 1978), p. 258.

10. Office of Juvenile Justice and Delinquency Prevention, *Offenders in Juvenile Court, 1993* (Washington, DC: Government Printing Office, 1996).

11. Bureau of Justice Statistics, *Felony Sentences in State Courts, 1996* (Washington, DC: Government Printing Office, 1999).

12. Bureau of Justice Statistics, *Felony Sentences in State Courts, 1996.*

13. Joan Petersilia, *Racial Disparities in the Criminal Justice System* (Santa Monica: Rand, 1983), p. 21.

14. Lawrence W. Sherman and Barry Glick, *The Quality of Police Arrest Statistics* (Washington: The Police Foundation, 1984).

15. Rothwax, *Guilty.*

16. Cassia Spohn, John Gruhl, and Susan Welch, "The Impact of the Ethnicity and Gender of Defendants on the Decision to Reject or Dismiss Felony Charges," *Criminology* 25(1) (1987): 175–91. For a provocative discussion on whether sentencing guidelines, which are designed to increase the visibility or "transparency" of the sentencing process, achieve that result see Ulmer, *Social Worlds of Sentencing.*

17. Petersilia, *Racial Disparities in the Criminal Justice System,* pp. 20–30.

18. Bureau of Justice Statistics, *Felony Sentences in the United States, 1992* (Washington, DC: Government Printing Office, 1996), Table 4.

19. Bureau of Justice Statistics, *Felony Sentences in State Courts, 1996.*

20. James Lynch, "Crime in International Perspective," in James Q. Wilson and Joan

Petersilia, eds., *Crime* (San Francisco: ICS Press, 1995), pp. 11–38.

21. Marc Mauer, *Americans Behind Bars: A Comparison of International Rates of Incarceration* (Washington, DC: The Sentencing Project, 1991).

22. Lynch, "Crime in International Perspective." Considerable controversy prevails over these comparative crime rates. In particular, many observers question the findings of the International Crime Survey (ICS) that U.S. violent crime rates are not that much higher than those of other countries: Jan van Dijk, P. Mayhew, and M. Killias, *Experiences of Crime Across the World* (Boston: Klewer, 1990).

23. Lynch, "Crime in International Perspective."

24. Bureau of Justice Statistics, *Crime and Justice in the United States and in England and Wales, 1981–1996* (Washington, DC: Government Printing Office, 1998).

25. Samuel Walker, *Taming the System: The Control of Discretion in Criminal Justice, 1950–1990* (New York: Oxford University Press, 1993); Michael R. Gottfredson and Don M. Gottfredson, *Decision Making in Criminal Justice*, 2d ed. (New York: Plenum, 1988).

26. Nardulli et al., *Tenor of Justice*, p. 39.

27. Malcolm Feeley, "Perspectives on Plea Bargaining," *Law and Society Review* 13 (Winter 1979): 199.

28. Frederick Suffett, "Bail-Setting: A Study in Courtroom Interaction," *Crime and Delinquency* 12 (1966): 318–331.

29. Alissa Pollitz Worden, "The Judge's Role in Plea Bargaining: An Analysis of Judges' Agreement with Prosecutors' Sentencing Recommendations," *Justice Quarterly* 12 (June 1995): 273.

30. John Rosecrance, "Maintaining the Myth of Individualized Justice: Probation Presentence Reports," *Justice Quarterly* 5 (June 1988): 235–56.

31. Nardulli et al., *Tenor of Justice*, p. 41.

32. Ulmer, *Social Worlds of Sentencing*, especially table 8.1.

33. Barry C. Feld, *Justice for Children: The Right to Counsel and the Juvenile Courts* (Boston: Northeastern University Press, 1993), p. 55.

34. Malcolm Feeley, *Court Reform on Trial* (New York: Basic Books, 1983), p. 173.

35. Campaign for an Effective Crime Policy, *The Impact of "Three Strikes and You're Out" Laws: What Have We Learned?* (Washington, DC: Campaign for an Effective Crime Policy, 1996).

36. William A. Geller and Michael S. Scott, *Deadly Force: What We Know* (Washington, DC: Police Executive Research Forum, 1992), p. 503.

37. Terance D. Miethe and Charles A. Moore, *Sentencing Guidelines: Their Effect in Minnesota* (Washington, DC: Government Printing Office, 1989). Bureau of Justice Statistics, *Sourcebook of Criminal Justice Statistics–1998* (Washington, DC: Government Printing Office, 1999), p. 491.

38. Department of Justice, *State and Federal Prisons: Report*, press release (December 3, 1995).

39. Raymond T. Nimmer, *The Nature of System Change* (Chicago: American Bar Foundation, 1978), p. 181.

40. Eisenstein et al., *Contours of Justice*, p. 294.

41. Cassia Spohn and Julie Horney, *Rape Law Reform: A Grassroots Revolution and Its Impact* (New York: Plenum, 1992), pp. 171–73.

42. Ibid., pp. 291–305.

43. Feeley, *Court Reform on Trial*, p. 184.

44. *Furman v. Georgia*, 408 U.S. 238 (1972); Raymond Paternoster, *Capital Punishment in America* (Lexington, MA: Lexington Books, 1991).

45. Campaign for an Effective Crime Policy, *The Impact of "Three Strikes and You're Out" Laws.*

46. William Claiborne, "'Three Strikes' Tough on Courts Too," *Washington Post* (March 8, 1995), pp. 1, 14; Fox Butterfield, "Tough Law on Sentences is Criticized," *New York Times,* 8 March 1996: A8.

47. Pamala L. Griset, "The Politics and Economics of Increased Correctional Discretion over Time Served: A New York Case Study," *Justice Quarterly* 12 (June 1995): 307–323.

48. "Death Row's Living Alumni," *The New York Times,* 22 August 1999, Section 4, p. 1.

49. C. Ronald Huff, Arye Rattner, and Edward Sagarin, "Guilty Until Proven Innocent: Wrongful Convictions and Public Policy," *Crime and Delinquency* 32 (October 1986): 518–44; C. Ronald Huff, Arye Rattner, and Edward Sagarin, *Convicted but Innocent* (Beverly Hills, CA: Sage, 1996).

50. Hugo Adam Bedeau and Michael L. Radelet, "Miscarriages of Justice in Potentially Capital Cases," *Stanford Law Review* 40 (November 1987): 21–179.

4

The Career Criminal

The career criminal has been a major focus of crime control policy for over 25 years. Several important crime control policies—preventive detention, major-offender prosecution programs, selective incapacitation—are aimed at the so-called career criminal. Anticrime rhetoric has always conjured up images of "hard-core" criminals, "repeaters," or "chronic recidivists." In the past, these terms were based largely on myth and stereotypes. We are indebted to Marvin Wolfgang and his associates for giving us a detailed profile of these people. Their landmark study, *Delinquency in a Birth Cohort,* one of the most important pieces of criminal justice research in the last thirty years, has had a profound influence on thinking about crime policy.[1]

WOLFGANG'S BIRTH COHORT

Wolfgang's birth cohort included all the males born in Philadelphia in 1945 and traced their careers through their eighteenth birthday in 1963. Using official records, such as police and school records, the study reconstructed the criminal careers of a sample of 9,945 juveniles. The principal finding was that a small percentage of delinquents are responsible for a majority of all crimes and for about two-thirds of all violent crimes.

As Table 4-1 indicates, 35 percent of the cohort had at least one *officially recorded contact* with the police. Of that group, 46 percent had no more contacts. Wolfgang labeled them "one-time offenders." He divided the remaining

Table 4-1 Wolfgang's birth cohort

	Number	Percentage of original sample	Total criminal offenses	Percentage of total offenses
Original sample	9,945			
Delinquents	3,475	34.9%	10,214	
One officially recorded contact with police	1,613	16.2	1,613	15.8%
Two to four contacts	1,235	12.4	3,296	32.3
Five or more contacts	627	6.3	5,305	51.9

SOURCE: Marvin Wolfgang, Robert M. Figlio, and Thorsten Sellin, *Delinquency in a Birth Cohort* (Chicago: University of Chicago Press, 1972).

1,862 juveniles into two groups. The 1,235 with two, three, or four contacts were labeled the "nonchronic recidivists." The remaining 627 with five or more contacts were the "chronic delinquents." They represented 6 percent of the original cohort and 18 percent of the 3,475 delinquents. These 627 are the so-called career criminals.

Several comments about Wolfgang's data are in order. Most important, he measured delinquency in terms of officially recorded police contacts. Obviously, many delinquents were never caught, and the actual prevalence of criminal behavior was higher than 35 percent. Also, many of the "one-time delinquents" committed other illegal acts but were never caught. And, finally, some "nonchronic delinquents" committed more than four crimes. Despite this limitation, however, the cohort study highlighted a general pattern: Most delinquents stop committing illegal acts at some point, and most of them stop relatively early. We do not know what makes them stop. Some "mature out." Others may be deterred by their contact with the police. Still others may be helped by the treatment program included in their juvenile court disposition. All we know for sure is that most eventually stop.

The amount of undetected criminality is an important question. Frank Dunford and Delbert Elliot tried to measure this through self-report interviews. Of 242 delinquents they defined as "career offenders" (either three index offenses in any two consecutive years or twelve delinquent acts in two consecutive years), 86 percent were never arrested. Twelve percent had between one and four arrests, while only 2 percent of the total had five or more.[2] These data reinforce the point we made in Chapter 3—that the risk of arrest is fairly low and that the low risk of apprehension is the weakest part of the entire criminal justice system.

The significance of Wolfgang's 627 "chronic recidivists" is dramatized when we see that they were responsible for more than half (52 percent) of all the crimes committed by the entire cohort. This amount included 63 percent of all the index crimes committed by the cohort and 71 percent of the murders, 73 percent of the rapes, and 82 percent of all the robberies. The one-time offenders committed only 16 percent of the total; the nonchronic recidivists, the remaining 32 percent.

The policy implications of these data are obvious: If we could identify and control that 6 percent, we could achieve a major reduction in serious crime. This idea generated much excitement among policy makers. Moreover, it does not make any difference what your basic crime policy perspective is. If you are a liberal who believes in rehabilitation, then identifying and treating that 6 percent will achieve a huge reduction in crime. If you are conservative, you will get the same results by incapacitating in prison or jail that same 6 percent.

OTHER COHORT STUDIES

Wolfgang's original findings have been confirmed by other cohort studies. He and his associates conducted a follow-up study of males and females born in Philadelphia in 1958. This was a larger cohort (28,338 subjects) and more representative in terms of race and sex. Following their criminal careers between 1968 and 1974 (age 10 to 18), they found a similar pattern in criminal behavior: 33 percent had at least one recorded contact with the police, whereas the chronic recidivists represented 7.5 percent of the total cohort (compared with 6.3 percent in the original study).[3]

The 1958 cohort did commit more crimes. Remember, this study covered the late 1960s, when the crime rate soared. The murder rate was three times higher and the robbery rate five times higher than for the 1945 cohort. Thus, about the same percentage of cohort members became delinquent, but those who did committed more crimes and far more serious ones.

Some people might question whether Philadelphia is representative of the rest of the country. Lyle Shannon studied three cohorts in Racine, Wisconsin, tracing the careers of 6,127 persons born in 1942, 1949, and 1955. Unlike Wolfgang, he followed his subjects into adulthood. Members of the 1942 cohort were 33 years old when the study ended.[4] Shannon found that most of his subjects had at least one contact with the police: 68 percent of the 1942 group, 69 percent of the 1949 cohort, and 59 percent of the 1955 cohort (but the members of this last cohort were only 22 years old when the data collection ended, so it missed part of their high-crime years). These figures may seem frightening until we learn that most of the arrests were for relatively minor crimes. Part I index crimes represented only 12.7 percent of all the arrests for the 1942 cohort and 15.9 percent and 24.6 percent for the other two cohorts, respectively. These data confirm what criminologists have long known: that most males in this country break the law at some point in their lives but that most of the law breaking involves minor crimes such as vandalism.

The career criminal patterns in Racine resembled those in Philadelphia. Shannon found that 9.5 percent of the 1942 cohort had 51 percent of the police contacts, 8 percent of the 1949 group had 50.8 percent of the contacts, and 5.8 percent of the 1955 group had 50.8 percent of that group's police contacts. Looking at felony arrests only, he found that people with four or more contacts represented 0.6 percent of the 1942 cohort but accounted for

27.1 percent of the felony arrests. For the 1949 group, 1.7 percent of the cohort had four or more contacts and were responsible for 44.1 percent of the felony contacts; for the 1955 group, 3.5 percent of the cohort had four or more and accounted for 63.8 percent of the felony contacts.

The fact that the Racine findings parallel those from Philadelphia is fairly significant. Racine is a relatively small Midwestern community, with a population of only 71,000 in 1950 and 95,000 in 1970. Racial minorities constituted only 11 percent of the population in 1970. Philadelphia in 1970 was then the third largest city in the country, with a minority population of 33.6 percent. The Racine study suggests that Wolfgang's most important finding holds true for other communities. Additional support comes from David Farrington's study of young men in London. Farrington found that 6 percent of his sample accounted for 49 percent of all the criminal convictions in the cohort.[5] In short, a near-universal pattern seems to exist in which a small group of offenders account for a very high proportion of all the crimes committed by their cohort.

Before going any farther, it is useful to clarify some of the terminology used in career criminal research.[6] First, we can distinguish *criminal careers* from *career criminals*. Every offender has a criminal career. Some have short ones; others have long ones. Everyone who goes to school has an academic career. If you drop this and every other course tomorrow and never return to school, you have an academic career—a very short one. The kid who commits one act of minor vandalism has a criminal career—a short one. The career criminal is the person with a long criminal career.

Another basic issue is the *prevalence* of criminality. We define this in terms of *participation,* which distinguishes between those who commit at least one crime and those who do not commit any. To identify the real career criminals, we need to know the *frequency* of offending—that is, the rate at which active criminals commit crimes. Determining the *seriousness* of offending is also important, because we want to identify those who commit the more serious crimes. The beginning of a criminal career is referred to as the *onset.* Do career criminals begin earlier than do one-time offenders? If they do, we might be able to spot them that way. *Persistence* refers to continuing criminal activity and *desistance* to stopping. The amount of time between onset and desistance is the *career length.*

FROM RESEARCH TO POLICY

Wolfgang's original birth cohort study generated an enormous amount of excitement, stimulating research and influencing public policy. The study was published at a politically opportune moment. By 1972, crime rates had been rising dramatically for a decade. The public was disillusioned with the liberal rehabilitation-oriented policies of the 1960s. They were ready for programs that promised to "get tough" with hard-core criminals.[7] Wolfgang's data suggested that it might be possible to identify that small group.

This book examines some of the specific policies inspired by the career criminal research. They include police programs that target suspected career criminals for intensive surveillance (Chapter 5), pretrial detention of "dangerous" offenders (Chapter 7), career criminal prosecution programs (Chapter 8), and selective incapacitation for repeat offenders (Chapter 7). Many of the treatment-oriented crime control policies proposed by liberals are also designed to deal with particular classes of offenders. Intensive probation programs (Chapter 11) are designed for "high-risk" offenders, whereas boot camps are designed for special categories of offenders.

The data in Table 4-1 make it look simple: Spot the chronic recidivists, and either treat or punish them accordingly. There is only one problem, however. Nothing is simple in the real world of criminal justice. Ideas that sound good in theory do not necessarily work out in practice. Let us look at some of the problems that arise when we try to translate Wolfgang's birth cohort research into crime control policy.

As is so often the case with path-breaking research, *Delinquency in a Birth Cohort* raised more questions than it answered. Identifying that 6 percent was a major breakthrough, but it was only the beginning. Criminologists have devoted an enormous amount of time and energy to answering some basic questions. Exactly who are the career criminals? Can we identify them early in their careers? How much crime does each one commit? What kinds of crime do they commit? When do they start their careers in crime? How long do they remain active criminals? When do they stop? Why do they stop? And are there criminal justice programs or interventions that cause them to stop earlier than they otherwise would have?

These questions are fundamental to any program targeting career criminals. The challenge, however, is to identify and control these offenders *and only them*. It is a waste of time and money to imprison one-time offenders who do not repeat. Traditionally, criminal justice officials believed that they could identify the repeat offenders or the truly dangerous criminals. Judges denied bail to defendants they "knew" were dangerous. Judges granted some convicted offenders probation because they "knew" they were not going to commit more crimes. Most of these decisions were based on hunch, guesswork, or just plain bias. At best, they relied on the seriousness of the immediate offense and the offender's prior record.

This issue is illustrated by the famous story about how one Supreme Court justice defined pornography. In the *Jacobellis* case (1964), Justice Potter Stewart admitted that he could not define "hard-core pornography" but said "I know it when I see it."[8] Many criminal justice officials believe they know a career criminal when they see one.

In the real world of criminal justice, career criminal programs run into two serious problems. The first is identifying the career criminal. We call this the *prediction problem*. The second is accurately estimating how much crime these career criminals actually do—and thus how much crime we will prevent by either imprisoning or treating them. Let us look at both of these problems in detail.

THE PREDICTION PROBLEM

We can use three basic methods for predicting criminal behavior. The first is an *actuarial* approach that relies on patterns of behavior among individuals with similar characteristics. Insurance companies use this method. The data indicate that young drivers have more accidents than middle-age drivers and that young men have much worse records than young women. Thus, insurance companies charge higher insurance rates for young people.

A second approach uses the *prior history* of the individual. You flunked the first test in this course; therefore, we predict that you will flunk the next one. As we learned in Chapter 3, criminal justice officials typically use prior criminal record to assess offenders. Sentencing guidelines build prior record into the matrix, assigning more points for each offense.

A third approach is *clinical evaluation*. Here, predictions about future behavior are based on the assessments of trained experts. A psychologist or social worker, for example, might conduct a personal interview, review the individual's social history (family, employment record, and so forth), and possibly

Table 4-2 Number of youths predicted to be violent and nonviolent who proved to be violent and nonviolent, California, 1972

	Predicted violent	Predicted nonviolent
Actual violent	True positives: Violent persons correctly identified as violent and incarcerated	False negatives: Violent persons incorrectly identified as nonviolent and not incarcerated
	52	52
Actual nonviolent	False positives: Nonviolent persons incorrectly identified as violent and needlessly incarcerated	True negatives: Nonviolent persons correctly identified as nonviolent
	404	3,638

SOURCE: Ernst A. Wenk, James O. Robison, and Gerald W. Smith, "Can Violence Be Predicted?" *Crime and Delinquency* 18 (October 1972): 393–402.

administer a psychological test. Presentence investigations by probation officers are an example of clinical evaluations.

The question is: Can these techniques be used to successfully predict future criminal behavior? A good test was conducted on behalf of the National Council on Crime and Delinquency (NCCD) by Ernst A. Wenk, James O. Robison, and Gerald W. Smith. The results were not reassuring. Wenk and his colleagues began with a sample of 4,146 youths committed to the California Youth Authority. Of this group, 104 subsequently became "violent recidivists." Wenk and his colleagues sought to develop a prediction instrument that would have identified these 104 individuals if it had been used in advance. Their instrument involved a combination of prior record and clinical assessment, using each juvenile's prior criminal record, history of violence and substance abuse, among other factors. Clinical assessments were based on psychological tests and interviews.[9]

Table 4-2 indicates the results. As is obvious, the method successfully identified only half (52) of the 104 who subsequently committed a violent act. This group, referred to as the "true positives," were correctly and positively identified as likely to commit a violent act. The other 52 slipped through the net, however. We call them the "false negatives." They were falsely (or incorrectly) predicted not to be violent. From this perspective, the prediction instrument was only 50 percent accurate; it missed half of those who actually became violent.

There is an additional problem, however. As Table 4-2 indicates, 404 people were incorrectly predicted as likely to become violent. These are referred to as the "false positives." What this means is that the method used by Wenk and his associates incorrectly identified about eight people for every one who was successfully identified as likely to become violent. From this perspective, the prediction instrument is accurate only about 12 percent of the time (52 out of the total of 456 predicted to be violent). To translate this figure into real-world terms, it would mean imprisoning eight nonrecidivists for every violent recidivist correctly identified. Obviously, the costs in terms of dollars and unnecessary deprivation of liberty would be enormous.

The Wenk study reveals the difficulty in predicting human behavior. Even with the extensive data available, the study's method produced large number of both false positives and false negatives. Even though many people think they "know" career criminals "when they see one," in fact it is very difficult to predict future behavior accurately.

One way of illustrating this problem is to apply it to Wolfgang's birth cohort. If juvenile court officials used the same prediction instrument to identify the 627 chronic recidivists, they would first miss half of them (313) and then needlessly lock up 2,500 juveniles who would not have become chronic recidivists.

The Rand Selective Incapacitation Study

A second exercise in prediction was conducted by the Rand Corporation in its report *Selective Incapacitation*.[10] For this exercise they used the Rand Inmate Survey (RIS), which involved self-report interviews with prison inmates in California, Texas, and Michigan. The survey asked inmates how many crimes they had committed between arrests.

Then, using the actuarial method of prediction, the Rand researchers correlated the self-reported criminal activity with the social histories of the 2,190 inmates. They identified thirteen characteristics that were correlated with high rates of criminal activity. Only those characteristics that were legally relevant and appropriate were used. An offender's race is not a legally appropriate factor, for example. Rand then used this data to develop a seven-point prediction scale (Table 4-3). Offenders with four or more points were then predicted to be high-rate offenders; those with two to three points were predicted to be medium rate, and those with only one or no points were low-rate offenders.

In the next stage, Rand retrospectively correlated the prediction scores with inmates' actual reported criminal activity. The results appear in Table 4-4. The prediction device was correct only 51 percent of the time. This represents

Table 4-3 Seven-point scale of factors affecting prediction of offense rates

1. Prior conviction for the instant offense type
2. Incarcerated more than 50 percent of preceding two years
3. Conviction before age 16
4. Served time in a state juvenile facility
5. Drug use in preceding two years
6. Drug use as a juvenile
7. Employed less than 50 percent of the preceding two years

SOURCE: Peter W. Greenwood, *Selective Incapacitation* (Santa Monica, CA: Rand, 1982), p. 50.

Table 4-4 Predicted versus self-reported offense ratio for robbery and burglary

		Self-reported offense rates (%)			
Score on prediction scale		Low	Medium	High	Total
Low	(0–1)	14	10	3	27
Medium	(2–3)	12	22	10	44
High	(4–7)	4	10	15	29
Total		30	42	28	100

SOURCE: Peter W. Greenwood, *Selective Incapacitation* (Santa Monica, CA: Rand, 1982). p. 59.

the combination of the predicted low-risk offenders who proved to be low risks (14 percent), the predicted medium risks who proved to be medium risks (22 percent), and the predicted high risks who actually proved to be high risks (15 percent). A 51 percent accuracy rate is not very good. You could do as well flipping a coin.

At the same time, the prediction device was *grossly* wrong in 7 percent of the cases: the 4 percent who were predicted to be high risks but who turned out to be low risks (false positives) and the 3 percent who were predicted to be low risks but proved to be high risks (false negatives). The prediction device was only *moderately* wrong in the remaining 42 percent of the cases. (Consider for a moment the real-world implications of the 4 percent error rate for those incorrectly predicted to be high risks. Given our current prison population, that translates into about 50,000 people needlessly imprisoned.)

We can hardly expect any system to be perfect. The relevant question is whether the Rand prediction device is better than existing sentencing practices. If it leads to a substantial improvement, even though less than perfect, the device would be useful. Peter Greenwood took his sample of offenders and categorized them as low, medium, or high risks according to the sentences they had actually received. These sentences were "correct" 42 percent of the time. That is, in 42 percent of the cases, the sentencing judges had correctly identified the high-rate offenders and sentenced them to long prison terms and correctly identified low-rate offenders and sentenced them to short terms. Meanwhile, the judges were grossly wrong 12 percent of the time. In short, the extremely sophisticated Rand prediction device was only slightly better than what judges had in fact already done with these offenders (51 percent versus 42 percent).

Several years later, Rand researchers made another attempt at predicting career criminals. They used two samples. One group included 2,700 men who had been committed to the California Youth Authority (CYA) as juveniles between 1966 and 1971. The second group included 200 Rand Inmate Survey (RIS) inmates who had been incarcerated for either burglary or robbery and had been released at least two years before the new study. Rand used the original seven-point prediction scale for the RIS group and a modified five-point scale for the CYA group.[11]

The results of this study are expressed in the subtitle of the Rand report: *Why the High-Rate Offenders Are Hard to Predict.* The authors concluded that "high rate offenders cannot be accurately identified, either prospectively or retrospectively, on the basis of their arrest rates alone,"[12] and they conceded that the earlier Rand conclusions about the ability to identify high-rate offenders and reduce crime by selectively incapacitating them were "overly optimistic."[13]

HOW MUCH CRIME DO THEY DO?

The second problem in translating career criminal research into policy involves estimating how many crimes the average high-rate offender commits. The estimate has important practical ramifications. Let us assume we want to lock up all armed robbers for a minimum of five years. How many crimes will we prevent? How much additional crime prevention will we achieve if we lock them all up for ten years?

The Rand Inmate Survey (RIS) attempted to estimate annual offending rates through interviews with inmates in three states: Michigan, Texas, and California. The RIS was one of the most influential studies, and its findings have been widely used. The self-report method was a major advance because official records (e.g., arrest reports) do not provide a complete picture of a criminal's criminal behavior. Many crimes are not reported and, obviously, most crimes do not result in an arrest.

The RIS estimated high rates of criminal activity, but with some important variations. California robbers averaged 53 robberies per year, compared with 77 for Michigan robbers but only nine a year for those in Texas. The RIS also found that criminals do not specialize in one type of crime. California robbers also averaged 90 burglaries, 163 thefts or frauds, and 646 drug offenses each year. Texas robbers, meanwhile, averaged 24 burglaries and 98 thefts each year.[14]

Why were the rates so much higher for Michigan and California compared with those for Texas? The best explanation is that Texas judges send more robbers to prison. As a result, the Texas sample includes a higher proportion of low-rate offenders than the Michigan and California samples do, thereby dragging down the group's average. California judges were incarcerating only the worst robbers, with the result that the inmates in that state had much higher annual crime rates.

The difference may seem like a minor technical point, but it has tremendous practical consequences. We need a precise estimate of the annual offending rate to calculate the amount of crime reduction we will get. The annual offending rate is expressed as *lambda*. If the lambda is large, then we can expect a substantial reduction in crime for every career criminal who is imprisoned or rehabilitated. But if the lambda is low (that is, if the average career criminal commits relatively few crimes each year), then the payoff will be much lower.

Estimates of lambda by respected scholars vary enormously. Alfred Blumstein and Jacqueline Cohen estimated that adult arrestees committed an annual average of 3.4 robberies and 5.7 burglaries in Washington and 4.7 robberies and 5.3 burglaries in Detroit. The National Youth Survey estimated that active offenders committed an average of 8.4 robberies and 7.1 burglaries per year.[15] At the other end of the scale, Edwin W. Zedlewski, in *Making Confinement Decisions,* used an estimate of 187 felonies per year.[16] The practical implications of these different estimates are obvious. If we accept Zedlewski's figure, we could expect a great reduction in crime. But if we accept Blumstein and Cohen's figure, we will get a much smaller payoff for locking up each offender. When we discuss incapacitation as sentencing policy in Chapter 7, we will take a critical look at Zedlewski's use of his 187 figure.

A major part of the problem here is the concept of *average* offending rates. The RIS data clearly indicate that there is no such thing as an "average" career criminal. The median annual robbery rate for the RIS inmates was five per year. The top 10 percent, however, averaged 87 robberies per year.[17] It is important to remember that the RIS inmates are a pretty select group: they got caught and were sent to prison because judges regarded them as dangerous offenders. The top 10 percent of the RIS sample, then, are the worst of the worst.

From a practical standpoint, to get some real payoff in terms of crime reduction, it is necessary to identify this small group from among all the other "serious" offenders. Say, for example, that you wanted to send most robbers (five per year) to five-year prison terms and give the really high-rate robbers (87 per year) 15 years. You would have to make very precise predictions.

We will examine this subject again in Chapter 7 when we discuss incapacitation as a crime control strategy. It is worth pointing out, however, that despite all the initial excitement about the possibilities of applying career criminal research through *selective* incapacitation, we have in practice abandoned that goal and adopted a policy of *gross* incapacitation. The prison population has soared because we are locking up lots of people without making fine distinctions.

CONCLUSION

The subject of career criminals is an excellent example of the difficulties of translating research into policy. No one seriously questions Wolfgang's original finding about the fact that a small group of offenders is responsible for a huge percentage of all crime. Subsequent research has tended to confirm it. Nor does anyone seriously question the argument that we could make a substantial reduction in crime *if* we could correctly identify those people and keep them from committing more crime.

The key word here, of course, is *if.* Research on the prediction problem indicates that it is difficult, if not impossible, to precisely identify in advance the small group of high-rate offenders. This difficulty is compounded by the fact that estimates conflict on how much crime these high-rate offenders actually do. If the averages are in fact low, we will not get that much payoff in terms of crime reduction.

The problems we have identified here have a direct impact on many of the crime control policies we will examine in the chapters ahead. As we mentioned earlier, the administration of justice consists of a series of discretionary decision points. Many of those decisions involve predictions about who is and who is not dangerous.

NOTES

1. Marvin Wolfgang, Robert M. Figlio, and Thorsten Sellin, *Delinquency in a Birth Cohort* (Chicago: University of Chicago Press, 1972).

2. F. W. Dunford and D. S. Elliott, "Identifying Career Offenders Using Self-Reported Data," *Journal of Research in Crime and Delinquency* 21 (1984): 57–86.

3. Paul E. Tracy, Marvin E. Wolfgang, and Robert M. Figlio, *Delinquency in Two Birth Cohorts* (Chicago: University of Chicago Press, 1985).

4. Lyle W. Shannon, Judith L. McKim, James P. Curry, and Lawrence J. Haffner, *Criminal Career Continuity: Its Social Context* (New York: Human Sciences Press, 1988).

5. The findings of all the longitudinal studies are reviewed in David P. Farrington, Lloyd E. Ohlin, and James Q. Wilson, *Understanding and Controlling Crime: Toward a New Research Strategy* (New York: Springer, 1986), see especially pp. 50–52.

6. Alfred Blumstein, Jacqueline Cohen, Jeffrey Roth, and Christy A. Visher, eds., *Criminal Careers and "Career Criminals"* (Washington, DC: National Academy Press, 1986).

7. Samuel Walker, *Popular Justice: A History of American Criminal Justice,* 2nd ed. (New York: Oxford University Press, 1998).

8. *Jacobellis v. Ohio,* 378 U.S. 184, 197 (1964).

9. Ernest A. Wenk, James O. Robison, and Gerald W. Smith, "Can Violence Be Predicted?" *Crime and Delinquency* 18 (October 1972): 339–402.

10. Peter W. Greenwood and Allan Abrahamse, *Selective Incapacitation* (Santa Monica, CA: Rand, 1982).

11. Peter W. Greenwood and Susan Turner, *Selective Incapacitation Revisited: Why the High-Rate Offenders Are Hard to Predict* (Santa Monica, CA: Rand, 1987).

12. Greenwood and Turner, *Selective Incapacitation Revisited,* p. x.

13. Greenwood and Turner, *Selective Incapacitation Revisited,* p. 49.

14. The data are in Greenwood and Abrahamse, *Selective Incapacitation.* The original report is Joan Petersilia, Peter W. Greenwood, and Marvin Lavin, *Criminal Careers of Habitual Felons* (Santa Monica, CA: Rand, 1977).

15. Alfred Blumstein and Jacqueline Cohen, "Estimating Individual Crime Rates from Arrest Records," *Journal of Criminal Law and Criminology* 70 (1979): 561–85; Blumstein et al., *Criminal Careers and "Career Criminals."*

16. Edwin W. Zedlewski, *Making Confinement Decisions* (Washington, DC: Government Printing Office, 1987).

17. Petersilia et al., *Criminal Careers of Habitual Felons.*

❖

PART II

"Get Tough":
The Conservative Attack
on Crime

Conservatives argue that we can reduce serious crime if we just "get tough" with criminals. Their crime control agenda, which has not changed in 30 years, includes the following items. First, we can reduce crime if we would just unleash the cops and give them more power and resources. We will look at several strategies for unleashing the cops in Chapter 5. Second, we can deter crime through swifter, more certain, and more severe punishments. We will take a close look at the theory of deterrence and some deterrence-oriented programs in Chapter 6. Third, we should lock up more criminals by sending more to prison and for longer prison terms. This represents a strategy of incapacitation. We will look at several incapacitation programs in Chapter 7. Fourth, conservatives believe that too many criminals "get off" through loopholes in the criminal justice system. We will examine four proposals designed to close loopholes in Chapter 8. Conservatives and some policy analysts believe that the recent reduction in crime is a result of these policies.

The 1994 Violent Crime Control Act incorporates much of the conservative agenda. It authorized $9 billion to hire 100,000 additional police officers, extended the death penalty to 60 different federal crimes, provided mandatory imprisonment for certain crimes, increased the penalties for certain drug offenses and other crimes, and offered financial assistance to states where persons convicted of violent crimes serve at least 85 percent of their prison terms.

The fact that President Bill Clinton sponsored and signed this law indicates the extent to which many liberals have adopted the conservative crime control agenda. Now let us take a look at these and other conservative crime control policies.

5

Unleash the Cops!

Conservatives believe we can reduce crime if we just "unleash" the cops. Give them more resources and powers, this argument goes, and the police will deter more crime and arrest more criminals. Two basic strategies are proposed for accomplishing this goal: hiring more police officers and removing the procedural restraints on obtaining evidence and confessions. Let us look at these and some other proposals to see whether they are likely to reduce crime.

MORE COPS

The 1994 Violent Crime Control and Law Enforcement Act authorized $9 billion to support the hiring of 100,000 additional police officers. The idea of putting more police on the street is very popular with the public. When the National Crime Survey asked people what improvement in policing they would like, both whites and African Americans said they wanted more police.[1] The fact that President Bill Clinton enthusiastically supported this idea is a good example of how many liberals have adopted traditional conservative crime control ideas in recent years.[2] There is a certain commonsense logic to this idea: If police patrol prevents crime, then more police will reduce crime even further. Let's see if there is any evidence to support it.

Table 5-1 Police-population ratios, major cities, 1997

	Sworn officers per 1,000 population
Washington, D.C.	6.7
New York City	5.2
Philadelphia	4.6
Detroit	4.1
Los Angeles	2.7
Minneapolis	2.5
San Diego	1.7
San Jose	1.6

SOURCE: Bureau of Justice Statistics, *Law Enforcement Management and Administrative Statistics, 1997* (Washington, DC: Government Printing Office, 1999), table 1a.

The Police and Crime

A lot of mythology exists about the relationship between the police and crime rates. Simply hiring more police officers does not necessarily mean that more patrol officers will be on the street or that they will be used effectively in fighting crime.

The standard measure of the level of police protection is the police-population ratio: the number of officers per 1,000 people.[3] Table 5-1 indicates that police-population ratios vary enormously. For instance, the fact that Washington, D.C., has more than twice as much police protection as Los Angeles and almost four times as much as San Diego hardly makes it a safer city.

Unfortunately, the police-population ratio is a virtually meaningless figure because it does not tell us how police departments *use* their officers. If a department does not put those officers on the street, or if it uses inefficient two-officer patrols, additional officers will not have any real impact. Table 5-2 illustrates the point by comparing two hypothetical police departments, one that is very efficiently operated and one that is not. Both are in cities with populations of 500,000. One has 900 sworn officers, the other 600. The department with 900 officers, however, assigns a lower percentage to patrol. Many officers are probably assigned to desk jobs. The department also does not assign its patrol officers according to a rational workload formula, leaving the busy evening shift understaffed. Finally, it employs two-officer patrol units, which are much less efficient than one-officer units. The net result is that the city with the higher police-population ratio actually has fewer patrol units on the street during the high-crime evening shift. The citizens are paying more for police protection but getting less.

Even more important is the question of what officers actually *do* when they are on the street.[4] Later in this chapter we will examine some recent innovations in problem-oriented policing that are designed to alter what police

**Table 5-2 Deployment of patrol officers
in two hypothetical cities**

	City X	City Y
Population	500,000	500,000
Sworn officers	900	600
Percentage of officers assigned to patrol	50	70
Officers assigned to patrol	450	420
Percentage of patrol officers assigned to 4 P.M.–12 A.M. shift	33	50
Patrol officers, 4 P.M.–12 A.M. shift	148	210
One-officer patrols	20	190
Two-officer patrols	64	10
Total patrols, 4 P.M.–12 A.M.	84	200

officers do to reduce crime. A department may put a lot of officers on patrol, but if they do little real police work, or do not do anything that is different from what they have normally done, the public will not get much in the way of actual crime fighting. In short, simply adding more police to an already inefficient department is throwing money—or cops, in this case—at the problem. Conservatives are fond of attacking liberals for throwing money at social problems. This criticism applies to the idea of hiring more police.

The Lessons of Kansas City

The idea that a visible police presence deters crime has been the core principle of modern policing since Robert Peel created the London Metropolitan Police in 1829. For nearly 150 years everyone accepted this idea on faith, without any scientific evidence to back it up. This traditional assumption was finally tested in the Kansas City Preventive Patrol Experiment (1972–73), one of the most important events in police history.[5]

The experiment divided the South Patrol District into three groups of patrol beats. *Proactive* beats received two or three times the normal level of patrol. *Reactive* beats received no routine patrol. Police cars entered those areas only in response to a citizen's call for service. Officers handled the call and then left the beat area. *Control* beats kept the normal level of patrol. Using a victimization survey, the experiment examined the effect of different levels of patrol on criminal activity and citizen perceptions of police protection. Unlike earlier experiments, they controlled for other variables that might affect the level of criminal activity: temporary or random changes in criminal activity, unreported crime, the possible displacement of crime into neighboring areas, and the reactions of both police officers and citizens to changes in police activity.

The Kansas City experiment found that the level of patrol had no effect on either crime or citizen perceptions. Crime did not increase in the reactive beats where there was less patrol and did not decline in the proactive beats where there was more patrol. Moreover, people did not seem to notice the differences in the level of patrol. Fear of crime did not go up in the reactive beats and did not go down in the proactive beats.[6]

It is important to emphasize that the experiment did *not* prove that patrol has absolutely no effect on crime. No beats ever had no police presence whatsoever for any extended period of time. Patrol cars entered the reactive beats to handle calls, while officers in other units (for example, juvenile) entered these beats to handle their own assignments. Law-abiding citizens and potential criminals alike saw a marked police car and assumed that the police were patrolling the area. This phenomenon has been described as the *phantom effect:* even if there are no police around, patrol works if people believe they are.

Most important for our purposes, the experiment found that *more* police patrol does not *reduce* the criminal activity. The subsequent Newark Foot Patrol Experiment, meanwhile, found that additional foot patrol had no effect on the crime rate, although it did reduce citizen fear of crime.[7]

Why is there no deterrent effect of adding for patrol officers? Deterrence theory assumes that the threat of apprehension is *communicated* to its target audience, that it is *perceived* as a threat, and that people make *rational decisions* on the basis of that information.[8]

First, patrol is spread very thin even in the best of circumstances. A patrol car actually passes each point in its assigned beat very few times in any seven-day period. Doubling the number of patrol units still leaves a very thin layer of coverage. That is to say, the threat of arrest and punishment is not communicated to its intended audience

Second, many actual or potential offenders do not perceive police patrol as a meaningful threat. Nor do they necessarily act rationally. Many believe that they will not be caught. A sense of invincibility is common among teenagers, for example. Experienced criminals, meanwhile, are fatalistic and assume that sooner or later they will be caught. In either case, offenders are not making rational calculations about the risk of arrest and punishment. Analyzing the *Rand Inmate Survey* (RIS), James Q. Wilson and Alan Abrahamse found that most inmates were fatalistic and thought there was a good chance they would be arrested, convicted, or even injured as a result of doing crime.[9]

Third, many crimes are inherently not "suppressible" by patrol. The majority of murders and assaults, and about half of all rapes, occur between people who know each other. Because they usually occur indoors and in the heat of passion, the amount of police patrol out on the street is not going to affect them. Robbery, burglary, and auto theft, which do occur outside, are at least theoretically "suppressible" through patrol.

Our conclusion, then, is as follows:

PROPOSITION 6

Simply adding more police officers will not reduce crime.

But what about the 100,000 additional police officers authorized by the 1994 Violent Crime Control Act? Have they had any impact? Aren't they responsible for the reduction in crime? Probably not. First, many were added by suburban and small-town police departments, which do not have serious crime problems. Serious crime is concentrated in particular neighborhoods of the largest cities. Yet a 1997 General Accounting Office (GAO) audit found that big cities had received only 23 percent of all grant funds to that point.[10] The primary conclusion of the Maryland *Preventing Crime* report is that efforts should be directed toward "the urban neighborhoods where youth violence is heavily concentrated."[11] In short, in terms of crime reduction, many if not most of the new officers are not likely to have much of an impact.

Second, it is not clear that new officers hired through the federal funding program are actively engaged in effective crime reduction programs. There is evidence that some departments accepted the federal funds but are not really doing community policing at all. Other departments have adopted the rhetoric of community policing but without significantly changing police operations.[12]

Third, there is still no conclusive evidence that community policing has any direct impact on crime.[13] Some recent narrowly focused programs do offer some evidence of success, however, and we now turn our attention to them.

Focused Police Officer Activities

If there is a strong consensus among police experts that simply adding more police will not reduce crime, there is also growing evidence that certain kinds of carefully planned and focused police activities can be effective. It is important to distinguish, however, between the traditional police "crackdowns" and more recent problem-oriented policing programs.

Traditional Crackdowns Law enforcement crackdowns are a classic "get tough" program. Essentially, a *crackdown* is a short burst of intensive law enforcement, directed toward either a particular area or a particular crime.[14]

One well-known antidrug crackdown was Operation Pressure Point (OPP) in New York City. In the early 1980s, OPP targeted an open drug market on the city's Lower East Side that had been described as a "drug buyer's paradise." An additional 240 officers flooded the area, dispersing crowds, stopping and questioning suspected drug buyers and sellers, writing traffic tickets, and making a high volume of arrests (more than 2,000 in the first month alone). Also, the police department ended its Desk Appearance Ticket (DAT) policy, which allowed persons charged with misdemeanors to be released immediately, and the U.S. attorney's office agreed to process many of the drug arrests in federal court where the defendants would face harsher sentences.[15]

Although an evaluation of Operation Pressure Point claimed that it effectively reduced the level of drug trafficking in the neighborhood, a number of important questions were left unanswered. OPP did not control for the possible displacement of drug trafficking into other neighborhoods. Moreover, drug dealers adapted to the crackdown with more sophisticated techniques, such as using lookouts and steerers to insulate the actual dealers from the police. The cost effectiveness of the arrests was not evaluated. Finally, the evaluation mentioned, but did not discuss in detail, the implications of the police misconduct that the program encouraged. Officers disrupted drug dealing by harassing potential buyers and scaring them off.[16]

Perhaps even more significant, the drug problem in the city as a whole only got worse after Operation Pressure Point. With the arrival of crack in the mid-1980s, entire neighborhoods were overtaken by open drug dealing. Police officers in those neighborhoods have conceded that large numbers of arrests do little good. As one put it, for every person arrested "there is always a replacement."[17]

Problem-Oriented Policing Recent problem-oriented policing programs (POP) represent a more sophisticated kind of focused police activity. Most draw upon three important new developments in policing. First, the POP approach involves carefully planning under the SARA model (Scanning, Analysis, Response, Assessment).[18] Second, many programs draw heavily on the concept of "hot spots." Lawrence W. Sherman's analysis of 911 calls in Minneapolis found the astonishing fact that 5 percent of the addresses in the city accounted for 64 percent of all 911 calls. A very few places, which he labeled "hot spots," were consuming the vast majority of police time and effort.[19] Third, they utilize the community policing and POP principles of involving other government agencies and noncriminal justice resources in crime fighting.

The SMART program was directed toward specific drug hot spots in Oakland, California. The police were part of a multiagency task force. In addition to increased law enforcement activity by the police (more patrol, field interrogations, arrests), SMART mobilized officials from the housing, fire, and public works departments to enforce local building codes and clean up the physical appearance of the neighborhood. A training program for landlords was designed to help them screen prospective tenants and evict existing tenants for rules violations. Lorraine Green's evaluation of SMART found that it reduced the level of drug activity in the target areas. Moreover, it not only did not displace crime to nearby areas, but had a "diffusion" effect of improving surrounding areas.[20]

Three key factors, acting in combination, distinguish the SMART program from the traditional approaches of adding more patrol and "crackdowns." First, it represents a change in police *activity,* as opposed to the mere number of police officers. Second, it focuses narrowly on specific "hot spots," as opposed to unfocused patrol of the entire community. Third, it enlists other agencies and uses non-criminal justice tactics to address underlying causes of crime. This approach is consistent with the integrated and place-focused crime prevention strategy recommended by the Maryland report on *Preventing Crime.*[21]

A problem-oriented policing program in Jersey City, New Jersey also found that focused crime prevention activities by the police were successful in reducing crime. The program first identified 12 pairs of areas in the city where there were high rates of violent crime ("hot spots"). In each pair, one area received focused crime prevention police work, while the other served as a control. An evaluation of the program identified 28 different police strategies applied to the experimental areas. The twelve most commonly used strategies are listed in Table 5-3. What is notable about this list is that only four represent traditional law enforcement activities. The other eight are nontraditional activities and are the responsibility of other government agencies (e.g., increased lighting, trash removal). The evaluation found that the program reduced crime and disorder without displacing them to neighboring areas (there was also no diffusion of benefits as had been the case in the SMART program, however).[22]

The lessons of these recent and successful problem-oriented policing programs seem to be that *some* kinds of police law enforcement activity *can* make a difference. These programs, however, must (1) involve careful planning and administration; (2) be focused on particular places and/or offenses; and (3) involve other, nonlaw enforcement agencies in a comprehensive attempt to improve the quality of life in particular areas. In Chapter 10, we will look at

Table 5-3 Police strategies used in Jersey City

Strategy	Number of places used
Aggressive order maintenance	12
Drug enforcement	9
Required store owners to clean store fronts	5
Public Works Dept. removed trash from streets	5
Robbery investigations	4
Increased lighting of areas	4
Housing code enforcement	3
Erected fences around vacant lots	3
Vacant lots cleaned	3
Abandoned buildings boarded and fenced	3
Hung signs explaining rules of behavior (e.g., no drinking)	3
Videotape surveillance of places	3

SOURCE: Anthony M. Braga et al., "Problem-Oriented Policing in Violent Crime Places: A Randomized Controlled Experiment," *Criminology* 37.3 (1999): 544, table 2. Reprinted with permission.

another focused police activity, the Kansas City Gun Experiment, designed to reduce the number of handguns in high-crime areas.

> ## PROPOSITION 7
> Carefully planned problem-oriented policing strategies, directed toward limited geographic areas and involving non-criminal justice resources, can be successful in reducing crime and disorder.

Sorting Out the Issues

A lot has been happening with respect to policing in recent years (community policing, 100,000 new officers, etc.), and it is important to sort out the different changes and specify the effects, if any, of each one.

New York City represents a good example of the difficulty of specifying causes and effects. New York City has experienced one of the greatest reductions in crime in the entire country. And because the city is the media capitol of the country and local officials have not been shy about claiming credit for reducing crime. There have been three major developments with the police department that need to be considered. First, the number of sworn officers increased by more than a third between 1990 and 1995, from about 25,000 to 40,000. Second, the NYPD adopted a "zero-tolerance" policy focusing on less serious quality of life offenses such as public urination and failure to pay subway fares. NYPD officials claim that tough enforcement related to small offenses had a direct payoff in terms of serious crime. Kids arrested for minor offenses, they claim, were often found to be illegally carrying a weapon.[23] Third, the NYPD adopted COMPSTAT, a management tool that provides immediate data on crime by precinct and involves regular meetings where precinct commanders are held accountable for crime trends in their areas.[24]

Did these developments, independently or in combination, contribute to the reduction in crime? Some skepticism is warranted. First, most cities have enjoyed major reductions in crime with any of these three developments. San Diego, for example, experienced a reduction in crime equal to New York's between 1990 and 1995 with only a modest increase in the number of police, only one-third the police-population ratio, and no aggressive zero-tolerance policy.[25] Second, most criminal justice experts are reluctant to attribute the national reduction in crime to any single development, and many believe that the most important factor has been changes in drug markets, primarily a sharp decline in the use of crack.[26]

In short, we need to be very skeptical about claims regarding successful police crime reduction efforts—particularly when they come from politicians or police chiefs who want to show that it was *their* programs that did the trick. The problem-oriented policing programs described earlier do offer some evidence of success, but these were carefully planned and narrowly focused programs. Moreover, no one involved with them makes claims that are not supported by the evidence.

FASTER RESPONSE TIME

Many people believe that we could reduce crime if the police got to crime scenes faster. This idea has a basic, commonsense logic to it: The faster the police get there, the greater the likelihood they will arrest the offender. More arrests, meanwhile, will deter or incapacitate more criminals and lower the crime rate. Let us take a look at this idea.

Faster response time will not produce more arrests because the police are called to very few crimes in progress. At most, only about 30 percent of all patrol dispatches involve criminal activity. Some studies put the figure as low as 17 percent. Moreover, about 75 percent of these crime-related calls involve "cold" crimes: typically, a burglary that occurred many hours earlier. The offender is long gone, and it makes no difference whether the police get there in three minutes or three hours.[27]

The remaining 25 percent of crime-related calls are "involvement" crimes, meaning a confrontation exists between the victim and a suspect. Response time rarely makes a difference in these crimes, either. In many cases, the victim and offender are acquaintances. The victim can identify the suspect no matter when the police arrive. Also, victims usually do not call the police immediately. Traumatized and confused, they often try to compose themselves, decide whether to even call the police and often call a friend or family member first. This delay in calling the police renders the police travel time irrelevant in terms of catching the offender. Faster police response might make a difference in a very small number of crime calls: about 3 percent, according to a study by the Police Executive Research Forum. Commercial robberies are the best example. If someone calls the police while the crime is in progress, a very quick response time might improve the chances of catching the offender at the scene. But these kinds of crime are rare events.[28]

This leads to our next proposition:

PROPOSITION 8
Faster response time will not produce more arrests or lower the crime rate.

MORE DETECTIVES

As we have already pointed out, arrest is the weakest point in the criminal justice system. The police clear only about 21 percent of all Index crimes. Some people believe that we could increase the clearance rate if we just had more detectives or made other improvements in detective work. Let us take a look at this idea.

Myths and Realities of Detective Work

Some of the most durable myths about policing surround detectives. Movies and television cop shows portray criminal investigation as fast-paced, exciting, and dangerous work, with frequent shootings, car chases, and confrontations with dangerous criminals. In the classic television show from the 1950s, *Dragnet,* Sgt. Jack Webb always caught the offender. This media image of the police as "crime fighters" is pure mythology.

The reality of criminal investigation is very different from the media myth. It is generally boring, unglamorous, and highly unproductive. Instead of kicking in doors, ducking bullets, and wrestling with dangerous sociopaths, detectives spend most of their time writing reports. The Rand study of criminal investigation found that the typical case gets an average of about four hours' work, and most of that involves paperwork.[29]

Most of the crimes that are cleared are readily solved. The victim or a witness either knows the offender or can provide a good lead to the first police officer who arrives on the scene.[30] In many acquaintance crimes, the offender is still there when the police arrive, so that no real "detective" work is required. This explains why between 60 and 80 percent of all arrests are made by patrol officers instead of detectives.[31]

The importance of having a good lead at the very beginning was documented by the President's Crime Commission in a study of 1,905 cases handled by the Los Angeles police (Figure 5-1). The police cleared 86 percent of the 349 cases in which a suspect was immediately identified by the victim or

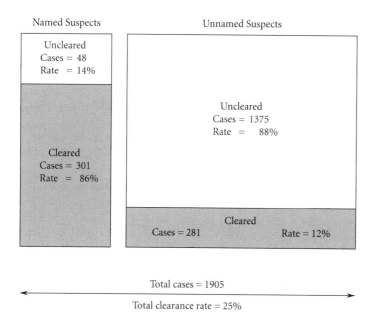

FIGURE 5-1 Clearance of crimes with named and unnamed
suspects, Los Angeles Police Department, 1966.

SOURCE: President's Commission on Law Enforcement and Administration of Justice, *Task Force
Report: Science and Technology* (Washington, DC: Government Printing Office, 1967), p. 8.

witness. But they cleared only 12 percent of the remaining 1,556 cases in
which no suspect was immediately identified.[32]

The key to solving crimes and making arrests, in short, is information
about a suspect. Where no good information to work with is available at the
very beginning of a case, the chances of clearing the crime are very limited. In
other words, the chances of solving a crime depend primarily on the circumstances of the crime rather than the number of police officers or the amount
of detective work. Increasing the number of detectives is not going to help.
Having twice as many detectives, or spending twice as much time on a case, is
not going to overcome the lack of any good leads. Detectives always complain
about being overworked, and it is true that they are swamped with cases.
Information, not time however, is the critical factor.[33]

We should not be distracted by celebrated cases. Every now and then
detectives do solve a crime—often a high-profile murder or robbery—as a
result of extensive detective work. But these are rare events and not typical of
most cases. The famous Unabomber case is a good example of how crimes are
solved. A nationwide manhunt by the FBI produced nothing for twenty years.
A suspect was finally identified when his own brother, who had access to the
suspect's writings and recognized a similarity to the Unabomber's manifesto,
tipped off the FBI.

For the same reasons, better training for detectives is not likely to increase
the clearance rate. Even the smartest and best-trained detective is not likely to

solve a "cold" crime for which there are no leads. The Rand study of criminal investigation found that the quality of training made little difference in clearance rates between departments.[34] Training is not completely irrelevant. An incompetent detective can easily lose a case by bungling the interrogation or mishandling the evidence. Skill does make a difference and training can improve skills. But this assumes that there is some evidence to begin with.

A Word about Fingerprints. A great deal of mythology surrounds fingerprints. The FBI has elevated fingerprints to near-mythical status in the solving of crimes. The Bureau now has nearly 225 million fingerprint cards on file, representing about 79 million individuals. (In the 1930s, the FBI launched an abortive campaign to fingerprint the entire population.) The mystique of fingerprints was designed to project an image of the Bureau as an incredibly efficient agency—efficient because it was backed by the massive weight of "science."

In reality, fingerprints are rarely the critical factor in solving crimes. It is extremely difficult to get usable prints from a crime scene. The New York City police obtain useful prints in only about 10 percent of all burglaries. And in only 3 percent of those cases do the prints help with the arrest. In Long Beach, California, a suspect was identified through fingerprints in only 1.5 percent of all cases.[35]

Targeting Career Criminals

One of the hot new ideas of the 1980s called for the police to target a small number of suspected career criminals. Like selective incapacitation and major-offender prosecution programs, these programs are based on Wolfgang's birth cohort study, which we examined in Chapter 4. The assumption is that if detectives succeed in arresting this small group of high-rate offenders, a significant reduction in crime will follow.

The Repeat Offender Project (ROP, pronounced "rope") in the Washington, D.C., police department involved a special unit of 60 officers targeting suspects they believed were committing five or more Index crimes a week. The list of suspects was developed by cross-indexing information from other units in the department, such as Investigation Services, the Career Criminal Unit, the Warrant Squad, the Court Liaison Division, the district commanders, and the Youth Division. ROP officers surveilled these suspects to arrest them for felonies.[36]

An evaluation of Washington's ROP program revealed mixed results. Around-the-clock surveillance of suspects quickly proved to be "time-consuming, frustrating, and unproductive." ROP officers got bored waiting and watching. As a result, ROP shifted its emphasis to suspects with arrest warrants on file. Eventually, half of the unit's time was devoted to this activity. In this respect, then, ROP essentially became an intensified warrant enforcement unit. Like many other supposed innovations, it called for officers to do what they always said they were doing.

The ROP unit officers succeeded in arresting 58 percent of their targeted group, significantly more than the 8 percent arrested among a control group of potential suspects. Nonetheless, the overall arrest productivity of ROP officers was less than that of a comparison group of officers. The 62 ROP officers produced 66 convictions by the end of the first year, or a little more than one per officer. Whether this is money well spent is a good question. Even more disturbing is the 37.2 percent conviction rate for ROP arrests (66 of 177). This seems to defy the basic rationale of career-criminal programs that supposedly target people who are believed to be active, high-rate offenders. You would expect a high conviction rate for these suspects. Given the cost of the program and the reduction of nonarrest activities (such as order maintenance) by ROP officers, the evaluation raised serious questions about the cost-effectiveness of the program.[37]

Arrest is the weakest point in the criminal justice system. Unfortunately, there does not appear to be any way to increase the clearance rate significantly. The ability of the police to solve crimes is primarily determined by the nature of individual crimes, and in particular whether there is a good lead about a suspect.

This leads to our next proposition:

PROPOSITION 9

More detectives, or other changes in detective work, will not raise clearance rates or lower the crime rate.

ELIMINATE THE "TECHNICALITIES"

Conservatives firmly believe that the courts have "handcuffed" the police with procedural rules that limit their power to investigate and solve crimes. According to this view, these "technicalities" of criminal procedure allow streetwise criminals to "beat the system" and avoid punishment. In a sweeping indictment of the criminal justice system, Judge Harold Rothwax of New York argues that the system is geared for "anything but the truth." Procedural rules designed to ensure "fairness" undermine the search for truth about guilt or innocence, with the result that "criminals go free."[38]

Conservatives direct their fire at the Supreme Court, particularly the Warren Court (1954–1968), which issued a series of decisions protecting the rights of suspects and limiting the powers of the police. The two most famous decisions, *Mapp* (1961) and *Miranda* (1966), coincided with the great increase in crime between the early 1960s and early 1970s. Consequently, many people blame the Court for our high rates of crime.[39]

Repeal the Exclusionary Rule

The Supreme Court established the exclusionary rule in the 1961 *Mapp v. Ohio* decision. The Court held that "all evidence obtained by searches and seizures in violation of the Constitution is, by that same authority, inadmissible in a state court."[40] Prosecutors cannot use evidence obtained in violation of the Fourth Amendment's guarantee of "the right of the people to be secure in their persons, houses, papers, and effects, against unreasonable searches and seizures." Evidence obtained illegally is "excluded" or inadmissible in court.

Mapp produced a storm of controversy that has continued for 40 years. Critics charge that the exclusionary rule has limited the ability of the police to gather evidence necessary to convict criminals. Actually, the exclusionary rule was nothing new in 1961. The Supreme Court had applied it to federal proceedings in 1914 (*Weeks v. United States*). By 1961, it was already in effect in more than half of the states, mainly through decisions by state supreme courts. *Mapp* simply applied the exclusionary rule to all the states.

The exclusionary rule has three basic purposes: to protect the rights of individuals against police misconduct, to maintain the integrity of the judiciary, and to deter the police from misconduct. The rule has always evoked far more outrage than the equally famous *Miranda* warning. *Miranda* excludes confessions that have been obtained improperly. Even many law-and-order advocates concede that a coerced confession is wrong. But the *Mapp* exclusionary rule applies to physical evidence that speaks for itself, no matter how it was obtained. Therefore, they believe it should be allowed as evidence.

The Exclusionary Rule and Crime Fighting Several studies indicate that the exclusionary rule has virtually no impact on the crime-fighting capacity of the police. James J. Fyfe argues that the impact is "minuscule" and "infinitesimal."[41] Very few cases are "lost" because the evidence is excluded as a result of an improper search. Drug cases are the only area where the rule has any noticeable impact, and even there the effect is fairly small. Take another look at the data in Table 3-2 in Chapter 3. It indicates that due process problems account for a very small percentage of all rejections and dismissals and that not all of those due process problems involve the exclusionary rule.

When we consider the realities of police work, we can understand why the exclusionary rule has such a limited impact. As we pointed out earlier, the police solve crimes when they immediately obtain a good lead about a suspect, from either the victim or a witness. Physical evidence, independent of some other kind of identification of the suspect, is rarely the primary factor in making an arrest and convicting an offender.

The limited impact of the exclusionary rule is mainly confined to drug possession, weapons possession, and gambling cases. It is not hard to see why. The most important element of a drug possession case is whether the defendant actually had the drugs and how the police obtained the evidence. Robbery cases, on the other hand, are more likely to depend on eyewitness identification of the suspect. Physical evidence is rarely the crucial factor.

Once in court, few defendants try to use the exclusionary rule, and even fewer succeed. Procedurally, the defense attorney asks the court to exclude or suppress the evidence. Judges have the discretion to grant or deny the motion. Peter F. Nardulli found that motions to suppress physical evidence were made in fewer than 5 percent of all cases and were successful in only 0.69 percent of the total. A General Accounting Office (GAO) study of the federal courts found that motions to suppress evidence were filed in only 11 percent of all cases and that between 80 and 90 percent were denied. Finally, a study of search warrants by the National Center for State Courts showed that only 5 percent of all motions to suppress were successful.[42]

Defense lawyers file motions to suppress evidence because they have a professional obligation to represent their clients' interests. Not filing such motions might raise questions about their competence. Most of the time, however, they are just going through the motions, if you will pardon the expression. They are not the "crafty" lawyers of popular folklore. Most felony cases are handled by public defenders who are conscientious but extremely overworked. They have little time to devote to any one case, and in some jurisdictions they meet their clients only moments before entering the courtroom.

Even when a motion to exclude evidence succeeds, the defendant will not necessarily go free. He or she can still be convicted on other evidence. If an appeals court overturns a conviction under the exclusionary rule, the prosecutor can refile charges on the basis of the remaining evidence. A study of search warrant cases found that 12 of the 17 defendants (70 percent) who succeeded in having evidence suppressed were subsequently convicted on other charges.[43]

Judges vary greatly in their willingness to invoke the exclusionary rule. Sheldon Krantz and his colleagues found in his study of Boston that one judge granted 45.4 percent of the motions to suppress, whereas another granted only 22.2 percent. Three judges denied all motions presented to them. Motions to suppress were successful in only 2 percent of all the gambling and drug cases that Krantz et al. studied.[44]

A controversial 1982 study by the National Institute of Justice produced a much higher estimate of the rule's impact. It found that in 520,993 felony arrests in California between 1976 and 1979 prosecutors rejected a total of 86,033 cases for various reasons. Illegally obtained evidence accounted for 4,130 of those rejections. The Justice Department claimed that the 4,130 represented 4.8 percent of the 86,033 rejections.[45] In a pair of stinging critiques, Thomas Y. Davies and James J. Fyfe argued that it was more accurate to consider the 4,130 rejections as a percentage of the original 520,993 cases. This produces a rejection rate of only 0.8 percent (a figure that is very close to some of the other studies).[46]

In short, the exclusionary rule does not let "thousands" of dangerous criminals loose on the streets, and it has almost no effect on violent crime. Judge Rothwax and other critics of the exclusionary rule are guilty of reacting to a few celebrated cases. Yes, some convictions are overturned, and some of those defendants who are factually guilty are released, but these are rare events.

Our position, therefore, is:

PROPOSITION 10

Repeal or modification of the exclusionary rule will not help the police reduce serious crime.

The Positive Impact of the Exclusionary Rule Far from impairing police work, the exclusionary rule has played a major role in improving the professionalism of police work. Myron Orfield's study of narcotics officers in Chicago found that the exclusionary rule produced a number of significant reforms. The Chicago police and the Illinois state's attorney office developed a closer working relationship, the state attorney scrutinized applications for warrants more closely, and the police department improved its own training and supervision. The result was better police work. Interviews with Chicago narcotics detectives found that they supported the rule and were very concerned that weakening it would open the door to police abuse. Officers said that the experience of having evidence excluded in court was a valuable learning experience—the best on-the-job training they ever got.[47]

Response to the exclusionary rule depends on the professionalism of a police department. Craig Uchida and Tim Bynum studied the impact of the 1984 *Leon* decision which allowed a "good faith" exception to the exclusionary rule. Like the earlier studies, they found that the overall impact of the exclusionary rule in seven jurisdictions was "slight." Less than 1 percent (0.9) of all motions to suppress evidence obtained by search warrants were successful. In three of the seven jurisdictions, no motions to suppress evidence were successful. Those sites had a high degree of cooperation between police and prosecutors that included training of police officers and supervision of warrants. In "River City," however, the police were less professional and had an antagonistic relationship with prosecutors. Motions to suppress were filed in 57 percent of all cases, and 14 percent of them were successful.[48]

Many thoughtful law enforcement executives now accept and even welcome the rule. Former FBI Director William Sessions said that "protections that are afforded by the exclusionary rule are extremely important to fair play and the proper carrying out of the law enforcement responsibility."[49] Because of the rule, law-abiding citizens do not have to fear overzealous and intrusive action by a cop, and so the police enjoy greater public respect.

Instead of abolishing the exclusionary rule altogether, some critics propose modifying it to permit "good-faith" searches: cases in which the officer made an honest mistake (as in getting a number wrong on a street address). The Supreme Court adopted the good faith exception in *United States v. Leon* (1984), ruling that evidence could be admitted if it were obtained under a valid search warrant even though it was later found that there was not probable cause to issue the warrant.[50]

The good-faith exception, however, presents several problems. First, it complicates rather than simplifies search-and-seizure cases by opening the door to appeals based on whether the search was in good or bad faith and whether the officer made an honest mistake or a deliberate one. Fyfe argues that this makes the judge's job even harder. Second, the good-faith exception encourages police incompetence. It gives officers an incentive to claim that they made a minor mistake instead of prodding them to do a professional job in the first place. One of the main effects of the exclusionary rule has been to stimulate police professionalism.[51]

Finally, and most important in terms of crime fighting, the good-faith search is not going to significantly increase the number of convictions because few convictions are being "lost" owing to the exclusionary rule's existence.

Abolish *Miranda*

The *Miranda* warning is the second major "technicality" that conservatives believe "handcuffs" the police. The 1966 *Miranda v. Arizona* decision held that to ensure a suspect's Fifth Amendment protection against self-incrimination, the police must advise a criminal suspect of certain rights: Prior to any questioning, the person must be warned that he has a right to remain silent, that any statement he does make may be used against him, and that he has a right to the presence of an attorney, either retained or appointed.[52]

Conservatives have been angry about *Miranda* ever since. In the original decision, Justice Byron White dissented on the grounds that it "return[s] a killer, a rapist or other criminal to the streets and to the environment which produced him, to repeat his crime whenever it pleases him." Other opponents have repeated this criticism for thirty years.[53]

Almost thirty-five years later, the *Miranda* warning is the most widely known and probably most misunderstood element of police procedure. Hollywood and television writers love it. The warning adds a special dramatic complication to the plot. In one movie, a narcotics detective wrestles the suspect to the ground with one arm while reading from the *Miranda* warning card he holds in the other hand. Get it? The police have one hand tied behind their backs. A 1991 public opinion poll on the two-hundredth anniversary of the Bill of Rights found that while only 10 percent knew why it was originally adopted, 80 percent knew about their right to remain silent if arrested.[54] A recent book observed that "School children are more likely to recognize the *Miranda* warnings than the Gettysburg Address."[55]

Miranda in Operation   Does the *Miranda* warning really handcuff the police? Let us look at it in operation. First, let us clear up a few myths about the decision. The *Miranda* warning does not have to be given at the moment of arrest but only before questioning. If a suspect blurts out a confession ("Why did I do it?"), the confession is admissible. Also, a suspect can waive his or her rights by agreeing to talk and agreeing to talk without a lawyer. In fact, many suspects do waive their rights.

Paul G. Cassell, a strong critic of *Miranda,* properly raises the question of how we should measure the impact (or the "cost") of *Miranda*. He makes a persuasive argument that we should not look at the number of convictions overturned because of a *Miranda* violation but the number of confessions the police do not get. Surveying all of the studies done to date, he estimates that the rate of confessions has declined by 16 percent because of *Miranda*. But that is not the whole story, because some offenders are convicted even without a confession. He estimates that confessions are needed in about 24 percent of all cases. Thus, the net effect is that *Miranda* results in a "loss" of convictions in 3.8 percent of all cases (16 percent of 24 percent = 3.8 percent). Despite Cassell's own claims, this is not a very significant impact.[56]

Stephen J. Schulhofer, moreover, argues that Cassell's study suffers from a number of methodological flaws. One of the more serious is his failure to take into account the fact that confession rates were dropping in the years before

Miranda, for reasons unrelated to the decision. Factoring in a continuation of this trend, and adding in the effect of other methodological problems, Schulhofer estimates that the "loss" due to *Miranda* is not 3.8 percent but less than 1 percent (0.78%). "For all practical purposes," he concludes, *Miranda's* empirically detectable net damage to law enforcement is zero."[57]

The best study of *Miranda* in operation is Richard Leo's "Inside the Interrogation Room," in which he directly observed a total of 182 police interrogations in three police departments. Leo found that 78 of the suspects waived their *Miranda* rights and cooperated with the police. (Cassell found that 84 percent of the suspects in Salt Lake waived their *Miranda* rights).[58] As a result, two-thirds (64 percent) made a full confession, a partial confession, or some incriminating statement. What tactics did the police use to get them to cooperate? In over 80 percent of the cases, the police either confronted them with evidence of their guilt or appealed to their self-interest (it will help you if you talk), or both.[59]

In short, the *Miranda* warning was no barrier to successful police work. In the vast majority of the cases, the police got suspects to waive their rights, to confess or make an incriminating statement, and they did so through lawful means. It should be noted, however, that in 30 percent of the cases the police lied by confronting the suspects with false information about their guilt, as in falsely telling them that their partner had confessed. This evidence supports keeping the *Miranda* warning.

Why do suspects waive their rights and confess? Why do only about 20 percent of suspects take advantage of their right to remain silent? The first point is that the police do not arrest very many suspects. They only clear about 26 percent of all robberies and 14 percent of all burglaries. Thus, they usually have some evidence against the few suspects they do arrest. This leaves a small group of cases in which there is reasonably strong evidence. And as Leo discovered, detectives confront 85 percent of all suspects with evidence of their guilt. The suspects in these remaining cases have powerful incentives to cooperate and confess. They know that they committed the crime, and they realize that the police have some fairly good evidence against them. A lot of them feel guilty about it. Leo found that detectives appealed to suspects' conscience in 23 percent of all cases. Some hope to get a better deal in a plea bargaining. The detectives in Leo's study appealed to the suspects' self-interest in 88 percent of the cases.[60]

The image of the tough streetwise criminal who is skilled at manipulating the rules is another myth. Some suspects do invoke their *Miranda* rights, but the majority cooperate with the police. Felony suspects are typically young, poorly educated, and in many instances functionally illiterate. Most failed to learn how to manipulate the public school bureaucracy to their advantage, and they are not much more successful in the criminal justice system. The typical robber or burglar is so disorganized and impulsive that he does not even plan his crimes very well. The Rand Inmate Survey found that 40 percent of the juvenile robbers and 25 percent of the adults had not even intended to rob anyone when they left home. As one kid put it, "It was just a sudden thing. I didn't really mean to do it. I didn't plan nothing; it just happened." Among the adult "career criminals," only 40 percent bothered to visit the sites of their crimes in advance, and as few as 22 percent made an effort to check on police patrol in the area.[61]

In custody, young offenders may strike a tough pose, but it is usually nothing more than that—a pose, an act. A skilled professional detective can get most suspects to talk.

Modifying Miranda In 1984, the Supreme Court finally accepted the conservative argument and created a "public safety" exception to the *Miranda* warning. In *New York v. Quarles,* the Court held that when the safety of an officer or a citizen is threatened, as by the presence of a gun, the officer may ask questions before advising a suspect of his or her rights.[62] The decision represents a major victory in the conservatives' 30-year campaign to reverse the rules laid down by the Warren Court. Given the limited impact of the *Miranda* warning on confessions, however, it is hard to imagine that this limited exception would result in many more arrests or any significant crime reduction.

Consequently, our conclusion is:

> ## PROPOSITION 11
> Repeal or modification of the *Miranda* warning
> will not result in more convictions.

CONCLUSION

The police are the front line of the criminal justice system. Patrol is the primary strategy for preventing crime, and arrest is the "gatekeeping" point for all criminal cases. Many people believe we could reduce crime significantly if we would just "unleash" the cops: give them more resources and more powers. We have found that these ideas are not likely to reduce crime. The only promising strategies involve some of the new focused police programs, such as "hot spots" and some community policing programs.

NOTES

1. Department of Justice, *The Police and Public Opinion* (Washington, DC: Government Printing Office, 1977).

2. Bill Clinton and Al Gore, *Putting People First* (New York: Times Books, 1992), p. 72.

3. Police-population ratios are regularly published in Federal Bureau of Investigation, *Crime in the United States* (Washington, DC: Government Printing Office, annual), and Bureau of Justice Statistics, *Law Enforcement Management and Administrative Statistics, 1997* (Washington, DC: Government Printing Office, 1999).

4. Lawrence W. Sherman and David Weisburd, "General Deterrent Effects of Police Patrol in Crime 'Hot Spots': A Randomized Controlled Trial," *Justice Quarterly* 12 (December 1995): 625–48.

5. George L. Kelling, Tony Pate, Duane Diekman, and Charles E. Brown, *The Kansas City Preventive Patrol Experiment: A Summary Report* (Washington, DC: The Police Foundation, 1974).

6. Kelling et al., *Kansas City Preventive Patrol Experiment.*

7. The Police Foundation, *The Newark Foot Patrol Experiment* (Washington, DC: The Police Foundation, 1981).

8. Franklin E. Zimring and Gordon J. Hawkins, *Deterrence: The Legal Threat in Crime Control* (Chicago: University of Chicago Press, 1973).

9. James Q. Wilson and Alan Abrahamse, "Does Crime Pay?" *Justice Quarterly* 9 (September 1992): 372–73.

10. General Accounting Office, *Community Policing: Issues Related to the Design, Operation, and Management of the Grant Program,* GAO/GGD-97-167 (September 1997).

11. University of Maryland, *Preventing Crime: What Works, What Doesn't, What's Promising* (Washington, DC: Government Printing Office, 1997), p. v.

12. For evidence that there has been relatively little change in basic police operations, see Jihong Zhao and Quint C. Thurman, "Community Policing: Where Are We Now?" *Crime and Delinquency* 43 (July 1997): 345–57.

13. See the summary of the evidence in University of Maryland, *Preventing Crime,* pp. 8-25–8-30.

14. Lawrence W. Sherman, "Police Crackdowns," in Michael Tonry and Norval Morris, eds., *Crime and Justice: An Annual Review of Research,* vol. 12 (Chicago: University of Chicago Press, 1990), pp. 1–48.

15. Lynn Zimmer, "Proactive Policing against Street-Level Drug Trafficking," *American Journal of Police* 9.1 (1990): 43–74.

16. Zimmer, "Proactive Policing."

17. "The World of the Drug Bazaar," *New York Times,* 1 October 1992; "Neighborhood Ruled by Drug Culture," *New York Times,* 2 October 1992.

18. Herman Goldstein, *Problem-Oriented Policing* (New York: McGraw-Hill, 1990).

Tara O'Connor Shelley and Anne C. Grant, eds., *Problem-Oriented Policing* (Washington, DC: Police Executive Research Forum, 1998).

19. Lawrence W. Sherman, Patrick R. Gartin, and Michael E. Buerger, "Hot Spots of Predatory Crime: Routine Activities and the Criminology of Place," *Criminology* 27 (No. 2, 1989): 27–55.

20. Lorraine Green, "Cleaning Up Drug Hot Spots in Oakland, California: The Displacement and Diffusion Effects," *Justice Quarterly* 12 (December 1995): 737–54.

21. University of Maryland, *Preventing Crime.*

22. Anthony A. Braga, David L. Weisburd, Elin J. Waring, Lorraine Green Mazerolle, William Spelman, and Francis Gajewski, "Problem-Oriented Policing in Violent Crime Places: A Randomized Controlled Experiment," *Criminology* 37 (No. 3, 1999): 541–80.

23. George L. Kelling and Catherine M. Coles, *Fixing Broken Windows* (New York: Free Press, 1996). William Bratton and Peter Knoblach, *Turnaround* (New York: Random House, 1998).

24. Jack Maple, *The Crime Fighter* (New York: Doubleday, 1999); Eli Silverman, *NYPD Battles Crime* (Boston: Northeastern, 1999).

25. Gary Cordner, "Problem-Oriented Policing vs. Zero Tolerance," in O'Connor and Grant, eds., *Problem-Oriented Policing,* pp. 303–14.

26. K. Jack Riley, *Crack, Powder Cocaine, and Heroin: Drug Purchase and Use Patterns in Six U.S. Cities* (Washington, DC: Government Printing Office, 1997). Timothy Egan, "A Drug Ran Its Course, Then Hid with Its Users," *New York Times,* 19 September 1999.

27. William Spelman and Dale K. Brown, *Calling the Police: Citizen Reporting of Serious Crime* (Washington, DC: Government Printing Office, 1984).

28. Spelman and Brown, *Calling The Police.*

29. Peter Greenwood, *The Criminal Investigation Process* (Santa Monica, CA: Rand, 1975).

30. Skogan and Antunes, "Information, Apprehension, and Deterrence."

31. Albert J. Reiss, *The Police and the Public* (New Haven, CT: Yale University Press, 1971), p. 104.

32. President's Commission on Law Enforcement and Administration of Justice, *Task Force Report: Science and Technology* (Washington, DC: Government Printing Office, 1967), p. 8.

33. John E. Eck, *Solving Crimes: The Investigation of Burglary and Robbery* (Washington, DC: Police Executive Research Forum, 1983).

34. Greenwood, *Criminal Investigation Process.*

35. Joan Petersilia, "Processing Latent Fingerprints—What Are the Payoffs?" *Journal of Police Science and Administration* 6 (June 1978): 157–67.

36. Susan E. Martin and Lawrence W. Sherman, "Selective Apprehension: A Police Strategy for Repeat Offenders," *Criminology* 24 (February 1986): 155–73; Susan E. Martin, "Policing Career Criminals: An Examination of an Innovative Crime Control Program," *Journal of Criminal Law and Criminology* 77 (Winter 1986): 1159–182.

37. Martin and Sherman, "Selective Apprehension."

38. Harold J. Rothwax, *Guilty: The Collapse of Criminal Justice* (New York: Random House, 1996), p. 15.

39. Samuel Walker, *Popular Justice: A History of American Criminal Justice,* 2nd ed. (New York: Oxford University Press, 1998).

40. *Mapp v. Ohio,* 367 U.S. 643 (1961).

41. James J. Fyfe, "The NIJ Study of the Exclusionary Rule," *Criminal Law Bulletin* 19 (May–June 1983): 253–60.

42. Peter F. Nardulli, "The Societal Costs of the Exclusionary Rule: An Empirical Assessment," *American Bar Foundation Research Journal* 1983 (Summer 1983): 585–690; Comptroller General of the United States, *Impact of the Exclusionary Rule on Federal Criminal Prosecutions,* Report #GGD-79-45 (April 19, 1979); National Center for State Courts, *The*

Search Warrant Process (Williamsburg, VA: National Center for State Courts, 1986).

43. National Center for State Courts, *Search Warrant Process.*

44. Sheldon Krantz, Bernard Gilman, Charles G. Benda, Carol Rogoff Hallstrom, and Gail J. Nadworny, *Police Policymaking* (Lexington, MA: Lexington Books, 1979), pp. 189–92.

45. National Institute of Justice, *The Effects of the Exclusionary Rule: A Study in California* (Washington, DC: Government Printing Office, 1982).

46. Fyfe, "The NIJ Study of the Exclusionary Rule"; Thomas Y. Davies, "A Hard Look at What We Know (And Still Need to Learn) about the 'Costs' of the Exclusionary Rule: The NIJ Study and Other Studies of 'Lost' Arrests," *American Bar Foundation Research Journal* (Summer 1983): 611–90.

47. Myron W. Orfield, Jr., "The Exclusionary Rule and Deterrence: An Empirical Study of Chicago Narcotics Officers," *University of Chicago Law Review* 54 (Summer 1987): 1016–055.

48. Craig Uchida and Tim Bynum, "Search Warrants, Motions to Suppress and 'Lost Cases': The Effects of the Exclusionary Rule in Seven Jurisdictions," *Journal of Criminal Law and Criminology* 81 (Winter 1991): 1034–066.

49. Sessions quoted in *New York Times,* 5 November 1987.

50. *United States v. Leon,* 468 U.S. 897 (1984).

51. James J. Fyfe, "In Search of the 'Bad Faith' Search," *Criminal Law Bulletin* 18 (May–June 1982): 260–64.

52. *Miranda v. Arizona,* 384 U.S. 436 (1966).

53. An invaluable collection of articles on the subject is Richard Leo and George C. Thomas, III, eds., *The Miranda Debate: Law, Justice, and Policing* (Boston: Northeastern University Press, 1998).

54. "Poll Finds Only 33% Can Identify Bill of Rights," *New York Times,* 15 December, 1991.

55. Leo and Thomas, III, eds., *Miranda Debate,* p. xv.

56. Paul G. Cassell and Bret S. Hayman, "Police Interrogation in the 1990s: An Empirical Study of the Effects of Miranda," *UCLA Law Review* 43 (February 1996): 860.

57. Stephen J. Schulhofer, "Miranda's Practical Effect: Substantial Benefits and Vanishingly Small Social Costs," in Leo and Thomas, eds., *Miranda Debate,* p. 205.

58. Paul G. Cassell, "Miranda's Social Costs: An Empirical Reassessment," *Northwestern University Law Review* 90 (Winter 1996): 387–499.

59. Richard A. Leo, "Inside the Interrogation Room," *Journal of Criminal Law and Criminology* 86 (No. 2, 1996): 266–303.

60. Leo, "Inside the Interrogation Room."

61. Joan Petersilia, Peter W. Greenwood, and Martin Lavin, *The Criminal Careers of Habitual Felons* (Washington, DC: Government Printing Office, 1978).

62. *New York v. Quarles,* 467 U.S. 649 (1984).

6

❖

Deter the Criminals

eterrence is an article of faith among conservatives: Punishment deters
crime; swifter, more certain, and more severe punishments will reduce
crime even further. In this chapter we will look at deterrence in theory
and practice. We are going to violate our own ground rules and discuss some
issues that fall outside the scope of our inquiry: the death penalty, drunk driving crackdowns, and domestic violence. They are not directly related to robbery and burglary, but they offer some important evidence about deterrence.

DETERRENCE THEORY

The theory of deterrence has a simple, intuitive appeal. People want to avoid
unpleasant experiences; if we make the punishment for crime more unpleasant, fewer people will commit crime. The basic theory is simple, but in actual
practice it is very complex, resting on a number of related assumptions that
may not work in the real world of the criminal justice.[1]

First, it is important to distinguish between the deterrent effect of the
criminal law and the criminal justice system on one hand and the more limited
deterrent effect of particular policies or programs on the other.

The criminal law and the criminal justice system have some general deterrent effect. The law defines the boundaries of acceptable behavior and specifies the consequences of crossing those boundaries. To a certain extent, this

deterrent effect works; the threat of punishment contributes to law-abiding behavior. Most of us do *not* commit serious crimes. We are not murders, robbers, and burglars. In the most comprehensive review of the subject, Daniel Nagin concludes that "the collective actions of the criminal justice system exert a very substantial deterrent effect."[2] The law and the justice system, however, are only two of the factors at work in shaping our behavior. Families, religious training, schools, and peers also exert powerful influences. In this broad social context, it is difficult to specify the independent effect of the law and the justice system.

Nagin goes on to point out that the real issue of deterrence is "whether a specific policy, grafted onto the existing structure, will materially add to the preventive effect."[3] That is precisely the point of this book: Are there policies that will reduce serious crime from its current level? On this point, Nagin is very cautious. There is a lack of clear and convincing evidence of policies that, from a deterrence perspective, produce real, long-term reductions in crime. To understand why we should be skeptical about the added deterrent effect of any criminal justice policy, let's examine the assumptions underlying deterrence.

Assumptions Underlying Deterrence

The theory of deterrence involves a number of basic assumptions. Deterrence assumes the existence of an information loop involving potential offenders' knowledge and perception of the potential punishment. First, offenders have to be *aware* of the penalty for particular crimes. They have to be aware, for example, of a new law imposing mandatory jail term for a first-offense drunk driving conviction. And, as we learned in Chapter 5, they have to be aware of increased police patrol in their neighborhood.

Second, potential offenders have to *perceive* the consequences of law breaking as *unpleasant* and therefore something to be avoided.

Third, they have to *believe* a real *risk* of arrest, conviction, and punishment is present. As Scott Decker and his colleagues point out, "Deterrence is essentially a psychological process that involves the balancing of personally held beliefs about possible punishment and anticipated gain."[4] Certainty and swiftness of punishment are regarded as essential to this process in order to heighten the connection between the crime and its consequences.

Finally, and perhaps most important, deterrence theory assumes that people are *rational actors* who weigh the relative costs and benefits of their actions and make conscious decisions about the best course of action. On this point, deterrence-oriented policy makers assume that we can influence behavior by altering the perceived costs and benefits. Thus, if we raise the costs by making punishment more certain and/or more severe, we will influence people not to commit crime. Or, if we educate kids about the personal costs of doing drugs, they will choose not to use illegal drugs.

Deterrence operates in two ways, depending on the target audience. *Specific* deterrence is directed at the individual offender. The punishment is intended to teach that person right and wrong, that criminal activity leads to

unpleasant consequences. *General* deterrence is directed at the society as a whole. Punishing a few criminals is designed to communicate a message to the larger audience.[5]

With respect to designing crime policies, an important distinction must also be made between *absolute* and *marginal* deterrence. The idea of absolute deterrence posits that a particular punishment deters crime (or a particular crime) completely. Marginal deterrence holds that a relatively more severe penalty will produce *some* reduction in crime.[6] No one realistically expects any punishment to eliminate crime completely. Therefore, in this book we are really concerned with policy that will make some marginal but significant reduction in crime.

After being out of favor among criminologists for decades, deterrence theory enjoyed a tremendous revival in the 1980s. The revival was not confined to criminal justice policy. Ronald L. Akers points out that the underlying theory of rational choice became a "hot topic" in many of the social sciences in the 1980s.[7] It was especially influential in economic theory and many aspects of social policy. Recent welfare reform, for example, rests on the assumption that traditional welfare programs provided too few incentives for finding employment. Cutting welfare benefits and putting a cap on the number of years of welfare eligibility, conservatives argue, encourages people to find employment and get off welfare.[8]

While deterrence theory is generally associated with conservatives, we need to point out that on certain issues many liberals also believe in deterrence. Many, for example, believe that the exclusionary rule deters illegal searches and seizures by police officers, or that citizen review of the police will deter police misconduct. Many liberals also believe that gun control laws with stiff penalties will deter illegal gun ownership.[9]

From Theory to Practice: Four Problems

Nagin gives four reasons for being skeptical about how effectively deterrence-oriented policies are translated into practice.[10] First, we know little about the long-term effects of policies. In theory, part of the "cost" of crime is the resulting social stigma. But if arrest and imprisonment are common experiences in a particular social group, they begin to lose their stigmatizing effect. Many observers believe that this is precisely what has happened with young African-American males as a result of the war on crime. So many people have been arrested and convicted that it is simply a "normal" life experience, with little deterrent effect.

Second, Nagin points out that we know relatively little about the process of how perceptions of risk are formed. Research on this subject is relatively recent, and little has been done with regard to serious offenders.

Third, the impact of particular policies depends upon how they are implemented in different jurisdictions. As we learned in Chapter 5, two police departments may add the same number of new police officers, but one may use them far more efficiently and effectively in terms of crime fighting. In California, the state's "three strikes" law has been used extensively in Los Angeles but to a very limited extent in San Francisco.

Fourth, as the preceding observations indicate, laws and policies are not always implemented as intended. As we learned in Chapter 3, the courtroom work group has a tremendous ability to undermine new laws or policies that disrupt the established going rate. The case of "three strikes" laws is an excellent example. With respect to domestic violence, we are not absolutely certain that police officers faithfully carry out mandatory arrest laws or policies.

The Risk of Crime: Some Preliminary Evidence

Because deterrence theory rests on the actual and perceived risk of crime, it is useful to review what we learned in Chapters 2 and 3 about the administration of justice. While the criminal law and the justice system may have some general deterrent effect, the fact is that the risk of apprehension and punishment for most crimes is very low. Only 37 percent of all Index crimes are reported to the police, and the police clear only 21 percent of those crimes. Thus, only 8 percent of all Index crimes result in arrest. Since about half of all felony arrests are dismissed, only 4 percent of all crimes are prosecuted (see Chapter

3, Box 3.1). In short, the overall risk of punishment (defined as conviction) is extremely low.

The risks are somewhat higher for particular crimes. Virtually all murders are reported, and the police clear about 68 percent of them. A Justice Department report found that 87 percent of all husbands tried for murdering their wives are convicted, and 81 percent of them are sentenced to prison.[11] Meanwhile, about 54 percent of all robberies are reported, and the police clear about 26 percent of them. This yields an overall apprehension risk of 14 percent, which is significantly higher than the rate for all Index crimes.

Looking at the risks of crime from the perspective of individual offenders, particularly career criminals, creates some additional problems for deterrence theory. The Rand Inmate Survey (RIS) found that offenders were extremely fatalistic about their chances of being arrested and punished. Unfortunately, neither the perceived risk nor the actual experience of imprisonment seems to deter them from criminal activity. James Q. Wilson and Allan Abrahamse conclude that the RIS offenders do not act rationally, as deterrence theory requires.[12] And in a study of 1,000 Nebraska prisoners, Julie Horney and Ineke Marshall found that offenders with higher arrest rates relative to self-reported crime also reported higher perceptions of the risk of arrest and punishment.[13]

Now let us turn our attention to some policies designed to deter crime and see what we can learn about deterrence theory in practice.

THE DEATH PENALTY

The death penalty is a good subject for examining deterrence theory for two reasons. First, many people believe that capital punishment deters crime; second, considerable research has been done on the subject.

Sorting Out the Issues

We can debate the merits of the death penalty in terms of three separate issues.[14] First is the moral question of whether it is a just form of punishment. Some people firmly believe the death penalty is a morally justifiable form of punishment for murder, whereas others believe it is morally wrong. This debate involves basic conceptions of morality and justice and is not subject to empirical proof one way or the other.

The question of whether the death penalty is constitutional is the second issue. Constitutional challenges began in the 1960s and eventually led to the 1972 *Furman v. Georgia* decision in which the U.S. Supreme Court ruled that the death penalty had been applied in an unconstitutionally arbitrary and capricious fashion.[15] It rejected the argument that capital punishment is inherently cruel and unusual. Four years later, in *Gregg v. Georgia,* the Court upheld the constitutionality of the death penalty where there were guidelines to control its application.[16]

Table 6-1 Homicide rates in death penalty states (Ohio, Indiana) and in a state without the death penalty (Michigan), 1920–1974 (homicides per 100,000 population)

Five-year periods	Michigan Rates	Ohio Rates	Number of executions	Indiana Rates	Number of executions
1920–1924	5.5	7.4	45	6.1	5
1925–1929	8.2	8.4	40	6.6	7
1930–1934	5.6	8.5	43	6.5	11
1935–1939	3.9	5.9	29	4.5	22
1940–1944	3.2	4.3	15	3.0	2
1945–1949	3.5	4.8	36	3.8	5
1950–1954	3.8	3.8	20	3.7	2
1955–1959	3.0	3.4	12	3.0	0
1960–1964	3.6	3.2	7	3.2	1
1965–1969	6.6	5.1	0	4.7	0
1970–1974	11.3	7.8	0	6.4	0

SOURCES: National Office of Vital Statistics, *Vital Statistics of the United States;* William J. Bowers, *Executions in America* (Lexington, MA: Heath, 1974), Appendix A; Thorsten Sellin, *The Penalty of Death* (Beverly Hills, CA: Sage, 1980), p. 144.

The third issue is whether the death penalty deters crime. This is the focus of our discussion here. The moral and constitutional questions are extremely important, but as we explained in Chapter 1, this book focuses on issues of crime policy.

Executions and Crime: Sellin's Studies

Some of the first attempts to study the deterrent effect of capital punishment were relatively simple comparative and longitudinal studies. The noted criminologist Thorsten Sellin compared neighboring states, two with and one without the death penalty. As Table 6-1 indicates, Ohio and Indiana, two death penalty states, did not have lower crime rates than Michigan, which does not have the death penalty. Murder rates in all three states changed in roughly the same direction, decreasing from the 1930s to the early 1960s and then rising sharply. This suggests that broad social factors common to all states, rather than executions, were the primary causal factors in homicide rates.[17] Sellin also examined individual states over time. Kansas, which had earlier abolished the death penalty, restored it in 1935. Its homicide trends were nearly identical to those in Missouri and Colorado, which had kept the death penalty throughout the period.

Sellin's research did not conclusively demonstrate the absence of a deterrent effect. His fairly simple methodology did not control for all the variables that might influence homicide rates. Now let us turn our attention to one controversial study that did attempt to control these variables.

Dr. Ehrlich's Magic Bullet

The debate over the deterrent effect of the death penalty entered a new phase in 1975, when economist Isaac Ehrlich produced a study of crime and executions between 1930 and 1969 purporting to prove that each execution deterred seven or eight murders.[18] If Ehrlich's analysis is correct, the death penalty has a powerful deterrent effect.

Did Ehrlich prove his case? His major contribution to death penalty research was his sophisticated formula that attempted to control for all of the variables that might have affected the murder rate. This included the probability of apprehension, the probability of conviction for murder, the probability of execution, the unemployment rate, the labor force participation of adults, the real per capita income, and the proportion of the population between the ages of 14 and 24. He explicitly embraced the rational choice theory of human behavior, explaining that the "propensity" to commit crimes "is influenced by the prospective gains and losses associated with their commission."[19]

Critics, however, quickly found flaws in Ehrlich's analysis. His sophisticated mathematical formula, which appeared to be the strongest part of his approach, also turned out to be his greatest weakness. The formula is highly sensitive to problems with the reliability of the data. Critics focused on the 1960s, when executions stopped and violent crime increased. As we already noted, this pattern leads many people to believe that the death penalty does deter crime. In their own analyses, Brian Forst, Peter Passell, and William Bowers and Glenn Pierce all argue that when you exclude the years from 1962 to 1969, the deterrent effect claimed by Ehrlich vanishes.[20] His formula does not explain the trends between the 1930s and the early 1960s, when executions declined while the crime rate either declined or remained stable.

We might add that the murder rate increased dramatically in the late 1980s at the same time that executions increased. The number of homicides increased from 18,980 in 1985 to 24,530 in 1993, despite an average of almost twenty executions per year in that period, with a peak of thirty-one in 1992.[21] The lesson here is that it is often easy—but inappropriate—to try to prove an argument by selecting a certain time period when the trends favor your position.

Ehrlich's critics also found serious problems with the official UCR data he used. The data on crime and arrests indicate that the certainty of apprehension declined from the 1930s through the 1960s. We have good reason to believe, however, that because of the lack of professionalism in most departments, these data seriously undercount the amount of crime. In New York City alone, for example, at least two well-documented episodes (in 1955 and 1965) occurred in which administrative changes in the police department produced huge increases in officially reported crime. In Chicago, meanwhile, reporters in 1983 caught the Chicago police unfounding a substantial number of crimes.[22] In other words, the apparent risk of apprehension was higher in the pre-1960 years because police record keeping kept the number of reported crimes artificially low. Consequently, the real risk of apprehension had not declined as much between 1930 and 1969 as Ehrlich asserted.

Research on the deterrent effect of the death penalty continues. The safest conclusion we can draw at this point is that no convincing evidence has surfaced indicating that the death penalty deters crime. This point leads us to the following proposition:

PROPOSITION 12

The death penalty does not deter crime.

Delays and Deterrence

Death penalty advocates reply to the critics by arguing that the deterrent effect is undermined by long delays in carrying out executions. In fact, the average time between conviction and execution is over eight years. Appeals in some cases take 15 years or more. Also, many death sentences are vacated, through appeal, executive clemency, or death by natural causes. In 1995, for example, 56 offenders were executed while nearly twice as many (105) were removed from death row by other causes.[23] Death penalty advocates argue that these factors undermine both the certainty and the swiftness of the death penalty. If we would eliminate these obstacles, the argument continues, the deterrent effect would work.

Long delays in death penalty cases are to be expected. Someone sentenced to die is going to explore every possible avenue of appeal. The process of appeal is an essential part of the criminal justice system, designed to protect against errors in the process. And mistakes do happen. Hugo Bedau and Michael Radelet identified a total of 350 miscarriages of justice in potentially capital cases since 1900. They define *miscarriage of justice* as a case in which "the defendant was erroneously convicted of a capital crime." Of the 350 cases they identified, 139 were given death sentences, and 23 were actually executed.[24] In January 2000, the governor of Illinois suspended all executions after 13 people were released from death row because they had been wrongly convicted.

The U.S. Supreme Court has substantially reduced the right of death row inmates to challenge their sentences in recent years. As a result, the pace of executions has increased. In 1999, 98 persons were executed, the largest number since the early 1950s.[25] Some advocates of the death penalty will argue that this increase is responsible for the drop in the crime rate in the mid-1990s. Yet as we already noted, homicides increased in the late 1980s at the same time as the number of executions was increasing. In short, you cannot cite trends over a short period of time and assume that a cause-and-effect relationship exists.

Brutalization Theory?

In a different challenge to deterrence theory, Bowers and Pierce argued that capital punishment may actually encourage crime. According to their *brutalization* theory, each execution is followed by a two- to threefold increase in the number of homicides the next month. They found in three California counties a "slight but discernible" increase in the number of murders in the ten days following an execution (0.25 per execution). A greater increase (1.6 per execution) in homicides occurred in Philadelphia within two months after an execution. Bowers and Pierce contend that the effect is felt among a limited group of people who, independently, have "reached a state of 'readiness to kill,'" in the sense of having an intended victim already in mind. The legal execution conveys the message that vengeance is justified.[26]

Bowers and Pierce concede that "there is room to quarrel" with their analysis, but Brian Forst reached a similar conclusion in his own study. Examining the years 1960 through 1970, he found no evidence that executions prevented crime and some evidence that they actually "provoked" homicides.[27]

Summary

Research on the effect of the death penalty on crime is extremely mixed. Because so many different factors influence criminal behavior, it may never be possible to determine the extent of any deterrent effect. For the moment, then, we can say that the advocates of capital punishment have not persuasively established the existence of a deterrent effect.

DETERRING THE DRUNK DRIVER

In the 1980s, a crusade against drunk driving arose and swept the country. Spurred by a wave of public outrage, virtually every state enacted new laws and policies, most of which were designed to deter drunk driving through tougher punishment.[28] Leading the national crusade was an organization called MADD (Mothers Against Drunk Driving), founded by Candi Lightner, whose 13-year-old daughter, Cari, was killed in a crash involving Clarence Busch, who had two previous drunk driving convictions and was out on bail on a third drunk driving charge. Cari Lightner's death confirmed the belief of many people that repeat drunk drivers beat the system.

The "Killer Drunk" and Other Myths

Like so many aspects of criminal justice, the subject of drunk driving is dominated by myths that inhibit the development of sound and effective policies. It is widely believed, for example, that drunk drivers are responsible for half of all traffic fatalities. One Justice Department report repeated the widely publicized claim that drunk driving kills 50,000 people every two years—"almost as many American lives as were lost in the entire ten years of the Vietnam war."[29] This grossly exaggerated estimate originated in a 1968 report by the Department of Transportation (DOT) and has been widely repeated ever since.

Current data indicate that 40.9 percent of all traffic fatalities in 1996 were "alcohol related," meaning that the driver tested positive for alcohol.[30] Alcohol was not necessarily the *cause* of each of those accidents, however. There is an important distinction between drivers who have been drinking and those whose driving is *impaired* by drinking. James B. Jacobs argues that only 30 percent of all traffic deaths are associated with drunk driving, and H. Laurence Ross believes that about a quarter of all fatalities involve a driver who is clearly drunk (that is, with a blood alcohol content of 0.10 percent or higher).[31]

Another myth is that many "killer drunks," people with a serious drinking problem and many arrests, frequently beat the system.[32] The myth of the killer drunk has several elements. First, it places the blame on a small number of dangerous people. Second, it emphasizes the killing of innocent people. Third, it puts much of the blame on the criminal justice system for not punishing these offenders and keeping them off the road. Fourth, it makes criminal punishment the primary focus of efforts to reduce traffic fatalities.

Ross argues that each of these elements distorts the reality of alcohol-related fatalities. First, the problem is not confined to a few dangerous people. Driving after drinking is fairly common. Ross estimates that about 20 percent of all drivers, or 33 million people, drive after drinking every year. That is a lot of people. Moreover, because about 20 to 30 percent of the population do not drink at all, the percentage of drinkers who drive after drinking is higher than 20 percent. Ross's point is that drinking and driving is a routine part of a society where driving is nearly universal (and practically necessary in terms of work) and drinking is an acceptable social custom. In short, we cannot address the problem by assuming that only a handful of people are responsible for it.[33]

Second, innocent drivers or bystanders are not the typical victims of alcohol-related crashes. About half of all the people killed are the drunk drivers themselves, and another 20 percent are passengers in their cars. Additionally, a large percentage of pedestrians who are killed by motor vehicles are drunk themselves.[34]

Third, the argument that the criminal justice system is "soft" on drunk drivers is one part of a general view of the criminal justice system which we have already discussed in Chapters 2 and 3. We will take a close look at the alleged loopholes in the criminal justice system in Chapter 8. Later in this chapter, we will look specifically at the handling of drunk driving cases.

In fact, most of the drivers killed in alcohol-related crashes do not have a history of drunk driving. It is not possible, therefore, to spot them in advance on the basis of their driving records. This is another example of the prediction problem. The crash that killed Cari Lightner, involving an innocent victim and a driver with a long record, is the classic "celebrated case" at the top of our criminal justice wedding cake.

Fourth, and perhaps most important in terms of reducing drinking and driving, both Ross and Jacobs argue that many different kinds of policies can contribute to reducing alcohol-related traffic fatalities.[35] Most do not involve deterrence-oriented enforcement. We will examine some of these policies in the "good news" section below.

Deterrence and Drunk Driving

Deterrence-oriented efforts to reduce drunk driving involve both short-term enforcement crackdowns and long-term changes in sentencing policy.[36] There are several reasons for thinking that tougher punishment is more likely to work with drunk driving than, for example, robbery or burglary. Because people who drink and drive are more representative of the general population, more of them will have a stake in society and therefore feel threatened by the stigma of arrest and the impact on their jobs and families. Reasons also abound for thinking that the probability of arrest is higher for drunk driving. It is a public crime, occurring in plain view over an extended period of time. The evidence does not necessarily support these assumptions, however.

One of the most famous drunk driving crackdowns involved the 1967 Road Safety Act in England. The law empowered the police to require a breath test of any driver and specified that refusal to submit to the test was punishable as an actual failure. It attempted to increase the certainty of apprehension, without changing the severity of punishment.[37]

As Figure 6-1 indicates, weekend traffic fatalities and serious injuries dropped to one-third of their previous levels after the law went into effect. Some observers saw this as evidence of a deterrent effect. But it is also obvious that the effect gradually wore off. Within three years, fatalities returned to their previous level. This decay appears to be a general phenomenon in enforcement crackdowns. A 1984 Justice Department evaluation of four anti–drunk driving campaigns found similar results and concluded that the deterrent effects of an enforcement effort, even when it exists, "appear to diminish over time."[38]

Lawrence Sherman characterizes decline in deterrent effect as "initial deterrence decay." He points out, however, that some deterrent effect remains, which he characterizes as "residual deterrence."[39] The challenge for policy makers is to increase the amount of residual deterrence over the long-term. Unfortunately, the evidence indicates that short-term crackdowns do not achieve this effect.

The British crackdown illustrates a phenomenon known as the *announcement effect*. The publicity surrounding a crackdown causes people to alter their behavior: People decide not to have another drink, or they ask someone else to drive them home; a bartender refuses to serve a drink, or friends tell someone that he or she has had enough to drink. In short, people do perceive the threat of punishment and make rational decisions to alter their behavior. In some instances, these changes occur before the law actually goes into effect as people's awareness of the potential penalty rises.

The announcement effect may also change the behavior of police officers, causing them to become more active in stopping drunk drivers. A Justice

FIGURE 6-1 The effect on traffic fatalities and serious injuries of a crackdown on drunk driving, United Kingdom, 1966–1970.

SOURCE: Reprinted by permission of the publisher, from *Deterring the Drinking Driver: Legal Policy and Social Control,* by H. Laurence Ross (Lexington, MA: Lexington Books, D.C. Heath and Company). Originally appeared in Ross, 1973, *Journal of Legal Studies,* University of Chicago Press.

Department evaluation of four anti–drunk driving campaigns, for example, found that arrests went up in three of them but not in the one in which "relatively little publicity" was made about the mandatory imprisonment law.[40]

As the publicity surrounding an enforcement effort diminishes, however, the effect wears off. Drinkers are less conscious of the risks and revert to their normal behavior. Police officers return to their normal levels of enforcement activity.

One of the main problems with drunk driving crackdowns is that the risk of arrest is extremely low. In his evaluation of the British experiments, H. Laurence Ross estimates that the probability of being asked to submit to a breath test is 1 per million vehicle miles driven. The risk is higher for drinking drivers because their behavior attracts the attention of the police, but it is still "low by any reasonable criterion." The U.S. Department of Transportation estimates that someone would have to drive drunk between 200 and 2,000 times to be apprehended—and even then would face only a 50 percent chance of being punished.[41]

Most people, moreover, believe the risk is low. A survey of Minneapolis and St. Paul residents found that 75 percent thought their chances of being arrested if they drove drunk were "unlikely" or "very unlikely."[42] And according to deterrence theory, the deterrent effect is weak or nonexistent if the perceived risk is low.

Looking at enforcement from the perspective of the police officer helps to explain why the risk is low. Both regular patrol officers and traffic unit officers are theoretically on the lookout for drunk drivers. Regular patrol officers, however, have many responsibilities—law enforcement, order maintenance, and service—and are primarily concerned with answering calls for service. Moreover, as we learned in the previous chapter, they are spread very thin and are responsible for patrolling streets that are not prime "hunting grounds" for drunk drivers. Traffic unit officers, meanwhile, represent no more than about 10 percent of the sworn officers in a department. They also have other responsibilities, such as watching for speeders. Drunk driving is heaviest at those hours when the police are busiest with other assignments. In short, not that many police officers are concentrating exclusively on drunk driving.

Certain disincentives affect aggressive traffic enforcement. Traffic stops are unpleasant and occasionally dangerous experiences for police officers. Citizens resent them and sometimes let the officer know it. Traffic situations are the fourth most hazardous situation for police officers in terms of officers killed on duty (and these situations include accidents resulting from pursuits).[43] In the absence of any strong incentives, such as ticket quotas, most cops prefer to avoid traffic stops except in the most serious cases.

When officers do make arrests, the law of diminishing returns comes into play. Processing an arrest may take up to two hours (or more, depending on local procedures). Thus, each arrest removes the police officer from the street and lowers the level of enforcement. While there may be some gain in specific deterrence related to the person arrested, there is an offsetting loss in general deterrence.

If the hunters are few, the hunted are many and well hidden among law-abiding drivers. Experts estimate that even during the peak drunk driving hours (Friday and Saturday nights), only about 3 to 4 percent of all drivers are legally drunk.[44] Perhaps another 5 percent have some detectable level of alcohol in their blood. But some drivers who are legally drunk may not be impaired, and their driving may not attract the attention of the police. The drive home from a neighborhood bar may be very short, leaving a small "window of opportunity" for detection.

Drunk Drivers in Court

Another factor undermining the deterrent effect of a crackdown is the fate of drunk driving cases in court. James B. Jacobs estimates that about 90 percent of all arrested drunk drivers are convicted through guilty pleas.[45] In this respect, the prosecution of drunk driving offenses closely resembles the handling of other criminal cases. Those data, however, reflect only convictions. The main purpose of crackdowns is to deter drunk driving by increasing the severity of punishment, usually through a mandatory jail or prison sentence.

Mandatory sentencing provisions can be evaded through dismissal, plea bargaining, or blatant disregard for the law. H. Laurence Ross and James P. Foley examined the implementation of new mandatory sentencing laws enacted in New Mexico and Indiana in the 1980s. The New Mexico law required a jail term of not less than 48 hours for offenders with a prior drunk driving conviction and prohibited suspended sentences. Ross and Foley found that in 238 cases the mandated sentence was imposed and served in only 106, or 45 percent of the total. In another 60 cases (25 percent) the mandatory sentences were imposed but there was no documented proof that the offenders served them. In 10 percent of the cases, the judge suspended the sentence, and in another 20 percent the offender served no jail sentence. The Indiana law mandated five days in jail, with at least 48 consecutive hours, or a minimum of 80 hours of community service, for offenders with a prior drunk driving conviction. Yet 30 percent of the convicted offenders did not serve the mandated sentence. Of 753 cases, 64 percent served the 48 consecutive hours, and another 6 percent did the required 80 hours of community service.[46]

Ross and Foley offer several possible explanations for this evasion of mandatory sentences. In some cases, the judges may have been ignorant of the offender's prior record. (We might ask whether they chose not to find out as a deliberate strategy for evading the mandatory sentencing provision.) In others, judges may have chosen to interpret the law as covering only certain kinds of prior convictions (for example, felonies and not misdemeanors). Judges may have simply ignored the law in some cases. For some sentenced offenders, the term "48 hours" may not have been interpreted literally. Correctional officials may have counted a few hours a day as representing the entire day; if the offender spent a few hours in jail spanning midnight, he might have been credited with having served both days. Similar evasions of mandatory sentencing have been found in studies of other crackdowns.

Evasion of the law by justice officials is not universal by any means. The Justice Department's evaluation of enforcement efforts in Seattle found that the incarceration rate for convicted drunk drivers went from 9 to 97 percent. In Memphis, it went from 29 to almost 100 percent.[47] A 1982 California law increased the statewide jail incarceration rate for second-time offenders from 83 percent in 1980 to 97.5 percent in 1984. In Sacramento County, the percentage of first-time drunk drivers sent to jail went from 10 percent to more than 50 percent. These data make it clear that second-offense drunk drivers were not getting off easy before passage of the new law. The most significant effect of the California law was on first-time offenders; the percentage going to jail increased from about 10 percent to over 50 percent.[48]

Nonetheless, as the Ross and Foley study suggests, a certain amount of evasion of mandatory sentencing persists in some jurisdictions that undermines both the certainty and severity of punishment. This compounds the low perceived and actual risk of arrest. In the end, most experts believe that enforcement crackdowns are not likely to deter drunk driving. After reviewing all the evidence, Ross concludes that "deterrence-based policies are questionable in the long run. No such policies have been scientifically demonstrated to work over time."[49] Jacobs agrees but adds that deterrence-based laws play a symbolic role in expressing society's moral condemnation of drunk driving.[50] Our conclusion can be stated as follows:

PROPOSITION 13
Enforcement crackdowns do not deter drunk driving over the long term.

Crackdown Costs

When a drunk driving crackdown does result in more punishment, it imposes significant costs on the criminal justice system. The most direct impact is on local jails and courts. Additional judges were needed in Seattle to handle the increase in cases. Cincinnati had to add an additional daily traffic court. In Sacramento County, California, more defendants insisted on going to trial, with the result that convictions at trial decreased. In Seattle, the county had to open a new jail facility just to handle the drunk drivers. In Memphis, some offenders had to wait six or seven months to serve their jail sentences. In two California counties, the jails became so overcrowded that courts found jail conditions unconstitutional.[51]

In short, as with other "get tough" policies, drunk driving crackdowns not only may not achieve their intended goals but may also impose unintended costs on the justice system.

Some Good News:
Alternative Strategies for Dealing with Drunk Drivers

Actually, there is considerable good news about trends in traffic fatalities. As Table 6-2 indicates, the motor vehicle *death rate per 100,000 vehicle miles* has dropped from 16.33 in 1927 to 3.35 in 1977 and 1.71 in 1997.[52] The long-term decline since 1930 is substantial, and the nearly 50 percent reduction since 1980 is a particularly significant achievement. How do we explain this success, especially in light of our conclusion that enforcement crackdowns do not work? The answer is that *some things do work*. Tougher enforcement by the criminal justice system undoubtedly contributed to this decline, but both Ross and Jacobs argue that at best it was only one factor. Other social policies also played important roles.

Most important, cars have become safer. Seat belts are required on all new cars, and their use is mandatory in every state except New Hampshire. The National Safety Council estimates that seat belts reduce the risk of death in an accident by 45 percent. Child restraints, meanwhile, saved an estimated 3,299 lives between 1982 and 1996, including 365 in 1996 alone. Air bags have saved an estimated 1,821 lives between 1987 and 1996.[53]

As a result of federal law, all states have raised the legal age for drinking to 21. Although this law has not necessarily curbed teenage drinking, it may have

Table 6-2 Motor Vehicle Deaths

Deaths per 100,000 vehicle miles

Year	Death Rate
1927	16.33
1937	14.68
1947	8.82
1957	5.98
1967	5.50
1977	3.35
1987	2.51
1997	1.71

SOURCE: National Safety Council, *Accident Facts, 1998* (Washington, DC: National Safety Council, 1998), pp. 104–105.

helped to reduce drunk driving by teenagers, and the DOT estimates that it saved 16,513 lives between 1975 and 1996.[54]

Another strategy is administrative license revocation, in which a police officer can revoke a driver's license on the spot if he or she fails a breath test. It is important to point out that this is a *civil* law rather than a criminal law approach. It rests on the theory that a driver's license is essentially a privilege that can be withdrawn without resort to the full criminal process. Ross argues that it is both swift and certain, resulting in the immediate incapacitation of the offender (in the sense that the person cannot drive legally, although obviously some people drive without a license). He cites studies indicating that this approach has been effective in reducing alcohol-related accidents and fatalities.[55]

Some of the long-term reduction in fatalities may also be the result of socialization. It is possible that the national anti–drunk driving crusade, with all of the attendant publicity, has had a long-term effect on attitudes and behavior. Public opinion surveys have found that the percentage of people saying they "sometimes" drive after drinking fell from 25 percent in 1983 to 16 percent in 1995. The percentage indicating that they "never" did rose correspondingly.[56] We have good reason to assume that these attitudes reflect real changes in behavior. Not only has the number of traffic fatalities fallen, but the percentage that are alcohol related fell from 57.3 in 1982 to 40.9 in 1996.[57]

In short, we have substantially reduced motor vehicle fatalities over the long term. This trend is probably related to genuine changes in attitudes and behavior related to drinking and driving. We will also examine the issue of long-term behavioral changes when we discuss drug policy in Chapter 13. Other examples of such long-term changes are evident. Consumption of red meat has declined, and consumption of fresh fruits and vegetables has increased, since 1970.[58] Smoking among adults is down substantially. These changes are a result of public concern about health. Safe-sex education programs, meanwhile, have produced a sharp decline in the incidence of new AIDS cases among gay men (but not among needle-drug users). In short, behavior does change over time, and some of those changes are the result of national-level efforts.

Two points need to be emphasized about this long-term success. First, the reduction in traffic fatalities has probably been the result of changes not directly related to deterrence-oriented enforcement (e.g., safer cars, seat belts, etc.). Attacking problems through a variety of strategies, including civil law enforcement, is identified by the University of Maryland report on *Preventing Crime* as a potentially successful approach.[59] In Chapter 5 we learned that successful crime reduction is not achieved simply by adding more police, but through problem-oriented programs involving agencies other than the police.

Second, we need to heed James B. Jacobs's cautionary observation that there "are limits to what can be accomplished through directed social change."[60] It appears that we can make some positive changes, but we cannot force people to change, particularly through the criminal law. The best evidence indicates that it requires a variety of strategies and measures to induce change over the long term.

DETERRING BURGLARS AND ROBBERS

So far, we have discussed deterrence in relation to the death penalty and drunk driving. But what about burglars and robbers? Are they deterred by a perceived higher risk of arrest, greater certainty of conviction, and probability of harsher punishment? As we indicated at the beginning of this chapter, the criminal law and the criminal justice system have some general deterrent effect. The real question is whether any particular change in policy will increase the deterrent effect and reduce crime.

As Nagin points out, until recently there has been little research on the crucial element of deterrence theory: how particular groups of people perceive the deterrent. Moreover, most of the social psychological research involves college undergraduates and relatively minor offenses. One critic derides this body of literature as "the science of sophomores."[61] Horney and Marshall's study of 1,000 prison inmates is one of the few that investigates the perceived risk of apprehension and punishment by serious offenders.[62]

In an imaginative study, Scott Decker and his colleagues interviewed a group of 48 active residential burglars and a control group of 40 nonoffenders drawn from two job training and recreation centers in the same city. Procedures were taken to ensure the anonymity of the active burglars (unlike subjects in most of the career criminal research, these individuals were not currently prison inmates). Both groups were given hypothetical situations that altered the risk of apprehension, the reward from doing the burglary, and the penalty if caught.[63]

Including the expected reward in the equation added an important element. As we already noted, deterrence theory assumes a rational choice between the relative costs *and* gains from doing crime. Virtually all of the deterrence research has focused only on the cost side: the effect of different punishments. Because the theory assumes a choice between alternatives, it is necessary to include the expected gains as well.

Decker and his colleagues found a "clear and highly significant difference" between the burglars and the control group.[64] The active burglars were much more likely to commit a crime than were members of the control group. Increasing the risk of apprehension lowered the willingness to commit a burglary for both groups. But only 10 percent of the controls indicated a willingness to commit a burglary when told that the risk of apprehension was only 1 percent. Meanwhile, even with a 50 percent chance of apprehension, slightly more than half (55.2 percent) of the active burglars would still commit a burglary.

For the active burglars, an increase in the severity of the penalty had some effect on their willingness to commit a burglary, but it was surprisingly modest. When the punishment was described as two years' probation, 61.5 percent said they would commit a burglary; increasing the penalty to five years in prison only reduced it to 52.5 percent. The burglars were more influenced by changes in the relative gain from the burglary; that is, they indicated a greater willingness to commit crime when the expected gain was higher than they had previously believed it to be.

The study provides little support for traditional deterrence theory. Decker and his colleagues concluded that neither the burglars nor the control group "were significantly affected by the severity of the threatened penalty on its own."[65] Certainty of apprehension did have some effect, but, as we learned in the previous chapter, the prospects for increasing clearance rates are not good.

The Rand Inmate Survey

The Rand Inmate Survey asked prisoners in three states (California, Michigan, Texas) to estimate the probable results of doing crime. Well over 80 percent believed they had an "even chance" of being arrested, imprisoned, or being injured or killed. Over 60 percent believed they had a "high chance" of arrest and imprisonment or that it was "certain." In short, the prisoners were extremely fatalistic about the consequences of criminal activity. Significantly, they were only half as likely to expect a high chance or certainty of enjoying the good outcomes of crime ("high living," having "expensive things," or "being own man").[66]

In their analysis of these data, James Q. Wilson and Allan Abrahamse posed the obvious question: If their estimate of bad consequences is so high and their estimate of good consequences so much lower, why do they commit crime? (Remember, these were imprisoned offenders, some of whom were classified as "high-rate" offenders). The answer is that they do not act on the basis of a rational calculation of costs and benefits. Wilson and Abrahamse, for example, found that they consistently overestimate the financial rewards of crime. They act impulsively, overestimating the immediate, short-term gains of crime and underestimating unpleasant consequences, such as imprisonment, which lies in the future.[67] They also may have felt that they have no alternatives in terms of legitimate work—in other words, that they perceived no positive rewards for a law-abiding lifestyle.

Like Decker's study of active burglars, the Rand Inmate Survey provides little support for traditional deterrence theory. Actual offenders do not appear to make their decisions about criminal activity on the basis of a rational and carefully calculated assessment of the costs and benefits.

DETERRING DOMESTIC VIOLENCE

Another area that has seen considerable research on the deterrent effect of punishment is arrest for domestic violence. Traditionally, police officers avoided arrest in domestic violence situations, especially when married couples were involved. In the 1970s, the women's movement challenged this practice, arguing that failure to arrest left the female victim vulnerable to further violence. Women's groups successfully sued the New York City and Oakland police departments on equal protection grounds and won settlements that included mandatory arrest policies. By the 1980s, a national movement was under way toward mandatory arrest or arrest-preferred policies. These have been implemented either through police department policy or state law.[68]

Most advocates of mandatory arrest for domestic violence believe that it deters future violence. The first study of this issue, the Minneapolis Domestic Violence Experiment, became one of the most publicized and influential experiments in criminal justice history. The experiment tested the effect of three different police actions: arrest, separation, and mediation. Through official police records and interviews with victims, it found lower rates of repeat violence over the following six months as a result of arrest compared with either of the other two alternatives. The experiment seemed to indicate that arrest deterred domestic violence. The authors of the experiment were careful to point out that the persons arrested were rarely prosecuted or incarcerated; the "punishment" was usually nothing more than arrest, or at most a night in jail.[69]

These findings had an enormous impact on public policy. Over the next few years, most police departments adopted mandatory arrest policies. By 1988, 60 percent of all big-city police departments mandated arrest, and another 30 percent specifically encouraged it.[70]

Replications of the Minneapolis experiment in Omaha, Charlotte, Miami, and Milwaukee, however, found no consistent evidence that arrest deters future violence. Moreover, the Milwaukee experiment found that arrest had different effects on different kinds of offenders. It seemed to increase the level of repeat violence among unemployed men compared with employed. It is probable that employed men have a greater stake in social conformity and are more likely to be deterred by the sanction of arrest than are unemployed men who have less of a stake in conformity.[71]

Lawrence Sherman, principal investigator on the original Minneapolis experiment, now argues that the impact of arrest in domestic violence situations is an extremely complicated matter and that we cannot assert conclusively that arrest deters violence.

CONCLUSION

The evidence on the death penalty, drunk driving, burglary and robbery, and domestic violence leads us to the following general conclusion:

PROPOSITION 14

Deterrence-oriented policies that rely exclusively on criminal law enforcement do not enhance the inherent deterrent effect of the criminal justice system.

The commonsense notion that people will avoid unpleasant things and that we can influence their decisions by increasing the unpleasantness does not necessarily work in the real world of criminal justice. Let us be careful about exactly what we are saying. As in so many other areas, it is not true that "nothing works." The criminal law does have some deterrent effect. Most of us, after all, do not become career criminals. The threat of punishment, however, probably plays a relatively minor role in influencing the behavior of law-abiding people. The threat works, but it just is not the major factor. In terms of controlling behavior, the broader processes of socialization are the primary factors. As Leslie Wilkins put it, there are "those of us who have never needed a deterrent."[72] When these processes have broken down, we should not expect the criminal justice system—and deterrence-oriented policies in particular—to fix the problem.

NOTES

1. The best treatment of the subject is still Franklin E. Zimring and Gordon J. Hawkins, *Deterrence: The Legal Threat in Crime Control* (Chicago: University of Chicago Press, 1973).

2. Daniel S. Nagin, "Criminal Deterrence Research at the Outset of the Twenty-First Century," in Michael Tonry, ed., *Crime and Justice: A Review of Research,* vol. 23 (Chicago: University of Chicago Press, 1998), p. 3.

3. Nagin, "Criminal Deterrence Research."

4. Scott Decker, Richard Wright, and Robert Logie, "Perceptual Deterrence among Active Residential Burglars: A Research Note," *Criminology* 31 (February 1993): 135.

5. Zimring and Hawkins, *Deterrence,* pp. 92–248.

6. Zimring and Hawkins, *Deterrence,* pp. 13–14.

7. Ronald L. Akers, "Rational Choice, Deterrence, and Social Learning Theory in Criminology: The Path Not Taken," *Journal of Criminal Law and Criminology* 81 (Fall 1990): 653–76.

8. See, for example, the extremely influential conservative argument in Charles Murray, *Losing Ground: American Social Policy, 1950–1980* (New York: Basic Books, 1984).

9. Dallin Oaks, "Studying the Exclusionary Rule in Search and Seizure," *University of Chicago Law Review* 37 (Summer 1970): 665–757.

10. Nagin, "Criminal Deterrence Research," pp. 4–6.

11. Bureau of Justice Statistics, *Spouse Murder Defendants in Large Urban Counties* (Washington, DC: Government Printing Office, 1995).

12. James Q. Wilson and Allan Abrahamse, "Does Crime Pay?" *Justice Quarterly* 9 (September 1992): 359–77.

13. Julie Horney and Ineke Haen Marshall, "Risk Perception among Serious Offenders: The Role of Crime and Punishment," *Criminology* 30 (1992): 575–94; Nagin, "Criminal Deterrence Research," p. 16.

14. Raymond Paternoster, *Capital Punishment in America* (Lexington, MA: Lexington Books, 1991), part IV, "Arguments for and against the Death Penalty," pp. 185–270.

15. *Furman v. Georgia,* 408 U.S. 238 (1972).

16. *Gregg v. Georgia,* 428 U.S. 153 (1976).

17. Thorsten Sellin, *The Penalty of Death* (Beverly Hills, CA: Sage, 1980).

18. Isaac Ehrlich, "The Deterrent Effect of Capital Punishment: A Question of Life and Death," *American Economic Review* 65 (1975): 397–417.

19. Isaac Ehrlich, "Participation in Illegitimate Activities: A Theoretical and Empirical Investigation," *Journal of Political Economy* 81 (1973): 521.

20. Brian Forst, "Capital Punishment and Deterrence: Conflicting Evidence," *Journal of Criminal Law and Criminology* 74 (Fall 1983): 927–42; Peter Passell, "The Deterrent Effect of the Death Penalty: A Statis-

tical Test," *Stanford Law Review* 28 (November 1975): 61–80; William J. Bowers and Glenn Pierce, "The Illusion of Deterrence in Isaac Ehrlich's Research on Capital Punishment," *Yale Law Review* 85 (1975): 187–208.

21. Bureau of Justice Statistics, *Sourcebook of Criminal Justice Statistics—1995,* pp. 324, 609.

22. Robert Hood and Richard Sparks, *Key Issues in Criminology* (New York: McGraw-Hill, 1980), pp. 40–41; Zimring and Hawkins, *Deterrence,* p. 334; Philip Wattley, "City Hit on Crime Data," *Chicago Tribune,* 28 April 1983: 1–2.

23. Bureau of Justice Statistics, *Capital Punishment 1995* (Washington, DC: Government Printing Office, 1996), table 11.

24. Hugo Adam Bedeau and Michael L. Radelet, "Miscarriages of Justice in Potentially Capital Cases," *Stanford Law Review* 40 (November 1987): 21–179.

25. Current data on the death penalty are available from a variety of web sites.

26. William J. Bowers and Glenn L. Pierce, "Deterrence or Brutalization? What Is the Effect of Executions?" *Crime and Delinquency* 26 (October 1980): 453–84.

27. Forst, "Capital Punishment and Deterrence."

28. The two best surveys of the subject are H. Laurence Ross, *Confronting Drunk Driving: Social Policy for Saving Lives* (New Haven, CT: Yale University Press, 1992), and James B. Jacobs, *Drunk Driving: An American Dilemma* (Chicago: University of Chicago Press, 1989).

29. Bureau of Justice Statistics, *Jailing Drunk Drivers: Impact on the Criminal Justice System* (Washington, DC: Government Printing Office, 1984).

30. National Safety Council, *Traffic Safety Facts 1998* (Washington, DC: National Safety Council, 1998), p. 86.

31. Jacobs, *Drunk Driving,* pp. 27–28; Ross, *Confronting Drunk Driving.*

32. Ross, *Confronting Drunk Driving,* pp. 21–22, 168–170.

33. Ross, *Confronting Drunk Driving.*

34. National Safety Council, *Traffic Safety Facts 1998,* p. 87.

35. Jacobs, *Drunk Driving*; Ross, *Confronting Drunk Driving.*

36. Lawrence W. Sherman, "Police Crackdowns: Initial and Residual Deterrence," in Michael W. Tonry and Norval Morris, eds., *Crime and Justice: An Annual Review of Research,* vol. 12 (Chicago: University of Chicago Press, 1990), pp. 1–48.

37. H. Laurence Ross, *Deterring the Drinking Driver: Legal Policy and Social Control,* rev. ed. (Lexington, MA: Lexington Books, 1984), pp. 24–34.

38. Bureau of Justice Statistics, *Jailing Drunk Drivers,* p. 2.

39. Sherman, "Police Crackdowns: Initial and Residual Deterrence."

40. Sherman, "Police Crackdowns."

41. Ross, *Deterring the Drinking Driver,* pp. 33, 105.

42. Donald E. Green, "Past Behavior as a Measure of Actual Future Behavior: An Unresolved Issue in Perceptual Deterrence Research," *Journal of Criminal Law and Criminology* 80 (No. 3, 1989): 781–804.

43. Federal Bureau of Investigation, *Law Enforcement Officers Killed and Assaulted, 1997* (Washington, DC: Government Printing Office, 1998), p. 30.

44. Jacobs, *Drunk Driving,* p. 47.

45. Jacobs, *Drunk Driving,* pp. 98–100.

46. H. Laurence Ross and James P. Foley, "Judicial Disobedience of the Mandate to Imprison Drunk Drivers," *Law and Society Review* 21.2 (1987): 315–23.

47. Bureau of Justice Statistics, *Jailing Drunk Drivers,* p. 2.

48. Rodney Kingsworth and Michael Jungsten, "Driving under the Influence: The Impact of Legislative Reform on Court Sentencing Practices in Drunk Driving Cases," *Crime and Delinquency* 34 (January 1988): 3–28.

49. Ross, *Deterring the Drinking Driver,* p. 111.

50. Jacobs, *Drunk Driving,* p. 126.

51. Bureau of Justice Statistics, *Jailing Drunk Drivers*; Kingsworth and Jungsten, "Driving Under the Influence."

52. National Safety Council, *Accident Facts 1998* (Washington, DC: NSC, 1998), pp. 104–05.

53. National Safety Council, *Accident Facts 1998,* p. 88.

54. National Safety Council, *Accident Facts 1998,* p. 87.

55. U. S. Department of Transportation, *Reducing Highway Crashes Through Administrative License Revocation* (Washington, DC: Government Printing Office, 1986); Ross, *Confronting Drunk Driving,* pp. 63–67.

56. Bureau of Justice Statistics, *Sourcebook of Criminal Justice Statistics—1995* (Washington, DC: Government Printing Office, 1996), p. 302.

57. National Safety Council, *Accident Facts 1998,* p. 86.

58. *Statistical Abstract of the United States, 1995,* table 225, p. 147.

59. University of Maryland, *Preventing Crime* (Washington, DC: Government Printing Office, 1997).

60. Jacobs, *Drunk Driving,* p. 191.

61. Raymond Paternoster, "The Deterrent Effect of the Perceived Certainty and Severity of Punishment: A Review of the Evidence and Issues," *Justice Quarterly* 4 (June 1987): 173–217.

62. Horney and Marshall, "Risk Perceptions Among Serious Offenders."

63. Decker et al., "Perceptual Deterrence," pp. 135–47.

64. Decker et al., "Perceptual Deterrence," p. 139.

65. Decker et al., "Perceptual Deterrence," p. 145.

66. Wilson and Abrahamse, "Does Crime Pay?" p. 373.

67. Wilson and Abrahamse, "Does Crime Pay?" pp. 372–73.

68. Lawrence W. Sherman, *Policing Domestic Violence: Experiments and Dilemmas* (New York: Free Press, 1992).

69. Sherman, *Policing Domestic Violence.*

70. Sherman, *Policing Domestic Violence.*

71. Sherman, *Policing Domestic Violence.*

72. Quoted in Zimring and Hawkins, *Deterrence,* p. 97.

7

Lock 'Em Up

GETTING CRIMINALS OFF THE STREET

The main conservative crime control strategy is to get criminals off the street. This includes three "lock 'em up" proposals: preventive detention, incapacitation, and mandatory sentencing. All three are based on the assumption that the criminal justice system turns dangerous criminals loose on society, where they prey on law-abiding citizens. The new "three strikes" laws are the ultimate lock 'em up policy.

All of the "lock 'em up" strategies seek to limit the discretion of judges.[1] The underlying assumption is that judges have too much discretion to release dangerous criminals on bail, grant them probation, or sentence them to inappropriately short prison terms. Conservatives believe that the misuse of judicial discretion is the result of two factors. First, too many judges are "bleeding hearts" who are too lenient with convicted offenders. Second, many of our policies encourage not locking people up. American law has traditionally embodied the principle of a right to bail. The philosophy of rehabilitation, meanwhile, encourages alternatives to prison for convicted felons. Conservative proposals attack these laws and policies as soft on crime.

PREVENTIVE DETENTION

Conservatives believe that people released on bail commit a large number of crimes. President Ronald Reagan's Task Force on Victims of Crime declared in 1982, "A substantial proportion of the crimes committed in this country are committed by defendants who have been released on bail or on their own recognizance."[2] Conservatives believe that preventive detention, a policy that allows denying bail to high-risk criminal defendants, can prevent these crimes.

Preventive detention raises both *constitutional* and *empirical* questions. The constitutional question is whether the Eighth Amendment to the U.S. Constitution prohibits detaining someone solely for the purpose of preventing crime. The Eighth Amendment guarantees that "excessive bail shall not be required." As with many other parts of the Bill of Rights, the exact meaning of the Eighth Amendment is ambiguous. Traditionally, it was interpreted to mean that all criminal defendants have a right to bail, with the exception of persons accused of "capital" crimes, or those crimes punishable by the death penalty. The purpose of bail in Anglo-American law was to ensure the defendant's appearance at trial. Preventive detention, then, represents a fundamental change in the purpose of bail.[3]

The Supreme Court answered the constitutional question in 1987, when it upheld the preventive detention provision of the 1984 federal Bail Reform Act. In *United States v. Salerno,* the Court ruled that there is no absolute right to bail and that preventive detention is a legitimate "regulatory" measure.[4]

The empirical question that is central to our inquiry involves the amount of crime committed by people released on bail. How much crime will we prevent by keeping certain offenders in jail?

A Short History of Bail Reform

The demand for preventive detention is a backlash against the bail reform movement of the 1960s. The civil rights movement focused public attention on the plight of the poor in the criminal justice system. The President's Crime Commission found that 52 percent of all people in jail were awaiting trial. Critics labeled America's jails the "new poorhouses." Wealthy organized crime figures easily raised large bail amounts, whereas poor people remained in jail.[5] Caleb Foote's pioneering studies of bail in Philadelphia in the 1950s found that defendants not released on bail were more likely to be convicted and imprisoned.[6] Thus, the money bail system compounds the denial of a basic constitutional right by increasing the chance of conviction and imprisonment. Unnecessary pretrial detention also raises the cost of operating the jails and often results in jail overcrowding.

Current data support Foote's earlier finding about the impact of pretrial detention. According to the National Pretrial Reporting Program (NPRP), 79 percent of those detained in 1992 were convicted, compared with only 61 percent who were released. Additionally, 70 percent of those detained were convicted of a felony, compared with only 45 percent of those released.

Finally, among those convicted, 89 percent of those who had been detained were sentenced to incarceration, compared with only 59 percent of those who were released.[7]

The bail reform movement sought to correct these problems with programs to facilitate pretrial release. The most popular innovation was *release on recognizance* (ROR), which allows a defendant to be released without any financial considerations. Evidence of a job, family ties, or other roots in the community are used to evaluate whether the person is likely to appear for scheduled court dates. The 1966 federal Bail Reform Act directed federal courts to develop ROR procedures. Many states, meanwhile, developed their own ROR programs and/or adopted 10 percent plans that allowed defendants to post 10 percent of the formal bail amount.[8]

The bail reform movement achieved many of its goals. The percentage of people in jail who were being held for trial dropped from 52 percent in 1967 to 33 percent in 1971. In some cities, reform had a dramatic impact. The percentage of defendants held for more than 24 hours in Philadelphia dropped from 75 percent in 1954 to only 25 percent in 1975. Similar reductions were also found in other cities. Some evidence, however, indicates that the "get tough" policies of recent years have reversed these trends. In 1992, 50 percent of all jail inmates were defendants awaiting trial.[9]

The first bail reform movement did not achieve all of its goals, however. Because employment status is a major criterion for ROR, it discriminates against the unemployed and the marginally employed. Nearly three-quarters (72 percent) of employed defendants were released in 1990, compared with 46 percent for unemployed.[10] Bail reform also did not eliminate the practice of detaining certain defendants by simply setting high bail.

The first bail reform movement coincided with the great rise in serious crime. Between 1963 and 1973, the robbery rate tripled, while the burglary rate went up two and a half times. Conservatives argue that bail reform contributed to this by releasing many dangerous offenders.

The focus of the backlash was Washington, D.C. Because of rising crime rates, Congress passed a *preventive detention* law for the District of Columbia in 1970. By the 1980s, public support for preventive detention was widespread, and nearly all states had adopted it. Some states amended their state constitutions to limit the right to bail. The Michigan constitution allows preventive detention in four kinds of crimes when the judge finds a possibility of "danger" if the defendant were to be released.[11]

Let us take a look at how preventive detention works in practice.

Preventive Detention in Operation: Washington, D.C.

The 1970 District of Columbia law offered the first evidence of how preventive detention might work. The law allowed a judge to hold without bail for 60 days a defendant charged with a crime of violence or a dangerous crime. Several procedures were designed to protect defendants' rights. A formal hearing was required to determine that substantial probability of guilt existed and that no other release procedure could guarantee public safety. The defendant must have been convicted of a crime in the preceding ten years, be a narcotics addict, or currently be on pretrial release, probation, or parole. Finally, if the trial were not held within sixty days, the defendant had a right to release on bail.

Something funny happened in Washington, however: the law was hardly ever used. Judges detained very few defendants without bail. A study by Georgetown University and the Vera Institute found that in the first six months prosecutors filed detention motions against only 20 of 6,000 felony defendants (or less than one-third of 1 percent!). These motions resulted in nine formal hearings and eight actual detentions. Another two defendants were detained through judicial initiative. Thus, only ten defendants were detained in six months.[12]

This is not the end of the story, however. Five of the ten detentions were reversed on appeal or reconsideration. Another was dismissed when the grand jury refused to indict the suspect. Thus, a grand total of four people were fully detained during the entire ten-month period.

What happened? Federal prosecutors in the District of Columbia had full discretion to use or not use the law. It is easy to explain why they chose not to. In most cases, they did not need to. They could detain someone simply by setting bail at a level beyond his or her financial means. Because most robbers are poor, unemployed, or marginally employed, establishing an inaccessible bail amount is not hard to do. Setting bond at a high figure is the traditional means by which the courtroom work group has covertly undermined the nominal right to bail. In effect, it says, "Sure you have a right to bail—how much *can't* you afford?" Remember from our discussion of the courtroom work group in Chapter 3 that disagreement rarely erupts over bail.[13] In other words, all members of the work group are in agreement over the real impact of a high bail amount.

This practice continues today. In 1992, the median bail for all robbery defendants was $10,000. Those who succeeded in obtaining release, however, faced a median bail of only $5,000. Under a 10 percent plan, they would only need to post $500. Those who did not obtain their release faced a median bail of $20,000. In short, robbery defendants can be categorized into two classes: one group gets relatively low bail, whereas the other, which the courtroom work group wants to detain, gets high bail and is not released.[14]

The 1984 Federal Bail Reform Act

The 1984 Bail Reform Act allows federal judges to detain a defendant without bail if "no condition or combination of conditions . . . will reasonably assure . . . the safety of any other person and the community." The law has had a very different impact than the 1970 law. Federal judges are using it very extensively. The number of defendants detained by federal judges increased from 2,733 in the first six months of 1987 (before the Supreme Court upheld the law) to 4,470 in the last six months of 1988. The war on drugs accounted for much of this increase: more people were arrested for drug offenses, and prosecutors requested detention for drug defendants far more often than for other crimes. Between 70 and 75 percent of the prosecutors' requests for detention were granted.[15] The heavy use of the 1984 law, compared with the 1970 one, is an index of the "get tough" mood of the period.

Closer inspection, however, reveals that the overall detention rate did not increase greatly. The percentage of all federal defendants detained before trial only increased from 24 percent to 29 percent. The major change was a shift in the *method* of detention. Before the 1984 law, virtually all of the detained defendants remained in jail because they could not raise sufficient bail. Of the 29 percent detained after the law went into effect, 19 percent were detained under the preventive detention law, and 10 percent were detained because they could not raise bail. (By 1996, the percentage of federal defendants denied bail had increased to about 32 percent of all defendants.)[16] In short, the 1984 law gave judges legal authority to do what they had previously done covertly.

The important question, from our perspective, is whether preventive detention has helped reduce crime. None of the studies of bail reform evaluates the impact on the overall crime rate. Evaluations have focused on crime by persons released on bail and have found no significant impact on pretrial crime. The percentage of federal defendants granted pretrial release who were rearrested for a felony increased from 1.2 percent in 1983 to 1.3 percent in 1985. The percentage arrested for misdemeanors went from 0.6 percent to 0.7 percent. By 1996, 1.8 were rearrested for a felony.[17] It is important to note how small a percentage of defendants were being rearrested before 1984. If anything, the percentage should have gone down, since judges were now able to detain suspected repeat offenders. These data force us to take a closer look at the whole question of crime by persons out on bail.

Crime on Bail: Myths and Reality

The failure of the Bail Reform Act to reduce pretrial crime comes as no surprise to most experts. Substantial research has found that contrary to popular belief, the amount of crime committed by persons out on bail is relatively small. Let us take a look at success and failure of defendants on pretrial release.

A defendant released on bail can "fail" in one of two ways: either by committing a crime or by failing to appear (FTA) at a scheduled court hearing. Both types of failure are complex, and it is necessary to examine the data carefully.

Not all crimes by persons on bail are equally serious. In terms of the "cost" to society, a felony is far more serious than a misdemeanor, and a violent crime is more serious than a property crime. Arrest, meanwhile, is not the same as conviction. If you use the total number of failures—*all* arrests and *all* FTAs—the failure rate for people on bail will be relatively high. It will be much lower, however, if we only measure convictions for violent offenses.

The National Pretrial Reporting Program (NPRP) reports that in 1992, 14 percent of all felony defendants released before trial by county courts were rearrested in the next twelve months (in 1994 it was still only 15 percent); 10

Table 7-1 Felony defendants arrested while on pretrial release in the 75 largest counties, by selected defendant charactertics, 1992[a]

Defendant characteristics	Number of defendants	Percentage of felony defendants			
		Not re-arrested	Rearrested		
			Total	Felony	Mis-demeanor
All released defendants	30,051	86%	14	10	3
MOST SERIOUS ORIGINAL ARREST CHARGE					
Violent offenses	6,991	88	12	8	3
Property offenses	10,147	86	14	11	4
Drug offenses	10,146	84	16	13	4
Public-order offenses	2,765	91	9	7	2
SEX					
Male	24,839	85	15	11	3
Female	5,164	91	9	6	3
RACE					
Black	15,830	85	15	12	4
White	11,329	89	11	8	3
Other	365	95	5	5	0
RACE/HISPANIC ORIGIN[b]					
Non-Hispanic					
Black	11,292	85	15	11	4
White	6,313	91	9	7	3
Other	361	94	6	6	0
Hispanic, any race	5,126	84	16	12	4
NUMBER OF PRIOR CONVICTIONS					
10 or more	1,154	62	38	27	11
5 to 9	2,393	74	26	19	7
2 to 4	4,691	82	18	14	4
1	4,122	86	14	10	4
None	15,670	91	9	7	2

NOTE: Rearrest data were collected for one year. Rearrests occuring after the end of this one-year study period are not included in the table. Information on rearrests in jurisdictions other than the one granting the pretrial release was not always available. Rearrest data were available for 94 percent of released defendants.
[a] Detail may not add to total because of rounding.
[b] Data on race combined with Hispanic origin were available for 77 percent of defendants.

SOURCE: U.S. Department of Justice, Bureau of Justice, *Pretrial Release Defendants, 1992*, Bulletin NCJ-148818 (Washington, DC: U.S. Department of Justice, 1994), p. 11.

percent were rearrested for a felony and about 3 percent for a misdemeanor (Table 7-1). (Note that these rearrest rates are far higher than for federal court defendants.) Interestingly, persons originally charged with a violent crime were rearrested at a slightly lower rate (12 percent) than were persons charged with property (14 percent) or drug (16 percent) offenses. Of all those who were rearrested, 61 percent were convicted on the new charge, but only 45 percent were convicted of a felony. Thus, only about 6 percent of all defendants released before trial were convicted of a new felony.[18] Although the overall reconviction rate is fairly low, it is clear that some types of defendants are rearrested and reconvicted at fairly high rates. Not surprisingly, 38 percent of those with ten or more prior convictions were rearrested, compared with only 9 percent of those with no prior convictions.

Now let us look at the failures to appear. Most FTAs are not intentional. Usually, the defendant forgets the date or is confused about the court proceedings. The really serious FTAs, which we should be concerned about, are those in which the defendant deliberately flees. In 1992, 25 percent of all felony defendants failed to appear in court (in 1994 it was 24%). Yet about two-thirds of these were eventually returned to court. Thus, only 8 percent of all defendants released before trial were actual fugitives from justice.[19]

The Prediction Problem Revisited

The relatively low rearrest and reconviction rates bring us back to the prediction problem that we discussed in Chapter 4. The problem facing a judge is to spot in advance the defendants likely to commit a crime on bail. The point of preventive detention is to detain them and *only* them. How successful are judges likely to be in this effort?

Predicting Dangerousness: Pretrial Drug Testing Many people believe that testing arrestees for drug use would be a reliable method of predicting whether or not a criminal defendant is likely to be rearrested if released before trial. The underlying assumption is that the combination of an arrest and illegal drug use is a good indicator of a lifestyle that includes a high rate of criminal activity.

A National Institute of Justice study investigated pretrial misconduct by arrestees in six sites (Washington, D.C.; Prince George's County, Maryland; Milwaukee, Wisconsin; Maricopa County, Arizona; Manhattan, New York, and Dade County, Florida). The study found, however, that "except for heroin use, pretrial drug testing did not appear to help predict rearrests." In fact, even those defendants who tested positive for more than one drug were not more likely to be rearrested. Heroin use, however, did predict rearrest, and was a particularly strong predictor in three of the six sites. Cocaine use was a predictor of failure to appear (FTA). In the end, the best predictor of rearrest was the number of prior arrests.[20] In short, testing for drug involvement does not help judges improve their decisions related to pretrial misconduct.

A Natural Experiment A 1984 Supreme Court case on preventive detention for juveniles produced a natural experiment in predicting dangerousness. A New York law authorized preventive detention of juveniles who posed a "serious risk" of committing another crime if released. The law was challenged, and in 1981 a federal district court judge declared it unconstitutional and enjoined its operation. New York appealed, and in 1984 (*Schall v. Martin*) the U.S. Supreme Court ruled that preventive detention for juveniles was constitutional.[21]

The lower-court decision had a quirk, however. The district court judge only enjoined the commissioner of corrections from holding allegedly dangerous juveniles but not the judges who ordered them held. Thus, judges continued to order some juveniles detained. These kids were turned over to the commissioner of corrections, who was forced to release them. This arrangement produced a natural experiment that allows us to examine how accurate the judges were in predicting the dangerousness of a small group of juvenile defendants.[22]

Jeffrey Fagan and Martin Guggenheim identified 69 juveniles who were judged "at risk," ordered detained by judges, but then released. These juveniles were compared with a control group of 64 who had similar backgrounds and were not ordered held. After ninety days, 40 percent of the at-risk group had been rearrested, compared with only 15.6 percent of the control group. In short, the judges were reasonably accurate in identifying juveniles who posed a higher risk than comparable offenders. This was achieved, however, at the cost of false positives: 60 percent of the at-risk group were not rearrested. Moreover, only 19 percent were rearrested for a violent crime, so the judges were even less successful in predicting violent behavior.

Fagan and Guggenheim argue, as others have, that the goal of policy reform is not to achieve perfection but to improve on current practice, to make some *marginal* improvement in predictive accuracy. If you used an actuarial method for making preventive detention decisions based on objective criteria and applied it to all the juveniles in their study, you would detain members of the control group. Remember that they were comparable to an at-risk group in terms of their background characteristics (about 90 percent of both groups had some prior criminal record, for example). Yet only 15.6 percent of the control group were arrested within 90 days (think of them as false negatives). Applying the same objective prediction formula to the control group would result in detaining the 84.4 percent of the control group who were not rearrested. This outcome translates into five false positives for every true positive. (Recall that the Wenk prediction study we covered in Chapter 4 produced eight false positives for every true positive.)

Fagan and Guggenheim conclude that "the accuracy of prediction of dangerousness during the pretrial period remains questionable." And because of the costs and limited marginal gains likely to be achieved, "preventive detention appears to be unjustified."[23] As we will see, shortly, the Rand Corporation reached a similar conclusion regarding the prediction of high-rate criminal offenders.

Because only a small percentage of people on bail are rearrested, and because we cannot predict which ones will commit more crime, we conclude:

PROPOSITION 15

Preventive detention will not reduce serious crime.

Speedy Trial: A Better Way

If we want to prevent both crime on bail and failure to appeal, speedy trial is a much better approach. The 1992 NPRP data indicate that among those who were rearrested, 8 percent were rearrested in the first week and 37 percent within a month.[24] Disposing of all cases within five to six weeks would prevent about half of the crime committed by persons out on bail (this assumes that most will be convicted and sentenced to some confinement). Speedy disposition would also reduce the FTA rate and preserve two constitutional rights: the right to bail and the right to a speedy trial. Therefore, we can draw the following conclusion:

> ## PROPOSITION 16
> Speedy trials can reduce crime while preserving constitutional rights.

Actually, we have tried this approach. Congress and many states have enacted speedy-trial laws. Yet, as Malcolm Feeley found in his research on court reform, these laws were often evaded by the courtroom work group.[25] Thus, we face another dilemma: how to achieve a desired reform in the face of resistance by the courtroom work group. One possibility might be expedited trials only for those offenders who are high risks. This policy would preserve their constitutional rights to both bail and a speedy trial as well as protecting the public.

INCAPACITATION

Incapacitation seeks to reduce crime by imprisoning repeat offenders. It represents the same logic underlying preventive detention: Keep criminals off the street so that they cannot commit more crimes. The strategy further assumes that if we keep them in twice as long, we will prevent twice as many crimes. As a sentencing philosophy, incapacitation does not try to rehabilitate offenders; it is only intended to get them off the street.[26]

There are actually two kinds of incapacitation. *Selective incapacitation* is designed to lock up only the few high-rate offenders, or career criminals. Like preventive detention, it builds on Wolfgang's career criminal research, which we discussed in Chapter 4. The alternative is *gross incapacitation,* which involves locking up large numbers of people regardless of their criminal histories. The new "three strikes" laws are the ultimate form of gross incapacitation.

Selective Incapacitation: The Rand Formula

Selective incapacitation was one of the hot ideas in criminal justice in the 1970s and 1980s. James Q. Wilson endorsed it in his 1975 book, *Thinking about Crime,* claiming that serious crime could be reduced by *one-third* if each person convicted of a serious crime received a mandatory three-year prison sentence. He cited an earlier study that claimed that selective incapacitation could reduce crime by 80 percent.[27]

These extravagant claims generated much excitement, and a number of criminologists attempted to develop more sophisticated selective incapacitation policies. The most notable was a 1982 study, *Selective Incapacitation,* by Peter Greenwood and his associates at the Rand Corporation.[28] We have already discussed this work in Chapter 4 on the subject of career criminals. Let us take another look at it from the perspective of sentencing policy.

Selective Incapacitation estimated that a fine-tuned sentencing policy could reduce robbery by 15 percent while also reducing prison populations by 5 percent (an unselective policy would have to increase the prison population by 25 percent to achieve the same reduction in crime). The reduction in the prison population (with the resulting cost savings) would be achieved because the longer prison terms for career criminals would be offset by reduced punishments for low-risk offenders (shorter prison terms or probation).[29] Like so many crime control proposals, the policy seems to offer the best of all possible worlds: more effective crime control at less cost.

As we mentioned in Chapter 4, the Rand proposal is based on the earlier Rand Inmate Survey (RIS). Interviews with 2,190 prison and jail inmates in California, Texas, and Michigan are used to develop estimates of the *average annual offending rates* for offenders.[30] These estimates are the subject of considerable controversy, and the particular rate you choose has enormous policy implications. If the average career criminal commits more than a hundred crimes a year, incapacitation will achieve significant crime reduction. But if the average is only about five a year, the payoff will be relatively small.[31] Think of it in terms of Wolfgang's birth cohort, which we studied in Chapter 4: an ideal selective incapacitation policy would successfully identify and incarcerate the 6 percent of the cohort who are the career criminals, and only that group.

Rand developed a prediction instrument by correlating inmates' background characteristics with their self-reported criminal behavior. The result is a seven-point scale of factors associated with high rates of criminal behavior (see Table 4-3, p. 69). Offenders are then classified as low risk (one point), medium risk (two to three points), and high risk (four to seven points).

Rand then correlated inmates' predicted offense category with their actual self-reported level of criminal activity (see Table 4-4, p. 70). The prediction scale was correct 51 percent of the time. The 51 percent figure is calculated by adding the predicted low rate and actual low rate (14 percent), the predicted medium risk and actual medium risk (22 percent), and the predicted high risk and actual high risk (15 percent). The prediction device was grossly wrong 7 percent of the time (the 4 percent who were predicted high but actually low, and the 3 percent predicted low but actually high). In the remaining 42 percent of the cases, the prediction scale was only moderately accurate.[32]

Once again, the challenge is to improve on current practice. When the Rand experts correlated their predictions with inmates' actual sentences, they found that the judges imposed a "correct" sentence (that is, a long sentence for a predicted high-rate offender) 42 percent of the time. In short, this figure is only a marginal improvement over what judges are currently doing.[33]

Why such a small marginal improvement? The Rand system has several problems. The first is our old friend the prediction problem. As other studies have found, prior criminal records and other indicators such as drug use are relatively weak predictors of future behavior. We consistently get significant numbers of false positives and false negatives. In fact, in the face of widespread criticism, Rand took another look at its own proposal five years later and admitted that its earlier estimates were "overly optimistic." It concluded that "there are no reliable methods for either measuring or predicting future offense rates."[34]

One of the problems with selective incapacitation schemes involves the estimated annual offending rates. The overall rates are *averages* that are inflated by the extremely high rates for the very worst offenders. The Rand report observes that "most offenders reported fairly low rates of crime." The median robbery rate was only five per year, but the worst 10 percent (or the 90th percentile) averaged 87 per year![35] Incapacitating a member of the 90th percentile will produce a significant crime reduction, but the payoff for locking up all the others is relatively small.

The most shocking aspect of the Rand prediction scale is the use of employment history as a criterion for sentencing. An offender acquires one point for having been unemployed for more than half of the two preceding years. It carries the same weight as a prior conviction for the same offense. Under the formula, an additional point might reclassify the offender from a low-risk to a medium-risk offender, and thus it would mean the difference between jail and prison.

When you take out any one of the seven factors in the prediction scale, the entire scheme begins to collapse. With only six factors, the success rate will fall below the 51 percent that Rand estimates. You would then be doing no better than judges currently do, using a combination of presentence investigations and pure hunch.

It is outrageous that imprisonment might be contingent on unemployment. The Rand formula takes us back two hundred years to the days of imprisonment for debt. Even if such a policy were to become practice somewhere, it would immediately be challenged in court. The fact is that unemployment *is* highly correlated with criminal activity, but that correlation is not something we should translate into crime policy. An alternative response to the problem would be not to punish people for being unemployed but to provide greater employment opportunities.

Finally, the Rand *Selective Incapacitation* proposal faces a major political obstacle. The idea of not imprisoning low-risk and medium-risk offenders is exactly what liberal reformers have been advocating for decades. The National Council on Crime and Delinquency, the Edna McConnell Clark Foundation, the Sentencing Project, the Campaign for an Effective Crime Policy, and others have long maintained that we lock up too many people and for prison

terms that are unnecessarily long.[36] In 1980, as the prison binge was beginning, the American Bar Association's *Standards for Criminal Justice* stated that
"in many instances prison sentences which are now authorized, and sometimes
required, are significantly higher than are needed in a vast majority of cases."[37]
Because of the public mood, these recommendations have been consistently
rejected in favor of a policy of gross incapacitation.

If selective incapacitation seems too good to be true, that is because it is.
Because of the prediction problem and the political obstacles, we have to conclude as follows:

PROPOSITION 17
Selective incapacitation is not a realistic strategy for reducing serious crime.

Gross Incapacitation: Zedlewski's New Math

Selective incapacitation is a fine-tuned surgical instrument that involves making careful distinctions between criminal offenders. The political reality is that
we have completely ignored this approach and adopted instead a policy of gross
incapacitation: locking up a lot of people and sending them to prison for long
terms. This is the reason that the prison population tripled between 1980 and
1995. Let us take a look at the impact of gross incapacitation on the crime rate.

One of the most extraordinary endorsements of incapacitation is Edwin J.
Zedlewski's report, *Making Confinement Decisions*.[38] He reached the startling
conclusion that imprisonment actually *saves* money. Challenging the liberal
conventional wisdom about the high cost of imprisonment, he calculated that
for every dollar we spend imprisoning a criminal, we save $17 in total social
costs. Although Zedlewski focused on the dollar costs of crime, his formula
has important implications for crime reduction.

How did Zedlewski reach such an amazing conclusion? Let us take a look
at his figures. First, he estimated that crime cost American society a total of
about $100 billion in 1983. This included $33.8 billion for criminal justice system expenditures, $35 billion in victim losses (medical care, lost wages, prop-
erty damage, and so on), $26.1 billion for private security expenses, and so
forth. The NCVS, meanwhile, estimates that 42.5 million crimes were committed in 1983. Thus, Zedlewski calculated that each felony costs society
$2,300 ($100 billion ÷ $42.5 million).

Using the Rand Inmate Survey (RIS), Zedlewski then estimated that each
criminal commits an average of 187 crimes a year. Locking up each offender
for one year, therefore, "saves" society $430,000 ($2,300 × 2 × 187 =
$430,000). After you subtract the cost of imprisonment ($25,000 per year),
you get a net social "savings" of $405,000 for each offender imprisoned (or
about 17 times the $25,000 cost of incarceration).

If this seems too good to be true, it is because it is. Franklin Zimring and
Gordon Hawkins demolished the key assumptions underlying Zedlewski's

computations.[39] The first and most serious problem is the estimate of 187 crimes a year. They point out that Zedlewski does not mention the great disagreement among career criminal specialists over annual offending rates. Many put the figure at about 18 crimes a year, and some use an even lower estimate. If the average is only 18, then locking up one criminal saves only $43,000 a year, according to Zedlewski's formula.

It was professionally dishonest of Zedlewski not to mention the debate over annual offending rates and to use one of the highest possible estimates. As we mentioned in Chapter 1, faith often triumphs over fact in discussions of crime policy. Here we have a case of someone deliberately misrepresenting the facts to make a point. Zedlewski also did not take into account the problem of diminishing returns. As we lock up more people, we quickly skim off the really high-rate offenders and begin incarcerating more of the less serious offenders. Because they average far fewer crimes per year (perhaps as few as five, according to the RIS), we get progressively lower returns in crime reduction and dollar savings.

The estimate of the dollar savings is also flawed. A reduction in crime does not produce a direct reduction in criminal justice system costs. If the crime rate goes down by 25 percent, we are not going to cut police department budgets by 25 percent. Also, because 80 to 90 percent of all department budgets involve personnel costs, that would really mean laying off one-quarter of all the officers. In fact, police departments have not reduced their size as crime rates have fallen in the 1990s. Police officers do a lot more than fight crime. About 70 to 80 percent of patrol work involves order maintenance and service activities.[40] These are important tasks that people want the police to continue performing. The same is true for other criminal justice system costs. If crime drops by 25 percent, the cost of running the criminal courts will not automatically decline by the same percentage.

In the most devastating attack on Zedlewski, Zimring and Hawkins show that his own formula leads to absurd estimates of crime reduction. We have been running a natural experiment in gross incapacitation. They point out that between 1977 and 1987 the prison population increased by 230,000. If each criminal did an average of 187 crimes a year, that should have "prevented" 43 million crimes ($230,000 \times 2 \times 187 = 43$ million). Yet this figure is more than the number of crimes that the NCVS reported as occurring in 1987. In short, Zedlewski's formula predicts the complete elimination of all crime by 1986!

Of course that did not happen. First, criminals do not average 187 crimes a year, as Zedlewski estimated. And second, he did not consider the replacement factor: As some drug dealers are arrested, others take their place. You can do your own update of Zimring and Hawkins's critique with more recent data. Compute the increase in the prison population from the mid-1980s to the present and, using the estimated annual rate of 187 crimes per offender, estimate the amount of expected crime reduction. Compare that figure with the NCVS estimate of actual number of crimes committed. Crime has declined since the early 1990s.

Incapacitation: A Sober Estimate

Having demolished Zedlewski's fantastic estimates, Zimring and Hawkins undertook their own study of incapacitation, examining incarceration and crime trends in California. Using a variety of sophisticated models, they concluded that the incarceration of each offender in California in the 1980s prevented 3.5 crimes per year. We should note that this is one-fiftieth of the 187 figure used by Zedlewski and is even lower than the estimates of many experts on career criminals. The huge increase in the state prison population (115,000) reduced the crime rate by 15 percent.[41]

As Zimring and Hawkins pursued their analysis, however, some problems surfaced. For burglary, juvenile arrests declined significantly, but adult arrests increased. This is "exactly the opposite" of what the incapacitation model would predict, because most of those incarcerated were adults. A similar pattern appeared with larceny and rape, but not robbery. Consequently, Zimring and Hawkins conclude that it is not absolutely clear that incapacitation was the "primary cause" of the drop in crime.[42]

Zimring and Hawkins also did a cross-state comparison of changes in incarceration rates and crime rates in seventeen states during the 1980s. California stood at one extreme, with the greatest increase in imprisonment and the greatest reduction in crime. Yet Georgia had a very high increase in imprisonment but one of the highest rises in crime. Minnesota, meanwhile, had almost no increase in incarceration and virtually no change in the crime rate. In short, Zimring and Hawkins could detect "no clear patterned relationship" between incarceration rates and crime rates.[43]

Serious crime has declined in the 1990s, but we should be skeptical of claims that incapacitation is the sole or even the primary cause. Remember that we have been on an imprisonment binge for 25 years. Imagine going to a doctor, getting a prescription, taking the medicine (two pills a day), but not getting any better. You go back to the doctor, who increases the dosage (four pills a day). But you still do not get any better. The doctor then raises the dosage again (six a day). You repeat this process for 20 years. Finally, in about the nineteenth year, you begin to get better. Was it the medicine? Probably not. You cannot claim success for a prescription (pills/prisons) that failed for 19 years and then suddenly appeared to work in the twentieth year.

Because no clear link between incarceration and crime rates is apparent, and because gross incapacitation locks up many low-rate offenders at a great dollar cost to society, we conclude as follows:

PROPOSITION 18

Gross incapacitation is not a realistic policy for reducing serious crime.

MANDATORY SENTENCING

The third lock 'em up strategy for preventing crime is mandatory sentencing. Actually, mandatory sentencing is a *means* to an end. In this case there are actually two ends. Mandatory imprisonment is a means of achieving incapacitation or deterrence or both. Mandatory sentencing usually means two things: mandatory imprisonment for a certain crime and/or a mandatory minimum prison term.

Mandatory sentencing is an extremely popular crime policy. A Justice Department report on sentencing policies found that all fifty states had some form of mandatory sentencing by 1994. Most of these laws apply to specific offenses. Forty-one states have it for repeat offenders, 31 for certain drunk driving offenses, 32 for certain drug offenses, and 42 for some weapons offenses.[44] Meanwhile, by 1996, about 22 states had adopted "three strikes" laws, which represent an extreme form of mandatory sentencing.[45]

The popularity of mandatory sentencing can be explained in part by the celebrated case syndrome we discussed in Chapter 2. Public opinion is heavily influenced by a few highly publicized cases. The O. J. Simpson trial convinced many people that spouse murderers are frequently acquitted at trial. But as the BJS data on spouse murder indicate (see Chapter 2), most people who murder their spouse are convicted and imprisoned. Another good example is the Polly Klass case. Twelve-year-old Polly was brutally murdered by Richard Allen Davis, who was out on parole and had been twice convicted of kidnaping. The public uproar over her case led to the California "three strikes" law and similar ones in other states.

Two Case Studies

Let us review two case studies of mandatory sentencing laws in practice, one from the past and one current example.

Case 1: "The Nation's Toughest Drug Law." Most current mandatory minimum sentencing laws are modeled after a 1973 New York law, which was immediately advertised as the "nation's toughest drug law."[46] The law contained three major provisions designed to incapacitate drug offenders and deter future drug use: mandatory and long prison terms for heroin dealers, restrictions on plea bargaining for heroin dealers, and mandatory prison terms for certain categories of repeat offenders.

The prescribed prison terms were considered awesome at the time. The law established three categories of heroin dealers. Class A-I offenders (major dealers, defined as people who either sold one ounce of heroin or possessed two ounces) would serve minimum prison terms of 15 or 25 years and a maximum of life imprisonment. Class A-II (middle-level dealers, defined as those who sold one-eighth of an ounce of heroin or possessed one to two ounces) would serve prison terms of at least six to eight and one-third years and a maximum of life. Class A-III offenders (minor "street" dealers, defined as anyone who sold less than one-eighth of an ounce of heroin or possessed up to one ounce) would serve a minimum prison term of at least one to eight and one-third years and a maximum term of life. In short, anyone caught selling heroin would definitely go to prison and would face the possibility of life imprisonment.

The law attempted to prevent abuse of plea bargaining. Anyone arrested for either an A-I or A-II offense could plead guilty to an A-III charge, but people originally charged with an A-III offense could not plead to anything lower. The result was a floor that meant at least some prison time and a potential life term. The law also included a habitual-criminal provision, imposing mandatory prison terms on anyone with a prior felony conviction. To cope with the anticipated increase in the criminal courts' workload as a result of the law, New York added forty-nine new judges, thirty-one of them in New York City.

In practice, the law was a paper tiger. An evaluation concluded that "the threat embodied in the words of the law proved to have teeth for relatively few offenders."[47] An enormous amount of slippage or leakage occurred between arrest and conviction. Between 1972 and 1976, the percentage of drug arrests leading to indictment declined from 39 percent to 25 percent. Meanwhile, the percentage of indictments resulting in a conviction fell from 86 percent to 80 percent. Thus, the overall percentage of arrests leading to conviction fell from 33.5 percent to 20 percent.

The law was not a total failure. For those who were convicted, the rate of incarceration went up from 33 percent to 55 percent. Nonetheless, if only 55 percent were going to prison, about half the defendants were evading the supposedly "mandatory" sentencing provisions. Overall, however, little changed.

The percentage of people arrested for sale of heroin who went to prison was 11 percent in 1972–1973, and it was 11 percent in 1976.

The law did produce longer prison terms. Among those sentenced to prison, the percentage receiving a sentence of three years or longer rose from 3 percent of all those convicted to 22 percent.

The slippage that occurred in the application of the New York law is consistent with the long history of mandatory sentencing laws. The process can be explained in terms of the thermodynamics of the criminal justice process, which we discussed in Chapter 3. An increase in the severity of the potential punishment creates pressure to avoid its actual application. In this case, the controls over plea bargaining did not prevent a rise in dismissals. The enormous increase in the potential prison terms, meanwhile, encouraged defense attorneys to go to trial. The percentage of defendants demanding a trial increased from 6 percent to 15 percent. Because a tried case takes 15 times as long to process as a case that is not tried, the addition of even a few trials significantly disrupts the process. Disposition time for all drug cases doubled under the new law despite the addition of the new judgeships (and for some unexplained reason, the new courts were noticeably less efficient than previously established courts were).

Finally, and most important, the law had no significant effect on crime or drug use. Heroin use in New York City was as widespread in 1976 as it had been in 1973. Serious property crime, the kind generally associated with heroin users, increased 15 percent between 1973 and 1975, but neighboring states had similar increases. Nor did the law appear to deter convicted felons from committing additional crimes. According to the National Household Survey, drug use did begin to decline in the late 1980s, but this trend was nationwide, and we cannot say that the New York law had any special impact in that state.[48]

Adaptation. As we argued in Chapter 3, the criminal justice system adapts to major changes in the going rate. Our law of thermodynamics has been clearly at work in New York in the years since the 1973 drug laws were enacted. The state has taken one step backward, another step forward, and then another step backward again.

The "nation's toughest drug law" proved to be too much for the system. In 1976, the chief prosecutor of drug cases in New York City quietly announced that he would no longer enforce the law's prohibitions on plea bargaining. Three years later, the legislature formally eliminated these same prohibitions and permitted more flexibility in sentencing. It also allowed resentencing of some offenders given extremely long sentences under the original law.[49]

An important part of the slippage occurs after sentencing. As states have sent more offenders to prison and for longer terms, prisons have become seriously overcrowded. All prisons were 15 percent over capacity in 1995; Virginia was 40 percent over its officially rated capacity and Ohio was 70 percent over.[50] States have responded by releasing prisoners early through a variety of schemes. Some of them are overt emergency release procedures. But others are covert backdoor schemes embedded in changes in correctional practices. Pamala Griset's study of correctional trends in New York, which we discussed in Chapter 3, illustrates the extent to which this strategy involves both a hidden form of sentencing and a device for undermining the intent of mandatory sentencing laws.[51]

New York supplemented the 1973 drug law with two additional mandatory sentencing laws in 1978, covering juveniles and certain violent felonies. Prison overcrowding resulted, and because of the state's financial problems, the needed prison cells were not constructed. The state responded in 1987 and 1989 with laws creating three early release programs: shock incarceration, earned eligibility, and CASAT (Comprehensive Alcohol and Substance Abuse Treatment). These programs transfer enormous discretion to correctional officials over how much time offenders will actually serve.

Shock incarceration, like many boot camp programs we will examine in Chapter 11, involves early release after a short six-month program. Griset found that about 40 percent of those admitted to the program had been convicted of a second felony and that about 99 percent were immediately paroled upon completing the program. Many of these offenders were technically subject to the state's mandatory sentencing law regarding second offense felons. Yet on the basis of decisions by correctional staff—and not sentencing judges —they were released sooner than the law "mandated."

The second program, earned eligibility, speeds up an inmate's date of first eligibility for parole. Inmates who participate in treatment, educational, and work programs obtain a certificate of earned eligibility from correctional staff that grants them a virtual presumption of parole release (82 percent of those with certificates were paroled). As Griset explains, correctional staff have full discretion over whether to grant the certificate of earned eligibility.[52] Thus, actual control over the actual amount of time served passes from the legislature and judges to correctional officials.

Similarly, under the CASAT program inmates with alcohol or drug histories may be released up to eighteen months earlier than the expiration of their minimum sentence. As with the other two programs, correctional officials have full discretion to grant admission to CASAT.

The net result of these three programs, Griset explains, is that the reality of sentencing diverges from the rhetoric. New York politicians retained mandatory minimum sentencing but quietly authorized correctional officials to let prisoners out early.[53] On one hand, this is a cynical political maneuver: talking tough about crime while not facing up to paying the bill. At the same time, it is a classic example of how criminal justice thermodynamics often undermine the intent of "tough" sentencing laws.

Case 2: The Federal Sentencing Guidelines. The Federal Sentencing Guidelines that went into effect in 1987 include a number of mandatory sentencing provisions, and they have contributed to the increase in the federal prison population. To achieve "truth in sentencing," the guidelines reduced the range of possible sentences and abolished discretionary parole release. The percentage of convicted federal offenders sentenced to prison increased from 51 percent

in 1982 to 65 percent in 1994. Also, the average prison term increased 27 percent, from an average of 48 to 61 months.[54]

A basic question is whether prosecutors and judges are complying with the
Federal Sentencing Guidelines. There is mixed evidence on this issue. A study
by the Federal Judicial Center found that slightly less than half of the offenders
who were eligible under a mandatory minimum provision actually received it.
This is a fairly high rate of slippage and leakage.[55]

Another problem is plea bargaining—specifically, charge bargaining that
allows defendants to plea to a lesser offense and avoid a long mandatory minimum. Section 5K1.1 of the Federal Sentencing Guidelines allows a departure
from the presumptive sentence where the defendant "has provided substantial
assistance in the investigation or prosecution of another person who has committed an offense."[56] In other words, a defendant can reduce his or her potential sentence by cooperating and naming other criminals.

Ilene H. Nagle and Samuel J. Schulhofer examined plea bargaining in
three federal district courts and found that departures from the guidelines
occurred in between 15 and 25 percent of all cases, with the national average
about 17 percent. They conclude that circumvention of the guidelines is not
the norm and that it is not necessarily unfair. They did, however, find some
cases in which defendants won substantial sentence reductions: in one case,
from 168 to 21 months; in another, from 69 months to nine.[57] These reductions may be excessive compared with what most defendants receive.

The point is that through prosecutorial discretion, "mandatory" sentences
are not necessarily mandatory in practice. As we will see shortly, the mandatory provisions of "three strikes" laws are ignored in most states. The various
adaptations, moreover, because they are often hidden, increase the arbitrariness
of decisions and the possibility of discrimination.

Mandatory Sentencing and Crime

The basic question, of course, is whether mandatory sentencing effectively
reduces crime. A 1982 Justice Department report concluded that "it is difficult, perhaps fundamentally impossible, to substantiate the popular claim that
mandatory sentencing is an effective tool for reducing crime."[58] By fifteen
years later, we had much more experience with mandatory sentencing. A 1996
report on structured sentencing in a variety of states found no correlation
between incarceration rates and crime rates.[59] Zimring and Hawkins's multi-
state comparison of incapacitation, which we cited earlier, also did not find
any clear correlation between incarceration rates and crime rates.[60]

After reviewing all of the evidence on mandatory sentencing, Michael
Tonry, one of the leading experts on sentencing, declared, "Mandatory penalties do not work."[61] In his view, they are widely circumvented, tend to shift
discretion from justices to prosecutors, and often result in punishments that are
"unduly harsh." We agree. Our position is as follows:

PROPOSITION 19

Mandatory sentencing is not an effective means of reducing serious crime.

THREE STRIKES—WE ARE ALL OUT

The most popular new idea in mandatory sentencing is "three strikes and you're out." The basic concept is a mandatory life prison sentence for anyone convicted of a third felony, although in actual practice there are many variations. The state of Washington passed the first law, the Persistent Offender Accountability Act, in November 1993. The idea really caught fire after the brutal murder of Polly Klass in California by Richard Allen Davis, a man with a long criminal record who had been paroled only three months earlier. California passed its "three strikes" law in March 1994. Twenty-six states and the federal system have some kind of "three strikes" law. But as we point out later, almost all states have had repeat offender or habitual criminal law.[62]

Considerable variation exists among "three strikes" laws. The Washington law mandates life without parole for conviction to a "most serious offense" if the person had two prior convictions to "most serious offenses," which included a wide range of felonies. The California law has separate "two strikes" and "three strikes" provisions. The "second strike" provision doubles the sentence for a person convicted of a felony who has a prior felony conviction to a designated "strikeable" offense. The "third strike" provision mandates life imprisonment, with no parole eligibility before 25 years, to someone convicted of a felony who has two prior convictions to designated "strikeable" offenses. The 1994 Georgia law mandates life without parole for a second conviction to a "serious violent felony."[63]

The "three strikes" idea has been almost universally condemned by criminologists and other experts on sentencing. Franklin Zimring calls it "the voodoo economics of California crime." Jerome Skolnick says it represented the values of "the dark ages." A book labels it "Vengeance as Public Policy." Princeton's John J. DiIulio is one of the few to support it, arguing that "society has a right not only to protect itself from convicted criminals but to express its moral outrage at their acts by, among other things, keeping them behind bars."[64]

Actually, the basic principle underlying three strikes is nothing new. Most states have had some kind of repeat offender law for many decades. The first such law in the United States was passed in 1797. A famous 1926 New York law mandated life in prison for conviction to a third felony. A national survey of repeat offender laws by William F. McDonald in the mid-1980s found that they were "rarely used" and widely regarded as a "dead letter."[65] Forty-one states had some kind of repeat offender or habitual offender law on the books in February 1994, before the "three strikes" movement took off.[66]

"Three strikes" laws raise the same questions we have already considered in this book. First, will a law in fact be implemented or simply evaded by the courtroom work group? Second, assuming it is implemented, what impact will it have on the criminal justice system? Third, will it reduce serious crime?

PROPOSITION 20
Three strikes and you're out laws are a terrible crime policy.

Implementation

With the exception of California, and to a certain extent Georgia, states have not used their "three strikes" laws. An early study found Wisconsin used its law only once in the first year and a half, while Tennessee, New Mexico, and Colorado did not use theirs at all.[67] Local prosecutors simply do not file the necessary charges. In some instances, the law becomes a plea-bargaining tool. Many cases can be filed either as felonies or misdemeanors (say, misdemeanor assault versus felonious assault). The law gives the prosecutor a powerful weapon to get a guilty plea to a misdemeanor; in Sacramento, California, there were charge reductions in 67 percent of all the eligible cases. Even in California, application of the law varied tremendously. Two-thirds of all cases under the law originated in Los Angeles County. Officials in San Francisco, meanwhile, have publicly stated that they will not use it in certain kinds of cases, including drug cases.[68]

Impact

In the California counties where the "three strikes" law has been used, the effect has rippled through the local criminal justice system. More defendants have demanded jury trials, preferring to take their chances on acquittal at trial than plead guilty to certain third-strike sentences. In the first year, potential second- and third-strike cases in Los Angeles represented 3 percent of all cases but 24 percent of jury trials. The increase in criminal trials raised the costs of handling cases (in the state of Washington, a full jury trial costs as much as $50,000, compared with $600 for a routine plea-bargained case) and caused more delays in civil cases.[69]

The increase in the number of defendants waiting trial initially produced severe jail overcrowding. As a result, other offenders sentenced to short jail terms were being released early. Offenders sentenced to one-year jail terms were being released after 71 days, compared with an average of 200 days beforehand. The law had cost Los Angeles County alone an extra $169 million in just the first two years.

An early report by the Rand Corporation estimated that full implementation of the law in California would cost the state an extra $5.5 billion a year over the next 25 years.[70] Most of this cost involves building new prisons (at an estimated cost of $97,000 per prisoner) and operating these prisons (at an estimated cost of $20,800 per prisoner). One important factor with "three strikes" laws is that the cost of incarcerating an elderly prisoner is three times the normal cost ($60,000) because of the medical care and security needs of frail inmates. The number of these inmates will increase dramatically under the life terms imposed by "three strikes" laws.

Most criminologists doubt that "three strikes" laws will reduce crime very much. With respect to incapacitation, they are highly *unselective,* imposing a rigid formula that does not take into account the full dimensions of an offender's criminal career or predicted propensity to commit a high rate of crimes in the future. Among other things, they are likely to catch many offenders who are well beyond the peak years for criminal activity (ages 14 to 24). Thus they will result in the incarceration of middle-aged and elderly people, at great dollar cost, who are not likely to commit many crimes if they were not imprisoned.

The amount of crime attributable to persons eligible under "three strikes" laws has been greatly exaggerated by the proponents of these laws. Frank Zimring and his colleagues estimate that all the people arrested in California who are potentially eligible under both the "two strikes" and "three strikes" provisions are responsible for only about 11 percent of all felonies in California. In short, the net reduction in crime if the law were fully enforced would be very small.[71] And, of course, the law is *not* fully enforced. Indeed, the harsh scale of punishments encourages many prosecutors to not use it at all. And in many other cases it distorts plea bargaining, shifting power to prosecutors.

"Three strikes" laws are the worst example of gross incapacitation. And in a classic example of the trickle-up or hydraulic effect, they sweep up many people convicted of relatively minor offenses. The first California case, in fact, involved Jerry Williams, who stole a slice of pepperoni pizza. The first woman prosecuted under the law was arrested for a $20 cocaine purchase that occurred 14 years after her second "strike." One of the first people sentenced to life in prison in the state of Washington had stolen $151 from a sandwich shop; his two previous strikes involved robberies totaling $460. About 85 percent of those sentenced under the law in California were convicted of a nonviolent crime. In March 1996, 192 were sentenced for marijuana possession, compared with 40 for murder and 25 for rape.

Summary: Striking Out

"Three strikes" represents all the worst aspects of the "get tough" approach to crime. First, it is a classic example of overreaction to celebrated cases. Second, it represents a crude, meat-ax policy that sweeps up many nondangerous criminals. Third, these laws are not consistently implemented and thus increase the arbitrariness of the administration of justice. Fourth, they upset the normal going rate and impose new costs on local criminal justice systems, including more trials, delays, and greater dollar costs. Finally, no clear evidence indicates that they will reduce serious crime (and some good evidence shows that they incarcerate a lot of people who will not commit any crimes at all).

Rereading today William F. McDonald's 1986 report on the old repeat offender laws is a sobering experience. In effect, McDonald predicted all of the problems associated with "three strikes" laws. Surveying all of the states with such laws, he found: "Only a small fraction of eligible habitual offenders have been or are currently being sentenced as such." McDonald interviewed members of the courtroom work group (prosecutors, defense attorneys, judges) and found a general perception that "prior criminality is already being taken proper account of under the normal sentencing structure."[72] In short, as we argued in Chapter 3, the prevailing going rate did allow serious offenders to avoid significant punishment. For the most part, the old repeat offender laws were used as plea bargaining tools. Not surprisingly, prosecutors gave the laws generally favorable ratings, while defense attorneys and judges were highly critical.

McDonald's report also anticipated the conceptual confusion that surrounds "three strikes" laws. The old repeat offender laws failed to distinguish among seriousness, repetitiveness, intensity, and dangerousness. *Seriousness* refers to gravity of the particular crimes, including both the immediate crime for which an offender is being prosecuted or past crimes. *Repetitiveness* refers to a defendant's prior record or criminal career. *Intensity* refers to the rate at which a defendant has committed crimes in the past, as in the annual offending rate. *Dangerousness,* meanwhile, represents a predictive assessment of the amount of harm an offender might do to the community. McDonald found that practitioners believed that the old laws often sentenced offenders who were "not truly dangerous predators but comparatively petty offenders."[73] As we have seen, "three strikes" laws are blunt instruments that often result in the incarceration of persons convicted of relatively less serious offenses but whose records happen to fit a mechanical formula.

CONCLUSION

From a commonsense standpoint, "lock 'em up" strategies appear to be a simple and effective way to reduce crime. Unfortunately, it is not that simple in the real world of the criminal justice system. First, we cannot precisely identify the small group of high-rate offenders. Second, gross incapacitation policies create all sorts of problems in the justice system. Third, because of these problems, the courtroom work group often finds ways to evade extremely punitive laws. Fourth, no conclusive evidence indicates that locking up a lot of people actually produces the promised reductions in crime. Finally, even where some crime reduction does occur, it is not clear that it is worth the enormous dollar cost to society.

NOTES

1. On the general subject of discretion, see Samuel Walker, *Taming the System: The Control of Discretion in Criminal Justice, 1950–1990* (New York: Oxford University Press, 1993).

2. President's Task Force on Victims of Crime, *Final Report* (Washington, DC: Government Printing Office, 1982), p. 22.

3. Caleb Foote, "The Coming Constitutional Crisis in Bail," *University of Pennsylvania Law Review* 113 (May 1965): 959–99 and (June 1965): 1125–185.

4. *United States v. Salerno,* 481 U.S. 739 (1987).

5. On the background of the bail issue, see Wayne Thomas, *Bail Reform in America* (Berkeley: University of California Press, 1976).

6. Caleb Foote, "Compelling Appearance in Court: Administration of Bail in Philadelphia," *University of Pennsylvania Law Review* 102 (1954): 1031–079.

7. Bureau of Justice Statistics, *Pretrial Release of Felony Defendants, 1992*

(Washington, DC: Government Printing Office, 1994).

8. Thomas, *Bail Reform in America*.

9. Thomas, *Bail Reform in America*, p. 37; Bureau of Justice Statistics, *Pretrial Release of Felony Defendants, 1992*.

10. Bureau of Justice Statistics, *Pretrial Release of Felony Defendants, 1990* (Washington, DC: Government Printing Office, 1992).

11. John Goldkamp, "Danger and Detention: A Second Generation of Bail Reform," *Journal of Criminal Law and Criminology* 76 (Spring 1985): 1–74.

12. *Preventive Detention in the District of Columbia: The First Ten Months* (Washington, D.C.: Georgetown Institute of Criminal Law and Procedure, 1972); Thomas, *Bail Reform in America*, pp. 231–32.

13. Frederick Suffett, "Bail Setting: A Study of Courtroom Interaction," *Crime and Delinquency* 12 (1966): 318–31.

14. Bureau of Justice Statistics, *Pretrial Release of Felony Defendants, 1992,* table 5.

15. General Accounting Office, *Criminal Bail: How Bail Reform Is Working in Selected District Courts* (Washington, DC: Government Printing Office, 1987); Bureau of Justice Statistics, *Pretrial Release and Detention: The Bail Reform Act of 1984* (Washington, DC: Government Printing Office, 1988).

16. Thomas E. Scott, "Pretrial Detention under the Bail Reform Act of 1984: An Empirical Analysis," *American Criminal Law Review* 27.1 (1989): 1–51; Bureau of Justice Statistics, *Sourcebook of Criminal Justice Statistics—1998* (Washington, DC: Government Printing Office, 1999), p. 398.

17. Bureau of Justice Statistics, *Pretrial Release and Detention,* table 9; Bureau of Justice Statistics, *Sourcebook of Criminal Justice Statistics—1998*, p. 401.

18. Bureau of Justice Statistics, *Pretrial Release of Felony Defendants, 1992;* Bureau of Justice Statistics, *Felony Defendants in Large Urban Counties, 1994* (Washington, DC: Government Printing Office, 1998).

19. Bureau of Justice Statistics, *Pretrial Release of Felony Defendants, 1992*, p. 11; Bureau of Justice Statistics, *Felony Defendants in Large Urban Counties, 1994*.

20. William Rhodes, Raymond Hyatt, and Paul Scheiman, *Predicting Pretrial Misconduct with Drug Tests of Arrestees: Evidence from Six Sites* (Washington, DC: Government Printing Office, 1996).

21. *Schall v. Martin,* 467 U.S. 253 (1984).

22. Jeffrey Fagan and Martin Guggenheim, "Preventive Detention and the Judicial Prediction of Dangerousness for Juveniles: A Natural Experiment," *Journal of Criminal Law and Criminology* 86.2 (1996): 415–48.

23. Fagan and Guggenheim, "Preventive Detention," pp. 445, 448.

24. Bureau of Justice Statistics, *Pretrial Release of Felony Defendants, 1992*.

25. Malcolm Feeley, *Court Reform on Trial* (New York: Basic Books, 1983).

26. Franklin E. Zimring and Gordon Hawkins, *Incapacitation: Penal Confinement and the Restraint of Crime* (New York: Oxford University Press, 1995).

27. James Q. Wilson, *Thinking about Crime* (New York: Basic Books, 1975), pp. 200–202.

28. Peter Greenwood, *Selective Incapacitation* (Santa Monica, CA: Rand, 1982).

29. Greenwood, *Selective Incapacitation,* xix.

30. Jan M. Chaiken and Marcia R. Chaiken, *Varieties of Criminal Behavior: Summary and Policy Implications* (Santa Monica, CA: Rand, 1982).

31. Alfred Blumstein, Jacqueline Cohen, Jeffrey Roth, and Christy Visher, eds., *Criminal Careers and "Career Criminals"* (Washington, DC: National Academy of Sciences, 1988).

32. Blumstein et al., *Criminal Careers and "Careeer Criminals,"* p. 59.

33. Blumstein et al., *Criminal Careers and "Careeer Criminals,"* p. 60.

34. Peter W. Greenwood and Susan Turner, *Selective Incapacitation Revisited: Why the High-Rate Offenders Are Hard to Predict* (Santa Monica, CA: Rand, 1987).

35. Greenwood, *Selective Incapacitation,* table 4.3.

36. Edna McConnell Clark Foundation, *Overcrowded Time* (New York: Edna McConnell Clark Foundation, 1982);

Don C. Gibbons, *The Limits of Punishment as Social Policy* (San Francisco: National Council on Crime and Delinquency, 1988); Marc Mauer, *Americans Behind Bars: One Year Later* (Washington, DC: Sentencing Project, 1992); Campaign for an Effective Crime Policy, *What Every Policymaker Should Know About Imprisonment and the Crime Rate* (Washington, DC: Campaign for an Effective Crime Policy, 1995).

37. American Bar Association, *Standards for Criminal Justice,* "Sentencing Alternatives and Procedures," Standard 18-2.1 (Boston: Little, Brown, 1980), pp. 18–25.

38. Edwin W. Zedlewski, *Making Confinement Decisions* (Washington, DC: Government Printing Office, 1987).

39. Franklin E. Zimring and Gordon E. Hawkins, "The New Mathematics of Imprisonment," *Crime and Delinquency* 34 (October 1988): 425–36. See also Zimring and Hawkins, *Incapacitation.*

40. Eric J. Scott, *Calls for Service* (Washington, DC: Government Printing Office, 1981).

41. Zimring and Hawkins, *Incapacitation.*

42. Zimring and Hawkins, *Incapacitation,* p. 126.

43. Zimring and Hawkins, *Incapacitation,* pp. 106–07.

44. Bureau of Justice Assistance, *National Assessment of Structured Sentencing* (Washington, DC: Government Printing Office, 1996), pp. 24–25.

45. Campaign for an Effective Crime Policy, *The Impact of "Three Strikes and You're Out" Laws: What Have We Learned?* (Washington, DC: Campaign for an Effective Crime Policy, 1996).

46. U.S. Department of Justice, *The Nation's Toughest Drug Law: Evaluating the New York Experience* (Washington, DC: Government Printing Office, 1978).

47. U.S. Department of Justice, *Nation's Toughest Drug Law,* p. 18.

48. Bureau of Justice Statistics, *Drugs, Crime, and the Justice System* (Washington, DC: Government Printing Office, 1992), p. 30.

49. Malcolm M. Feeley and Sam Hakim, "The Effect of 'Three Strikes and You're Out' on the Courts," in David Shichor and Dale K. Sechrest, eds., *Three Strikes and You're Out: Vengeance as Social Policy* (Thousand Oaks, CA: Sage, 1996), p. 141.

50. Bureau of Justice Statistics, *Sourcebook of Criminal Justice Statistics—1995,* p. 94.

51. Pamala Griset, "The Politics and Economics of Increased Correctional Discretion over Time Served: A New York Case Study," *Justice Quarterly* 12 (June 1995): 307–23.

52. Griset, "Politics and Economics of Increased Correctional Discretion," p. 316.

53. Griset, "Politics and Economics of Increased Correctional Discretion," p. 321.

54. Bureau of Justice Statistics, *Sourcebook of Criminal Justice Statistics—1995* (Washington, DC: Government Printing Office, 1996), pp. 472–73.

55. Barbara Meierhofer, *The General Effect of Mandatory Minimum Prison Terms* (Washington, DC: Government Printing Office, 1992).

56. U.S. Sentencing Commission, *Federal Sentencing Guidelines Manual* (St. Paul, MN: West, 1990), p. 281.

57. Ilene H. Nagel and Stephen Schulhofer, "A Tale of Three Cities: An Empirical Study of Charging and Bargaining Practices Under the Federal Sentencing Guidelines," *Southern California Law Review* 66 (1992): 501–66.

58. U.S. Department of Justice, *Mandatory Sentencing: The Experience of Two States* (Washington, DC: Government Printing Office, 1982).

59. Bureau of Justice Assistance, *National Assessment of Structure Sentencing,* p. 117.

60. Zimring and Hawkins, *Incapacitation.*

61. Michael Tonry, "Mandatory Penalties," in Michael Tonry, ed., *Crime and Justice: A Review of Research,* vol. 16 (Chicago: University of Chicago Press, 1992), p. 243.

62. The best collection of material on "three strikes" laws is Shichor and Sechrest, *Three Strikes and You're Out.*

63. Michael G. Turner, Jody Sundt, Brandon K. Applegate, and Francis T. Cullen, "'Three Strikes and You're Out' Legislation: A National Assessment," *Federal Probation* 59 (September 1995): 16–35.

64. Jerome H. Skolnick, "Wild Pitch," *American Prospect* 17 (Spring 1994): 31–37; Shichor and Sechrest, *Three Strikes and You're Out*; John J. DiIulio, Jr., "Instant Replay," *American Prospect* 18 (Summer 1994): 12–18.

65. William F. McDonald, *Repeat Offender Laws in the United States: The Form, Use, and Perceived Value* (Washington, DC: Government Printing Office, 1986), p. 5.

66. Bureau of Justice Assistance, *National Assessment of Structured Sentencing*, pp. 24–25; Turner et al., "'Three Strikes and You're Out' Legislation."

67. Campaign for an Effective Crime Policy, *Impact of "Three Strikes and You're Out" Laws*.

68. Campaign for an Effective Crime Policy, *Impact of "Three Strikes and You're Out" Laws*.

69. Robert C. Cushman, "Effect on a Local Criminal Justice System," in Shichor and Sechrest, *Three Strikes and You're Out*, pp. 90–113.

70. Peter Greenwood, C. Peter Rydell, Allan F. Abrahmse, Jonathan P. Caulkins, James Chiesa, Karyn E. Model, and Stephen P. Klein, *Three Strikes and You're Out: Estimated Benefits and Costs of California's New Mandatory Sentencing Law* (Santa Monica, CA: Rand, 1994); this selection also appears as chapter 3 in Shichor and Sechrest, *Three Strikes and You're Out*, pp. 53–89.

71. Franklin Zimring, Gordon Hawkins, and Sam Kamin, *Punishment and Democracy: Three Strikes and You're Out in California* (New York: Oxford University Press, forthcoming).

72. McDonald, *Repeat Offender Laws in the United States*, abstract, n.p.

73. McDonald, *Repeat Offender Laws in the United States*, pp. 7, 19.

8

Close the Loopholes

Conservatives believe that many dangerous criminals beat the system and escape punishment: Their cases are dismissed, they plead guilty to lesser offenses, or if convicted they are not sent to prison. As a result, they return to the streets and commit more crimes. A major part of the conservative crime control agenda, therefore, is to close these perceived loopholes in the criminal justice system.

PROSECUTE THE CAREER CRIMINAL

To make sure that the really dangerous criminals are punished, a number of prosecutors have created special *major-offender* or *career criminal programs.* The basic idea is to focus special attention on them to make sure they are prosecuted, convicted, and incarcerated. Like some of the other programs we have examined, this idea is based on Wolfgang's career criminal research, which we examined in Chapter 4.

Getting Tough in San Diego

The San Diego Major Violator Unit targets robbery and robbery-related homicide cases in which the defendant is charged with three or more separate robbery-related offenses or has been convicted of one or more serious offenses in the preceding ten years.[1] The individual prosecutor assigned a major-violator case follows it through to completion. This policy provides *continuity of prosecution,* which is designed to prevent mistakes that might result from passing a case from one prosecutor to another as it moves through the system from the initial charge to preliminary hearing and eventual disposition. It is also designed to help maintain close contact between the prosecutor and the victim and witnesses. (Witnesses problems is one of the main reasons that cases are dismissed.) Prosecutors are involved in the preparation of the presentence investigation (PSI) report, and they submit an independent sentence recommendation to the judge, often asking for a stiff sentence.

Like other career criminal programs, the San Diego Major Violator Unit includes restrictions on plea bargaining.[2] Prosecutors may not "charge bargain" and can accept a plea only to the top felony count. This is designed to prevent the defendant from avoiding prison by pleading to a misdemeanor or a lesser felony. Despite these special procedures, however, the San Diego Major Violator Unit had only a modest impact on the prosecution of career criminals. The reason is simple: Prosecutors were already very tough on serious crime.

The Major Violator Unit won conviction in 91.5 percent of its cases. This figure sounds very impressive until we discover that San Diego normally convicted 89.5 percent of all career criminals. The unit did increase the percentage of convicted offenders sent to prison, from 77.1 percent to 92.5 percent. This change was less significant than it might appear, however. The percentage of convicted offenders who were incarcerated (either prison or jail) increased only slightly, from 95.3 percent to 100 percent. This point highlights an important but often misunderstood feature of felony sentencing.[3]

The category of incarceration includes both sentences to prison and *split sentences,* in which the offender does some time in jail followed by release on probation. Split sentences are actually fairly common. Nationally, about half of all convicted felons given probation actually serve some time in jail. The net result is that 69 percent of convicted felons are incarcerated (prison: 38 percent; jail: 31 percent; straight probation: 31 percent).[4]

These data on sentencing are extremely important in terms of public *perception* of how the system works. If you look only at the percentage of convicted offenders sentenced to prison (44 percent), the system looks somewhat weak. But when you include everyone who is incarcerated (70 percent), it looks a lot tougher. True, going to jail is not as serious as going to prison, but it is still an unpleasant experience, and these offenders are not beating the system.

The Major Violator Unit did, however, double the average length of incarceration. In this respect it significantly increased the severity of punishment. But it is important to recall that the length of prison terms has been rising across the country (particularly for serious crimes), so some of the increase in San Diego probably would have occurred even without the Major Violator Unit.

The important question for us is whether the San Diego Major Violator Unit had any impact on the crime rate. The evaluation of the program did not address this question. Common sense, however, suggests that it could not have had any significant effect, because the changes in the percentage of offenders convicted and the percentage incarcerated were so small.

Other Prosecution Programs

The results in San Diego were typical of outcomes in other jurisdictions. The National Institute of Justice found a similar pattern in three other career criminal programs. In Kalamazoo, Michigan, conviction rates went from 66.6 percent to 73.4 percent; in New Orleans, they rose from 81.8 percent to 88.7 percent; and they went from 73.9 percent to 76.4 percent in Columbus, Ohio. Incarceration rates rose slightly in two of the cities but actually declined in New Orleans. Sentence lengths went up in two cities but went down in Kalamazoo.[5]

A Phoenix, Arizona, repeat offender program (ROP) involves police officers in the prosecution effort, working with prosecutors as a team. Detectives "walk" warrants or information about additional charges through the courts to ensure a high bond so that the defendant is not released before trial. They also attend trials inconspicuously and provide feedback to prosecutors about the reaction of jurors. ROP detectives also personally contact probation officers and provide information for the presentence investigation report.

The results of the program were similar to those in San Diego. Over 98 percent of the ROP offenders were prosecuted, and 89.9 percent were convicted. The figures for the control group were nearly identical: 98.9 percent prosecuted and 86.4 percent convicted. The percentage incarcerated is almost the same, although a slightly higher proportion were sent to prison rather than given a split sentence.[6]

These data on the prosecution of so-called career criminals reveal an important point. Local prosecutors, without the benefit of a special program, are generally tough on major offenders—and have been getting tougher since the 1970s. They rely primarily on two important commonsense criteria: the seriousness of the offense and the defendant's prior record.[7] And as we pointed out in Chapter 3, these criteria are shared by all members as the courtroom work group.

Most people are surprised to find that the system is consistently tough on career criminals. This misperception can be explained in terms of our criminal justice wedding cake (Chapter 2). Public perception is heavily influenced by a few celebrated cases in the top layer: the armed robber who got probation; the rapist who plead guilty to misdemeanor assault; the O. J. Simpson trial. The typical career criminal case, however, falls into the second layer: successful prosecution, conviction, and a prison term. Additional public misunderstanding arises from aggregating second- and third-layer felonies. The relatively softer treatment of third-layer cases masks the tough response to the career criminals in the second layer.

In the end, it turns out that the alleged loophole of being soft on dangerous offenders does not exist. Therefore, we can draw the following conclusion:

> ## PROPOSITION 21
> **Career criminal prosecution programs do not produce either higher conviction rates or lower crime rates.**

ABOLISH THE INSANITY DEFENSE

John W. Hinckley never succeeded at much in life, but he is singlehandedly responsible for some significant changes in American criminal justice. Hinckley's acquittal for the attempted assassination of President Ronald Reagan in 1981 sparked a national outcry over the insanity defense.[8] Over the next two decades, almost every state and the federal government changed its insanity law. Twelve states adopted a new "guilty but mentally ill" (GBMI) standard and five abolished the insanity defense altogether.[9]

Hinckley's acquittal touched one of the raw nerves of public opinion: the sight of a guilty person "beating the rap" and "getting off" because of a "technicality." There was no question about whether John Hinckley shot and wounded the president; we all saw it on television. People were outraged over the Hinckley verdict of not guilty by reason of insanity (NGRI), which appeared to let him off. The fact is that he was institutionalized—in a hospital rather than a prison—and remains there today. Moreover, his notoriety will probably keep him there longer than if he had shot an ordinary person, pled guilty, and gone to prison.

For many people, the insanity defense is the classic loophole. It conjures up images of criminally insane persons roaming the streets in search of more victims. Insanity defense proceedings also anger many people. The parade of psychiatrists and expert witnesses on both sides of the case creates the impression that you can always find an expert somewhere to say what you want said. Like the O. J. Simpson trial, the Hinckley case supports the impression that the wealthy can buy lawyers and experts who will win them acquittal. In one public opinion survey, 87 percent of the respondents felt that the insanity defense is a loophole; about 40 percent regard it as a "rich person's defense."[10]

The conservative response to these perceptions is to try to close the loophole. Changes in the law over the past two decades fall into six categories: (1) abolishing the insanity defense altogether; (2) changing the test of insanity; (3) shifting the burden of proof to the defendant (instead of the state having to prove criminal intent, the defendant has to prove mental illness); (4) creating a new "guilty but mentally ill" verdict; (5) revising trial procedure for raising an insanity plea; raised; and (6) changing procedures for committing a person found not guilty by reason of insanity.[11]

Sorting Out the Issues

Changing the law on the insanity defense raises four separate issues. The first concerns the extent of the use of the defense. How many criminal defendants successfully win verdicts of not guilty by reason of insanity? A second issue involves the fate of those who do win acquittal. Do they return to the streets? How soon? Do they endanger the public? The third issue is predicting dangerousness. If some offenders are dangerous, how can we identify them? How can we tell when it is safe to release them? The fourth issue is the effect of abolishing the insanity defense. What is the impact on crime and the criminal justice system?

The Reality of the Insanity Defense

Despite all the attention it receives, the insanity defense is an extremely rare event. Very few defendants even try to use it, and few of them succeed. Studies have consistently found that the insanity defense is raised in less than 1 percent of all criminal indictments, and only between 15 and 25 percent of those efforts are successful.[12] Henry J. Steadman and his colleagues, for example, found that in four states (California, Georgia, Montana, New York), the insanity defense was *raised* in slightly less than 1 percent (0.90 percent) of all felony indictments. Only about 23 percent of these *succeeded* in getting an NGRI verdict.[13] The American Psychiatric Association (APA) Insanity Defense Work Group concluded, "While philosophically important for the criminal law, the insanity defense is *empirically unimportant* (involving a fraction of 1 percent of all felony cases").[14]

The extent of public misunderstanding about the frequency of the insanity defense is extraordinary. An Illinois poll found that people believed nearly 40 percent of all criminal defendants used the insanity defense. This misunderstanding explains the fact that nearly half of the respondents wanted the insanity defense abolished.[15] But if this alleged loophole were completely closed, the effect would not be noticed. Moreover, there would be absolutely no impact on robbery and burglary cases. The few successful insanity defense cases are the classic celebrated cases in the top layer of the criminal justice wedding cake. They are completely unrepresentative and tell us nothing about how most serious crimes are routinely handled.

Most successful uses of the insanity defense are the result of a plea bargain or a stipulated finding. That is, the prosecutor, defense attorney, medical experts, and judge all agree that the defendant is mentally ill. This is another example of the court room work group in operation. A study of 60,432 felony indictments in Baltimore, Maryland in 1991 found that the insanity defense was raised in only 190 cases; it was eventually dropped in 182 cases, and the remaining eight defendants were stipulated mentally ill by both prosecution and defense.[16] The main point is that the prosecutor agrees with this verdict. The defendant is not "beating the system."

Another popular myth about the insanity defense is that the people who use it are violent and dangerous. Not all of the defendants committed to mental health institutions by way of an insanity verdict have committed a violent offense, however. Of the 500 men in the Bridgewater (Massachusetts) State Hospital for the Criminally Insane, more than 100 had been charged with vagrancy.[17] These people are not dangerous sociopaths. Many are pathetic individuals who have serious mental health problems and cannot cope with their lives. Most sank through the various safety nets and ended up on skid row, where they finally were arrested.[18]

Aftermath of Acquittal

What happens to defendants who are committed to mental institutions after winning not guilty by reason of insanity verdicts is a matter of much controversy. Liberals generally contend that they are likely to spend more time in a mental hospital than if they had been found guilty of the crime and sent to prison. Conservatives argue that they get out too soon.

Several years ago, there was considerable truth to the liberal argument. Many allegedly mentally ill people were hospitalized for years, even decades, without any treatment or any evidence that they were really dangerous. Supreme Court decisions and new state laws, however, have led to greater protection of the rights of the confined. One of the most important is a mental patient's right to periodic review of his or her condition to determine whether continued confinement is justified. The landmark case of *Baxstrom v. Herold* (1966) forced the release of persons held for long periods of time in the New York State Hospital for the Criminally Insane and necessitated the development of new procedures for continued confinement.[19]

Nonetheless, persons hospitalized after being found not guilty by reason of insanity still spend more time confined in hospitals than comparable offenders spend in prison after being found guilty of the crime. Henry Steadman and his associates found that in New York, 88 percent of all NGRIs were hospitalized; of the 12 percent immediately released, a disproportionate share were women. Those who were charged with murder but found not guilty by reason of insanity spent an average of 6.4 years in the hospital; those acquitted of other violent crimes were hospitalized for an average of 5.2 years; and for nonviolent crimes, hospital stays averaged 2.8 years. For all the crimes except murder, these terms of confinement were longer than for offenders found guilty of similar crimes.[20]

In an earlier study, Steadman studied a group of defendants found incompetent to stand trial to see whether they "beat the rap." A defendant who is too mentally ill to comprehend the nature of a criminal trial is committed to an institution until he or she is able to understand the proceedings, at which point the criminal process resumes. Steadman found that those defendants deemed "nondangerous" spent less than two years in mental institutions, whereas the "dangerous" were confined an average of two years and two months. If they were subsequently convicted at trial, they faced the possibility of additional

prison time. Do you "beat the rap" by taking the mental health route? Steadman argues not: "Mental hospitals are simply an alternative place to do time."[21]
In short, the system is not turning hordes of dangerous psychotics loose on
society.

Danger to the Community

How dangerous are the criminally insane? We have had some "natural experiments" on this question as a result of court decisions that forced the release of
criminal defendants. A 1971 decision forced the clinical reassessment of 586
inmates of Pennsylvania's Fairview State Hospital for the Criminally Insane.
More than two-thirds were eventually released. Over the next four years, 27
percent were rearrested, but only 11 percent for a violent crime. Including
some others who were rehospitalized for a violent act, a total of 14.5 percent
of those released proved to be dangerous.[22] A recent review of the literature
concluded that the recidivism rate for persons acquitted by reason of insanity is
"no greater than that of felons."[23]

Once again we encounter the prediction problem. A decision to release or
confine persons alleged to be criminally insane involves a prediction about
their future behavior. Do they pose a danger to the community? The success
rate in predicting the dangerousness of the criminally insane is no better than
in other areas of criminal justice. Because only 14.5 percent of the Fairview
inmates committed another violent act, you could argue that the experts were
wrong about the other 85.5 percent. This translates into six false positives
(people unnecessarily locked up) for each true positive.

The Impact of Abolition

For many people, "abolishing" the insanity defense (like "abolishing" plea bargaining or parole) is a slogan. As we have seen, changing the law on the insanity defense can be done six different ways. Each of these changes involves
complex legal and practical problems.

Abolishing or modifying the insanity defense raises fundamental issues
about the criminal law. Our justice system rests on the principle that the
accused is innocent until proven guilty and that the prosecution must prove
guilt beyond a reasonable doubt. To prove guilt, the prosecution must establish
three things: The accused committed the act (*actus reus*), the accused had criminal intent (*mens rea*), and a connection exists between the two (that is, that the
accused did it and intended to do it).[24]

The key issue with the insanity defense is the *mens rea* requirement. The
criminal law has long recognized different degrees of intent. The law distinguishes between a planned murder (first degree) and one committed in the
heat of passion (second degree). It further recognizes that some homicides
occur without any criminal intent (manslaughter). Differences in the degree of
intent are reflected in the severity of the punishment. First-degree murder carries a potential death sentence in many states.

The law has historically recognized that some people lack full criminal intent because they do not understand what they are doing. One example is the 5-year-old who picks up the loaded handgun and accidentally kills his brother. This child does not have criminal intent; he does not understand the nature and consequences of firing the gun. Another example is the truly deranged person who kills because she hears voices from another planet. Like the child, this person does not appreciate the criminal nature of her act.[25]

Unfortunately, not all cases are as simple as these examples. The legal system has struggled for 150 years to develop a formula for resolving questions about the accused's mental state. The principle of insanity first entered English law in 1843 with the famous *M'Naughton* case, which established the "right-wrong test": Did the accused understand the difference between right and wrong? Because this test is somewhat crude, legal scholars have attempted to develop alternatives, such as the "irresistible impulse" test. Laypersons are often mystified by the arcane distinctions among those alternatives, none of which resolves the basic problem created by the intersection of medical diagnoses, with their inevitable shades of gray, and the legal system, with its requirement of an absolute verdict of guilt or innocence.[26]

Attempts to abolish the insanity defense run up against the *mens rea* requirement. Suppose a state adopted a law that said "mental condition shall not be a defense to any charge of criminal conduct." This might be interpreted as abolishing the *mens rea* requirement altogether. The prosecution would not have to prove anything about the accused's mental state, only that he or she did the crime. Among other things, it would wipe out the distinction between first-degree murder, second-degree murder, and manslaughter. It is doubtful that even the most ardent opponents of the insanity defense seriously want to take this approach, which would probably be found unconstitutional. Wisconsin (1909) and Mississippi (1928) abolished the insanity defense early in this century. In both cases, the new laws were declared unconstitutional under the due process clauses of their state constitutions.[27]

A more limited interpretation of "mental condition shall not be a defense to any charge of criminal conduct" would be that an affirmative plea of not guilty by reason of insanity could not be raised. The crucial distinction here is between affirmative and ordinary defenses. An *ordinary defense* is simply an attempt to show that the prosecution has failed to connect the accused with the crime. An *affirmative defense* is that, yes, the accused did kill the victim and intended to, but he or she does not have criminal responsibility for the act (because of self-defense, duress, insanity).

What would happen if we abolished insanity as an affirmative defense? As a recent review of the literature pointed out, we have little empirical evidence on this question, because so few states (five) have actually abolished the insanity defense and also because there are so few cases.[28] Put yourself in the shoes of a defense attorney, and the answer is obvious. You would directly attack the prosecution's case on the basic *mens rea* requirement and argue that your client lacked the necessary criminal intent. You would not win every time, of course, but you might win some of the time, with the net result that your client would be fully acquitted. The people who oppose the insanity defense would find this outcome even more outrageous than our current situation. Even if you did not win, you would force the prosecution to address your client's mental state. In short, the basic issues underlying the insanity defense would reappear in a different form. There is no getting around it; the *mens rea* requirement is a bedrock principle of our legal system.

The guilty but mentally ill (GBMI) alternative has three serious flaws. First, it strikes indirectly at the *mens rea* requirement, introducing the slippery notion that the accused had partial, but not complete, criminal intent. Second, it creates a lesser and included offense that judges and juries may choose simply as a compromise verdict. They may decide that the accused probably did something wrong and deserves some punishment, but they are unwilling to bring in a verdict of guilty on the top charge. The GBMI option would allow them to split the difference and choose the lesser verdict. Finally, the GBMI verdict does not guarantee treatment for the person who has been declared mentally ill.

Prisons and jails, many of which are overcrowded, cannot handle their current inmates with mental problems. A 1998 BJS survey found that 16 percent of all prison and jail inmates were mentally ill. This represented a total of 283,800 persons. Over 80 percent of the mentally ill prison inmates had a prior criminal conviction, and the majority of those were for a violent crime.[29] Although 60 percent of the prison inmates report receiving treatment (half were taking prescription medication; 44 percent were receiving counseling), there are good reasons for questioning the long-term effectiveness of those services. In 1996, state prison systems spent an average of only about 10 percent of their budgets on all forms of health care; obviously only a small part of those expenditures involve *mental* health care.[30]

For the GBMI offenders, we can imagine the sequence of events. The convicted offender is sentenced to prison, where his behavior becomes a problem. He is then transferred to the state mental hospital for treatment. After his behavior stabilizes, he is transferred back to prison, where because of the brutal conditions his behavior again deteriorates. The cycle then repeats itself. This is not to suggest that our mental hospitals are models of effective treatment and humane custody. They are not, and much of the "treatment" is meaningless. But sending an allegedly mentally ill person to prison is an even worse solution.

The GBMI option has already proved to be a bogus reform. A 1981 Illinois law added GBMI as an additional verdict, retaining the traditional insanity defense. In Cook County (Chicago), NGRI verdicts actually increased from 34 to 103 between 1981 and 1984. At the same time, GBMI verdicts went from 16 in 1982, the first year the option was available, to 87 in 1984. This represents a "hydraulic" effect that is contrary to the law's intent. GBMI verdicts appear to have involved people who would otherwise have been found guilty, not defendants who would have been found not guilty by reason of insanity.[31]

The Illinois GBMI law also failed to provide medical treatment for GBMI defendants. An evaluation found that "not a single GBMI offender has been transferred from the Department of Corrections to the Department of Mental

Health" for treatment. The law only "complicated rather than resolved [the] fundamental issues surrounding the insanity defense."[32] A study of the GBMI verdict in another state reached similar conclusions: There was no reduction in the number of insanity pleas, jurors were more likely to be confused about the legal issues, many offenders receiving a GBMI verdict were placed on probation, and offenders had no assurance that they would receive any medical treatment.[33]

The real function of the guilty but mentally ill option is symbolic, to appease public opinion. The public has little concern for the details of what actually happens to a mentally ill criminal defendant. Basically, it wants a symbolic statement of "guilty." In practice, as Richard Moran points out, the GBMI verdict has as much meaning as "guilty but brown eyes."[34]

In sum, the various proposals to abolish or modify the insanity defense fail on two counts. Not only do they fail to reduce crime, because the insanity defense is so rare, but they create new problems for the criminal justice system. We can state unequivocally:

PROPOSITION 22

**Abolishing or limiting the insanity defense
will have no impact on serious crime.**

Richard Moran offers the best verdict on this issue: "The insanity defense has been misinterpreted and abused"—not by criminal defendants but "by politicians and journalists who mistakenly attack it as a major loophole in the law."[35] A review of attempts to revise or abolish the insanity defense over the past 20 years concluded that all of these changes have "had little effect," in large part because "there is no real evidence that it is broken."[36]

ABOLISH PLEA BARGAINING

Everyone seems to dislike plea bargaining. Conservatives believe it is a major loophole through which criminals beat the system and avoid punishment. Liberals, meanwhile, believe that it is the source of grave injustices: Prosecutors deliberately "overcharge"; defense attorneys make deals rather than fight for their clients; defendants are coerced into waiving their right to a trial; some defendants get much better deals than others.[37]

In many instances, the process of plea bargaining makes a mockery of justice. In court the judge goes through the charade of asking the defendant whether any promises have been made in return for the guilty plea, and the defendant answers no. But, of course, a deal has been made.[38]

For a few years in the 1970s, calls were made for abolishing plea bargaining. Public outrage reached its peak in 1973, when Vice President Spiro Agnew, in perhaps the most famous plea bargain of all time, avoided going to prison on extortion charges by pleading no contest to a lesser charge. In 1973

the National Advisory Commission on Criminal Justice Standards and Goals recommended that plea bargaining be abolished within five years.[39]

Plea bargaining, of course, continues to survive. In 1996, 91 percent of all felony cases in state courts were settled by a guilty plea.[40] When we take a closer look at plea bargaining, including some of the attempts to abolish it, we can understand why.

Alaska Bans Plea Bargaining

The most ambitious attempt to abolish plea bargaining occurred in Alaska, when Attorney General Avrum Gross abolished plea bargaining in the entire state.[41] On July 3, 1975, he issued a memorandum that read, in part, as follows:

> I wish to have the following policy implemented with respect to all adult criminal offenses in which charges have been filed on or after August 15, 1975:
>
> (1) District Attorneys and Assistant District Attorneys will refrain from engaging in plea negotiations with defendants designed to arrive at an agreement for entry of a plea of guilty in return for a particular sentence. . . . (4) . . . While there continues to be nothing wrong with reducing a charge, reductions should not occur simply to obtain a plea of guilty. (5) Like any general rule, there are going to be some exceptions to this policy [which must be approved by the attorney general's office].

The new policy attacked plea bargaining in three ways: abolishing "sentence bargaining," abolishing "charge bargaining," and establishing procedures for supervising plea negotiations. Gross's action was possible in part because of the structure of Alaska's criminal justice system. Local prosecutors are appointed by and work under the supervision of the state attorney general. In other states, local prosecutors are elected and enjoy almost complete political and administrative independence.

What happened when Alaska banned plea bargaining? Contrary to popular expectations, the criminal courts did not collapse. The traditional defense of plea bargaining is that it is necessary to handle the heavy load of cases and that the courts would grind to a halt if it were abolished. The Alaska courts, however, continued to function pretty much as they had before with little change in the rate of guilty pleas. Trials increased, from 6.7 to 9.6 percent of all cases. True, this is about a 50 percent increase, but the total remains less than 10 percent of all cases.[42]

Other dire predictions also did not come true in Alaska. Many experts argue that discretion cannot be eliminated and that attempts to abolish it only serve to move it to other parts of the justice system. Restricting a prosecutor's discretion to accept guilty pleas, according to this argument, will shift discretion "upstream" to police officers or "downstream" to judges.[43] Specifically, some experts believe that banning plea bargaining will give judges more discretion and lead to more sentence bargaining.

No radical shift in discretion occurred as a result of the ban in Alaska. One way to measure this effect is to examine the pattern of rejections and dismissals of cases. Some experts believe if a prosecutor cannot settle cases by accepting pleas to lesser offenses, more cases will be dismissed altogether. The rate of dismissals in Alaska, however, remained consistently high— about 52 percent before and after the ban. Dismissals in drug possession and morals cases increased, but this seemed to be a function of the low priority prosecutors gave these cases rather than anything related to the ban on plea bargaining.[44]

One surprising result of the ban was that cases were processed faster than before. This was contrary to the expectation that there would be more delay because of more trials and a greater backlog of cases. In Anchorage, the mean disposition time for felony cases dropped from 192.1 months to 89.5 months. Case processing time also dropped in Fairbanks and Juneau. This unexpected effect has an obvious explanation. Restrictions on plea bargaining eliminate certain alternatives. With less to negotiate, the prosecutor and defense attorney reach agreements more quickly.[45]

The ban on plea bargaining had no apparent impact on cases involving defendants charged with serious crimes or those with substantial criminal records. An evaluation concluded that "the conviction and sentencing of persons charged with serious crimes of violence such as murder, rape, robbery, and felonious assault appeared completely unaffected by the change in policy."[46] Dangerous offenders had not been beating the system beforehand through plea bargaining (any more than they had in San Diego), and the ban did not make the system either weaker or tougher than before.

The ban did have an unexpected effect on the disposition of less serious cases, producing more severe sentences. A similar effect has been found in other reforms, called the *trickle-up* or *hydraulic* effect. Our wedding cake model helps explain this process. Policies directed toward second-layer cases actually have their greatest impact on third-layer cases. Under normal circumstances, third-layer cases—low-level assaults or burglaries where little of value is stolen —are often settled with pleas to even lesser offenses and sentences of proba- tion. A "get tough" policy, such as a ban on plea bargaining however, closes off this avenue of mitigation and produces both convictions on more serious charges and harsher sentences than would normally be the case. This process is characterized as a hydraulic effect because it lifts third-layer cases into the sec- ond layer. The problem, of course, is that these third-layer cases were not the original target of the policy change, and there is no impact on serious crime.

From the standpoint of our inquiry, the important question is whether the Alaska ban on plea bargaining affected the crime rate. The evaluation did not examine this issue. Nonetheless, the mere fact that the ban had no real effect on the disposition of cases involving serious crimes suggests that it probably had no impact on the crime rate.

Other Experiments

Other attempts to ban plea bargaining have focused on specific crimes. When Michigan enacted a law mandating prison terms for people convicted of gun- related crimes ("one with a gun gets you two"), the Wayne County (Detroit) prosecutor supplemented it with a ban on plea bargaining. They would no longer drop gun-related charges in return for a guilty plea. This seemed to be an important step, because many people believe that weapons charges are fre- quently dropped in return for a plea to a nongun charge (for example, from armed robbery to simple robbery) as a way of avoiding a prison sentence. Some people believe that these "mandatory" sentencing laws are evaded.[47]

An evaluation of the Michigan law found no significant change in the minimum sentences for homicide and armed robbery cases. The going rate for armed robbery was about six years in prison both before and after the law's passage. In other words, Wayne County prosecutors had not been lenient in plea bargaining with defendants charged with robbery beforehand. Once again, there was no loophole to be closed.

The Michigan policy had a trickle-up or hydraulic effect, however. Persons charged with aggravated assault began to receive higher minimum sentences. Prosecutors had previously treated aggravated assaults as third-layer cases, accepting pleas to lesser charges. The new law closed off this avenue and (as in Alaska) produced convictions on higher charges and longer sentences.

In Search of Plea Bargains

Plea bargaining has proven to be a phantom loophole. Despite the criticisms, it is not a device by which large numbers of serious offenders are beating the system. Attempts to abolish it either have no effect whatsoever or produce changes that are contrary to the intended result.

BOX 8-1   The War on Drugs and Plea Bargaining

In 1999, a major scandal erupted in Los Angeles involving allegations that LAPD officers had framed numerous citizens on alleged drug offenses. Prosecutors immediately recommended the release of dozens of convicted offenders because of police misconduct and began reviewing thousands of drug convictions.

The scandal exposed the fact that many innocent individuals pled guilty to crimes they did not commit. Why? One possible answer is the war on drugs.

One of the framed offenders faced a choice of pleading guilty to a lesser offense and serving eight years in prison or going to trial and, with a third felony conviction, being sentenced to life in prison. And as he and other defendants realized, neither judges nor jury members would take their word against the word of a police officer—even though the officer in this one case was blatantly lying.[51]

In a classic example of criminal justice thermodynamics, the harsh new sentencing laws upset the old going rate and give police and prosecutors enormous leverage in plea negotiations. The result is a gross distortion of the normal plea bargaining process.

Our discussion of the criminal justice wedding cake (Chapter 2) and the role of the courtroom work group (Chapter 3) helps explain why plea bargaining survives. As Malcolm Feeley suggests, we should think of the criminal courts as supermarkets, handling a high volume of business with fixed prices.[48] Once the work group reaches a consensus about the proper "going rate" for different kinds of cases, not much actual bargaining is necessary.

Virtually all of the studies of plea bargaining have found a high degree of regularity and predictability in the disposition of cases. One of the most systematic studies concluded that you can predict the outcome if you know the seriousness of the top charge and the defendant's prior record.[49] Courtroom work groups have accommodated themselves to sentencing guideline laws. Many observers have feared that by restricting the discretion of judges these laws would radically shift power to prosecutors and result in more charge bargaining and/or more trials. Studies of the impact of sentencing guideline jurisdictions, however, have found that most courtroom work groups conduct their business pretty much as before, with relative little change.[50] This is but another example of both the enduring strength of routine plea bargaining practices and the power of the courtroom work group to accommodate major change.

In short, plea bargaining is not a loophole that lets lots of offenders beat the system. Therefore, we can safely conclude:

PROPOSITION 23
Abolishing plea bargaining will not reduce serious crime.

RESTRICT APPEALS

Conservatives believe that postconviction appeals undermine the criminal justice system in several ways. First, some offenders win and thereby escape punishment altogether. Second, appeals delay final resolution of a case and undermine the deterrent effect of the law. Deterrence theorists argue that punishment needs to be swift and certain for the deterrent effect to work. Third, appeals transform the criminal process into a "sporting contest," a game rather than a search for truth. Liberals, on the other hand, see the absence of finality as a virtue. Protection of individual rights requires recognition of the possibility of error in the criminal justice process.[52]

Years ago, Judge Macklin Fleming argued that our obsession with postconviction appeals represented a quixotic search for "perfect justice." He listed twenty-six possible challenges available in California on search-and-seizure grounds alone, including moving for dismissal of all charges at the preliminary examination; appealing a denial of that motion to the state supreme court; moving to have the case transferred to federal court on grounds that federal civil rights had been violated; objecting to admission of the evidence at trial; if convicted, appealing for postconviction relief in the state supreme court; and if that failed, appealing the conviction in federal court.

Nor is this all. Fleming points out that "in almost every one of the foregoing steps the losing defendant can petition for a rehearing or reconsideration by the particular court that ruled against him."[53] Thus, innumerable potential challenges to a criminal charge can be made just on Fourth Amendment search-and-seizure issues. If these fail, many postconviction appeals are possible—for example, on grounds of inadequate assistance of counsel in violation of the Sixth Amendment. For the imaginative and determined offender, the possibilities are seemingly endless.[54] As we shall see, however, the key word here is *seemingly*.

Limiting Appeals

Conservatives believe that limiting appeals will close a loophole that undermines the criminal justice system. The 1981 Attorney General's Task Force on Violent Crime recommended a three-year statute of limitations on habeas corpus petitions and a prohibition on federal courts' holding evidentiary hearings "on facts which were fully expounded and found in the state court proceeding."[55]

Habeas corpus is one of the cornerstones of Anglo-American law. The British Parliament formalized it with the Habeas Corpus Act of 1679, and Americans wrote it into the U.S. Constitution. Article III, Section 9, of the Constitution reads, "The privilege of the writ of habeas corpus shall not be suspended, unless when in case of rebellion or invasion the public safety may require it." The writ of habeas corpus is a device to challenge the detention of a person taken into custody. A person under arrest or in prison may demand an evidentiary hearing before a judge to examine the legality of the detention.

The writ of habeas corpus is purely procedural: It guarantees only a right to a hearing and says nothing about the substance of the issues in the case.

The Supreme Court greatly expanded the ability of an offender convicted in a state court to obtain a rehearing in federal court in the 1963 decision *Fay v. Noia*. One of the underlying issues here is the role of the Supreme Court in a federal system. Conservatives have long argued that the Court, particularly under Chief Justice Earl Warren, intruded into matters that should be left to the states and to legislatures. Liberals, on the other hand, saw the Court as the principal guardian of individual rights.

Appeals in Practice

In actual practice, appeals play a very minor role in the administration of criminal justice. A national study of 10,000 habeas corpus petitions filed in federal district courts by offenders challenging their convictions found that only 1 percent succeeded. Federal judges dismissed 63 percent (usually for failing to exhaust state remedies) and ruled against the offender on the merits of the case in 35 percent. The typical habeas corpus petition was filed by someone convicted of a violent offense (23 percent had been convicted of murder) and sentenced to a long prison term. The most frequent claim raised was ineffective assistance of counsel.[56]

How many convicted offenders "abuse" the right to appeal? The study found a rate of fourteen habeas corpus petitions for every 1,000 prisoners—or only 1.4 percent of all imprisoned offenders. This figure confirms what we have already learned: that most convictions are obtained through plea bargains in which the facts of the case are not seriously contested. The study also found that the impact of habeas corpus petitions on the workload of the courts has been greatly exaggerated. These appeals represented only 4 percent of the civil case filings in U.S. District Courts.

In short, Macklin Fleming's nightmare vision of convicted offenders endlessly filing appeals on all of the theoretically possible issues is pure fantasy. Appeal of felony convictions through habeas corpus petitions is very much like the insanity defense: a procedure that is rarely used and even more rarely successful. There are two exceptions to this rule. People on death row do exhaust every possible appeal, and many appeals drag on for as long as fifteen years, or even longer. The fact is that mistakes do occur with the death penalty. In early 2000, the governor of Illinois ordered a halt to all executions in the state because 13 people sentenced to die had their convictions overturned—as many as had actually been executed since the death penalty was restored in that state. The possibility that innocent people might be wrongfully executed dramatizes the importance of keeping open all possible avenues of appeal.

A second exception involves the so-called "writ writers," prisoners who file innumerable appeals in federal court challenging their conviction or prison conditions. These individuals represent a tiny proportion of all inmates. Few succeed in winning their release, and those that ever do make a negligible contribution to the crime rate, even in the worst circumstances.

The available facts about the use of appeals do not support the conservative argument that multiple appeals contribute to crime. Conservatives argue that appeals delay "finality" and thereby undermine the deterrent effect of the criminal process. Several things are wrong with this argument. First, appeals are filed in so few cases that they cannot have any broad impact on criminal justice. Second, as we have also learned, many factors affect the deterrent effect (low probability of arrest, a relatively high probability of the charges being rejected or dismissed, whether the threat of punishment even works for certain categories of offenders, and so forth). Appeals are at best a very minor factor.

Like the insanity defense, postconviction appeals are mainly a *symbolic* issue. On occasion, a convicted offender is released through a successful appeal. But these are the few celebrated cases that do not represent the general pattern in the criminal justice system. Therefore, our proposition is:

> ## PROPOSITION 24
> Limiting habeas corpus appeals of criminal convictions
> will have no effect on serious crime.

CONCLUSION

We will not reduce serious crime by trying to close alleged loopholes in the criminal justice system. The reason for this is simple: Those loopholes do not exist. The idea that thousands of criminals beat the system through the insanity defense, or plea bargaining, or some other loophole is a perception based in a very small number of unrepresentative celebrated cases. The justice system is actually fairly harsh in dealing with those serious offenders who are arrested.

NOTES

1. U.S. Department of Justice, *An Exemplary Project: Major Violator Unit—San Diego, California* (Washington, DC: Government Printing Office, 1980).

2. Some examples are described in William F. McDonald, *Plea Bargaining: Critical Issues and Current Practices* (Washington, DC: Government Printing Office, 1985).

3. McDonald, *Plea Bargaining.*

4. Bureau of Justice Statistics, *Felony Sentences in State Courts, 1996* (Washington, DC: Government Printing Office, 1999), table 2.

5. Eleanor Chelimsky and Judith S. Dahmann, *National Evaluation of the Career Criminal Program: Final Report* (McLean, VA: MITRE, 1979).

6. Allan F. Abrahamse, Patricia A. Ebener, Peter W. Greenwood, Nora Fitzgerald,

and Thomas E. Kosin, "An Experimental Evaluation of the Phoenix Repeat Offender Program," *Justice Quarterly* 8 (June 1991): 141–68.

7. Michael R. Gottfredson and Don M. Gottfredson, *Decision Making in Criminal Justice: Toward the Rational Exercise of Discretion,* 2nd ed. (New York: Plenum, 1988).

8. Jack Hinckley, *Breaking Points* (Grand Rapids, MI: Chosen Books, 1985).

9. Randy Borum and Solomon M. Fulero, "Empirical Research on the Insanity Defense and Attempted Reforms: Evidence Toward Informed Policy," *Law and Human Behavior,* 23.1 (1999): 117–35.

10. Reported in Rita J. Simon and David E. Aaronson, *The Insanity Defense: A Critical Assessment of Law and Policy in the Post-Hinckley Era* (New York: Praeger, 1988), p. 166.

11. Simon and Aaronson, *Insanity Defense,* table 3.2, p. 40.

12. Borum and Fulero, "Empirical Research on the Insanity Defense," p. 120.

13. Borum and Fulero, "Empirical Research on the Insanity Defense," pp. 27–28.

14. American Psychiatric Association, *American Journal of Psychiatry* 140 (1983): 681–88.

15. Valerie Hans, "An Analysis of Public Attitudes toward the Insanity Defense," *Criminology* 24 (May 1986): 393–414.

16. Jeffrey S. Janofsky, Mitchell H. Dunn, Erik J. Ruskes, "Insanity Defense Pleas in Baltimore, County: An Analysis of Outcome," *American Journal of Psychiatry,* 153.11 (1996): 1464–468.

17. *Newsweek,* 24 May 1982.

18. For a good study of this subject, see Egon Bittner, "Police on Skid Row: A Study in Peacekeeping," *American Sociological Review* 32 (October 1967): 694–715.

19. *Baxstrom v. Herold,* 383 U.S. 107 (1966).

20. Steadman et al., *Before and After Hinckley* (New York: Guilford, 1993), pp. 58–61, 97–99.

21. Henry J. Steadman, *Beating a Rap? Defendants Found Incompetent to Stand Trial*

(Chicago: University of Chicago Press, 1979), p. 104.

22. Terence P. Thornberry and Joseph E. Jacoby, *The Criminally Insane: A Community Follow-up of Mentally Ill Offenders* (Chicago: University of Chicago Press, 1979). For another study with similar results, see Henry J. Steadman and James J. Cacozza, *Careers of the Criminally Insane* (Lexington, MA: Lexington Books, 1974).

23. Borum and Fulero, "Empirical Research on the Insanity Defense," p. 121.

24. Norval Morris, *Madness and the Criminal Law* (Chicago: University of Chicago Press, 1982).

25. Morris, *Madness and the Criminal Law.*

26. Morris, *Madness and the Criminal Law.*

27. Grant H. Morris, *The Insanity Defense: A Blueprint for Legislative Change* (Lexington, MA: Lexington Books, 1974).

28. Borum and Fulero, "Empirical Research on the Insanity Defense," p. 129.

29. Bureau of Justice Statistics, *Mental Health and Treatment of Inmates and Probationers* (Washington, DC: Government Printing Office, 1999).

30. Bureau of Justice Statistics, *Sourcebook of Criminal Justice Statistics, 1997* (Washington, DC: Government Printing Office, 1998), p. 13.

31. John Klofus and Ralph Weisheit, "Guilty but Mentally Ill: Reform of the Insanity Defense in Illinois," *Justice Quarterly* 4 (March 1987): 39–50.

32. Klofus Weisheit, "Guilty but Mentally Ill."

33. Kurt M. Bumby, "Reviewing the Guilty but Mentally Ill Alternative: A Case of the Blind 'Pleading' the Blind," *Journal of Psychiatry and the Law* 21.2 (1993): 191–220.

34. Moran, "Insanity Defense," p. 81.

35. Moran, "Insanity Defense, pp. 77–78.

36. Borum and Fulero, "Empirical Research on the Insanity Defense," p. 133.

37. The most critical view of plea bargaining is Abraham Blumberg, *Criminal Justice: Issues and Ironies,* 2nd ed. (New York: New Viewpoints, 1979). The best recent study is McDonald, *Plea Bargaining.*

38. On the "copout" ceremony, see Jonathan D. Casper, *American Criminal Justice: The Defendant's Perspective* (Englewood Cliffs, NJ: Prentice Hall, 1972), pp. 81–86.

39. National Advisory Commission on Criminal Justice Standards and Goals, *Courts* (Washington, DC: Government Printing Office, 1973), p. 46.

40. Bureau of Justice Statistics, *Felony Sentences in State Courts, 1996* (Washington, DC: Government Printing Office, 1999), p. 5.

41. Michael L. Rubinstein, Stevens H. Clarke, and Teresa J. White, *Alaska Bans Plea Bargaining* (Washington, DC: Government Printing Office, 1980).

42. Rubinstein et al., *Alaska Bans Plea Bargaining.*

43. Norval Morris and Gordon Hawkins, *Letter to the President on Crime Control* (Chicago: University of Chicago Press, 1977), p. 61.

44. Rubinstein et al., *Alaska Bans Plea Bargaining.*

45. This point is argued in Samuel Walker, *Taming the System: The Control of Discretion in Criminal Justice, 1950–1990* (New York: Oxford University Press, 1993), pp. 95–96.

46. Rubinstein et al., *Alaska Bans Plea Bargaining,* viii.

47. Colin Loftin and David McDowall, "One with a Gun Gets You Two: Mandatory Sentences and Firearms Violence in Detroit," *Annals of the American Academy of Political and Social Science* 455 (May 1981): 150–67.

48. Malcolm W. Feeley, "Perspectives on Plea Bargaining," *Law and Society Review* 13 (Winter 1979): 199.

49. Peter F. Nardulli, James Eisenstein, and Roy B. Flemming, *The Tenor of Justice: Criminal Courts and the Guilty Plea Process* (Urbana: University of Illinois, 1988).

50. Bureau of Justice Assistance, *National Assessment of Structured Sentencing* (Washington, DC: Government Printing Office, 1996), pp. 98–100. Jeffrey T. Ulmer, *Social Worlds of Sentencing* (Albany: State University of New York Press, 1997).

51. "Scandal Shows Why Innocent Plead Guilty," *Los Angeles Times,* 31 December 1999.

52. Herbert Packer, "Two Models of the Criminal Process," in Packer, *The Limits of the Criminal Sanction* (Stanford, CA: Stanford University Press, 1968), pp. 149–73.

53. Macklin Fleming, *The Price of Perfect Justice* (New York: Basic Books, 1974).

54. Fleming, *Price of Perfect Justice.*

55. U.S. Department of Justice, *Attorney General's Task Force on Violent Crime* (Washington, DC: Government Printing Office, 1981), p. 58.

56. Bureau of Justice Statistics, *Federal Habeas Corpus Review: Challenging State Court Criminal Convictions* (Washington, DC: Government Printing Office, 1995). See also Victor E. Flango, *Habeas Corpus in State and Federal Courts* (Williamsburg, VA: National Center for State Courts, 1994).

PART III

The Middle Ground:
Guns and Victims

On one thing, conservatives and liberals agree: Guns are a major part of the crime problem. They disagree, however, on the exact nature of the problem and the solution to it. Liberals focus on guns and want to limit their availability. Conservatives focus on criminals who use guns and want to get tough with them. The policies each side recommends reflect their fundamentally different assumptions about crime and criminals. There is also a certain amount of agreement with respect to crime victims. Both sides support certain programs designed to assist victims. In this section we will examine policies directed toward the victims of crime, guns, and gun-related violence.

9

❖

Protect Crime Victims

I n late 1999, the Judiciary Committee of the U.S. Senate passed and sent to the full Senate an amendment to the U.S. Constitution to protect the rights of crime victims. The proposed amendment would guarantee a victim the right to court-ordered financial restitution from offenders; the right to be notified of and not be excluded from any court proceeding related to his or her crime, the right to submit a statement related to any pending bail release, plea bargain, or sentence involving the offender; and other rights.[1]

The proposal for a victims' rights amendment represents the culmination of a thirty-year movement on behalf of crime victims. The movement emerged in the 1970s and reached its peak in the 1980s. President Ronald Reagan declared a national Crime Victims Week, the first ever, in 1981. A year later, his President's Task Force on Victims of Crime offered 68 policy recommendations designed to help victims.[2] The 1992 Attorney General's Report on Violent Crime made six recommendations related to crime victims,[3] listed in Figure 9-1.

The fact that President Bill Clinton also endorsed a victims' rights amendment (in 1997) is significant. Victims' rights has been primarily a conservative crime policy issue. Emilio Viano, one of the leading experts in the field, points out that national concern about crime victims is largely a result of the prevalence of conservative ideology in the 1980s.[4] Clinton's position is another indication of the extent to which, on this issue as on others, liberals have now adopted much of the traditional conservative crime policy agenda.

VI. Respecting the victim in the criminal justice process

19. Provide for hearing and considering the victims' perspective at sentencing and at any early release proceedings.
20. Provide victim-witness coordinators.
21. Provide for victim restitution and for adequate compensation and assistance for victims and witnesses.
22. Adopt evidentiary rules to protect victim-witnesses from courtroom intimidation and harassment.
23. Permit victims to require HIV testing before trial of persons charged with sex offenses.
24. Notify the victim of the status of criminal justice proceedings and of the release status of the offender.

FIGURE 9-1 Recommendations related to crime victims.

SOURCE: U.S. Department of Justice, *Combating Violent Crime* (Washington, DC: Government Printing Office, 1992), xii.

THE VICTIMS' RIGHTS MOVEMENT

The crime victim was long the forgotten person in American criminal justice. In modern Anglo-American law, the crime victim has no formal role in the criminal process. The prosecutor represents the public interest, including that of the victim. This is why, in some states, cases are formally titled "The People versus. . . ." As an ACLU handbook on *The Rights of Crime Victims* explains, "The victim is not a formal party to a criminal proceeding."[5]

It was not always this way. Until the mid-nineteenth century, crime victims represented themselves, bringing their own cases before magistrates and judges. The office of the modern prosecutor gradually emerged in the nineteenth century, assuming the role of representing the public in general and crime victims in particular.[6]

Having a professional public official handle criminal cases serves two important purposes. First, it establishes the idea that a crime is an offense against society as a whole and not just an individual. Second, it removes the element of vengeance from the handling of a case. A public official is more likely to be free of anger and personal animosity toward the offender. The desire to keep emotionalism out of the criminal process explains why in two cases the U.S. Supreme Court has ruled that victim impact statements at sentencing in death penalty cases are unconstitutional.[7] (The concept of restorative justice, which we will examine in Chapter 11, represents an attempt to debureaucratize the criminal justice system and bring back some of the older informal and communal approaches to justice.)

Another reason that crime victims have had no formal role in the criminal process is that Anglo-American law places a high priority on protecting indi-

vidual rights against possible violations by the state. For this reason, the Bill of Rights includes specific protections for criminal suspects and defendants: due process of law, the right to an attorney, protection against self-incrimination, and so on.

By the 1970s, however, a new victims' rights movement emerged, arguing that the victim was neglected by the criminal justice system. The movement found fault with all parts of the system: Police and prosecutors did not inform victims about the progress of cases; victims had no say in plea bargain agreements, sentencing, or parole decisions. An early survey found that in Alameda County, California (Oakland), only about 12 percent of victims had ever been notified that an arrest had been made in their case. Also, 45 percent of those who appeared in court had not been informed of the nature of their appearance, and about 42 percent were never notified of the outcome of the case.[8] In 1982, the chair of the President's Task Force on Victims of Crime declared: "The neglect of crime victims is a national disgrace."[9]

Although conservatives have dominated the victims' rights movement, groups representing other political persuasions have also been active. Feminists demanded new laws and policies to protect the victims of domestic violence and rape. Mothers Against Drunk Driving (MADD) organized an anti–drunk driving crusade primarily to protect the victims of drunk driving (see Chapter 6). The wave of "three strikes" laws was spurred by public outrage over victims such as Polly Klass, who was murdered by a recent parolee (see Chapter 7). Even the ACLU, which vigorously opposes many victims' rights proposals as unconstitutional, published a handbook on *The Rights of Crime Victims* in 1985.[10] The United Nations, meanwhile, adopted a Declaration of Basic Principles of Justice for Victims of Crime and Abuse of Power in 1985.

The Costs of Crime

The victims' rights movement has spurred interest in estimating the total cost of crime. A 1996 Justice Department report reached an estimate of $450 billion a year (based on 1987–1990 National Crime Victim Survey [NCVS] data).[11] The study took a comprehensive view of the costs of crime and included property loss; medical care; mental health care; loss of productivity at work; and the costs of police, fire, and victim assistance services. Most controversially, it included an estimate of the intangible "quality of life" costs. This category comprised 75 percent ($345 billion) of the total costs.

New Laws and Programs

The victims' rights movement has been very successful in achieving its legislative goals. By the early 1990s, every state had passed some kind of victims' rights law, and 29 had amended their constitution to include some victims' rights. Meanwhile, a series of federal laws—the 1970 Crime Insurance Act, the 1982 Victim Witness Protection Act, the 1984 Victims of Crime Act, the 1984 Justice Assistance Act, the 1990 Victims' Rights and Restitution Act, and the 1994 Violent Crime Control Act—have been enacted.[12]

Typical of many new state laws is the 1986 North Carolina Fair Treatment for Victims and Witnesses Act. The law guarantees a victim's right to information about emergency medical assistance, protection from harm, and financial compensation; a secure area in the courthouse; the right to make a victim impact statement at sentencing; information about the final disposition of the case; and notification about the offender's release or escape.[13]

Critics of the Movement

The victims' rights movement has many critics. Civil libertarians in particular have criticized proposals to limit individual rights in the name of helping crime victims. The most sweeping criticism has been made by Robert Elias. In a series of books, Elias has argued that victims have been manipulated to serve a conservative political agenda, that most of the new victims' rights laws and policies have not provided much in the way of tangible help, and that many serious forms of victimization (workplace injuries, environmental pollution, unsafe products, false advertising, among others) have been ignored despite their enormous toll in terms of human suffering and dollar cost. As Elias sees it, the victims' rights movement has been largely an exercise in "symbolic politics" that leaves crime victims "victims still."[14]

Sorting Out the Issues

The victims' rights movement does not have a single agenda. A variety of groups has recommended many different proposals. To make sense of all these proposals, it is useful to divide them into three general categories.

Victims' services. One set of proposals involves services for crime victims. The most important are financial compensation and counseling. Women's groups have led the fight for rape and domestic violence hot lines, counseling programs, and shelters.

Victims' voice laws. A second set of proposals includes laws to enhance the role of victims in the criminal justice system, in particular to allow them to make a statement about bail setting or plea bargain agreements, or at sentencing or parole hearings.

"Get tough on crime" laws. A third set of proposals are "get tough" ideas similar to ones we have considered in other chapters. These include proposals to deny bail to dangerous offenders, close loopholes in the criminal justice system, and give longer prison sentences. They usually do not mention crime victims directly. The underlying assumption is that by getting criminals off the streets, there will be fewer crimes and crime victims.

The six recommendations of the Attorney General's Task Force on Violent Crime listed in Figure 9-1 include three in the area of victims' services, one related to victims' voices, and two designed to get tough on crime.

Criteria for Evaluation

What criteria should we use to evaluate the various crime victims' laws and policies?[15] Three different criteria are appropriate.[16]

Implementation. The first issue, of course, is whether a law or policy is in fact being implemented or is likely to be implemented. As we have learned, the courtroom work group has tremendous power to block or frustrate new policies if it upsets the established going rate. If a victims' rights law is not implemented, it will not have any impact on crime.

Impact on Crime Victims. A second issue is the impact of a crime victims' law on crime victims themselves. Does a particular law help them deal with the trauma of victimization, return to their normal lifestyle, and improve their evaluation of the criminal justice system?

Impact on the criminal justice system. A third issue is whether laws and policies designed to help crime victims have undesirable effects on the criminal justice system. Many, for example, call for radical changes in constitutional law. Even if they might reduce crime or help victims, the cost to the justice system may be too great. Remember that our goal in this book is to find policies that are effective, practical, and sound.

Crime reduction. The fourth issue is the concern of this book: Do victims' rights laws help to reduce serious crime? Some of the proposals we will examine may be sound, humane ideas that will genuinely help victims deal with their suffering. They should be supported for that reason. But the relevant question for us is whether they will reduce crime.

Table 9-1 Victim services that jurisdictions require prosecutors' offices to provide, 1994

| | Percentage of offices | | | |
| | | Full-time office (population served) | | |
Type of service	All offices	500,000 or more	Less than 500,000	Part-time office
NOTIFICATION/ALERT				
Notify victim	82	87	85	73
Notify witness	55	67	59	42
ORIENTATION/EDUCATION				
Victim restitution assistance	60	62	62	55
Victim compensation procedures	58	73	65	41
Victim impact statement assistance	55	78	60	40
Orientation to court procedures	41	57	48	24
Public education	15	20	17	9
ESCORT				
Escort victim	23	39	28	9
Escort witness	17	31	19	9
COUNSELING/ASSISTANCE				
Property return	38	46	39	35
Referral	32	46	37	18
Personal advocacy	17	26	22	5
Counseling	10	21	12	5
Crisis intervention	10	19	14	0
Number of offices	2,282	119	1,480	683

SOURCE: Bureau of Justice Statistics, *Prosecutors in State Courts, 1994* (Washington, DC: Government Printing Office, 1996), p. 9.

VICTIM ASSISTANCE PROGRAMS

Perhaps the most popular victims' rights idea has been victim–witness assistance programs. By the late 1980s an estimated 4,000 such programs existed around the country. The 1984 Victims of Crime Act provides about $50 million a year for local programs; by 1987, 1,364 programs were receiving federal funds. By 1997, one-third of all city police departments and sheriffs' departments had a special unit for victim assistance.[17]

Table 9-1 presents the range of services required by law in 2,282 prosecutors' offices in 1994. Note that the survey only asked prosecutors what services they were required to provide. It is not clear that all of these services are, in fact, provided. The survey found, for example, that some information, although required, was provided only upon the request of a victim.[18]

Victim–witness programs vary widely. Many provide emergency services in the form of shelter, security repair, financial assistance, and on-the-scene comfort. One national survey found that most provide follow-up counseling. Nearly all have some form of advocacy and support services, such as intervening with the victim's employer or landlord. Many help with insurance claims or efforts to obtain restitution. Nearly all provide court-related services concerned with the victim's role as witness for the prosecution, such as orienting victims or witnesses to court procedures, notifying them of court dates, giving transportation to court, escorting them at the court, and providing child care.

How well do these programs work? A survey of 62 victim service programs in North Carolina found that the state's 1986 Fair Treatment for Victims and Witnesses Act was meeting the needs of victims "only minimally."[19] Almost all of the programs were providing referral to social, restitution, and compensation services; notification about court cases; and allowances for victim impact statements. Nonetheless, 59 percent of crime victims surveyed in the state expressed dissatisfaction with the criminal justice system. Particularly significant was the fact that about one-third were not even aware of their right to make a victim impact statement. This suggests that a major provision of the law was not being fully implemented. An evaluation concluded that the programs primarily provided *witness* assistance rather than crime *victim* assistance.

A national evaluation of victims' rights laws found that in many cases the laws are not fully implemented. Even in states with "strong" victims' rights laws, for example, 60 percent of victims were not given advance notice about offenders' pretrial release hearings, as required by law. Over 90 percent received notification about the arrest and trial date of the offender in these states, but compliance was much lower for all other stages in the criminal process.[20]

What about the impact of victim-witness services on crime? Because most victim assistance programs operate after the crime has occurred, we have little reason to assume that they will reduce crime. We should not ignore one possible exception to this rule. Shelters for the victims of domestic violence may in fact protect women from immediate violence. This aspect of shelters has not been evaluated, however.

Even if they prove effective, shelters have no relationship to the crimes of robbery and burglary, which are the focus of this book. This leads us to the following proposition:

PROPOSITION 25
With the possible exception of domestic violence shelters, social service programs for crime victims will not reduce serious crime.

Police-Victim Recontact

A variation on the theme of victim services is to provide more contact between the police and crime victims. The President's Task Force on Victims of Crime recommended that police departments establish procedures for informing victims of violent crime about the status of the investigation of crimes.[21] Known as victim recontact programs, they are designed to overcome the problem of victims feeling alienated from the system because they never hear from the police.

Victim recontact is a sound and humane idea that is probably long overdue. There is absolutely no reason that the police should not keep victims informed and many reasons that they should. Mainly it would help build positive police-community relations. By 1997, about one-third of all city police departments and county sheriffs' departments had some kind of victim assistance program.[22] Meanwhile, almost all state prosecutors (93 percent) reported in 1990 that they informed victims of the outcome of cases. This compares with only 35 percent in 1974.[23]

Victim recontact may not deliver what its advocates expect, however. In one component of the Houston "fear reduction" experiment, police officers contacted crime victims to express sympathy and ask whether they needed any further assistance or information. An evaluation found that the program achieved none of its goals. Victims who were contacted did not express any less fear of crime or greater confidence in the police, compared with victims who were not contacted. Victims with poor English skills were actually more fearful than those who were not recontacted. They did not understand why the police were contacting them and became more fearful as a result.[24]

The Houston data suggest that perhaps victims' rights advocates have misinterpreted the victims' alienation from the criminal justice system. Many people may prefer just to be left alone. We should remember that according to NCVS, victims do not report 61 percent of all crimes. Many regard the crime as a private matter or say that it just was not important enough. In other words, even though something bad has happened to them, these people do not want any involvement with the criminal justice system.[25]

Most important, as far as we are concerned, victim recontact is not going to reduce crime. This leads us to another proposition:

PROPOSITION 26
Victim recontact programs will not reduce crime.

Victim Compensation

The most popular victims' rights program involves financial compensation. California passed the first crime victims' compensation law in 1965. By the 1980s, 44 states and the District of Columbia had similar laws. The 1984 Victims of Crime Act provides federal financial support for state and local programs.

Victim compensation can be seen as a government-supported insurance program, providing funds to help people recover from their losses. (The 1970 Crime Insurance Act was passed to provide insurance for businesses and individuals in high-crime areas who could not get coverage through private insurance companies.)[26] These losses include medical bills, lost wages, and other expenses. The Justice Department estimates that medical costs of crime are $18 billion a year.[27] State programs typically provide between $10,000 and $25,000, although at least two have no upper limit. Many programs limit compensation to victims of particular crimes, and virtually all have time limits on when people must file claims as well as procedures for documenting actual losses.

The national evaluation of victims' rights laws found, paradoxically, that victims in states with "strong" laws were less likely to have the judge order restitution than victims in states with "weak" laws. Moreover, when judges did order restitution, only 37 percent of the victims in "strong" law states actually received it.[28]

Evaluations of victim compensation programs have not been overly favorable. Many requests are denied. The New York State Crime Victims Board denied as many as 60 percent of all requests in the late 1980s. The most common reason for denying claims is the failure to provide sufficient documentation.[29] Even more disturbing, according to William Doerner's study of Florida crime victims, those who did receive compensation did not have more favorable attitudes toward the criminal justice system than did victims whose claims were denied.[30] This failure to affect the attitudes of crime victims is one of the reasons that Robert Elias feels that the victims' rights movement is largely an exercise in symbolic politics.[31]

Despite these problems, victim compensation is a worthy idea that is long overdue. The heavy toll that crime takes on people gives the government good reason to maintain some kind of insurance or compensation program. Yet we have no reason to believe that compensation will reduce crime in any way.

PROPOSITION 27

Victim compensation programs may help crime victims, but they will not reduce serious crime.

EXPANDING THE VICTIM'S VOICE

One of the major goals of the victims' rights movement has been to expand the role of victims in the criminal process, giving them a greater voice in bail decisions, plea bargains, sentencing, and parole release decisions. The President's Task Force on Victims of Crime recommended amending the Sixth Amendment to read: "Likewise, the victim in every criminal prosecution shall have the right to be present and to be heard at all critical stages of judicial proceedings."[32] The 1999 proposed constitutional amendment embodies the same idea.

The idea of expanding victims' voices has two goals. One is to give crime victims a feeling of participating in the justice system and to end their feelings of isolation and alienation. We should see this as a victim service program. The other goal is ensure that offenders are properly punished and not allowed to get off too easily. The assumption is that the victim will object to a too lenient plea bargain or sentence. We should regard this as a "get tough" program.

Several states have enacted victims' voice laws. Proposition 8, adopted by California voters in 1982, provided that "the victim of any crime, or the next of kin of the victim . . . has the right to attend all sentencing proceedings . . . [and] to reasonably express his or her views concerning the crime, the person responsible, and the need for restitution."[33] The judge is required to take the victim's views into account in imposing sentence.

Opponents of victims' voice laws fear that it brings vengeance (as opposed to justice) into the criminal process. One of the functions of a professional criminal justice bureaucracy is to ensure fair and impartial treatment of all accused persons. A professional is someone who is not emotionally involved in a case and acts impersonally on the basis of the facts and circumstances. A lawyer, for example, has a professional obligation to prosecute or defend a criminal defendant regardless of his or her personal feelings about the person or what he is accused of doing.

The Supreme Court has shared some of these fears about the danger of vengeance and emotionalism distorting the criminal process. In *Booth v. Maryland* (1987) and *South Carolina v. Gathers* (1989), the Court reversed death sentences because of statements read to the jury about the victim. In *Gathers,* for example, the prosecutor read from religious material that had been in the possession of a murder victim and also mentioned that he was a registered voter.[34] The Court ruled that this information was not related to the circumstances of the crime. Two years later, however, in *Payne v. Tennessee* (1991), the Court ruled that victim impact statements were not unconstitutional.[35]

The Impact of Victims' Voice Laws

There is very mixed evidence about the impact of victims' voice laws. On the one hand, many victims do not take advantage of the opportunities to participate in the process. Also, those who do are not always seeking severe punishment. Nonetheless, some evidence exists of harsher punishment for offenders in cases in which victims do in fact participate.

A recent national study found that among those victims who were notified about hearings (and many were not, as we have seen), over 90 percent chose to make an impact statement at sentencing. Active participation was much lower for other stages in the criminal process, however. Less than 40 percent of those who were notified made a statement at bail hearings. And less than 20 percent chose to attend parole hearings.[36]

Does victim participation make a difference in the outcome? A study of 500 Ohio felony cases between June 1985 and January 1989 found several notable effects. First, victim impact statements (VISs) were submitted in about half (55 percent) of all cases. Under the program, VIS staff solicited information from victims at the time of grand jury hearings. Only 18 percent of victims appeared at trial or sentencing, and only 6 percent exercised their right to speak. Victim participation was heavily influenced by the seriousness of the crime. VISs were filed in 73 percent of "aggravated or special felony" cases, including 81 percent of sexual offenses, but only 49 percent of property crime cases, and only 13 percent of those that were handled as misdemeanors. Somewhat surprisingly, 61 percent of male victims filed a VIS, compared with only 28 percent of females.[37]

Of those who did submit a VIS, 60 percent requested that the offender be incarcerated. Convicted offenders were somewhat more likely to be incarcerated if a VIS was filed or if the victim appeared in court or requested incarceration (but, surprisingly, not if the victim only spoke in court). Also, filing a VIS statement, appearing in court, and requesting incarceration were associated with longer prison terms. The overall impact of the VIS law was somewhat limited, however. Case outcomes were primarily affected by offense severity and offenders' prior record.[38]

An earlier study of sexual assault cases in Ohio found that 60 percent of the victims made statements at sentencing. This study concluded that the statements had little effect on sentencing. A high level of agreement was noted between the sentence the victim recommended and the sentence the judge considered appropriate.[39]

A study of parole hearings in Pennsylvania, however, found that victim impact statements had a very significant effect on the chances of an offender being paroled. The Pennsylvania Board of Probation and Parole denied parole in 43 percent of 100 cases in which there was some victim input but in only 7 percent of a comparable set of 100 cases in which there was no input.[40] These findings lend support to concerns about the possible undesirable effects of victim impact statements. Whether a victim makes a statement may be a matter of chance, and it means that one offender will serve longer than another who committed the same crime because of an arbitrary factor unrelated to the crimes they committed.

In any event, apart from the satisfaction VISs may give to the victims themselves, no evidence indicates that they have any effect on serious crime. Some offenders may serve longer prison terms, but, as we have already seen, there is no evidence that they are any less likely to eventually recidivate.

PROPOSITION 28
Victim impact statements will not reduce crime.

SPEEDY TRIAL

Holding speedy trials is another popular victims' rights proposal. The underlying assumption appears to be that justice delayed is justice denied for the victim as well as the defendant. The irony is that the speedy trial has traditionally been seen as a defendants' rights issue, since the Sixth Amendment guarantees a speedy trial for the accused.

Congress passed a federal speedy trial law in 1974 and 18 states have followed suit. As we have already learned, however (Chapter 7), these laws have not worked as intended. Courtroom work groups frequently subvert the laws, often because attorneys on both sides have reasons for wanting to delay the case.[41] In short, it is not true that everyone wants a speedy trial or that holding a speedy trial is in the best interest of crime victims.

As we pointed out in Chapter 7, however, speedier trials might help reduce crime. Most of the crimes committed by persons out on bail occur after the sixtieth day of release.[42] Speedy trials, particularly for robbers, might reduce the number of these crimes. We should not expect too much crime reduction here, however. As we have also learned, crimes committed by persons out on bail are a small proportion of the total.

GETTING TOUGH ON CRIME

Many victims' rights proposals are essentially designed to "get tough on crime." The President's Task Force on Victims of Crime, for example, recommended legislation "to abolish the exclusionary rule," "to abolish parole," to permit hearsay evidence at preliminary hearings, and to authorize preventive detention.[43] Few of these proposals address crime victims directly. The underlying assumption is that locking up more offenders will reduce crime and therefore result in fewer crime victims.

We have considered many of these proposals in other chapters. Our conclusion has been that they will not reduce serious crime. In Chapter 5, we found that repealing the exclusionary rule or the *Miranda* warning will not reduce crime. In Chapter 7, we found that limiting the right to bail through preventive detention is not likely to reduce violent crime. In Chapter 11, we will examine whether abolishing parole would have any effect on crime.

Modifying the exclusionary rule may in fact backfire on victims. California's Proposition 8 attacked the exclusionary rule with a "truth-in-evidence" section permitting introduction of "all relevant evidence." This provision was designed to close an alleged loophole and tip the balance in favor of the prosecution. Within weeks of the proposition's enactment, it was clear that the truth-in-evidence clause might benefit suspects more than victims. The term "all relevant evidence" covers a lot of territory. It could include questions about a rape victim's background and character, allowing the defense to raise doubts about the victim's innocence. Although Proposition 8 specifically excludes the admission of evidence concerning a rape victim's past sexual activity, other evidence about her lifestyle is admissible. One defense attorney obtained an acquittal by introducing evidence concerning the victim's "colorful" background. The result has undermined years of progress toward the elimination of questioning about the past sexual conduct of rape victims.[44]

Equally dangerous is the President's Task Force recommendation that hearsay evidence should be admissible at preliminary hearings. The idea is that this will protect the victim from the trauma of testifying in person. Relaxing the established rules of evidence to permit hearsay testimony at any stage in the criminal process sets a dangerous precedent. Allowing it only at preliminary hearings, moreover, is silly and misleading. It will be little help in convicting the offender if it is inadmissible at trial. This leads us to the following conclusion:

PROPOSITION 29

Policies intended to get tough on crime will not reduce crime, not help crime victims, and may instead damage the criminal justice system.

Mandatory Arrest for Domestic Violence

Mandatory arrest for domestic violence is designed to protect female victims of crime. Feminists argued that police failure to arrest men for domestic assault leaves women at risk of being attacked again. Women's groups successfully sued police departments over their failure to arrest, charging denial of equal protection of the law. One of the major results of this movement has been the development of mandatory arrest policies. By 1997, 97 percent of all city police departments have a written policy on domestic disturbances.[45] Some of these policies are "mandatory arrest," whereas others are "arrest preferred."

The first study of the impact of arrest on domestic violence, the Minneapolis Domestic Violence Experiment, concluded that arrest deterred violence over the next six months more effectively than either mediation or separation. These findings encouraged the rapid spread of mandatory arrest policies.[46] Unfortunately, subsequent studies in Charlotte, Milwaukee, Omaha, and other cities found that arrest is not any more effective in deterring violence. The Milwaukee study, in fact, found that for certain groups of offenders, arrest actually led to higher levels of repeat violence than the other alternatives.[47]

CONCLUSION

The victims' rights movement is one of the more significant developments in recent criminal justice history. Twenty years ago, there was little concern about crime victims and few programs to assist them. Today new crime victim laws and programs are found in every jurisdiction.

Some of these laws and programs are good ideas, providing valuable assistance to people who have been harmed by crime. Some have not been fully implemented, however. Some of the others are positively dangerous, undermining important constitutional principles and likely to damage the justice system. Most important for our purposes, none of the programs we have discussed is likely to have any impact on serious crime.

NOTES

1. Data on current crime victims' legislation can be found on the web site of the National Center for Victims of Crime (www.ncvc.org). A critique of an earlier proposal by President Clinton is in Bruce Shapiro, "Victims and Vengeance: Why the Victims' Rights Amendment Is a Bad Idea," *The Nation,* 10 February 1997: 11–19.

2. President's Task Force on Victims of Crime, *Final Report* (Washington, DC: Government Printing Office, 1982).

3. Office of the Attorney General, *Combatting Violent Crime: 24 Recommendations to Strengthen Criminal Justice* (Washington, DC: Government Printing Office, 1992).

4. Emilio Viano, "Victim's Rights and the Constitution: Reflections on a Bicentennial," *Crime and Delinquency* 33 (1987): 443.

5. James H. Stark and Howard Goldstein, *The Rights of Crime Victims* (New York: Bantam, 1985), p. 19.

6. Allen Steinberg, *The Transformation of Criminal Justice: Philadelphia, 1800–1880* (Chapel Hill: University of North Carolina Press, 1989).

7. *South Carolina v. Gathers,* 490 U.S. 805 (1989). *Payne v. Tennessee,* 501 U.S. 808 (1991).

8. R. Lynch, "Improving Treatment of Victims: Some Guides for Action," in William McDonald, ed., *Criminal Justice and the Victim* (Beverly Hills, CA: Sage, 1976), pp. 165–76.

9. President's Task Force on Victims of Crime, *Final Report,* vii.

10. Stark and Goldstein, *Rights of Crime Victims.*

11. Ted R. Miller, Mark A. Cohen, and Brian Wiersma, *Victim Costs and Consequences: A New Look* (Washington, DC: Government Printing Office, 1996), p. 17.

12. Emilio C. Viano, "The Recognition and Implementation of Victims' Rights in the United States: Developments and Achievements," in E. C. Viano, ed., *The Victimology Handbook: Research Findings, Treatment, and Public Policy* (New York:

Garland, 1990). Dean G. Kilpatrick, David Beatty, and Susan Smith Howley, *The Rights of Crime Victims—Does Legal Protection Make a Difference?* (Washington, DC: Government Printing Office, 1998).

13. Robert A. Jerin, Laura J. Moriarty, and Melissa A. Gibson, "Victim Service or Self Service: An Analysis of Prosecution Based Victim-Witness Assistance Programs and Providers," *Criminal Justice Policy Review* 7.2 (1995): 142–54.

14. Robert Elias, *Victims Still: The Political Manipulation of Crime Victims* (Newbury Park, CA: Sage, 1993), *The Politics of Victimization: Victims, Victimology and Human Rights* (New York: Oxford University Press, 1990), and *Victims of the System* (New Brunswick, NJ: Transaction, 1984).

15. Elias, *Victims Still,* p. 39.

16. See the findings in Kilpatrick, Beatty, and Howley, *The Rights of Crime Victims— Does Legal Protection Make a Difference?*

17. Bureau of Justice Statistics, *Law Enforcement Management and Administrative Statistics, 1997* (Washington, DC: Government Printing Office, 1999), xix.

18. Bureau of Justice Statistics, *Prosecutors in State Courts, 1994* (Washington, DC: Government Printing Office, 1996), p. 9.

19. Jerin et al., "Victim Service or Self Service," p. 152.

20. Kilpatrick, Beatty, and Howley, *The Rights of Crime Victims—Does Legal Protection Make a Difference?*

21. President's Task Force on Victims of Crime, *Final Report.*

22. Bureau of Justice Statistics, *Law Enforcement Management and Administrative Statistics, 1997,* p. xix.

23. Bureau of Justice Statistics, *Prosecutors in State Courts, 1990* (Washington, DC: Government Printing Office, 1992).

24. Lee P. Brown and Mary Ann Wycoff, "Policing Houston: Reducing Fear and Improving Service," *Crime and Delinquency* 33 (January 1986): 71–89.

25. Bureau of Justice Statistics, *Criminal Victimization in the United States, 1993*

(Washington, DC: Government Printing Office, 1996), pp. 104–05.

26. Data on claims are in Bureau of Justice Statistics, *Sourcebook of Criminal Justice Statistics 1995* (Washington, DC: Government Printing Office, 1996), pp. 390–91.

27. Miller et al., *Victim Costs and Consequences,* p. 17.

28. Kilpatrick, Beatty, and Howley, *The Rights of Crime Victims—Does Legal Protection Make a Difference?,* p. 5.

29. Andrew Karmen, *Crime Victims: An Introduction to Victimology,* 2d ed. (Pacific Grove, CA: Brooks/Cole, 1990), p. 321.

30. William Doerner, "The Impact of Crime Compensation on Victim Attitudes toward the Criminal Justice System," *Victimology* 5.2 (1980): 61–77.

31. Elias, *Victims Still,* p. 42.

32. President's Task Force on Victims of Crime, *Final Report,* p. 114.

33. Edwin Villmoare and Virginia V. Neto, *Victim Appearances of Sentencing under California's Victims' Bill of Rights* (Washington, DC: Government Printing Office, 1987). Candace McCoy, *Politics and Plea Bargaining: Victims' Rights in California* (Philadelphia: University of Pennsylvania Press, 1993).

34. *South Carolina v. Gathers,* 490 U.S. 805 (1989); *Booth v. Maryland,* 482 U.S. 496 (1987).

35. *Payne v. Tennessee,* 501 U.S. 808 (1991).

36. Kilpatrick, Beatty, and Howley, *The Rights of Crime Victims—Does Legal Protection Make a Difference?* p. 6.

37. Edna Erez and Pamela Tontodonato, "The Effect of Victim Participation in Sentencing on Sentence Outcome," *Criminology* 28.3 (1990): 451–74.

38. Erez and Tontodonato, "The Effect of Victim Participation in Sentencing on Sentence Outcome."

39. Anthony Walsh, "Placebo Justice: Victim Recommendations and Offender Sentences in Sexual Assault Cases," *Journal of Criminal Law and Criminology* 77 (Winter 1986): 1126–141.

40. William H. Parsonage, Frances Bernat, and Jacquelin Helfgott, "Victim Impact Testimony and Pennsylvania's Parole Decision Making Process: A Pilot Study," *Criminal Justice Policy Review* 6.3 (1994): 187–206.

41. Malcolm Feeley, *Court Reform on Trial* (New York: Basic Books, 1982).

42. Bureau of Justice Statistics, *Pretrial Release of Felony Defendants, 1992* (Washington, DC: Government Printing Office, 1994).

43. President's Task Force on Victims of Crime, *Final Report,* pp. 17–18.

44. Cassia Spohn and Julie Horney, *Rape Law Reform* (New York: Plenum, 1992).

45. Bureau of Justice Statistics, *Law Enforcement Management and Administrative Statistics, 1997,* p. xix.

46. Lawrence W. Sherman and Richard A. Berk, *The Minneapolis Domestic Violence Experiment* (Washington, DC: Police Foundation, 1984).

47. Lawrence W. Sherman, *Policing Domestic Violence* (New York: Free Press, 1992).

10

Control Gun Crimes

THE PROBLEM WITH GUNS—
AND GUN POLICY

Firearms, especially handguns, are a serious problem in the United States. Even with the recent decline in violent crime, firearms are associated with thousands of deaths and injuries every year. In 1997, 32,436 people died as a result of firearms. This number included 13,000 homicides, 17,000 suicides, and about 1,000 accidental deaths. Another 96,000 people suffered nonfatal gunshot wounds.[1] In addition, handguns are used in over 40 percent of all robberies.[2] As we pointed out in Chapter 1, criminologists who study comparative crime rates argue that compared with other countries, the United States has a serious problem with *violent* (but not necessarily property) crime. Guns are a major part of the violent crime problem.

The good news is that gun-related crime is down, along with the rates for all serious crime. Between 1993 and 1997, the gun-related death rate declined 21.1 percent. This drop parallels a 21 percent decline for all violent crime during the period.[3]

The policy question—as we indicated in Chapter 1—is identifying what is responsible for the recent and substantial reductions in gun-related deaths. The Clinton administration, reflecting the liberal perspective, was quick to claim that it was the result of the new gun control laws it helped to enact: the ban on assault weapons and the Brady Bill waiting period for gun purchases. Conservative analysts argue that tough sentences and the great increase in the prison

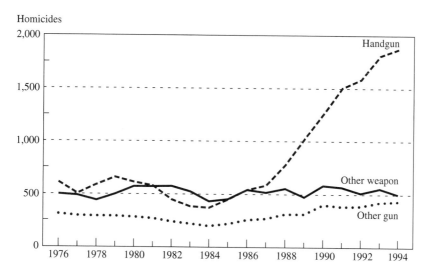

Homicides

FIGURE 10-1 Juvenile Homicides by Weapon.

SOURCE: James Alan Fox, *Trends in Juvenile Violence* (Washington, DC: Government Printing Office, 1996), p. 11.

population have both deterred and incapacitated offenders. Many criminologists believe that the decline is associated with the reduction in drug and gang-related violence, in particular the decline in the use of the drug crack.

The available data indicate a strong association among homicide rates, guns, juveniles, and crack usage. Juveniles accounted for the great increase in gun-related homicides between the late 1980s and the early 1990s. And as Figure 10-1 indicates, *all* of that increase involved handgun homicides. Juveniles are also responsible for most of the decline in gun murders in the mid-1990s. The firearm-related death rate declined 28 percent for persons age 15 to 24 between 1993 and 1997, compared with only 18 percent for those age 25 to 34.[4] Even if we assume that change in illegal drug use is the most important factor in this development, we still have to explain what caused that change. Was it community policing, the 100,000 new police officers, zero-tolerance policing, gun control laws, or incapacitation?

For decades, everyone has agreed that we need to do something about gun-related violence, but we have disagreed sharply over exactly what to do. Liberals generally believe that the problem is guns, supporting a number of policies designed to reduce their availability. As they put it, "Guns kill people." Conservatives, on the other hand, believe that criminals are the problem, supporting policies designed to either deter or incapacitate them. As they put it, "Guns don't kill people—people kill people."[5]

Public opinion polls reveal how deeply divided the public is over what to do about gun-related violence. Polls consistently indicate that more than 60 percent of the public believe that gun control laws should be "stricter," while only about 10 percent believe they should be less strict.[6] Yet that 60 percent figure conceals disagreement over what kinds of laws people think would be best. These divisions are reflected in recent federal and state legislation. The 1993 Brady Bill attempts to limit access to handguns by mandating a five-day waiting period for the purchase of a handgun; the 1994 Violent Crime Control Act bans 19 types of assault weapons. Several states, however, have passed "shall issue" laws requiring (as opposed to permitting) local law enforcement officials to issue permits to carry concealed weapons unless the applicant is legally disqualified (for example, because of a criminal record). While the federal laws seek to limit access, these state laws make guns more available to the public.[7]

The gun control issue arouses passionate debate for several obvious reasons. With the possible exception of drinking and driving, no other issue discussed in this book directly affects so many people as gun ownership. About 47 percent of all homes have some kind of firearm, and about 25 percent have a handgun. And although no one argues that drunk driving is acceptable, many people believe they have a right to own a gun. Gun owners argue that the Second Amendment establishes a constitutional right to own a gun, although the Supreme Court has never accepted that interpretation.[8]

GUN OWNERSHIP
AND GUN-RELATED VIOLENCE

Much misunderstanding persists about the exact nature of the problem related to guns, gun ownership, and gun-related violence. The leaders of both sides of the issue have often distorted the evidence to support their respective positions. Let us try to clear the air by establishing a few basic facts.

Types of Guns

The first problem is that there is a lot of confusion about exactly which weapons we are talking about. A basic distinction is among rifles, shotguns, and handguns.[9] Virtually everyone agrees that handguns are the real problem with respect to crime. Ninety-six percent of the firearms used in robberies are handguns. The so-called "Saturday night special" is one kind of handgun, small, easily concealable, and cheap. Assault weapons, meanwhile, are rifles or pistols that are capable of rapid-fire action. We will look at specific policy proposals directed at both the specials and assault weapons.

Gun Ownership

The Bureau of Alcohol, Tobacco, and Firearms (BATF) estimates there are over 200 million firearms in circulation in the United States. About 70 million are handguns, and 1.5 to 2 million new handguns are produced each year. It is important to keep these 70 million handguns in mind throughout this chapter, since any effective gun control policy has to take them into account.

Despite the tremendous increase in the total number of firearms, the percentage of households with some kind of firearm has remained fairly stable for forty years, at about 47 percent. The percentage with a handgun has risen slightly to just under a quarter of the households.[10] Handgun ownership is higher among men (32 percent versus 19 percent for women), whites (26 percent versus 16 percent for racial and ethnic minorities), higher-income people, Protestants, and southerners. People in the southeast United States are the most likely to own a handgun (32 percent), in large part because the region is very rural and there is a strong tradition of hunting. Handgun ownership is lowest in the urbanized northeast (13 percent).[11] Data from the National Opinion Research Center's (NORC) General Social Survey indicate that gun ownership is highly correlated with people "who are members of social groups where gun ownership is the norm." With respect to attitudes, gun owners are more likely to distrust government and be part of a cultural tradition of private retribution.[12]

Handgun-Related Violence

The facts about handgun violence in the United States are grisly. In 1992, the most recent peak year for violent crime, 930,700 handgun crimes were committed. This included 13,200 murders, or almost 60 percent of all murders; 11,800 rapes; 339,000 robberies; and 566,800 assaults.[13] In addition, two-thirds of all police officers feloniously killed in the line of duty are slain by handguns.[14] Note that we use the term *gun-related fatalities.* To say that guns "are responsible for" or "caused" deaths is to accept the liberal gun control position on this issue. *Gun-related* is a policy-neutral term.

As we have already noted, the most alarming development in the 1980s was the dramatic increase in gun-related homicide among juveniles. While the murder rate among people age 24 and older remained stable, the rate among people under the age of 18 more than doubled between 1985 and 1995 (see Figure 1-1, p. 4). Virtually all of the increase involved gun-related murders. The rate of nongun murders among 10- to 17-year-olds has remained stable.[15]

The profile of handgun crime *victims* closely resembles the profile of gun crime *users.* Both groups are disproportionately young, African-American males. Juveniles are currently more likely to carry a gun than are adults. Analyzing data from the Drug Use Forecasting (DUF) survey, Scott Decker and his colleagues found that whereas 14 percent of all arrestees carried a gun all or most of the time, 20 percent of the juvenile males and 31 percent of gang members did.[16]

Handguns as Self-Protection

Most of those arrestees who carry a weapon, say they do so for protection or self-defense. The result is a self-perpetuating gun culture. As more juveniles carry guns, their peers feel the need to carry one also for self-protection. As James D. Wright explains, these individuals "live in a very hostile and violent environment, and many of them have come to believe, no doubt correctly, that their ability to survive in that environment depends critically on being adequately armed."[17] They are "highly motivated gun owners who are not easily persuaded that they should not have one."

Handguns are fired in only 13 percent of all the robberies in which they are used, and the victim is actually struck by a bullet in only about 15 percent of these incidents (or 2 percent of all robberies). Handguns are primarily used to *intimidate* victims, and in this regard they are extremely efficient.[18] They are used in 78.8 percent of all the *completed* robberies and 48.7 percent of the *completed* rapes.

Although many people say that they have a gun for self-protection, crime victims rarely use a weapon. Analyzing NCVS data from 1979 to 1985, Gary Kleck and Miriam DeLone found that robbery victims used a gun to resist the offender in only 1.2 percent of all robberies (this figure included both completed and attempted robberies). Very few of these incidents involved a shootout between victim and offender. Nonetheless, Kleck and DeLone argue that when victims do use guns, they are frequently successful in preventing a completed robbery. In short, victims use them in the same way armed criminals do: to intimidate the other person.[19]

GUN-RELATED LAWS

It is a myth that the United States has no laws designed to control gun-related crime. In fact, we have innumerable federal, state, and local laws regulating ownership and use of guns, along with other laws imposing harsher punishment for using a gun in a crime.[20] The real question is whether these laws are effective in accomplishing their stated purposes. We use the term *gun-related laws* because many laws are directed at gun use by criminals and not gun ownership.

State and local laws vary considerably. Some are far more restrictive than others. Some cities have banned the ownership of handguns, and at least 14 have outlawed the sale of Saturday night specials. The result is that someone can easily buy a handgun in a state with weak regulations and carry it to a state or city with very restrictive laws. A congressional report issued in 1997 found that many guns sold in Virginia, Florida, South Carolina, Georgia, and Texas —states with some of the weakest laws—ended up being seized in other states. In one report, the BATF identified 1,234 guns sold in Florida that were later used by criminals in other states, including 181 in New York.[21]

The Policy Alternatives

The question is: What should we do to reduce gun-related violence? Generally, liberals adopt a *supply reduction* approach, seeking to reduce the availability of firearms, especially handguns. They cite the fact that compared with other countries, the United States has both the most permissive gun ownership laws and the highest rates of gun-related violence. These facts lead them to the conclusion that reducing gun availability would reduce violent crime.

Conservatives generally prefer a *demand reduction* approach designed to deter use of guns in crime. They argue that criminals, not guns, are the problem and that we have high rates of violent crime because we fail to punish offenders who use firearms. Tougher penalties such as mandatory prison terms, they believe, will both deter and incapacitate criminals. Pro-gun advocates have introduced a new issue in the gun policy debates, supporting laws that permit the carrying of concealed weapons. Allowing law-abiding citizens to carry weapons, they argue, will enable them to protect themselves and prevent victimization.[22]

We will encounter the distinction between supply reduction and demand reduction when we discuss drug policy in Chapter 13. As Mark Moore suggests, it is helpful to think comparatively about strategies for controlling guns, drugs, and alcohol.[23]

Public Attitudes toward Gun Control

It is often reported that a majority of Americans favor gun control. This statement is only partly true. When some people say they favor "gun control," they may mean only restrictions on the purchase of guns rather than a ban on ownership, or they may actually mean tough penalties for criminals who use guns. It depends on exactly which gun control policy you are referring to. The percentage of Americans favoring a ban on the possession of handguns has remained steady at about 40 percent since the early 1980s. A large majority of the public supports regulation of gun ownership. Over 70 percent consistently support requiring a police permit to buy a gun along with the registration of all guns. Meanwhile, 90 percent favor a waiting period of 7 to 21 days for a gun purchase.[24] At the same time, 83 percent support mandatory prison sentences for offenders who use a gun.[25]

Now let us review the various policy alternatives and see whether any evidence indicates that they work or might work.

BAN HANDGUNS

The most extreme gun control proposal is to ban handguns. The idea of "banning" handguns actually consists of several different policies: outlawing possession, outlawing bullets, prohibiting the manufacture and sale of handguns, and banning only Saturday night specials or assault weapons.

Ban Possession

A few cities have actually banned the possession of handguns. Their experience gives us some idea of what this approach can and cannot accomplish. The District of Columbia banned the purchase, sale, transfer, and possession of all handguns in 1975. It exempted handguns and long guns previously registered under a 1968 gun registration law. The nation's capital represents a tough test of banning handguns because it is a major city with a lot of violent crime.

What happened as a result of the law? The U.S. Conference of Mayors, a leading gun control advocate, claimed that the law was responsible for a "significant reduction in both firearm and handgun crime." Other analysts, however, believe that the mayors' report was flawed and inconclusive. Edward Jones found that comparable cities experienced even greater reductions in gun-related crime during the same period, without the benefit of gun control. Jones conceded that the law may have made some contribution to reducing handgun crime, but it was impossible to argue that it was the only or even the most important cause.[26]

Murder trends in Washington over the last twenty years suggest that the 1975 law was not effective. Murders declined significantly in the late 1970s and early 1980s, reaching a low of 147 in 1985. They skyrocketed to 482 by 1991, mainly as a result of the arrival of crack. Clearly, young men in Washington who wanted to obtain a handgun had little trouble getting one.

Evanston, Illinois, enacted what Gary Kleck calls "the toughest gun law in America" in 1982 by banning the possession of handguns within city limits (except for possession by police, private security guards, licensed gun dealers, and a few gun collectors).[27] The impact of the law on crime was insignificant. Between 1981 and 1984, trivial increases in murder and assault occurred, and armed robbery decreased slightly.

The Limits of "Banning" Handguns

The Washington, D.C., and Evanston experiences illustrate the limits of attempting to outlaw possession of handguns. The main problem is the 70 million handguns that already exist. No one has offered a realistic plan for how they might be removed from circulation. As law professor John Kaplan once pointed out, crusaders who seek to outlaw a product (alcohol, drugs, guns) always focus on the alleged dangers of the item and spend "little time and energy" estimating the costs of enforcement and the likelihood of effectiveness.[28]

A sizable black market in handguns and other weapons already exists. A majority of the arrestees in the Drug Use Forecasting (DUF) survey indicated that they obtained their guns through the illegal firearms market. Over half (55 percent) said that guns are easy to obtain: more than a third (37 percent) said they could obtain one in less than a week, and 20 percent said they could get one in a day or less. Thirteen percent said that they had stolen a gun at some point in their life.[29] A federal ban on handgun possession would probably foster the growth of the black market, just as the prohibition of alcohol (1920–1933) stimulated the growth of organized crime. We will discuss the consequences of attempting to outlaw certain products—alcohol, guns, drugs—in more detail in Chapter 13.

Any truly effective attempt to ban ownership of guns would require a federal law. No strong support for such a law exists at present, however. Also, it is safe to predict that millions of gun owners would refuse to turn in their weapons. In Evanston, Illinois, only 116 handguns were voluntarily turned in after the 1982 ban went into effect, despite the fact that there were over 5,000 admitted handgun owners.[30] Not only do 25 percent of all American households currently have handguns, but many of those people fiercely believe that they have a constitutional right to own those weapons.[31] A federal law would create a situation resembling Prohibition in the 1920s, when tens of millions of people drank alcoholic beverages despite a constitutional amendment prohibiting them. Any attempt to enforce such a ban would require highly intrusive measures by the police. Many right-wing groups already express intense hostility toward the BATF, and a federal ban would only inflame the situation further.

Ban Bullets

Some groups, including the U.S. Conference of Mayors and the Consumer Product Safety Commission, have recommended banning the manufacture and sale of bullets on the grounds that they are a health hazard. This is a politically motivated strategy designed to sidestep the strong public opposition to outlawing guns themselves. The obvious problem with this approach is that bullets are easily made at home. Many hunters already pack their own. Outlawing bullets would only stimulate a large cottage industry in homemade bullets and a black market.

A variation of the bullet ban is a 1986 federal law prohibiting the manufacture, importation, and sale of so-called "cop-killer" bullets. These bullets are made of hard metals capable of piercing the bulletproof vests worn by police officers. Law enforcement organizations actively supported the law. When pressed, however, advocates of the law could not cite any cases of a police officer's actually being killed by one of these bullets. Meanwhile, only 18 cases were reported of criminals caught in possession of such bullets over an 18-year period![32]

The cop-killer bullet issue is a classic example of a general phenomenon in crime control policy debates: the habit of some activists and politicians to seize on a small but seemingly important part of the problem. It is usually a cop-out: a way of appearing to have a solution to the problem while actually ignoring the hard questions related to the larger problem.

Ban the Manufacture and Importation of Handguns

Another way to reduce the availability of handguns in the United States is to outlaw their manufacture and importation. This approach is designed to dry up the supply of handguns over the long run. In practice, however, it would only stimulate an international black market like the one that already dominates the drug trade. Also, it has been estimated that the current supply of handguns is enough to last for the next hundred years.[33]

Buy Back Handguns

Another strategy for drying up the supply is for law enforcement officials to buy back handguns, offering either cash or coupons good for discounts at local stores in exchange for handguns. St. Louis conducted two buy-back programs, bringing in 7,500 guns in 1991 and another 1,200 in 1994. Richard Rosenfeld evaluated the program and found "little evidence" of any impact on gun assaults or homicides in the city. An evaluation of a buy-back program in Seattle also failed to find any reduction in crime. Trying to put a more optimistic interpretation on his findings, Rosenfeld argues that buy-back programs are more likely to be effective in achieving other goals such as strengthening community bonds and building support for community leadership and that they should be evaluated on those terms.[34]

Buy-backs have serious limitations. The available supply of guns is so huge that it is probably impossible to significantly reduce the number in any community. Many guns are turned in by people who are among the least likely to commit a gun crime (e.g., the elderly). Many simply wanted to dispose of an unwanted weapon. In St. Louis, 62 percent of those turning in a gun retained another weapon in the home. In short, there is no evidence that buy-back programs reduce crime.

Ban Saturday Night Specials

A compromise strategy for banning handguns advocated by some liberals is to outlaw only the so-called Saturday night specials.[35] The BATF defines the special as a gun of 0.32 caliber or less, with a barrel less than 3 inches in length and priced at $50 or less. In 1996, Los Angeles became the fourteenth city in the United States (along with the state of Maryland) to outlaw the sale of specials, specifically prohibiting twenty-three different weapons.[36] Advocates of outlawing the specials believe these weapons are favored by criminals because of their price and concealability.

Outlawing only Saturday night specials probably will not accomplish what many people think it would. The role of the specials in crime has been greatly exaggerated. Gary Kleck found that far from being the "preferred" weapon of criminals, they represent only between 10 and 27 percent of all handguns used in crimes.[37] Banning only the specials might produce a *substitution effect,* in which criminals simply move up to a larger weapon.

Kleck further argues that specials are the primary self-defense weapon for low-income people. Banning them would deprive poor people, who are victimized by violent crimes more than middle-class people, of one of their principal means of self-protection.[38]

The proposal to ban only the Saturday night specials is essentially a political cop-out. It allows people to appear to be doing something about the gun problem without directly threatening most gun owners. The same can be said about banning cop-killer bullets: it focuses on a small part of the problem, one that has high symbolic power, while avoiding the hard questions associated with the real problem.

Ban Assault Weapons

The rise of gang-related violence in the 1980s aroused public concern about so-called assault weapons. There was much publicity about gangs being heavily armed with Uzis, AK-47s, and similar weapons. The term *assault weapon* generally refers to "semiautomatic firearms with a large magazine of ammunition that [are] designed and configured for rapid fire and combat use."[39] They can be pistols, rifles, or shotguns. The BATF estimated in 1993 that about 1 percent of the 200 million guns in private hands were assault weapons. Many people want to ban them because they are not legitimate hunting weapons and have no purpose other than killing people. The 1994 Violent Crime Control Act outlawed the manufacture and sale of 19 specific types of assault weapons.[40]

A 1999 evaluation of the assault weapons ban found no persuasive evidence that it reduced violent crime. At best, the report concluded that "the ban *may* [emphasis added] have contributed to a reduction in the gun murder rate and murders of police officers by criminals armed with assault weapons," but the evidence was far from conclusive.[41] As with Saturday night specials, the importance of assault weapons has been greatly exaggerated. Kleck points out that the ordinary handgun remains the gun of choice among robbers. Virtually all of the police officers feloniously killed are killed with handguns. In short, although extremely deadly, assault weapons are not the real problem in gun-related crimes.[42]

Summary

All of the policies designed to eliminate the possession of handguns or certain types of guns run up against the same basic problems: millions of these weapons already are in circulation (including 70 million handguns), there is no practical plan for eliminating them, a black market already exists, and any kind of ban would only foster the growth of the black market. This leads us to the following conclusion:

> ## PROPOSITION 30
> Attempts to ban handguns, or certain kinds of guns, or bullets, are not likely to reduce serious crime.

REGULATE THE SALE
AND POSSESSION OF HANDGUNS

The basic American strategy for controlling handguns is to regulate their sale, purchase, and ownership. Innumerable federal, state, and local laws are designed to keep handguns out of the hands of convicted offenders, people with a history of mental illness, and juveniles. This is essentially a "bad person" strategy. The 1993 Brady Law requires a five-day waiting period so that a background check can be conducted on applicants. The Youth Handgun Safety Act of 1994 outlaws possession of handguns by juveniles and the private sale or transfer of a handgun to a juvenile.[43] The 1996 Lautenberg Amendment, meanwhile, outlaws gun ownership by anyone convicted of a domestic violence crime. (The law had enormous implications for police officers and members of the military who must use weapons as part of their jobs.)

The Brady Bill has been one of the major policy achievements of the Clinton Administration. In 1997 about 69,000 would-be gun purchasers were denied guns as a result of the Brady Bill. This represented about 3 percent of all applications. A total of 207,000 applications were denied between the time the law went into effect in March, 1994 and late 1998. In 1998, 63 percent of all rejections were due to a felony indictment or conviction on the part of the applicant.[44]

The White House quickly claimed that this was an important factor in the nationwide reduction of violent crime. Skeptics have raised serious doubts about these claims, however. There are serious problems with official criminal history data. The most serious problem is with offenders whose records do not show up in the files (think of these as false negatives). There are also false positives: people inaccurately listed as having a criminal record (a mistaken identity, data that were entered inaccurately, mistakes that were not expunged, and so forth). The mentally disturbed gun buyer represents an even more serious problem. There is no national data file of people with mental health problems —and some serious civil liberties questions exist about whether we would want such a file. What is meant by having a history of mental illness? Being hospitalized? That only covers a small number of people with problems. What about people who were treated by a private physician or counselor? Requiring these professionals to report all of their clients would be a serious invasion of privacy. And what level of seriousness would trigger the ban on gun owner-ship? Mild depression? That covers a lot of people. And of course millions of people with serious mental health problems never see a doctor or counselor.

Another problem with the Brady Bill is that some of the people denied a purchase simply turn to the black market and obtain a gun. This is particularly true of people who want a gun for the purpose of committing a crime.[45]

The gun black market is a major issue affecting all current or proposed gun policies. Mark H. Moore estimates that between 500,000 and 750,000 gun transactions take place between private individuals every year.[46] Many of these do not involve active or potential criminals: They are sales or gifts between friends, family members, gun collectors, and hunters. But many do involve illegal sales among active criminals. James D. Wright found that only one-sixth of all gun-using felons acquired their guns through legal, retail transactions. Half had stolen a gun at one time or another.[47] An estimated 341,000 firearms are stolen every year, 180,000 of which are handguns. By definition, these guns go directly into the hands of people (thieves) who are barred from own-ing them.[48]

For all of the same reasons that banning ownership of handguns seems futile, regulations designed to deny ownership to certain categories of "bad" people are not likely to succeed. Seventy million handguns are in existence, an active black market thrives in guns, and criminals themselves say that they have or would have no trouble quickly obtaining a weapon. People intent on com-mitting a crime are particularly motivated to obtain a gun. James D. Wright sums it up very well when he argues that it is not very efficient or sensible to try to control ownership of guns by the public at large when the real problem is the behavior of a very small part of the population—violent criminals.[49]

PROPOSITION 31

Attempts to deny ownership of handguns to certain categories
of "bad" people are not likely to reduce serious crime.

RESTRICT THE USE OF HANDGUNS

Instead of attempting to deny ownership of handguns, another serious group of policies is aimed at limiting how people *use* handguns. Let us take a look at this approach.

Restrict the Carrying of Handguns

Most states have traditionally had laws regulating the carrying of handguns outside the home, usually by prohibiting the carrying of concealed weapons or by requiring some kind of permit. The most famous variation of this approach was the 1975 Massachusetts Bartley-Fox Law, which mandates a one-year prison term for people who are caught carrying a handgun outside their homes without a permit. The law prohibits plea bargaining to a lesser offense and denies the possibility of either probation or parole. The intent was simple: "If you are caught with a gun, you will go to prison for a year and nobody can get you out."[50]

The Bartley-Fox Law is closely related to other crime control policies we discuss in this book. First, it is an exercise in mandatory sentencing (Chapter 7). It is also a strategy of deterrence, seeking to prevent crime through the threat of certain punishment (Chapter 6). Finally, it is an attempt to close the alleged loophole of plea bargaining (Chapter 8). Here we are primarily interested in its impact on crime and on gun-related crime in particular.

As a gun control measure, Bartley-Fox is a strategic compromise. It does not challenge people's right to own guns and keep them at home. Thus, it sidesteps much of opposition from gun owners. It attempts to reduce gun-related crime by keeping the guns at home. This strategy has strong empirical support. Many violent crimes are unplanned, spontaneous events: The person left home with no intention of committing a crime. As interviews with criminals have found, most carry a gun for self-defense. Nonetheless, some of these people end up committing a gun crime. Having the gun may have emboldened them to commit a crime once a situation arose. As we have already argued, guns are terribly efficient as threats. Without the gun, a robber may not have attempted or completed the crime. Thus, a strategy to deter people from carrying a gun in the first place might reduce crime.

Bartley-Fox has been intensively evaluated. The data on crime trends indicated that in Boston assaults with a gun declined by 13.5 percent between 1974 and 1975 and by 11.7 percent between 1974 and 1976. Four other cities, however, experienced even greater reductions in gun assaults without the benefit of a similar law. They went down 21.3 percent in Philadelphia and 26 percent in Chicago. Meanwhile, in Boston assaults with other kinds of weapons went up by 40.4 percent between 1974 and 1976. Thus, there may have been a substitution effect as people kept their guns at home and shifted to other weapons.[51]

Gun robberies in Boston went down a substantial 35.5 percent in the 1974–1976 period, whereas robberies committed without guns increased slightly. Again, however, other cities that did not have a similar law experienced even greater reductions. Armed robberies went down 43.5 percent in Chicago and 36.7 percent in Philadelphia. Meanwhile, gun murders declined by 55.7 percent in Boston. This decrease was part of a national decline in murders; the comparison cities had reductions of between 30 and 45 percent. An *announcement effect* (see Chapter 6) may have been at work. Gun-related crimes began to decline in the months just before the law went into effect, perhaps as a result of all the publicity (as has been the case in some drunk driving crackdowns), but this point is not entirely clear.

Some evidence indicates that officials undermined the "mandatory" provisions of Bartley-Fox, as police officers reportedly became a little more cautious about frisking people for weapons. Police reports on gun incidents declined by 25 percent in Boston between 1974 and 1976. Seventy of 79 officers interviewed admitted to being more selective because they did not want to catch "otherwise innocent" people violating the law. This is a classic example of how police officers' discretion reflects their judgment about the moral character of possible suspects. Meanwhile, the percentage of cases dismissed went from 18 percent to 38 percent. Despite its attempt to close plea-bargaining loopholes, the law did not restrict outright dismissal. Acquittals in the remaining cases increased from 16 percent in 1974 to 40 percent in 1975 and then declined to 33 percent in 1976. Finally, the number of appeals of convictions went from 21 percent to 96 percent.[52]

The net effect was that fewer people were sentenced for carrying a gun. The percentage of defendants actually sentenced dropped from 41 percent in 1974 to only 17 percent in 1976. This appears to be a classic illustration of criminal justice thermodynamics at work: As the nominal punishment went up, actual punishment went down. A follow-up study of the law in six Massachusetts counties found that it was still being implemented, with no evidence of systematic lowering or dropping of charges.[53]

Boston: Operation Cease Fire

Of course, in the long run the Bartley-Fox Law did not insulate the state against the dramatic upsurge in gun violence in the mid-1980s. Along with other cities, Boston experienced a sharp increase in murders, from 88 in 1985 to 152 in 1990.

In response, the city adopted a multipronged gun violence reduction effort consisting of several different programs. The most important were the Boston Police Department's Operation Cease Fire, involving zero-tolerance enforcement directed at known gang members, and the Boston Gun Project, a coordinated effort by the police department and federal agencies to disrupt the illegal gun market. In addition there were a number of other crime prevention programs, particularly involving local churches.[54] One of the most important elements of Operation Cease Fire was the recognition that many gang members were highly vulnerable to zero-tolerance law enforcement. Many if not most were on probation or parole or had outstanding warrants. In addition, many often drank in public or committed other minor offenses. All of these potential enforcement possibilities were directed toward known or suspected gang members.[55] Operation Cease Fire was conceptualized in terms of problem-oriented policing, similar to the programs described in Chapter 5.

Boston officials claimed enormous success for their antigun violence efforts. The number of juvenile gun homicides dropped to zero in 1996. Attorney General Janet Reno hailed Boston's efforts as a model for the rest of the country, and Operation Cease Fire received the prestigious Herman Goldstein Award for problem-oriented policing.

Were the Boston programs really that successful? We should be careful before we give them all the credit. The juvenile gun homicide trends in Boston closely paralleled the national trends, rising dramatically after 1985 and then falling almost as dramatically in the early 1990s. Since this pattern occurred in cities without Operation Cease Fire or any of the other Boston programs, it is difficult to give them full credit.

Guns at Airports and Schools

Another set of laws attempts to keep people from carrying guns in certain places such as airplanes and schools.

Airports. A federal law prohibits the carrying of a weapon on an airplane, and all passengers are electronically screened at the gate. The electronic screening at airports makes enforcement fairly effective. Every year about 2,500 firearms are confiscated.[56] Many of the people carrying them apparently forgot that they had a gun with them. This point is a testimony to the prevalence of guns in American society, the casualness with which they are carried around, and the limited deterrent effect of a well-known law. Nonetheless, the law has been effective in curbing airplane hijacking. The number of hijackings decreased from 40 in 1969 to only one attempted hijacking each in both 1990 and 1991, and none in either of the next two years.[57]

The strategy of preventing airplane hijackings by prohibiting guns on planes is consistent with the place-oriented approach discussed by the University of Maryland *Preventing Crime* report.[58] The antihijacking effort appears to have been successful, but there are serious limits on its application to other areas of society. Airports are special locations: confined spaces, involving a very small number of people, all of whom can be channeled through a metal detector. It is not clear how this strategy could be applied to society at large for the purpose of reducing ordinary robbery and burglary.

Schools. Another problem involves guns in school. Because of a series of sensational crimes—the 1999 massacre in Littleton, Colorado, and several other highly publicized incidents—there has been great national concern about guns and violence in public schools. Several strategies have been adopted to keep guns out of schools. The 1994 Gun Free Schools Act requires schools receiving federal education funds to have a policy mandating the expulsion of students who bring firearms to school. Some schools have instituted metal detectors similar to those used at airports.

The evidence, however, indicates that this is yet another example of the celebrated case phenomenon discussed in Chapter 2. Surveys of students consistently find that less than 10 percent have ever taken a gun to school. In 1997, 7 percent of students reported that they had been threatened with a weapon at school.[59] Additionally, despite the sensational episodes such as Littleton, there has been no increase in school crime in the 1990s. There was some increase in student victimization by violent crime between 1989 and 1995, but even in that latter year only 4.5 percent were the victim of a violent crime.[60]

Get Guns Off the Street: The Kansas City Experiment

The most innovative recent approach to reducing gun crimes is the Kansas City Gun Experiment.[61] The experiment involved intensive enforcement of existing laws on the illegal carrying of handguns. Funded by the federal Weed and Seed program, it represents a combination of two important innovations in policing: *problem-oriented policing,* in which the police focus on a specific problem, and *hot spots,* in which patrols focus on a particular area (see Chapter 5).[62]

The experiment was conducted in a particularly high-crime-rate precinct in Kansas City, where the 1991 murder rate was 177 per 100,000, or about 20 times higher than the national average. Two two-officer patrol cars, working overtime, patrolled for six hours every night, concentrating exclusively on detecting and seizing illegally possessed guns. The officers would stop cars on legitimate legal grounds (for example, a traffic violation) but focus on weapons seizures. Almost half (45 percent) of all the guns eventually seized were found through a search incident to arrest, another 21 percent were found in plain view, and 34 percent were found in frisks as authorized by the Supreme Court in the 1968 *Terry* decision.

Over the course of 29 weeks, the gun unit officers seized a total of 29 guns. Meanwhile, regular patrol officers in the target beat seized another 47 guns, for a combined total of 76. The number of gun crimes in the target beat declined by 49 percent, but only by 4 percent in a control beat. The experiment controlled for a possible displacement effect and found that gun crimes went up in some of the neighboring beats and down in others. The reduction in gun crimes could have occurred as a direct result of removing guns from the area, or through deterrence, or through the incapacitation of potential offenders who were arrested and imprisoned. The Kansas City Gun Experiment represents another example of problem-oriented policing as well as the kind of place-oriented and hot spots approach described in the Marlyand *Preventing Crime* report.[63]

The Kansas City Gun Experiment seems to suggest that a clearly focused program to remove guns from the streets can reduce gun-related crime. A number of questions about the program remain, however. It is extremely expensive when measured in terms of the cost per gun seized or crime prevented. It is not clear that a police department could afford to run such a program as a part of normal operations. Also, when Sherman replicated the program in Indianapolis, some serious questions were raised about the data and some of the claims made for its success.[64]

The safest conclusion at this point is that the gun seizure approach may prove to be an effective strategy for reducing gun-related violence, but more research is needed.

PROPOSITION 32

Focused, proactive enforcement strategies may be effective
in reducing gun-related crime in targeted areas.

More Guns?

Some gun owners believe that the best way to reduce crime and protect law-abiding citizens is to have more guns on the street. The debate over guns and crime took a new direction in 1996 with a paper by University of Chicago professors John R. Lott and David B. Mustard arguing that "allowing citizens to carry concealed weapons deters violent crimes and it appears to produce no increase in accidental deaths."[65]

The idea that more guns should be on the street (at least in the hands of law-abiding people) flies directly in the face of policies such as the Bartley-Fox Law and the Kansas City Gun Experiment. A fair amount of support is expressed for this position: Between 1977 and 1992, ten states enacted "shall issue" laws related to carrying weapons. These laws create a presumptive right to a permit to carry a weapon, as opposed to the traditional approach in which law enforcement officials had broad discretion to grant or deny permits.

Using county-level data on crime, Lott and Mustard estimate that if states without "shall issue" laws adopted them, it would prevent about 1,570 murders, 4,177 rapes, and over 60,000 aggravated assaults every year. In an early critique, Frank Zimring and Gordon Hawkins raise serious questions about the crime reduction claims made for the "shall issue" laws. As was the case with Isaac Erhlich's study of the death penalty (see Chapter 6), the data have a few serious problems. Zimring and Hawkins argue that, at best, "shall issue" laws are likely to produce "modest benefits" because so few people will actually exercise their right to take out gun permits (they estimate that "fewer than 2 percent" of the population do so). "Large reductions in violence are quite unlikely," however.[66]

Lott and Mustard have, if nothing else, altered the debate over guns and crime. Their work will undoubtedly spark further research. For the moment, their claims, like those of so many other policy advocates we consider in this book, seem extravagant and unwarranted.

GET TOUGH ON WEAPONS OFFENSES

The primary conservative policy on gun-related crimes is to get tough on offenders convicted of using guns. This approach reflects two basic conservative views: first, that criminals and not guns commit crimes; and, second, that the criminal justice system is soft on crime and criminals. The basic policy recommendation calls for mandatory prison terms for gun-related crimes and longer prison terms. Such laws are extremely popular. In 1994, 41 states had mandatory minimum sentencing laws for illegal weapons possession.[67] A 1975 Florida law is typical of those in other states. It imposed a mandatory minimum sentence of three years in prison for use of a weapon in the commission of certain crimes and prohibited the granting of certain types of good-time credit during the mandatory minimum period.[68]

National data indicate that, contrary to widespread belief, the criminal jus-tice system is not soft on gun-related crimes. In 1994, 69 percent of all persons convicted of a weapons offense in state courts were incarcerated—the same figure as for drug offenses. The average prison sentence was four years, and the average jail term was six months.[69] Federal courts were considerably tougher, sentencing 77 percent to prison, for average terms of just over six years.[70] (State court sentences have been getting shorter, down from an average of fifty-six months since 1985, whereas federal prison sentences have been get-ting longer, up from forty-two months in 1985.) But both state and federal prisoners serve about the same amount of time: twenty-two months for state prisoners and twenty-three months for federal prisoners.[71]

Getting Tough in Detroit

In 1977, Michigan passed a law mandating two years in prison for any gun-related crime. The law precluded either probation or parole and was advertised as "one with a gun gets you two." At the same time, the Wayne County (Detroit) prosecutor announced a new policy prohibiting plea bargaining of gun charges under the new law.

An evaluation by Colin Loftin and David McDowall focused on two ques-tions: Did the law increase the certainty and severity of punishment, and did it lower the crime rate? The key issue in regard to the severity of sentences con-cerned the effective minimum prison terms; that is, how much time could a convicted offender reasonably expect to do before becoming eligible for release, when reductions for both good time and parole were taken into account? They found "no statistically significant change in the expected mini-mum sentence" for gun-related murders and armed robberies, but a significant increase in the expected minimum sentences for gun-related assaults.[72]

Two factors—the going rate and the trickle-up phenomenon—explain what happened in Detroit. The expected minimum sentences for murder and robbery did not increase because the going rate for these crimes was already high. Armed robbers in Detroit had been serving prison terms averaging six years before the new law, and few convicted robbers ever got probation. The system was not soft on crime beforehand, and the supposed "get tough" law did not change things.

Sentences for assaults increased because the going rate for those offenses had been rather low. Probation and suspended sentences were common, and incarcerated offenders got an average of six months. Much of this seeming leniency stems from the ambiguity of the crime of assault. The nature of the act is often difficult to specify with precision; it may also be difficult to deter-mine who initiated the altercation. Moreover, as we argued in Chapter 3, criminal justice officials routinely treat assaults between people who know each other as essentially private disputes and frequently dismiss the charges or settle the case with a plea to a lesser offense. The new law raised the severity of sentences by eliminating this opportunity for mitigating punishment.

Loftin and McDowall also found that "the gun law did not significantly alter the number or type of violent offenses committed in Detroit." Murder, robbery, and assault did decline, but the decrease in the rate began five months before the law went into effect—long enough in advance to rule out the possibility of the announcement effect that has appeared with other laws toughening criminal penalties.[73]

The impact of mandatory sentences for gun crimes is extremely complex. When McDowall and Loftin (in collaboration with Brian Wiersma) pooled the results from six different studies, they reached somewhat different conclusions.[74] Mandatory sentencing appeared to reduce homicides in all six cities. In Detroit, there was a 14 percent reduction, with an average of 5.5 lives saved each month. On the other hand, there were no significant reductions in gun assaults or robberies in any of the sites. The authors characterized the results as a "logical puzzle," conceding that they did not know which features of the sentencing policy were "responsible for the preventive effects." More research is clearly needed, and we should be cautious about simplistic assertions on either side of the debate: that mandatory sentencing deters crime or that it does not work at all.

Evidence from California also suggests that the system is not overly soft on gun-related crimes. Gun-related crimes were 34 percent more likely to be accepted for prosecution at the initial screening than were nongun crimes and 24 percent more likely to be accepted at the preliminary hearing stage. Gun users were less likely to plead guilty, and 67 percent of the gun wielders who were convicted at trial went to prison, compared with only 33 percent of other offenders. Moreover, the use of a gun added nearly two years (600 days) to the average sentence. Pleading guilty did not help defendants accused of gun crimes. Seventy-four percent of those who pleaded guilty went to prison, compared with 45 percent of all others who copped a plea. And for their plea they got 400 additional days of prison time. These figures hardly paint a picture of a system soft on gun crimes.[75]

In short, as we argued in Chapter 2, the justice system has always been tough on gun-related crimes. Trying to "get tough[er]," especially through mandatory sentences, will not produce any additional reductions in crime.

PROPOSITION 33
Trying to "get tough" on gun crimes, especially through mandatory prison sentences, will not reduce gun-related crime.

CONCLUSION

Gun-related violence is a serious problem in American society. There is no obvious solution, however. Banning guns is an empty gesture, given the number of handguns already in circulation. Trying to keep guns out of the hands of "bad" people also appears to be futile. Nor does it appear that threats of severe punishment will deter or incapacitate offenders in a way that will significantly reduce crime. Policies directed at how people use guns, such as the Bartley-Fox Law or the approach taken in the Kansas City Gun Experiment, might have some positive impact on reducing the number of guns on the street and, as a consequence, gun-related crimes.

NOTES

1. Center for Disease Control and Prevention, *Morbidity and Mortality Weekly Report,* 48.45 (19 November 1999).

2. Bureau of Justice Statistics, *Sourcebook of Criminal Justice Statistics—1998* (Washington, DC: Government Printing Office, 1999), p. 274.

3. Center for Disease Control and Prevention, *Morbidity and Mortality Weekly Report* (19 November 1999).

4. Center for Disease Control and Prevention, *Morbidity and Mortality Weekly Report* (19 November 1999).

5. Philip J. Cook and Mark H. Moore, "Gun Control," in James Q. Wilson and Joan Petersilia, eds., *Crime* (San Francisco: ICS Press, 1995), p. 271. The most comprehensive treatment of gun violence and gun control policies is Gary Kleck, *Point Blank: Guns and Violence in America* (New York: Aldine de Gruyter, 1991).

6. Bureau of Justice Statistics, *Sourcebook of Criminal Justice Statistics—1995,* pp. 190, 191. Trend data on polls are in John T. Young, David Hemenway, Robert J. Blendon, and John M. Benson, "The Polls —Trends: Guns," *Public Opinion Quarterly* 60 (1996): 634–49.

7. John R. Lott, *More Guns, Less Crime* (Chicago: University of Chicago Press, 1998).

8. For a useful collection of articles on the debate, see Jan E. Dizard, Robert Merrill Muth, and Stephen D. Andrews, Jr., eds., *Guns in America: A Reader* (New York: New York University Press, 1999).

9. A basic classification scheme is in Bureau of Justice Statistics, *Guns Used in Crime* (Washington, DC: Government Printing Office, 1995).

10. Young et al., "The Polls—Trends: Guns," 639–40.

11. Young et al., "The Polls—Trends: Guns." p. 189.

12. Edward L. Glaeser and Spencer Glendon, "Who Owns Guns? Criminals, Victims, and the Culture of Violence," *American Economic Review* 88 (May 1998): 458–62; Gary Kleck, "Crime, Culture Conflict and the Sources of Support for Gun Control, *American Behavioral Scientist* 39 (February 1996): 387–404.

13. Bureau of Justice Statistics, *Guns and Crime* (Washington, DC: Government Printing Office, 1994).

14. Federal Bureau of Investigation, *Law Enforcement Officers Killed and Assaulted* (Washington, DC: Government Printing Office, annual).

15. Michael Tonry and Mark H. Moore, eds., *Youth Violence* (Chicago: University of Chicago Press, 1998).

16. Scott H. Decker, Susan Pennell, and Ami Caldwell, *Illegal Firearms: Access and Use by Arrestees* (Washington, DC: Government Printing Office, 1997).

17. James D. Wright, "Ten Essential Observations on Guns in America," *Society* (March/April 1995): 66.

18. Bureau of Justice Statistics, *Handgun Crime Victims* (Washington, D.C.: Government Printing Office, 1990).

19. Gary Kleck and Miriam A. DeLone, "Victim Resistance and Offender Weapon Effects in Robbery," *Journal of Quantitative Criminology* 9 (No. 1, 1993): 55–81.

20. A chart indicating the major state laws is found in Bureau of Justice Statistics, *Sourcebook of Criminal Justice Statistics— 1997,* p. 90. The best discussion of gun control laws appears in Kleck, *Point Blank.*

21. "Report Links Crimes to States with Weak Gun Controls," *New York Times,* 9 April 1997.

22. John R. Lott, *More Guns, Less Crime.* (Chicago: University of Chicago Press, 1998).

23. Mark H. Moore, "Controlling Criminogenic Commodities: Drugs, Guns, and

Alcohol," in James Q. Wilson, ed., *Crime and Public Policy* (San Francisco: ICS Press, 1983).

24. Young et al., "The Polls—Trends: Guns," p. 645.

25. James D. Wright, Peter H. Rossi, and Kathleen Daly, *Under the Gun: Weapons, Crime, and Violence in America* (New York: Aldine de Gruyter, 1983), p. 223.

26. Edward D. Jones, "The District of Columbia's 'Firearms Control Regulations Act of 1975': The Toughest Handgun Control Law in the United States—Or Is It?" *Annals* 455 (May 1981): 138–49.

27. Kleck, *Point Blank,* pp. 408–11.

28. John Kaplan, "The Wisdom of Gun Prohibition," *Annals* 455 (May 1981): 11–23.

29. Decker et al., *Illegal Firearms.*

30. Kleck, *Point Blank,* pp. 409–10.

31. Wayne LaPierre, *Guns, Crime, and Freedom* (New York: HarperCollins, 1995).

32. LaPierre, *Guns, Crime, and Freedom,* pp. 82–83.

33. Wright et al., *Under the Gun,* p. 320.

34. The St. Louis and Seattle evaluations, along with other articles are in Martha Plotkin, ed., *Under Fire: Gun Buy-Backs, Exchanges, and Amnesty Programs* (Washington, DC: Police Executive Research Forum, 1996).

35. Robert Sherrill, *The Saturday Night Special* (New York: Charterhouse, 1973).

36. "Los Angeles Bans the Sale of Inexpensive, Small Guns," *New York Times,* 8 September 1996.

37. Kleck, *Point Blank,* p. 85; see also "Los Angeles Bans the Sale of Small, Inexpensive Guns."

38. Kleck, *Point Blank,* pp. 85–86.

39. Bureau of Justice Statistics, *Guns Used in Crime,* p. 6.

40. For a critical discussion of the federal law and popular views about assault weapons, see David B. Kopel, ed., *Guns: Who Should Have Them?* (Amherst, NY: Prometheus Books, 1995), chap. 4.

41. Jeffrey A. Roth and Christopher S. Koper, "Impacts of the 1994 Assault Weapons Ban: 1994–96," (Washington, DC: Government Printing Office, 1999).

42. Gary Kleck, "Assault Weapons Aren't the Problem," *New York Times,* 1 September 1992; Kleck, *Point Blank,* pp. 70–82.

43. Office of Juvenile Justice and Delinquency Prevention, *Reducing Youth Gun Violence* (Washington, DC: Government Printing Office, 1996), p. 1.

44. Bureau of Justice Statistics, *Presale Handgun Checks, the Brady Interim Period, 1994–98* (Washington, DC: Government Printing Office, 1999).

45. For a criticism of the waiting period strategy, see Kopel, ed., *Guns: Who Should Have Them?* chap. 2.

46. Mark H. Moore, "Keeping Handguns from Criminal Offenders," *Annals* 455 (May 1981): 92–109.

47. James D. Wright, *The Armed Criminal in America* (Washington, DC: Government Printing Office, 1986); James D. Wright and Peter H. Rossi, *Armed and Considered Dangerous: A Survey of Felons and Their Firearms* (New York: Aldine de Gruyter, 1986).

48. Bureau of Justice Statistics, *Guns Used in Crime,* p. 4.

49. Bureau of Justice Statistics, *Guns Used in Crime.*

50. Glenn L. Pierce and William J. Bowers, "The Bartley-Fox Gun Law's Short-Term Impact on Crime," *Annals* 455 (May 1981): 120–37.

51. Pierce and Bowers, "The Bartley-Fox Gun Law's Short-Term Impact."

52. Pierce and Bowers, "The Bartley-Fox Gun Law's Short-Term Impact."

53. Committee on Criminal Justice, *The Bartley-Fox Gun Sentencing Study: Final Report* (Boston: Committee on Criminal Justice, 1991).

54. U.S. Attorney General, *Youth Violence: A Community-Based Response. One City's Success Story* (Washington, DC: Office of the Attorney General, 1996).

55. Boston Police Department, *Operation Cease Fire* (Boston: Boston Police Department, n.d.).

56. Bureau of the Census, *Statistical Abstract of the United States, 1995,* p. 657.

57. Bureau of the Census, *Statistical Abstract of the United States, 1995.*

58. University of Maryland, *Preventing Crime: What Works, What Doesn't, What's Promising?* (Washington, DC: Government Printing Office, 1997), chap. 7; airports are covered on pp. 7-29–7-30.

59. Howard N. Snyder and Melissa Sickmund, *Juvenile Offenders and Victims: 1999 National Report* (Washington, DC: Government Printing Office, 1999), p. 68.

60. Snyder and Sickmund, *Juvenile Offenders and Victims,* p. 31. Kathryn A. Chandler, et al., *Students' Reports of School Crime: 1989–1995* (Washington, DC: U.S. Department of Education, 1998).

61. Lawrence W. Sherman, James W. Shaw, and Dennis P. Rogan, *The Kansas City Gun Experiment* (Washington, DC: Government Printing Office, 1995).

62. Herman Goldstein, *Problem-Oriented Policing* (New York: McGraw-Hill, 1990).

63. University of Maryland, *Preventing Crime* (Washington, DC: Government Printing Office, 1997).

64. "Indy Gun-Interdiction Drive Proves an Inviting Target," *Law Enforcement News,* 20 July 1995.

65. John R. Lott, Jr., and David B. Mustard, "Crime, Deterrence, and Right-to-Carry Concealed Handguns," *Journal of Legal Studies* 26 (January 1997): 1–69; John R. Lott, *More Guns, Less Crime.*

66. Franklin Zimring and Gordon Hawkins, "Concealed Handguns: The Counterfeit Deterrent," *The Responsive Community* 7 (Spring 1997): 58–59.

67. Bureau of Justice Statistics, *National Assessment of Structured Sentencing* (Washington, DC: Government Printing Office, 1996), pp. 24–25.

68. William D. Bales and Linda G. Dees, "Mandatory Minimum Sentencing in Florida: Past Trends and Future Implications," *Crime and Delinquency* 38 (July 1992): 309–29.

69. Bureau of Justice Statistics, *Felony Sentences in State Courts, 1994* (Washington, DC: Government Printing Office, 1997).

70. Bureau of Justice Statistics, *Sourcebook of Criminal Justice Statistics—1995,* p. 470.

71. Bureau of Justice Statistics, *Weapons Offenses and Offenders,* pp. 5–6.

72. Colin Loftin and David McDowall, "'One with a Gun Gets You Two': Mandatory Sentencing and Firearms Violence in Detroit," *Annals* 455 (May 1981): 150–67.

73. Loftin and McDowall, "One with a Gun Gets You Two."

74. David McDowall, Colin Loftin, and Brian Wiersma, "A Comparative Study of the Preventive Effects of Mandatory Sentencing Laws for Gun Crimes," *Journal of Criminal Law and Criminology* 83.2 (1992): 378–94.

75. Alan Lizotte and Marjorie S. Zatz, "The Use and Abuse of Sentence Enhancement for Firearms Offenses in California," *Law and Contemporary Problems* 49 (1986): 199–221.

PART IV

Reform:
The Liberal Prescription

L iberals take a very different approach to crime policy than do conservatives. As we indicated in Chapter 1, liberals are much more optimistic about our capacity to reduce crime by either changing people or society. In the two chapters that follow, we will take a close look at the two most important components of liberal crime policy. Chapter 11 examines both the concept of rehabilitation and specific programs designed to change criminal offenders into law–abiding citizens. Chapter 12 looks at potential reforms in the criminal law and the criminal justice system that might reduce the incidence of criminality.

11

Treat 'Em!

REHABILITATING CRIMINALS

The concept of *rehabilitation* is the cornerstone of traditional liberal crime control policy. Although the rhetoric has changed over the years, the basic idea remains the same: reduce crime by treating criminals and "correcting" their behavior. The terminology used by state agencies reflects the continued commitment to rehabilitation. We have departments of "corrections" but no departments of "punishment." Why do we use this terminology? Charles Logan and Gerald Gaes explain that the term *corrections* embraces "the language of medicine, psychology, and education" and that this coinage reflects an effort to acquire "some of the perceived legitimacy and prestige of those other professions."[1]

The Philosophy of Rehabilitation

What exactly is rehabilitation? The National Academy of Sciences defines it as "any planned intervention that reduces an offender's further criminal activity."[2] The key words here are *planned* and *intervention*. As Wolfgang's career criminal research indicates (see Chapter 4), most lawbreakers stop sooner or later. It is well established that criminal activity peaks between the ages of 14 and 24 and then declines sharply. Aging is the best crime reduction policy we know about.[3] The goal of rehabilitation is to make offenders stop sooner rather than later through a program of planned intervention.

The principal strategy for rehabilitating offenders is to reintegrate them into the community. Prisons offer programs designed to facilitate this process: academic and vocational education program, drug and alcohol counseling, and so on. Advocates of rehabilitation have traditionally preferred community-based correctional programs, primarily probation and parole, on the grounds that they are more likely to reintegrate offenders into law-abiding lives than is institutional confinement.

In the 1990s, a new set of *intermediate punishments* appeared, designed to place offenders in the community but under closer surveillance than is the case with traditional probation and parole.[4] These programs include boot camps, electronic monitoring, home confinement, and intensive probation or parole supervision. Some observers believe that these measures represent a revival of rehabilitation as criminal justice policy. Others, however, are not so sure. This chapter examines first traditional rehabilitation-oriented programs and then looks at the new intermediate punishments to see if they are more effective. Our goal in this chapter is to try to identify correctional treatment programs that are relatively more effective than others and that, if adopted, would help reduce crime.

Throughout our examination of this subject, it is important to keep in mind the admonition of the University of Maryland *Preventing Crime* report. Too often a false dichotomy is drawn between enforcement or punishment-oriented programs favored by conservatives and so-called crime prevention programs favored by liberals. The Maryland report correctly points out that regardless of philosophy, all criminal justice programs are designed to prevent crime. They differ in terms of the means to that end.[5] Rehabilitation represents a philosophy that seeks to prevent crime by correcting criminals' behavior through some form of planned intervention.

The Politics of Rehabilitation:
The Willie Horton Furlough

Rehabilitation-oriented programs are often the subject of bitter political controversy. The 1988 presidential election campaign is one famous example. Republican candidate George Bush ran a television ad about a convicted murderer, Willie Horton, who had been released from prison into the community on a weekend furlough during which he raped a woman. Bush used the incident to attack his opponent, Michael Dukakis, as a liberal Democrat who was soft on crime. The fact that Horton was black and the rape victim a white woman injected a divisive racial element into the election campaign.[6]

Furloughs are a classic type of rehabilitation program, designed to reintegrate a prisoner into the community through gradual release. They have been used for many years and are very common. In 1996, about 140,000 prisoners were granted furloughs through programs in 41 states (although more than half were in Florida, which furloughed over 87,000 offenders). Generally, furloughed offenders behave themselves. A 1990 survey found that only 31 of the 96,745 Florida offenders "failed." In Illinois, all of the 13,785 participants successfully completed the program. Connecticut had the highest failure rate, but even there only 29 of 3,398 inmates furloughed were arrested for a new crime. In Massachusetts, scene of the Willie Horton incident, none of the 438 furloughed inmates was rearrested while on release.[7]

The Willie Horton story is a classic example of the celebrated case in the top layer of our criminal justice wedding cake. As David C. Anderson observes in his thoughtful review of the case, exaggerating its significance and treating it as typical of general patterns is a "gross insult to truth."[8]

The case does dramatize the political controversy over rehabilitation. Liberals believe that furloughs are an effective program for reintegrating offenders into the community, while conservatives believe that they are a soft-hearted and misguided method of turning dangerous people loose on the community.

THE "NOTHING WORKS" CONTROVERSY

For over 25 years, discussions of rehabilitation have been dominated by the Martinson report. Criminologist Robert Martinson published an article in 1974 concluding that "with few and isolated exceptions, the rehabilitative efforts that have been reported so far have had no appreciable effect on rehabilitation."[9] His original article was titled "What Works?" but many people interpreted it to mean, "Nothing works." Martinson did not actually say nothing works; in fact, he found positive outcomes in 48 percent of the programs he cited. A few years later, he unequivocally stated that "some treatment programs do have an appreciable effect on recidivism," adding, "The critical fact seems to be the conditions under which the program is delivered."[10]

The Martinson report is a classic example of how social science research is often misinterpreted in the political arena. Many people wanted to believe that "nothing works" because they were disillusioned with rehabilitation. They were angry over (by then) ten years of soaring crime rates. Conservatives blamed rehabilitation programs for being soft on crime, whereas liberals attacked the same programs for violating standards of due process. The disillusionment with rehabilitation was part of a more general conservative mood in the mid-1970s.[11]

The story of Martinson's report is fascinating in itself. His team reviewed all evaluations of correctional programs published in English between 1945 and 1967. They were able to find only 231 that were acceptable by rigorous scientific standards. Most evaluations they rejected because these tests used unreliable measures, failed to specify the "treatment," did not use proper control groups, or drew questionable conclusions from the data.[12] Martinson exposed a scandalous case of professional irresponsibility: the correctional community's failure to develop a systematic process of evaluation. Programs routinely claimed "success" without any legitimate basis for doing so. The academic community shared much of the responsibility, as formal evaluations were done either by researchers under contract or by in-house professionals with academic training. Because his findings were so threatening, the state of New York did not release the report and even denied Martinson permission to publish it. He sued and eventually forced the report's release.

Was Martinson Right?

Was Martinson's assessment of correctional programs accurate? The National Academy of Sciences' Panel on Research on Rehabilitative Techniques reexamined his work and concluded that he was "essentially correct."[13] It supported Martinson's view that there was little evidence "to allay the current pessimism about the effectiveness of institutional rehabilitation programs as they now exist."

The debate sparked by Martinson continues to rage. Some, including Logan and Gaes, agree with Martinson that no convincing evidence exists regarding the effectiveness of correctional treatment.[14] Daniel Glaser and others, however, believe that there is enough evidence of success of particular programs to justify continued support for rehabilitation as a crime control strategy.[15]

How can we sort our way through this debate? As a first step, it is important to recognize, as Logan and Gaes point out, that the debate is as much ideological as it is empirical. Some advocates of rehabilitation regard it as a morally superior social policy regardless of the evidence about its success. Logan and Gaes, on the other hand, regard punishment as a morally legitimate social policy. "Legal punishment," they argue, "is a legitimate and . . . even a noble aspect of our culture."[16] No empirical evidence is going to resolve this aspect of the debate. It is a question of what values should underlie social policies.

Criminologists, meanwhile, continue to argue over the empirical evidence on the effectiveness of correctional treatment. In defense of rehabilitation, Glaser states that "certain sentencing and correctional policies, which differ according to the criminalization of the offender, are more likely than their alternatives to reduce recidivism rates."[17] That is essentially what Martinson concluded over 20 years ago, but the statement glosses over some basic problems.

The Prediction Problem Revisited

First of all, Glaser's defense of rehabilitation assumes a good match between offender and treatment program. Some programs are effective for some offenders. Achieving this match, however, is more easily said than done, and the heart of the problem is our old friend the prediction problem. Sentencing a convicted offender to a community-based drug treatment program, for example, represents a prediction that he or she (1) is not a serious danger to the community, and therefore does not need to go to prison, and (2) will respond positively to the drug treatment. Drawing on the work of John Hagan, Glaser argues that some individuals are more deeply "embedded in crime" than others.[18] Those who are less deeply embedded are more "amenable" to community-based treatment.

So far, so good. The crucial question is whether judges and correctional officials can correctly identify the more "amenable" offenders and sentence them to the right treatment program. This task runs headlong into the prediction problem. We have already criticized conservative programs because of their failure to accurately predict which offenders are the really high-risk ones. As we examine probation, boot camps, and other rehabilitation-oriented programs in this chapter, the important question is whether they are any more successful in predicting behavior.

TRADITIONAL REHABILITATION PROGRAMS

Let us now examine the traditional rehabilitation-oriented programs—diversion, probation, and parole—to see what evidence there is regarding their effectiveness.

Diversion

Diversion was one of the great reforms of the 1960s. The President's Crime Commission endorsed it in 1967, and an estimated 1,200 separate diversion programs were established during the 1970s.[19] (Unfortunately, the standard sources of data such as the *Sourcebook of Criminal Justice Statistics* include no current figures on diversion programs.) Although diversion programs take many forms, they have a common goal of getting the individual out of the criminal justice system as early as possible.

Diversion was not new in the 1960s. Historically, a great many offenders have been diverted from the criminal justice system at an early stage. Police officers routinely exercise their discretion not to arrest, even when they have probable cause. Prosecutors dismiss cases when prosecution would not serve the "interests of justice." We can call these traditional practices the *old* diversion. The *new* diversion programs that appeared in the 1960s are characterized by officially stated goals, a professional staff, and treatment services.[20]

Diversion programs are designed to rehabilitate offenders (and thereby reduce crime) in two ways. First, they keep people accused of relatively minor offenses out of jails and prisons. This strategy reflects the labeling perspective in criminological theory that holds that processing by the criminal justice system (and imprisonment in particular) accentuates the tendency toward criminal behavior. The President's Crime Commission summed up the rehabilitative goals of all community-based corrections, including diversion: "Institutions tend to isolate offenders from society, both physically and psychologically, cutting them off from schools, jobs, families, and other supportive influences and increasing the probability that the label criminal will be indelibly impressed upon them."[21] As the Wolfgang cohort data suggest, most juveniles "mature out of" criminal behavior. The philosophy of diversion argues that the best approach is to intervene as little as possible.

Second, diversion programs are designed to provide social services that address the offender's real problems: drug or alcohol treatment, employment counseling, and so forth. Arrest may only aggravate those problems and overburden criminal justice agencies.

Finally, diversion programs are intended to reduce the costs of the criminal justice system, by avoiding the expenses of criminal prosecution or imprisonment.

In short, diversion promised the best of all possible worlds—more effective, more humane, and cheaper. An old adage says that if something seems too good to be true, it probably is. Let us take a look at diversion in practice.

The Manhattan Court Employment Project The earliest and most influential diversion program was the Manhattan Court Employment Project. Sponsored by the Vera Institute, the project provided employment services to arrested persons. The basic assumption was that because unemployment is a major cause of crime, facilitating employment will reduce subsequent criminal activity.

Each day staff members of the Court Employment Project reviewed the arrest docket and identified defendants who met the program's criteria: resident of New York City, between the ages of 16 and 45, unemployed or earning less than $125 a week, and charged with a felony other than homicide, rape, kidnapping, or arson. In addition, the defendant must have not had prior jail or prison experience of one year or longer. With the prosecutor's consent, the case was suspended for 90 days while the defendant received counseling, assistance in obtaining any short-term public assistance for which he or she might have been eligible, and referral to a job opening with one of the 400 cooperating employers. Charges were dropped completely if the defendant "succeeded" by keeping a job. If the person "failed" to secure employment, the case was prosecuted.

An early evaluation declared the Manhattan Court Employment Project a huge success. In its first three years, the project accepted 1,300 clients, about half of whom (48.2 percent) succeeded. About 70 percent of these 626 people had been unemployed at the time of arrest. Fourteen months later, about 80 percent of those who could be located were still employed. Only 15.8 percent of these successful clients committed another crime in the twelve months following their release from the program. This recidivism rate was half of that for both offenders who failed in the program and a control group. The program cost only $731 per client, or $1,518 per success.[22]

A subsequent evaluation, however, reached very different conclusions. According to this report, the project did not reduce recidivism and had no discernible effect on the employment record or the behavior of its clients. Moreover, it did not reduce pretrial detention time or lower the number of convictions. A major problem was that about half of the clients served by the program would not have been prosecuted at all if there had been no court employment project.[23] This is a classic example of "net widening." Because it affects so many well-intentioned reforms, we need to discuss net widening in detail.

The Net-Widening Problem   *Net widening* is the process by which more people are brought under some form of social control. The unwritten law of net widening is that less punitive alternatives tend to be applied to people who would otherwise not be under any social control at all—that is, they would not be arrested, prosecuted, or incarcerated.

Evaluations of early diversion programs found substantial net widening. More than half of the juveniles referred to 15 diversion projects in California would not have entered any kind of program under traditional practice. Thomas G. Blomberg found in his review of juvenile diversion programs that they produced a 32 percent increase in the total number of juveniles under some form of control. Other evaluations have found varying degrees of expansion but an expanding net nonetheless.[24] And as we shall see, net widening has plagued many of the new intermediate punishments such as boot camps.[25]

The dynamics of net widening are easy to understand. Officials continue to use the severe sanctions (for example, prison) for offenders they regard as really dangerous and the new less punitive program for less serious offenders. Thus, instead of diverting offenders out of the system, they divert additional new people in. As Tonry and Lynch explain, both politicians and correctional officials tend to be "risk averse": They want to avoid taking any risk that might eventually reflect badly on their judgment.[26] Judges worry that a defendant placed on bail might commit a serious crime while on release or that a convicted offender might commit a serious crime after being granted probation. In the case of diversion, a prosecutor worries that a defendant placed in a pretrial diversion program might commit a serious crime. Consequently, many diversion programs receive only the low-risk offenders. The problem, of course, is that most of those low-risk offenders would have succeeded without the benefit of the program. The program, therefore, provides no increase in crime reduction effectiveness.

The net-widening phenomenon suggests that the old diversion did a better job of achieving the basic goal of keeping people out of the system. When a police officer does not make an arrest, that person is truly diverted; when a prosecutor dismisses all charges, that defendant is genuinely diverted. New diversion programs, however, keep people under some form of control, thereby maintaining or even increasing the total costs to the system.[27]

Does Diversion Rehabilitate?   The most important question for us is whether diversion effectively rehabilitates offenders who are subject to formal programs. More precisely, the question is: Do diversion programs provide a treatment or intervention that reduces future criminal behavior more effectively than ordinary disposition through the system? A number of evaluations have found that they do not. The Law Enforcement Assistance Administration (LEAA) touted the Des Moines (Iowa) Adult Diversion Project as an "exemplary project" that other communities should adopt. An evaluation, however, found that it had "little impact in reducing recidivism among diverted, compared to nondiverted offenders." In another program, diverted offenders had lower recidivism rates than did juveniles sent to juvenile court but, alas, had higher recidivism rates than did kids released outright without the benefit of any "treatment."[28] More recent reviews have found similarly disappointing results.

Diversion programs suffer from a number of problems. The nature of the "treatment" can be vague and unspecific. Many do not actually deliver the services they claim to deliver. The early intensive probation supervision programs, for example, did not achieve a high rate of contacts between probationers and probation officers.[29] Questions also arise about the content and the impact of treatment services. Are the drug and alcohol treatment components of diversion programs effective in reducing substance abuse? How many of the offenders who succeed would have done so on their own, without the benefit of the treatment?

Additionally, if net widening occurs, the promised cost savings will not result because there are more rather than fewer clients. Finally, diversion programs introduce serious due process considerations. A person who agrees to enter a treatment program in the expectation of having criminal charges dropped is, in effect, admitting guilt. Rather than contest the charge, the person is saying, "Yes, I have done something wrong, and you have a right to force me to undergo treatment." By offering a seemingly more attractive alternative to prosecution and possible incarceration, the program coerces this tacit admission of guilt in a subtle but powerful way. In addition, the selection of the program's clients may be unfair.[30]

In the end, diversion offers a false promise. It fails to achieve its own goals, may well contradict them, and does not offer a realistic solution to the problem of serious crime. For the most part, diversion is not used for persons charged with robbery or burglary. Nor is there persuasive evidence that it rehabilitates lesser offenders in a way that keeps them from becoming serious offenders.

This leads us to the following proposition:

PROPOSITION 34
Diversion programs do not reduce serious crime.

Probation

Probation is the most widely used rehabilitation program in the entire criminal justice system. By the end of 1998, 3.4 million adults were on probation in the United States, more than twice as many as in the 1980s.[31] About 31 percent of all convicted felons are sentenced to "straight probation," and another 31 percent receive split sentences, with a jail term followed by probation. Thus, over half of all convicted felons serve some time on probation.[32]

Probation embodies the philosophy of rehabilitation by keeping convicted offenders in the community rather than sending them to prison. The "treatment" generally consists of some form of supervision and restrictions on behavior: reporting to a probation officer, drug or alcohol counseling, employment or evidence of seeking a job, and limitations on travel.

Probation serves a number of different purposes. From the stand point of proportionality in sentencing, it is often an appropriate sentence for someone convicted of a relatively less serious offense. It is also far cheaper than imprisonment—about $600 a year, compared with $17,000 to $20,000. Finally, we use probation as a matter of necessity. We simply could not afford to imprison all convicted felons even if we wanted to.

The Effectiveness of Probation Does probation work? Is it effective in rehabilitating offenders and reducing crime? Actually, there are two separate questions related to effectiveness: Is probation more effective than incarceration, and are some kinds of probation programs more effective than others? There is much debate over the effectiveness of probation. Evaluations have found failure rates that range from 65 to 12 percent.[33] Where does the truth lie?

The Rand study of felons on probation in California found very depressing results. After forty months on probation, 65 percent of the probationers had been rearrested, and 51 percent had been reconvicted of a new offense. Moreover, one-third of those reconvicted (18 percent of the original sample) were reconvicted of a serious violent crime. Nor do they wait very long to fail. Probationers reconvicted of a violent crime took an average of only eight months to recidivate, while those reconvicted of property offenses took an average of only five months.

In short, most offenders placed on probation "fail." What does this tell us about the effectiveness of probation as a crime reduction program? There are several possible answers to this question. The first is whether, despite the dismal results reported by Rand, probation is relatively more effective than prison. Unfortunately, no data indicate that it is. Offenders sentenced to prison and ultimately released either on parole or through mandatory release recidivate at almost the same rate. Therefore, one could continue to justify probation on either grounds of cost effectiveness (same results as prison but cheaper) or proportionality (a more just sentence for less serious offenses).

Another question, which is closer to the purpose of our inquiry, is whether some forms of probation are more effective than others. This raises the question of what accounts for the success of those people who do not recidivate. Can we identify the successful aspects of probation and enhance them? Or, to put it another way, are there some kinds of probation "treatment" that are more effective than others? We do not have good evidence on this issue. As Todd Clear and Anthony Braga point out, evaluation research has tended to focus on special forms such as intensive probation and house arrest, and as a result we do not know much about the effectiveness of conventional probation.[34]

Many experts have serious doubts about whether traditional probation programs provide any kind of meaningful treatment. The level of supervision has always been very minimal, involving a meeting with a probation officer (PO) once a month. The PO fills out the required reports, and that is that. Joan Petersilia found that offenders on regular probation in Los Angeles County met with their POs only once a month. Another report indicated that because of caseloads that exceeded a thousand probationers, POs in Los Angeles spent an average of 1 hour and 47 minutes *per year* with each offender.[35]

To overcome the problems associated with the delivery of services, a number of programs have adopted a *case management* approach. In case management, probation officers actively engage their clients in treatment, assess individual client needs, link clients with the relevant services (e.g., mental health services, or food stamps), monitor clients' behavior, and, if necessary, intervene with sanctions if clients do not comply with the terms of probation.[36] We should be skeptical about the claims made for this approach. In important respects, it seeks to repackage the traditional goals of probation in new terminology. At present, there is no persuasive evidence that probationers under case management programs do better than those under other programs.

Many experts believe that probation treatment has minimal impact on offenders. According to a 1995 survey, only 29 percent of all probationers were receiving alcohol abuse treatment and only 23 percent were receiving drug abuse treatment. Meanwhile, only 15 percent were in some kind of education or job training program.[37] And keep in mind, these data represent probationers who were *officially enrolled* in some kind of program. They say nothing about the content or quality of the programs, or about their impact on the probationers. It is important to recognize that most probation services to offenders represent *control* and *surveillance* rather than correctional treatment. We will discuss this issue in more detail later when we look at the new intermediate punishments.

Most probationers eventually rehabilitate themselves, through maturation, finding a job, getting married, and so on. John Hagan, drawing on the work of Mark Granovetter and others, argues that whether a person becomes law abiding or continues in a life of criminal activity depends on the extent to which he or she is "socially embedded" in legitimate or criminal opportunities. Some individuals have more contacts—for example, with family or people in the neighborhoods—that lead to jobs. These contacts, moreover, tend to multiply: A job results in additional contacts that lead to other and often better job opportunities. Such individuals are socially embedded in networks that lead to law-abiding lives, even when they had engaged in some initial criminal activity. This is particularly true of many white youths from blue-collar backgrounds. Other people, by contrast, have few of these positive networks. They are embedded in social circumstances that include few contacts with people who can refer them to jobs and more contacts with people who are engaged in criminal activity. This is particularly true of many racial and ethnic minority youths, who live in economically devastated areas where there are few jobs and relatively few people with contacts that lead to jobs.[38]

The idea that success or failure on probation is related to the social circumstances in which an offender lives is consistent with the University of Maryland *Preventing Crime* conclusion that crime prevention is likely to be more effective when it is multidimensional, addressing families, schools, the neighborhood, the local job market, and other factors related to the circumstances in which an offender is "socially embedded."[39] In short, a probation program operating in isolation from these other factors is not likely to be effective.

In addition to the traditional problems inherent with probation, the level of supervision has gotten even worse because of the increase in caseloads in recent years. The total number of people on probation more than tripled between 1979 and 1999, from 1 to 3.4 million. The average monthly caseloads for each PO in 1994 were as high as 294 in Rhode Island, 211 in Georgia, and 135 in Illinois. California reported an astounding average of 400 per probation officer (and perhaps as high as 1,000 in Los Angeles). States with lower caseload averages included Tennessee with 68 and Arizona with 60.[40]

This leads us to the following conclusion:

PROPOSITION 35

Probation is an appropriate sentence for many offenders, but there is no evidence that one kind of probation treatment is more effective in reducing crime than other kinds.

Can the effectiveness of probation be improved? The traditional means of improving probation has been through intensive supervision. It is one of several so-called *new intermediate punishments,* and it is often linked with other programs, such as house arrest. We will examine those programs later in this chapter.

Parole

Parole is the second most prevalent rehabilitation program. Most offenders sent to prison are released early under some form of supervision. Parole is seen as a rehabilitation program because, like probation, it seeks to reintegrate the offender into the community. In 1998, there were 704,964 adults on parole, more than three times as many as in 1980. Actually, the use of discretionary release parole has been declining as a result of the growth of sentencing guidelines. More offenders leave prison each year through supervised mandatory release (178,948 in 1995) than discretionary parole release (149,324 in 1995).[41]

Parole has historically been the unloved child of the criminal justice system. Everyone seems to criticize it. Conservatives argue that it turns dangerous offenders loose on society. Liberals, meanwhile, argue that parole release decisions are made without any scientific foundation, and the result is arbitrary and often discriminatory patterns in release.[42] Despite these criticisms, however, parole has demonstrated a remarkable capacity to survive in one form or another. It is important to recognize that parole consists of two elements: *discretionary release* and *postrelease supervision*. Fourteen states have abolished discretionary parole release, and another 21 have significantly limited the powers of parole boards to release prisoners. Nonetheless, all but two states still have some form of postrelease supervision.[43] Parole survives because it serves a number of purposes unrelated to rehabilitation: It offers prisoners an incentive to behave in prison, gives prison officials some power to control them, and serves as a safety valve for prison overcrowding.

Does Parole Work? Do prisoners who are released on parole have lower recidivism rates than those who serve longer prison terms? Does the prospect of earning early release encourage offenders to rehabilitate themselves? Does parole supervision facilitate rehabilitation? Do some forms of parole supervision work more effectively than others?

The effectiveness of parole has traditionally been measured in terms of the recidivism rate.[44] As with probation, an offender can fail either by committing a new crime or by a technical violation of parole conditions. In terms of a new crime, it depends on whether we measure failure in terms of being rearrested, reconvicted, or reincarcerated.

The data on parole outcomes are as discouraging as those for probation. The most recent and most thorough study of parole outcomes found that within three years 62.3 percent were rearrested for either a felony or serious misdemeanor. This was little different from the 64.8 rearrest rate for offenders released "unconditionally." About 47 percent were convicted of a new offense, and 41 percent were imprisoned for a conviction or a technical violation of their conditions of release.[45] These figures lend a great deal of support to the widespread belief that prison and parole are not successful in either deterring crime or rehabilitating offenders. The policy question is whether parole can be made to work more effectively.

One of the reasons for the high failure rate is that parole supervision generally provides very little in the way of treatment services. A study in California, for example, estimated that 10,000 parolees were homeless but only 200 shelter beds were available to them. Similarly, only four mental health clinics were available for an estimated 18,000 parolees with psychiatric problems. And there were only 750 beds in treatment programs for 85,000 parolees with alcohol or drug problems.[46] The lack of meaningful services has been one of the traditional problems affecting both probation and parole. The situation may, in fact, be getting worse. Most observers believe that in the last decade parole has become even more oriented toward enforcement rather than rehabilitation.

Intensive Parole Supervision   Intensive parole supervision (IPS) is one of the new intermediate punishments designed to improve parole. As already noted, IPS is often an integral part of other intermediate sanctions: boot camps, home confinement, and others. In 1996, about 4 percent of all parolees (24,800 total) were in an intensive supervision program.[47]

Like intensive probation supervision, intensive parole supervision is nothing new. California developed a pioneering Special Intensive Parole Unit (SIPU) program in the mid-1950s and maintained it for ten years.[48] Martinson reviewed the SIPU evaluations and found that three of the four phases produced no meaningful improvement in parolees' behavior. The phase involving smaller caseloads did appear to yield some positive results. Parolees in this phase appeared to be more successful because they were returned to prison more often for technical violations. Martinson concluded that this was a deterrent rather than a rehabilitative effect. Parolees behaved themselves a little better when they knew that they faced a real prospect of being sent back to prison.[49]

The Prediction Problem Again The parole reform strategy with the longest history is the attempt to improve parole release decision making: that is, to parole only those offenders who are ready for release into the community. The decision to release is a prediction that the offender will not recidivate. The sad fact of the matter, however, is that criminologists have been searching for better parole release criteria since the 1920s, but with little success.[50] Even though California developed a large correctional research unit in the 1950s, Martinson and others have found no evidence that California parole decision makers were more accurate in predicting offenders' behavior than were their counterparts in other states.[51] Conservatives, on the other hand, have criticized parole authorities for turning dangerous offenders loose on the community.

Abolish Parole? Disillusionment with parole reached such a point in the 1970s that several jurisdictions simply abolished it. The Determinate Sentencing Law enacted by California in 1976 abolished discretionary parole release. Release dates are mandatory once a prisoner has served the sentence imposed by the judge and good time has been deducted. A one-year period of parole supervision remains, however. The federal sentencing guidelines that took effect on November 1, 1987, also abolished parole and replaced it with presumptive sentences.[52] A total of fourteen states have now abolished discretionary parole release.

Abolition of discretionary parole release may or may not be a good idea. From the standpoint of this book, however, there is no evidence that one form of release from prison is more effective in reducing crime than a different form. The question of the abolition of parole, in short, is irrelevant to crime control.

Our position is as follows:

PROPOSITION 36
Abolishing parole will not reduce crime.

THE NEW INTERMEDIATE PUNISHMENTS

In their 1990 book *Between Prison and Probation,* Norval Morris and Michael Tonry leveled a major criticism of criminal sentencing in America. They argued that judges generally faced a choice between two extremes sentences, probation and prison. In many cases, however, prison is too harsh a punishment, while probation is too lenient. Part of the problem is that probation involves neither meaningful treatment nor effective control of offenders in the community. Consequently, Morris and Tonry called for the development of a range of intermediate punishments that would be less extreme than prison but with more content that traditional probation.[53]

Correctional officials and politicians across the country responded to this recommendation by developing a set of new programs. The most important of these are boot camps (BC), shock incarceration (SI), intensive probation supervision (IPS), home confinement (HC), and electronic monitoring (EM). Taken as a group, the new intermediate punishments represent what Joan Petersilia calls "an important landmark" in American crime policy.[54]

Ted Palmer and some other observers regard the new intermediate punishments as a revival of rehabilitation. It this true? Palmer's own choice of words, however, raises some doubts. He refers to *correctional intervention* instead of *rehabilitation*. The difference is more than a matter of semantics. As we shall see later in this chapter, the new intermediate punishments put special emphasis on surveillance and control of offenders, often with little emphasis on traditional treatment components. As some critics have pointed out, they are often more punishment than rehabilitation oriented. This trend reflects the extent to which recent developments in corrections have been completely dominated by the conservative crime control agenda.

It is important to recognize that many of the new intermediate punishments often overlap and include two or more different programs. Boot camps (BC) are often defined as a form of *shock incarceration* (IS) and frequently include a period of intensive parole supervision (IPS) following release. That IPS might include home confinement (HC), which may be enforced through electronic monitoring (EM).[55] All of these programs may include frequent random drug tests. In examining a particular intermediate punishment, therefore, it is important to look beyond the label and determine exactly what program elements it contains.

Boot Camps

The most highly publicized new intermediate sanction is the *boot camp.* By 1996, there were shock incarceration programs in 32 states and the federal prison system. Most had beds for about 150 inmates, although New York was the largest, with a capacity of about 1,400, while some states handled as few as 30 or 40 at any one time. Some of these programs emphasized the military aspects of boot camps more than others.

What exactly is a boot camp? Generally they involve (1) a short period of incarceration (typically three to six months), (2) in a facility separate from a regular prison, (3) for young first-time offenders (many exclude offenders con-

victed of violent crimes), (4) with program of rigorous physical, educational, and substance abuse programs. The short term of incarceration followed by (5) a period of intensive supervision in the community. Many of the initial boot camps emphasized the purely military aspects: "Military drill and ceremony, hard labor, physical training, and strict rules and discipline."[56] As time passed, correctional officials gave more emphasis to the treatment elements, such as drug counseling.

Along with other intermediate punishments, boot camps have multiple and often conflicting goals. They are simultaneously intended to rehabilitate, punish, control, and reduce prison overcrowding.

The basic idea underlying boot camps is nothing new. Judges have routinely given split sentences: short periods of incarceration followed by probation. Boot camps are different primarily by virtue of the military rhetoric that surrounds them and the intensive probation supervision that usually follows release.

Boot camp programs vary considerably in terms of how participants are selected, the content of the boot camp program, and the nature of the post-release supervision. In some states, judges sentence offenders directly to boot camp (these are sometimes referred to as *front-end* intermediate punishments). In others, correctional officials select participants (referred to as *back-end* programs). In some states, boot camp participation is voluntary, meaning that an offender must choose it. In others, it is mandatory for those sentenced to them. Offenders in some states can voluntarily drop out of the boot camp and return to prison.[57]

In terms of content, Doris Mackenzie and her colleagues found that one of the greatest differences between the boot camps in the eight states they evaluated was "the amount of time in the daily schedule that is devoted to work, drill, and physical training versus such treatment-type activities as counseling, drug treatment, or academic education."[58] Some boot camps are almost entirely military-style programs, whereas others put much more emphasis on traditional rehabilitative programs.

Do boot camps work? A review of evaluations concluded that the "emerging consensus" of informed opinion is "discouraging": "Most boot camps have no discernible effect on subsequent reoffending."[59] That is, boot camp graduates are no less likely to reoffend that individuals either sent to prison or placed on traditional probation. A number of problems affect boot camp programs. One-third or a half of offenders fail to complete the program. There also appears to be significant net widening, as judges or correctional officials place low-risk offenders in boot camp programs. As a result, overall system costs often increase rather than decrease. One problem that has affected all new intermediate punishment programs is that the more intensive surveillance (e.g., more contacts with parole officers, frequent drug tests) identifies more technical violations of the conditions of release. This increases the failure rate and results in sending more offenders back to prison, a development that eliminates the potential cost savings.

Some critics argue that the emphasis on military drill may be fundamentally misguided. Yelling at inmates, treating them with disrespect, and forcing them to undergo painful physical exercises may be counterproductive, teaching inmates that disrespect and verbal abuse are the keys to success in life. Such programs also value the most aggressive definition of masculinity. Finally, the legendary rigors of Marine boot camp at least offer a reward at the end: entry into the proud fellowship of the Corps. If prison boot camps offer nothing of comparable positive value at the end but only a return to the same neighborhood with the same bleak prospects (what Hagan refers to as a life socially embedded in crime), they are not likely to have a long-term positive impact on the people who pass through them.[60]

This leads us to the following conclusion:

PROPOSITION 37
Boot camps do not reduce crime.

Intensive Probation Supervision

Intensive probation supervision (IPS) is designed to make the probation treatment more effective. In 1995, 10 percent of all people on probation were reportedly in some kind of IPS program.[61]

Although often presented as a great innovation, IPS is not really new. Intensive supervision in both probation and parole was tried in the 1960s. One of the most important was the San Francisco Project, conducted by the federal probation system. Probationers were randomly assigned to probation officers with caseloads of various sizes. Two IPS groups involved caseloads of only 20 probationers; two other groups had caseloads of 40, and another group had caseloads of several hundred clients. All other offenders were assigned to groups with normal levels of supervision, meaning that probation officers had between 70 and 130 clients.[62] An evaluation of the program found no significant difference in the recidivism rates of offenders in the various groups. Intensive supervision did not consistently reduce the failure rate. In a development that would reappear in many subsequent new intermediate sanction programs, more intensive supervision resulted in more technical violations of the conditions of probation.

The most serious problem with the program was that the basic assumption underlying it was flawed. It was assumed that the key to effectiveness is the "intensity" of supervision as measured by caseload size and the frequency of contact.[63] It appears, however, that mere contact has little impact on a probationer's behavior and that increasing the number of contacts makes no difference. In many respects, this problem is similar to the flawed assumptions underlying police patrol that we examined in Chapter 5: that routine patrol deters crime and, therefore, that more patrol will deter crime more effectively.

The new IPS programs attempt to overcome some of the problems associated with the early programs. In addition to smaller caseloads (between 19 and 40 in three California programs) and more frequent contacts (one survey found that 32 percent of all IPS programs involve 5 to 14 contacts per month, whereas another 38 percent involve 15 to 24 contacts), there are usually a much wider range of restrictions on offenders' behavior. These include home confinement (82 percent of all California programs in one study), mandatory drug tests (76 percent), alcohol tests (74 percent), and electronic monitoring (56 percent).[64]

Are the new IPS programs effective? That is, are they more effective than traditional probation? Joan Petersilia found the results in three California programs "particularly discouraging." After one year, about 35 percent of the IPS probationers had been rearrested, another 40 percent committed technical violations of probation conditions, and only 25 percent had no violations of any sort. Admittedly, the offenders assigned to these IPS programs were "high risk," but a 75 percent failure rate after only one year is a very poor showing. Perhaps even more significant, their rearrest rates were no different from those of other probationers. This outcome suggests that the intense supervision did not stop them from committing crime. Once again, more intensive supervision resulted in much higher rates of technical violations. This result is hardly surprising, because that is what frequent contacts and drug tests are designed to detect.[65]

Why are IPS programs no more successful than regular probation in reducing recidivism? The answer may be that no form of probation supervision—intensive or minimal—has any real impact on offenders' behavior. The "treatment" may not address the real problems that offenders have.

Confused Goals IPS suffers from both confused goals and exaggerated promises. Its advocates claim it will rehabilitate offenders and keep them under control and reduce prison overcrowding and save money—all at the same time. As
some critics point out, if all this were true, IPS would be "the wonderchild of
the criminal justice system."[66] Yet as many observers have pointed out, current
IPS programs emphasize surveillance and control rather than rehabilitation. A
Justice Department report on *Performance Measures for the Criminal Justice System*
argues that if the goal is surveillance and control, then a high failure rate is a
positive indicator of the program's performance: Offenders who violate the
terms of probation or commit another crime are taken off the streets and sent
to prison.[67]

Many IPS programs do not necessarily serve the clients for whom they
were designed. Although generally intended for "high-risk" offenders, only 20
percent of the clients in the Georgia and New Jersey programs fit that definition. Georgia officials privately conceded that 25 percent of the IPS clients
were not "true" diversions from prison. There were also rumors that New Jersey judges sentenced some offenders to prison only to make them eligible for
"diversion" through IPS.[68]

The very intensity of the supervision in IPS programs has introduced an
entirely new problem. Joan Petersilia reports that one-third of those offenders
eligible for intensive probation in Marion County, Oregon, chose to go to
prison. In New Jersey, 15 percent of those who applied for IPS withdrew their
applications when they found out what IPS would be like.[69]

It is easy to see why offenders choose prison. The Oregon IPS program
included home visits two or three times a week, with telephone checks on
other days, unannounced searches for drugs, and periodic urine tests for drug
use. Offenders were required to perform community service work and were
forbidden to associate with certain people. This regime would last for two
years. The alternative was a two- to four-year prison sentence that usually
resulted in three to six *months* of actual time served, followed by two years of
routine parole supervision, which meant only one visit per month and none of
the other IPS requirements. The IPS program was far more intrusive and
punitive than prison and parole.[70]

This leads us to the following conclusion:

PROPOSITION 38
Intensive supervision, with either probation or parole, will not reduce crime.

More about Gun Crimes in Boston Chapter 10 described the various programs in
Boston designed to reduce gun crimes, particularly by young gang members.
Probation and parole officers were a major part of that effort, particularly
Operation Night Light, a police-corrections partnership. As explained earlier,
officials realized that many, if not most, gang members were on probation and
parole and were highly vulnerable to aggressive enforcement of existing release

conditions (e.g., curfews, or limits on associating with known criminals, etc.).[71]

Officials in Boston claim that Operation Night Light and related programs are responsible for the very dramatic drop in homicides in the city. Two things need to be said about these claims, however. First, as noted in Chapters 1 and 10, other cities have experienced similar declines in homicide and serious crime, so we should be skeptical about crediting the Boston programs. Second, and more to the point of this chapter, the Boston programs are aggressive *enforcement* efforts and the involvement of probation and parole officers has nothing to do with the traditional rehabilitation goals of probation or parole.

Home Confinement and Electronic Monitoring

Home confinement (HC) and *electronic monitoring* (EM) are designed to keep the offender in the community but under a fairly strict form of surveillance and control. HC is essentially a curfew. In some cases, the curfew is enforced through EM; in others, it is not. Critics have pointed out that both HC and EM have the same mixture of goals as does IPS. They are designed to simultaneously reduce prison overcrowding, and both control and rehabilitate the offender.

The current interest in electronic monitoring began in 1983, when Judge Jack Love of Albuquerque adopted the Gosslink system for a convicted offender. The idea quickly caught on. By 1996, there were 13,868 probationers and 8,491 parolees in EM programs.[72] An early report by the Rand Corporation gave electronic monitoring a cautiously favorable assessment. It was far cheaper than imprisonment: as low as $1,350 per year, versus $20,000 for prison. Basically two different EM technologies are available. Passive monitoring radio frequency (RF) systems place a transmitter on the offender (a tamperproof bracelet or anklet) and a dialer on the telephone. If the probationer leaves the premises, the signal is interrupted, and the dialer automatically calls the probation office. Active monitoring programmed contact (PC) systems involve periodic, usually random telephone calls to the probationer's home. The calling may be done automatically by machine or by the PO's personal phone call.

Initially, the largest group of offenders in EM programs were those convicted of major traffic offenses. By 1989, property offenders and drug offenders had become the two largest categories. This result suggests that as the program grew, judges felt more confident about committing different kinds of offenders to it. Sentences generally ran from 60 to 120 days. A Justice Department survey found that most failures occurred within the first two months. About 4 percent of the total sample committed a new offense, and half of those occurred in the first 60 days. About 22 percent of the sample committed a technical violation of the terms of their confinement.[73]

Many people initially opposed EM because it conjured up images of George Orwell's famous novel *1984,* with Big Brother continuously monitoring everyone's private behavior. In actual practice, EM may not deliver on its promises. Gary Marx argues persuasively that it is advertised as another tech-nological fix for the crime problem. It is the proverbial free lunch or "painless dentistry." EM systems have run into serious technical problems. Certain kinds of housing construction, for example, can disrupt the signal. Random calls in the middle of the night not only disrupt the probationer's sleep (not such a good idea if we want that person to hold a steady job) but also require that a staff person be on duty to respond to a violation.

Additionally, EM programs produce relatively small cost savings for the criminal justice system. The 12,000 offenders in EM programs in 1992 (proba-tion and parole combined) represented a minuscule fraction of the 4.8 million under correctional supervision that year.[74]

The intensive surveillance that EM (and IPS) provides creates additional problems. It is designed to detect failures, and it succeeds in doing so. More offenders are cited for technical violations than for new criminal acts, and many of them are sent to prison. As the report *Performance Measures for the Criminal Justice System* points out, disagreement persists over whether a high rate of technical violations is an indicator of success or failure. If the purpose of EM is to control offenders and detect misbehavior, then it is an indicator of success. If the purpose is to reintegrate the offender into the community, then it suggests failure.[75]

Most important for our purposes, evaluations indicate that offenders under IPS, HA, and EM have the same rearrest rate as those on regular probation. In short, they are no more effective in reducing crime than conventional prison or probation programs.

The question of effectiveness is complicated by the issue of the high rate of technical violations, however. If we assume that a technical violation of proba-tion (for example, violation of curfew) is a predictor of more serious failures, such as committing another crime, then sending the offender back to prison for that technical violation does reduce crime. If the intermediate punish-ments succeed in this respect, however, it is important to see them as *incapaci-tation* rather than rehabilitation programs. In other words, we should discuss them in Chapter 7 rather than in this chapter. We are still left searching for an effective rehabilitation program.

This leads us to conclude:

PROPOSITION 39
Home confinement and electronic monitoring will not reduce crime.

Summary:

Lessons of the Intermediate Punishment Movement

Joan Petersilia reviewed the first 10 to 15 years of the intermediate punish-ment movement and reached some sobering conclusions. Most of the pro-grams were "more symbolic . . . than substantive."[76] Most important, there was no evidence that intermediate sanctions were more effective than traditional programs in reducing recidivism. In many cases, this was the result of implementation problems: lack of adequate funding and program resources; selection of inappropriate offenders, and so on. The one "tantalizing" positive finding, according to Petersilia is the evidence that offenders who participate in a range of programs—substance abuse treatment, community service, employment programs—did have lower recidivism rates than comparable offenders who did not.[77] Although not definitive, this finding lends further support to the conclusion of the Maryland *Preventing Crime* report that effective crime reduction programs need to be multidimensional. Some experts refer to this as "neighborhood parole" or the "full service model" of probation and parole. It is still too early to pronounce a final judgment on this approach. Nonetheless, it does expose one of the traditional weaknesses of probation, parole, and other rehabilitation-oriented programs—and about how we have thought about those programs. No single program, working in isolation from the community context and the full range of offender needs, is likely to be effective.

RESTORATIVE JUSTICE

A radically new approach to criminal justice policy involves the concept of restorative justice. This approach is an alternative to the basic ethos of our legal system and its emphasis on formal bureaucratic procedures, the requirement that the state prove guilt, and its emphasis on both the individual responsibility of the offender and the harm done to the individual victim. *Restorative justice* has a more communitarian ethos, emphasizing both harm to the community at large and the responsibility of the offender to the community. As the term itself implies, it seeks not so much to punish offenders but to *restore* the bonds between the person who has done wrong, the victim, and the community at large.[78]

Instead of the traditional Anglo-American adversarial process, restorative justice emphasizes dialogue, negotiation, and the reestablishment of a positive relationship between victim and offender. In practice, restorative justice programs have often used financial restitution, community service, and mediation, usually in the form of face-to-face acknowledgment of guilt. The restorative justice movement draws heavily on communal peace-making traditions among Native Americans and other indigenous peoples.

The leader of the restorative justice movement is John Braithwaite, whose book *Crime, Shame and Reintegration* sparked the movement. Emphasizing shaming as the key to controlling crime, he argues that informal sanctions "imposed by relatives, friends or a personally relevant collectivity have more effect on criminal behavior than sanctions imposed by a remote legal authority."[79] Although Braithwaite is critical of traditional rehabilitation-oriented programs, his concept of restorative justice can be seen as a form of rehabilitation, particularly with its emphasis on reintegrating offenders into the community. Some programs, in fact, operate as diversion programs, referring cases to mediation conferences as an alternative to prosecution.

Restorative Justice in Operation

In a recent elaboration of restorative justice principles, Braithwaite argues that this approach is more effective in controlling crime than policies based on punishment, deterrence, incapacitation, and even rehabilitation. The U.S. Justice Department has recommended incorporating restorative justice into community policing programs.[80] How well does restorative justice work in practice? Like many of the so-called new intermediate punishments we discussed earlier, the restorative justice programs of financial restitution and community service are nothing new. They have been used for many years but have been seen primarily as alternative sentences within the basic sentencing framework, appropriate for less serious offenses, and not a radical alternative to the basic principles of the justice system.

Evaluations of experimental restitution, community service, and mediation programs have tended to find slightly lower recidivism rates for offenders compared with traditional sentences of prison or probation. The differences are not always consistent, however, and many questions remain regarding the implementation and outcomes of such programs.[81] Some of the most promising findings are closely related to the concept of procedural justice discussed in Chapter 12. In the most ambitious experiment in Australia, preliminary findings indicate that restorative justice conferences result in lower levels of anger, fear, and alienation from the legal system among both victims and offenders than does traditional court processing.[82]

We have many reasons for being skeptical about restorative justice as a response to serious crime. First, although it may well be appropriate for less serious crimes, especially minor property offenses, many people will question whether, from the standpoint of proportionality and just deserts, it is appropriate for serious crimes. Second, although it may be appropriate for first-time offenders, there are questions about whether is it appropriate for fourth- or fifth-time offenders. And finally, there are questions about whether it effectively reduces serious crime. A careful reading of Braithwaite's long 1999 essay in defense of restorative justice reveals that it is long on theory—and discussions of what it might accomplish—and fairly short on proven results.[83]

The most serious problem with Braithwaite's concept is that the necessary conditions he identifies do not exist in modern urban society. Common sense suggests that the informal sanctions of family, friends, or community are likely to be more effective in controlling behavior than the threats and actions of remote official agencies. But a major part of the crime problem in the United States today is the collapse of families, peer groups, and communities for many people. As Hagan's theory of social embeddedness suggests, some individuals are deeply embedded in lives that encourage law breaking rather than law abiding. In our poorest, most economically ravaged and drug-ridden neighborhoods, "community," in the positive sense of the term, has disappeared. The structure of families has collapsed for too many people. The peer group influence too often leads to drugs and crime. The concept of restorative justice may well be appropriate and effective for the young juvenile delinquent in a middle-class neighborhood but irrelevant for those aspects of our society that are the center of most serious crime.

Not only does restorative justice draw heavily on Native American traditions of communal justice, but it also reflects a nostalgic view of community in the United States. The informal mechanisms of social control that he prizes —disapproval of family, friends, and neighbors—were in fact the primary means of crime control in seventeenth-century colonial New England. They worked because those communities were small and extremely homogenous (almost entirely white, English, and Protestant). As this country grew into a large and diverse nation, characterized not only by different racial, ethnic, religious, and cultural groups but also by largely anonymous social relations, the old mechanisms no longer worked. That is one of the main reasons that Americans created the modern criminal justice system in the early nineteenth century. There is no returning to this vanished society.[84]

This leads us to the following conclusion:

PROPOSITION 40
The promise of restorative justice remains unproven in reducing serious crime.

CONCLUSION:
IS REHAB RUNNING ON EMPTY?

In the end, the evidence on rehabilitation does not look very good. We do not seem to have devised any "planned intervention" programs that substantially reduce recidivism rates. None of the much-publicized innovations seem to be more successful than the traditional forms of probation and parole. It is true that some things work: As Glaser and others argue, some programs work for some offenders. The problem, however, is that the liberals who advocate rehabilitation are no more effective in predicting future behavior than are the conservative advocates of incapacitation.

The recent innovations in corrections—intensive supervision, home confinement, electronic monitoring, boot camps—emphasize surveillance and control of offenders, often with little in the way of meaningful services. Insofar as they succeed in detecting misbehavior and sending offenders to prison, these programs should be considered incapacitative "lock 'em up" programs rather than rehabilitation programs. As Frank Williams and Marilyn McShane suggest, few if any really innovative ideas in corrections have been proposed. Instead of genuine innovations, reformers have been "running on empty."[85]

The new intermediate punishments, along with the spectacular increase in the number of offenders on probation and parole (triple the number 15 years ago), adds an important perspective on the traditional liberal calls for making greater use of alternatives to incarceration. For years, groups such as the National Council on Crime and Delinquency (NCCD), the Sentencing Project, and others have argued that we imprison too many people and that we should use more alternative sentences. It is undeniable that we lock up an enormous number of people. But it is also true that we have also increased the number of people in community-based alternatives. These alternatives may very well be less expensive and more humane than prison, but we do not have any persuasive evidence that they are any more effective in reducing recidivism and, as a result, lowering the level of serious crime.

NOTES

1. Charles H. Logan and Gerald G. Gaes, "Meta-Analysis and the Rehabilitation of Punishment," *Justice Quarterly* 10 (June 1993): 245–63.

2. Lee B. Sechrest, Susan O. White, and Elizabeth Brown, *The Rehabilitation of Criminal Offenders: Problems and Prospects* (Washington, DC: National Academy of Sciences, 1979), pp. 18–19.

3. Michael Gottfredson and Travis Hirschi, "The True Value of Lambda Would Appear to be Zero: An Essay on Career Criminals, Criminal Careers, Selective Incapacitation, Cohort Studies, and Related Topics," *Criminology* 24 (1986): 213–34.

4. Michael Tonry and Mary Lynch, "Intermediate Sanctions," in Michael Tonry, ed., *Crime and Justice: A Review of Research,* vol. 20 (Chicago: University of Chicago Press, 1996), pp. 99–144.

5. University of Maryland, *Preventing Crime* (Washington, DC: Government Printing Office, 1997).

6. David C. Anderson, *Crime and the Politics of Hysteria* (New York: Times Books, 1995); The Sentencing Project, *The Lessons of Willie Horton: Thinking about*

Crime and Punishment for the 1990s (Washington, DC: The Sentencing Project, 1989).

7. The 1996 data are in Bureau of Justice Statistics, *Sourcebook of Criminal Justice Statistics—1997* (Washington, DC: Government Printing Office, 1998), pp. 513–14. The 1990 data are in Bureau of Justice Statistics, *Sourcebook of Criminal Justice Statistics—1991* (Washington, DC: Government Printing Office, 1992), p. 130.

8. Anderson, *Crime and the Politics of Hysteria,* pp. 270–71.

9. Robert Martinson, "What Works? Questions and Answers about Prison Reform," *Public Interest* 35 (Spring 1974): 22–54.

10. Robert Martinson, "Symposium on Sentencing: Part II," *Hofstra Law Review* 7.2 (1979): 243–58. The full report is published as Douglas Lipton, Robert Martinson, and Judith Wilks, *The Effectiveness of Correctional Treatment* (New York: Praeger, 1975).

11. Samuel Walker, *Popular Justice: A History of American Criminal Justice,* 2nd rev. ed. (New York: Oxford University Press, 1998).

12. Lipton et al., *The Effectiveness of Correctional Treatment.*

13. Sechrest et al., *The Rehabilitation of Criminal Offenders,* pp. 14, 31, 102.

14. Logan and Gaes, "Meta-Analysis and the Rehabilitation of Punishment."

15. Daniel Glaser, "What Works, and Why It Is Important: A Response to Logan and Gaes," *Justice Quarterly* 11 (December 1994): 711–23.

16. Logan and Gaes, "Meta-Analysis and the Rehabilitation of Punishment,"p. 255.

17. Glaser, "What Works?" p. 721.

18. Glaser, "What Works?"; see also John Hagan, "The Social Embeddedness of Crime and Unemployment," *Criminology* 31 (November 1993): 465–91.

19. Raymond T. Nimmer, *Diversion: The Search for Alternative Forms of Prosecution* (Chicago: American Bar Foundation, 1974).

20. Nimmer, *Diversion,* pp. 11–18, 41–51.

21. President's Crime Commission, *The Challenge of Crime in a Free Society* (Washington, DC: Government Printing Office, 1967), p. 165.

22. Vera Institute of Justice, *The Manhattan Court Employment Project: Final Report* (New York: Vera Institute of Justice, 1972).

23. U.S. Department of Justice, *Diversion of Felony Arrests: An Experiment in Pretrial Intervention* (Washington, DC: Government Printing Office, 1981).

24. Thomas G. Blomberg, "Widening the Net: An Anomaly in the Evaluation of Diversion Programs," in Malcolm W. Klein and K. S. Teilman, eds., *Handbook of Criminal Justice Evaluation* (Beverly Hills, CA: Sage, 1980), pp. 572–92.

25. Tonry and Lynch, "Intermediate Punishments."

26. Tonry and Lynch, "Intermediate Punishments," p. 101.

27. Eugene Doleschal, "The Dangers of Criminal Justice Reform," *Criminal Justice Abstracts* 14 (March 1982): 133–52. A different perspective on criminal justice reform is in Samuel Walker, *Taming the System: The Control of Discretion in American Criminal Justice, 1950–1990* (New York: Oxford University Press, 1993).

28. Blomberg, "Widening the Net," p. 592.

29. Joan Petersilia and Susan Turner, *Intensive Supervision Probation for High Risk Offenders: Findings from Three California Experiments* (Santa Monica, CA: Rand, 1990).

30. Jamie Gorelick, "Pretrial Diversion: The Threat of Expanding Social Control," *Harvard Civil Rights—Civil Liberties Law Review* 10 (1975): 180–214.

31. Bureau of Justice Statistics, *Probation and Parole in the United States, 1998* (Washington, DC: Government Printing Office, 1999).

32. Bureau of Justice Statistics, *State Court Sentencing of Convicted Felons, 1996* (Washington, DC: Government Printing Office, 1999).

33. Todd R. Clear and Anthony A. Braga, "Community Corrections," in James Q. Wilson and Joan Petersilia, eds., *Crime* (San Francisco: ICS Press, 1995), p. 431.

34. Clear and Braga, "Community Corrections," p. 431.

35. Petersilia and Turner, *Intensive Supervision Probation for High Risk Offenders,* p. 47; Petersilia, "Measuring the Performance of Community Corrections," p. 62.

36. Kerry Murphy Healey, *Case Management in the Criminal Justice System* (Washington, DC: Government Printing Office, 1999).

37. Bureau of Justice Statistics, *Characteristics of Adults on Probation, 1995* (Washington, DC: Government Printing Office, 1997).

38. John Hagan, "The Social Embeddedness of Crime and Unemployment," *Criminology* 31 (November 1993): 465–91.

39. University of Maryland, *Preventing Crime.*

40. Bureau of Justice Statistics, *Sourcebook of Criminal Justice Statistics—1995* (Washington, DC: Government Printing Office, 1996), p. 81.

41. Bureau of Justice Statistics, *Sourcebook of Criminal Justice Statistics—1997,* p. 515.

42. David J. Rothman, *Conscience and Convenience: The Asylum and Its Alternatives in Progressive America* (Boston: Little, Brown, 1980); Jonathan Simon, *Poor Discipline: Parole and the Social Control of the Underclass, 1890–1990* (Chicago: University of Chicago Press, 1993).

43. Joan Petersilia, "Parole and Prison Reentry in the United States," in Michael Tonry, ed., *Crime and Justice: A Review of Research,* vol. 26 (Chicago: University of Chicago Press, 1999), p. 496, table 1.

44. Petersilia, "Measuring the Performance of Community Corrections."

45. Petersilia, "Measuring the Performance of Community Corrections," p. 512.

46. Petersilia, "Measuring the Performance of Community Corrections," p. 502.

47. Bureau of Justice Statistics, *Correctional Populations in the United States, 1996,* p. 124.

48. Simon, *Poor Discipline,* pp. 80–84.

49. Robert Martinson and Judith Wilks, "Save Parole Supervision," *Federal Probation* 41 (September 1977): 23–27.

50. Walker, *Popular Justice.*

51. Robert Martinson, "California Research at the Crossroads," *Crime and Delinquency* (April 1976): 180–91.

52. Bureau of Justice Statistics, *A National Assessment of Structured Sentencing.*

53. Norval Morris and Michael Tonry, *Between Prison and Probation* (New York: Oxford University Press, 1990).

54. Joan Petersilia, "A Decade of Experimenting with Intermediate Sanctions: What Have We Learned?" *Federal Probation* 62 (December 1998): 3–9; Tonry and Lynch, "Intermediate Sanctions."

55. Richard A. Ball, C. Ronald Huff, and J. Robert Lilly, *House Arrest and Correctional Policy* (Beverly Hills, CA: Sage, 1988).

56. Doris Layton MacKenzie, Robert Brame, David McDowall, and Claire Souryal, "Boot Camp Prisons and Recidivism in Eight States," *Criminology* 33 (August 1995): 351.

57. For a discussion of the "front-end," "back-end" distinction, see Tonry and Lynch, "Intermediate Sanctions," pp. 110–11.

58. MacKenzie, et al., "Boot Camp Prisons and Recidivism in Eight States," 351.

59. Tonry and Lynch, "Intermediate Sanctions," p. 110.

60. Merry Morash and Lila Rucker, "A Critical Look at the Idea of Boot Camp as a Correctional Reform," *Crime and Delinquency* 36 (April 1990): 204–22.

61. Bureau of Justice Statistics, *Sourcebook of Criminal Justice Statistics—1997,* p. 471.

62. J. Banks, A. A. Porter, R. L. Rardin, T. R. Silver, and V. E. Unger, *Evaluation of Intensive Special Probation Projects* (Washington, DC: Government Printing Office, 1977).

63. Todd Clear and Patricia Hardyman, "The New Intensive Supervision Movement," *Crime and Delinquency* 36 (January 1990): 42–60.

64. Petersilia and Turner, *Intensive Supervision Probation for High Risk Offenders.*

65. Petersilia and Turner, *Intensive Supervision Probation for High Risk Offenders.*

66. Todd Clear, S. Flynn, and C. Shapirto, "Intensive Supervision in Probation," in Belinda McCarthy, ed., *Intermediate Punishments* (Monsey, NY: Willow Tree Press, 1987), pp. 10–11.

67. Petersilia, "Measuring the Performance of Community Corrections," p. 67.

68. Clear and Hardyman, "The New Intensive Supervision Movement."

69. Joan Petersilia, "When Probation Becomes More Dreaded than Prison," *Federal Probation* 54 (March 1990): 23–27.

70. Petersilia, "When Probation Becomes More Dreaded than Prison."

71. Boston Police Department, *Operation Cease Fire* (Boston: Boston Police Department, 1998).

72. Bureau of Justice Statistics, *Correctional Populations in the United States, 1996* (Washington, DC: Government Printing Office, 1999), p. 124.

73. Marc Renzema and David T. Skelton, *Use of Electronic Monitoring in the United*

States: 1989 Update (Washington, DC: Government Printing Office, 1990).

74. Bureau of Justice Statistics, *Correctional Populations in the United States, 1992.*

75. Bureau of Justice Statistics, *Performance Measures for the Criminal Justice System* (Washington, DC: Government Printing Office, 1993), pp. 67–68.

76. Petersilia, "A Decade of Experimenting with Intermediate Sanctions," p. 3.

77. Petersilia, "A Decade of Experimenting with Intermediate Sanctions," p. 6.

78. John Braithwaite, "Restorative Justice," in Michael Tonry, ed., *Crime and Justice: A Review of Research,* vol. 25 (Chicago: University of Chicago Press, 1999), pp. 1–127.

79. John Braithwaite, *Crime, Shame and Reintegration* (New York: Cambridge University Press, 1989); Braithwaite, "Restorative Justice," p. 69.

80. Braithwaite, "Restorative Justice"; Caroline G. Nicholl, *Community Policing, Community Justice, and Restorative Justice* (Washington, DC: Government Printing Office, 1999).

81. See the various contributions to Burt Galaway and Joe Hudson, *Criminal Justice, Restitution, and Reconciliation* (Monsey, NY: Willow Tree Press, 1990), especially Laurie Ervin and Anne Schneider, "Explaining the Effects of Restitution on Offenders: Results from a National Experiment in Juvenile Courts," pp. 183–206.

82. The preliminary findings of the Australia experiment are discussed in Braithwaite, "Intermediate Sanctions."

83. Braithwaite, "Intermediate Sanctions."

84. This is one of the central themes of Walker, *Popular Justice,* 2nd ed.

85. Marilyn D. McShane and Frank P. Williams, "Running on Empty: Creativity and the Correctional Agenda," *Crime and Delinquency* 35 (October 1989): 562–76.

12

Reform the Law
and the System

Two traditional liberal proposals for reducing crime involve reforming the criminal justice system. One calls for eliminating injustices in the system, particularly race discrimination The other involve decriminalizing certain kinds of behavior. Let's take a look at these proposals and see whether they might reduce serious crime.

ELIMINATE INJUSTICE

A major liberal goal for improving criminal justice is to eliminate injustice from the system itself. The most important injustices involve discrimination based on race and ethnicity, gender, or social class.

As Chapter 1 explained, many critics believe that the war on drugs involves serious patterns of racial and ethnic discrimination in the criminal justice system. While African Americans comprise about 14 percent of the U.S. population, they represent about half of all state and federal prisoners, and two-thirds of federal prisoners incarcerated for drug offenses.[1] Jerome Miller characterizes the justice system's approach to young African-American men as one of "search and destroy."[2]

There is much controversy over the extent of discrimination in the criminal justice system. Coramae Richey Mann sees systematic race discrimination throughout the system.[3] William Wilbanks, on the other hand, argues that the idea that the system is racist is a "myth."[4] The data on such topics as arrest, plea bargaining, and sentencing is extremely ambiguous because racial disparities are often confounded by other variables. In *The Color of Justice*, Walker, Spohn, and DeLone argue that discrimination is *contextual* rather than systematic.[5] That is, some discrimination exists in many points of the justice system, but it is not blatant in every part of the system.

Walker illustrates contextual discrimination with reference to the police.[6] It is a mistake to think that all police officers in all departments engage in discriminatory acts all the time. That would represent *systematic* discrimination. A contextual analysis holds that discrimination is likely to be found in particular police department units, or areas of law enforcement, or certain officers, or certain departments. Narcotics units in particular appear to target racial and ethnic minorities. This tendency reflects a policy decision by command officers and not bias on the part of individual officers. Similarly, the most persuasive evidence of *racial profiling* (e.g., that police make traffic stops for "driving while black") involves state police engaged in drug enforcement on interstate highways (as opposed to enforcement patterns by traffic units in local police departments).[7] There is also persuasive evidence that particular officers have much worse records in use of force and citizen complaints than do other officers in the same department working similar assignments. Finally, some police departments have much worse records in use of deadly force, use of excessive force, or corruption than do other departments. The recent scandal in the Los Angeles Police Department, for example, is far worse than anything that has been found in any other department.

Two aspects of contextual discrimination deserve comment. First, Marjorie Zatz argues that relatively small amounts of discrimination at different points in the system have an enormous cumulative effect.[8] That is, some racial disparity takes place in arrests, but when this is combined with equally small disparities in the decision to prosecute, to convict, and to sentence to prison and in the length of prison sentences, the end result is quite significant.

Perhaps even more important than the statistically measurable evidence of discrimination is the social and political impact of particular cases or incidents. Consider the case of racial profiling in traffic stops. Even if only one or two incidents occur in one city in any given year, each of those incidents resonate with both the individual and members of racial and ethnic minority communities. African Americans are consistently more likely to report that they know someone who has been mistreated by the police than are whites.[9] Such incidents are perceived to be indicative of broader patterns of injustice at the hands of the criminal justice system and reinforce the sense that American society as a whole is racist. In short, the significance of particular incidents lie in how they are perceived more than in their statistical incidence.[10]

The most persuasive evidence of race discrimination in the justice system involves drug offenses. The Sentencing Project reports that African Americans represent an estimated 13 percent of all drug users but 35 percent of persons arrested for drug offenses.[11] This disparity in drug arrests is not necessarily the result of arrest discrimination by individual officers on the street but of department-level enforcement strategies that concentrate drug enforcement efforts in racial minority neighborhoods. The evidence of racially disparate arrest patterns for drug offenses coexists with very mixed evidence regarding race discrimination in arrests for other offenses. Studies have consistently found either no clear and consistent pattern of discrimination or very weak racial effects. In short, the discrimination in arrests is contextual: concentrated in enforcement related to a specific set of offenses.[12]

There is also strong evidence of disparate racial effect in the sentences for cocaine-related offenses in the federal sentencing guidelines, with much longer sentences for crack cocaine, which is more heavily used by African Americans, than for powder cocaine, which is more heavily used by whites. As with arrest, the evidence of discrimination in sentencing is very strong for a specific offense but very mixed for sentencing in general.[13]

Does Justice Matter?

Since the purpose of this book is to identify ways to reduce serious crime, the question becomes: Does discrimination contribute to criminal behavior? Or, to turn it around: Would eliminating or reducing discrimination help to reduce serious crime?

A valuable perspective on this issue is provided by the field of procedural justice.[14] In brief, the concept of *procedural justice* holds that people's satisfaction with the justice system depends heavily on how they feel they were treated by the system. Of particular importance is whether they feel they had a chance to tell their side of the story and that someone listened to them. Procedural justice is distinct from *distributive justice,* which involves actual case outcomes. Think of it in terms of a grade appeal. You appeal the grade you received in a course. The concept of procedural justice holds that having an opportunity to tell your side of story (e.g., a meeting or hearing) is more important to you than the actual outcome of the appeal. You may still be unhappy about your grade, but you feel that at least the process was fair.

Does a sense of fairness and justice make a difference in terms of law-abiding behavior? Tom R. Tyler investigates this question in his book *Why People Obey the Law.*[15] Tyler's study was based on interviews with 1,575 Chicago residents, 804 of whom were reinterviewed a year later. Respondents were asked about their own law breaking (e.g., speeding, littering, shoplifting), and their perceptions of and experience with the police and the courts. The latter questions were designed to determine respondents' sense of the legitimacy of the justice system. Tyler concluded: "Citizens who view legal authority as legitimate are generally more likely to comply with the law."[16]

One of the important implications of Tyler's study is that in terms of achieving compliance with the law, deterrence has been overrated. That is, people are not primarily motivated by fear of punishment. Instead, they are more likely to be influenced by positive feelings toward the law and the justice system.

Casper, Tyler, and Fisher found that among several hundred male felony defendants in three cities, procedural justice issues were associated with their evaluation of their experience in criminal court. Particularly important was how they felt they were treated by the police (e.g., did the officer "treat you in a businesslike manner?" or "use disrespectful language?") and the amount of time their lawyer spent with them. Interestingly, defendants' evaluations were not affected by whether they had a private attorney or a public defender, or whether they pled guilty or went to trial. In short, how they felt they were treated shaped their level of satisfaction with the system.[17]

A reanalysis of the Milwaukee Domestic Violence Experiment, meanwhile, found that aspects of procedural justice were associated with lower recidivism rates. Arrestees who felt they were treated in a procedurally fair manner had recidivism rates that were as low as the rates for those given a more favorable outcome (e.g., warned but not arrested).[18]

Does justice matter? There is some small but suggestive evidence supporting Tyler's argument that a *sense of justice* does matter in terms of law-abiding behavior. It is premature to generalize too broadly from his study. His data on law breaking involved relatively minor offenses (the most serious of which was shoplifting an inexpensive item). The study did not investigate the relationship between perceptions of the fairness of the justice system and serious crimes such as robbery and burglary. Nonetheless, it is reasonable to speculate that perceptions of discrimination do make a difference and that people who feel that the criminal justice system is unfair—and beyond that, American society in general offers them no place—are more likely to break the law.

Realistically, someone is not likely to perceive injustice and go out and commit an armed robbery. But it is reasonable to assume that a perception of injustice weakens a young person's respect for the law and contributes to minor law breaking (e.g., vandalism, petty theft) and that the resulting involvement in criminal behavior and the criminal justice system leads to more serious offending later on. From this perspective, respect for the law becomes the linchpin in serious crime.

This leads us to the following conclusion:

PROPOSITION 41

Reducing discrimination, and the perception of injustice, may help to reduce serious crime.

DECRIMINALIZATION

In their 1970 book *The Honest Politician's Guide to Crime Control,* Norval Morris and Gordon Hawkins call decriminalization a "first principle." Specifically, they propose removing criminal penalties on (1) public drunkenness; (2) purchase, possession, and use of all drugs; (3) all forms of gambling; (4) disorderly conduct and vagrancy; (5) abortion; (6) private sexual activity between consenting adults; and (7) juvenile "status" offenses.[19]

It is important to clarify exactly what kinds of behavior are involved in the list offered by Morris and Hawkins. Public drunkenness is included but not drunk driving. The person drunk on the street may be a nuisance but poses no threat of harm to anyone else. The drunk driver does pose such a threat. Sexual activity between consenting adults is covered but not sex between an adult and a child. In short, the standard decriminalization proposal covers a limited range of activity and not a general repeal of all criminal laws governing drinking or sex.

Some of these proposals are also supported by libertarian conservatives. As we will discuss in detail in Chapter 13, a number of prominent conservatives now support the legalization of drugs. In short, just as many liberals have adopted traditional conservative crime control ideas, so have some conservatives embraced some traditional liberal ideas.

Decriminalization or legalization of drugs is a major policy alternative today. We will consider that issue in detail in Chapter 13, which deals with drugs and drug policy. This chapter places the issue of decriminalization in a broader perspective, examining the likely impact on crime of decriminalizing other offenses.

The Rationale for Decriminalization

The basic assumption underlying decriminalization is the longstanding belief among liberals that the criminal law in the United States covers too much behavior. This problem is referred to as the *overreach* of the criminal law. In his classic work *The Limits of the Criminal Sanction,* Herbert L. Packer argues, "The criminal sanction is indispensable, [but] we resort to it in far too indiscriminate a way."[20]

The overreach of the criminal law has several undesirable consequences.[21] First, it overburdens the justice system with relatively minor offenses, such as public drunkenness, leaving it with less resources for the really serious crimes of murder, rape, robbery, and burglary. Public drunkenness is a good example. A 1971 book published by the American Bar Foundation defines the problem as *Two Million Unnecessary Arrests.*[22] Actually, the number of arrests for drunkenness has been declining steadily, from 1.2 million in 1975 to 713,000 in 1994 and 509,764 in 1997.[23] Nonetheless, 700,000 arrests consume a large amount of police and court resources.

A second problem is that no strong public consensus prevails about whether some behavior should be criminalized. Packer argues that "the criminal sanction should ordinarily be limited to conduct that is viewed, *without significant social dissent,* as immoral" (emphasis added).[24] The problem, however, is that there is much dissent on many issues. Americans have very mixed attitudes about gambling, for example; they feel that something is immoral about it, but they love to bet on sports nonetheless.

One of the results of conflicting public attitudes is selective and often arbitrary law enforcement. This practice violates the principle of equal protection

of the law and leads to cynicism about law enforcement among the public and police officers. Packer argues that "respect for law generally is likely to suffer."[25]

A third problem is that making various forms of recreation illegal leads to the development of criminal syndicates that provide the goods and services people want. Thirty years ago, the President's Crime Commission argued, "The core of organized crime activity is the supplying of illegal goods and services . . . to countless numbers of citizen customers."[26] Gambling was historically the principal source of revenue for organized crime, and the U.S. demand for illegal drugs sustains vast international networks and neighborhood drug gangs. In this sense, the law becomes criminogenic, creating forms of criminal behavior.

Fourth, the criminal syndicates that are created by making gambling and other activities illegal corrupt the justice system. The Knapp Commission investigation into police corruption in New York City in the early 1970s found that police officers were receiving a weekly "pad" of between $300 and $1,500 a month for protecting illegal gambling.[27] Twenty years later, the Mollen Commission found that the worst forms of police corruption and brutality in New York City were associated with drug trafficking.[28] Finally, the huge corruption and brutality scandal that was discovered in the Los Angeles Police Department in 1999 was clearly associated with the war on drugs, which created a climate in which LAPD officers felt they could get away with anything.[29]

Fifth, many people believe that certain kinds of recreation—sex and the use of some substances—is a matter of private choice. The overwhelming majority of Americans believe that sex between two adults of the opposite sex should not be a crime. About half of all Americans today now believe that sex between two adults of the same sex should not be a crime. Over 80 percent of Americans believe that women have a right to terminate a pregnancy by abortion.[30]

Sixth, many criminal justice and public health experts believe that the problems associated with drinking, gambling, and sex are really social, psychological, and medical problems that should not be addressed through the criminal law. The President's Crime Commission concluded that the criminal justice system "is not in a position to meet [the chronic alcoholic's] underlying medical and social problems."[31] Arrest and prosecution do nothing to help the chronic alcoholic deal with his or her drinking problem, and in many cases they make matters worse. Medical and social services would be a far more effective response.[32]

The Terms of the Debate

Not everyone agrees with the traditional arguments in favor of decriminalization. The debate between advocates and opponents of decriminalization raises fundamental questions about the role of the criminal law, involving issues of moral standards and the practical effects of criminalization.

Everyone does agree with the principle that the criminal law expresses (or should express) the basic values of society and defines the boundaries of acceptable conduct. Robbery is a crime because we believe that taking something that belongs to another person is wrong. Murder is a crime because taking another person's life is wrong. As Patrick Devlin puts it, "The criminal law as we know it is based upon moral principle."[33]

The question is not *whether* the law should express the values of society but *which values* it should express. As Packer says, "Whose morality are we talking about?"[34] Is gambling morally wrong or a legitimate form of entertainment? Is homosexual behavior morally wrong or a matter of private choice? Is abortion morally wrong (murder, in the eyes of anti-abortion activists) or a constitutionally protected private choice? Conservatives generally believe that these behaviors are morally wrong and therefore should be prohibited by the criminal law. Liberals generally believe that there is nothing immoral about these same behaviors and therefore they should not be made illegal. According to criminologist Gilbert Geis, certain forms of behavior are "not the law's business."[35]

Whether certain forms of behavior are wrong depends on how you define "harm." Advocates of decriminalization believe that gambling, for example, is a "victimless crime." Advocates of criminal prohibition believe that it produces real harms: that people can become addicted to gambling, that it can ruin their personal finances and harm their family, that it can lead to other crime as people try to pay off their gambling debts. Similarly, as we will discuss in Chapter 13, advocates of drug decriminalization believe that marijuana, for example, does not do the harm that it is alleged to do. Supporters of the current drug laws believe that marijuana does real physical, psychological, and social harm. Devlin sums up the prohibitionist position by arguing that "society is entitled by means of its laws to protect itself from dangers, whether from within or without."[36]

Decriminalization is also debated in terms of the practical consequences of making certain behavior illegal. As we mentioned earlier, advocates of decriminalization believe that criminal prohibition overburdens the justice system, leads to arbitrary enforcement, encourages corruption, and does not help people who have a medical or psychological problem. The advocates of criminalization would reply that the moral issues at stake outweigh the bad consequences. Even if the law does not completely deter drug abuse, society should still condemn this behavior through the criminal law.

The Impact of Decriminalization

Now let us take a look at some of the specific items on the old decriminalization agenda.

Public Disorder Crimes Public drunkenness, disorderly conduct, and vagrancy are essentially public nuisances rather than predatory crimes. They may offend our sensibilities, but they do not inflict tangible harm on someone the way robbery and burglary do.[37]

The crime control strategy underlying decriminalization of these offenses assumes an indirect effect. The assumption is that decriminalization will give the police more time to concentrate on serious crimes. As we indicated, 509,764 arrests were made for drunkenness in 1997, representing slightly less than 5 percent of all arrests and almost as many arrests as for all violent index crimes.[38]

The basic assumption is flawed. As we learned in Chapter 5, adding more patrol officers will not prevent more crime, and adding more detectives will not raise clearance rates. Insofar as decriminalization of public drunkenness saves police time and resources, it might be desirable as a cost-saving measure. We have no reason to assume, however, that it will help reduce serious crime.

Not everyone agrees with our analysis. Public-order offenses such as drunkenness and urinating in public are a central part of the zero-tolerance policy adopted by then New York City police commissioner William Bratton. He and others claim that aggressively enforcing the law on these minor crimes has contributed directly to the reduction of murder and other serious crimes.[39] Critics, however, point out that crime has also fallen in cities that do not have the zero-tolerance policy and that the decline began before Bratton became police commissioner.

Arrest trends indicate that we have been deemphasizing public-order arrests for many years. As we have already noted between 1975 and 1997, the number of arrests for drunkenness fell from 1.2 million to 509,764. Several factors accounted for this decline. First, some court decisions held that arresting someone because of a medical condition—as opposed to some behavior—was unconstitutional. In 1966, the U.S. Court of Appeals for the District of Columbia ruled in *Easter v. District of Columbia* that DeWitt Easter could not be convicted for public intoxication.[40] Second, states have decriminalized public intoxication (in part due to court rulings). Third, police departments informally deemphasized public-order offenses and concentrated on serious crimes.

Abortion Abortion was decriminalized by the famous 1973 Supreme Court decision *Roe v. Wade,* which declared existing criminal abortion laws unconstitutional.[41] We will not debate the morality of abortion here. It is important, however, to note that this issue dramatizes better than any other the moral basis of the criminal law and the conflict between different moral perspectives in our society. If you believe the fetus is a human being, then it logically follows that abortion is murder. But if you believe that the fetus is not a human being, then it follows that the abortion decision is a private choice.

Whatever your views on abortion might be, it is difficult if not impossible to find a connection between it and serious crime. Legalizing or criminalizing abortion has no effect on robbery and burglary.

Sex Between Consenting Adults States traditionally outlawed different kinds of sexual behavior, including activity between consenting adults such as adultery, cohabitation, homosexuality, and sodomy (which in some states includes "unnatural" sexual acts as well as acts between people of the same sex). By the mid-1980s, 13 states still had laws making it illegal for unmarried people to live together, and 13 had laws against "fornication" (sexual intercourse between people who are not married).[42] The 1910 Mann Act makes it a federal crime to take someone of the opposite sex across state lines for "immoral purposes." These laws are another good example of how the criminal law is used to define the moral boundaries of society.

In actual practice, the laws on sexual activity were rarely enforced, and as public attitudes about sex began to change in the 1960s, enforcement dropped even further. Many states abolished their laws in this area. About half the states, for example, no longer consider sex between adults of the same sex to be a crime.[43]

Whatever your views on adultery, cohabitation, or homosexuality, it is impossible to establish any connection between these activities and serious predatory crime. Legalizing or criminalizing cohabitation will have no effect on burglary or robbery.

One possible exception to this rule might be prostitution. In some instances, prostitution facilitates ancillary crimes: Customers are robbed; prostitutes are beaten by their pimps. It is possible that a system of legalized and regulated prostitution would remove streetwalkers from the streets and reduce some of these crimes.

Gambling The legal status of gambling in the United States has undergone a massive change in recent years. The old moralistic objections to gambling have collapsed as many states have created lotteries and authorized casino gambling.[44] Many Native American tribes have established betting casinos on tribal lands that are exempt from federal and state gambling laws. Despite the spread of legal gambling, however, many of the popular forms of illegal gambling—sports betting pools, the numbers game—continue to flourish.

Advocates of decriminalizing gambling see a number of possible benefits: saving scarce resources, ending arbitrary law enforcement, and undercutting the economic basis of organized crime, for instance. There is no expectation, however, that it would reduce predatory crime, which is the issue that concerns us.

Some opponents of legalized gambling believe that legalized gambling might actually lead to an increase in crime. They argue that gambling casinos attract a criminal subculture that involves more thefts, robberies, and other crimes. Several studies have examined this issue. The Illinois Criminal Justice Information Authority found that the advent of riverboat gambling had no impact on crime in Joliet, Illinois.[45] David Giacopassi and B. Grant Stitt found that casino gambling had a mixed impact on crime in Biloxi, Mississippi. Auto theft and larceny did rise, but no significant changes were noted for other crimes.[46] Finally, crime did increase in Atlantic City, New Jersey, after gambling was legalized there in 1976, but it was primarily "in-house" crime inside the casinos themselves. No increase occurred in the community generally.[47] In short, no consistent evidence indicates that legalized gambling leads to higher crime rates.

Summary

Many arguments exist for and against criminalizing the different kinds of behavior we have discussed. We can debate this issue on moral grounds, on grounds of the practical consequences of criminal penalties, or on both grounds. It seems very clear, however, that we have no reason to expect any reduction in serious crime. This leads us to the following conclusion:

> ### PROPOSITION 42
> With the possible exception of drugs (to be discussed in the next chapter), decriminalization will not reduce serious crime.

CONCLUSION

The emerging procedural justice perspective suggests that reforming the criminal justice system may in fact make a difference. Eliminating the sense of injustice, including the perceptions of discrimination, may enhance the legitimacy of the law and the justice system and promote law-abiding behavior. We do not want to overemphasize this point. The evidence is still very limited, but there is some evidence that justice does make a difference—and potentially makes a difference in terms of serious crime. The decriminalization of offenses other than those related to drugs, however, is unlikely to make any difference with respect to serious crime.

NOTES

1. Bureau of Justice Statistics, *Sourcebook of Criminal Justice Statistics—1998* (Washington, DC: Government Printing Office, 1999), pp. 498, 505.

2. Jerome G. Miller, *Search and Destroy: African-American Males in the Criminal Justice System* (New York: Cambridge University Press, 1996).

3. Coramae Richey Mann, *Unequal Justice* (Bloomington: University of Indiana, 1988).

4. William Wilbanks, *The Myth of a Racist Criminal Justice System* (Pacific Grove, CA: Brooks/Cole, 1987).

5. Samuel Walker, Cassia Spohn, and Miriam DeLone, *The Color of Justice*, 2nd ed. (Belmont, CA: Wadsworth, 2000).

6. Samuel Walker, *Police Interactions with Racial and Ethnic Minorities: Resolving the Contradictions between Allegations and Evidence* (Washington, DC: Police Executive Research Forum, 2000).

7. ACLU, *Driving while Black: Racial Profiling on Our Nation's Highways* (New York: ACLU, 1999).

8. Marjorie Zatz, "The Changing Forms of Racial/Ethnic Biases in Sentencing," *Journal of Research in Crime and Delinquency* 24 (February 1987): 69–92.

9. Sandra Lee Browning, Frances T. Cullen, Liqun Cao, Renee Kopache, and Thomas J. Stevenson, "Race and Getting Hassled by the Police: A Research Note," *Police Studies* 17.1, (1944): 6.

10. Walker, *Police Interactions with Racial and Ethnic Minorities.*

11. Marc Mauer and Tracy Huling, *Young Black Americans.* (Washington: The Sentencing Project, 1995).

12. The evidence is summarized in Walker, Spohn, and Delone, *The Color of Justice,* chap. 4.

13. Walker, Spohn, and DeLone, *The Color of Justice,* chap. 7.

14. E. Allan Lind and Tom R. Tyler, *The Social Psychology of Procedural Justice* (New York: Plenum, 1988).

15. Tom R. Tyler, *Why People Obey the Law* (New Haven: Yale University Press, 1990).

16. Tyler, *Why People Obey the Law,* p. 62.

17. Jonathan D. Casper, Tom Tyler, and Bonnie Fisher, "Procedural Justice in Felony Cases," *Law and Society Review* 22.3 (1988): 484–507.

18. Raymond Paternoster, Robert Brame, Ronet Bachman, and Lawrence W. Sherman, "Do Fair Procedures Matter? The Effect of Procedural Justice on Spouse Assault," *Law and Society Review* 31 (No. 1, 1997): 163–204.

19. Norval Morris and Gordon Hawkins, *The Honest Politician's Guide to Crime Control* (Chicago: University of Chicago Press, 1970), p. 3.

20. Herbert L. Packer, *The Limits of the Criminal Sanction* (Stanford, CA: Stanford University Press, 1968), p. 364.

21. The best overview of this issue is still Packer, *The Limits of the Criminal Sanction.*

22. Raymond T. Nimmer, *Two Million Unnecessary Arrests* (Chicago: American Bar Foundation, 1971).

23. Federal Bureau of Investigation, *Crime in the United States, 1975* (Washington, DC: Government Printing Office, 1976), p. 179. Bureau of Justice Statistics, *Sourcebook of Criminl Justice Statistics 1997* (Wash-

ington, DC: Government Printing Office, 1998), p. 338.

24. Packer, *Limits of the Criminal Sanction,* p. 264.

25. Packer, *Limits of the Criminal Sanction,* p. 287.

26. President's Commission on Law Enforcement and Administration of Justice, *The Challenge of Crime in a Free Society* (New York: Avon, 1968), p. 437.

27. Knapp Commission, *Report on Police Corruption* (New York: Braziller, 1973).

28. Commission to Investigate Allegations of Police Corruption and the Anti-Corruption Procedures of the Police Department, *Report* (New York: City of New York, 1994).

29. Los Angeles Police Department, Board of Inquiry, *Rampart Area Corruption Incident* (Los Angeles: Los Angeles Police Department, 2000).

30. Bureau of Justice Statistics, *Sourcebook of Criminal Justice Statistics—1995* (Washington, DC: Government Printing Office, 1996), p. 228.

31. President's Commission on Law Enforcement and Administration of Justice, *Task Force Report: Drunkenness* (Washington, DC: Government Printing Office, 1967), p. 3.

32. Nimmer, *Two Million Unnecessary Arrests.*

33. Patrick Devlin, *The Enforcement of Morals* (London: Oxf, 1995).ord University Press, 1965), p. 7.

34. Packer, *Limits of the Criminal Sanction,* p. 263.

35. Gilbert Geis, *Not the Law's Business* (New York: Schocken, 1979).

36. Devlin, *Enforcement of Morals,* p. 13.

37. President's Commission, *Task Force Report: Drunkenness.*

38. Federal Bureau of Investigation, *Crime in the United States, 1997,* p. 232.

39. George L. Kelling and Catherine Coles, *Fixing Broken Windows* (New York: Kessler, 1996).

40. *Easter v. District of Columbia,* 361 F.2d 50 (D.C. Cir. 1966).

41. *Roe v. Wade,* 410 U.S. 113 (1973).

42. Mitchell Bernard, Ellen Levine, Stefan Presser, and Marianne Stecich, *The Rights of Single People* (New York: Bantam, 1985), pp. 12–13.

43. Vincent J. Samar, *The Right to Privacy: Gays, Lesbians, and the Constitution* (Philadelphia: Temple University Press, 1991).

44. John D. Rosecrance, *Gambling without Guilt: The Legitimation of an American Pasttime* (Pacific Grove, CA: Brooks/Cole, 1988).

45. Illinois Criminal Justice Information Authority, *Riverboat Gambling and Crime in Illinois* (Springfield: ICJIA, 1994).

46. David Giacopassi and B. Grant Stitt, "Assessing the Impact of Casino Gambling on Crime in Mississippi," *American Journal of Criminal Justice* 18 (No. 1, 1994): 117–31.

47. Daniel Curran and Frank Scarpitti, "Crime in Atlantic City: Do Casinos Make a Difference?" *Deviant Behavior* 12 (No. 4, 1991): 431–50.

PART V

❖

The Drug Problem

One of the ground rules for this book is a focus on robbery and burglary. We are now going to violate that rule by examining drug policy. Why? The drug problem is at the center of the crime problem today, and it is pointless to discuss crime policy without reference to drugs. The drug crack was closely associated with the surge in gun violence in the 1980s, and drug enforcement has been the driving force behind the soaring prison population. Let us take a look at the problem of drugs, the drug-crime connection, and the larger question of drug policy.

13

Sense and Nonsense about Drugs

THE DRUG PROBLEM

To talk seriously about crime policy, we have to address the issue of drugs and drug policy. Drugs have been the focal point of the crime problem in the United States for many years. Directly or indirectly, they were responsible for the dramatic rise in the murder rate in the 1980s, gang violence, the soaring prison population, the worsening crisis in race relations, and the steady erosion of individual rights in Supreme Court rulings.[1]

Discussing drug policy allows us to apply much of what we have learned so far. Conservative drug policies emphasize getting tough with drug offenders through more arrests and tougher punishments, whereas liberal policies prefer prevention, education, and treatment. Because the purpose of this book is to find policies that will lower serious crime, we will not be able to undertake a full discussion of drugs and drug abuse. This chapter focuses on drug policies that might reduce serious crime.

Hysteria over Drugs

Public hysteria over drugs and drug-related crime inhibits sensible discussion of policy. It seems that this has always been the case. In the 1930s, a wave of national hysteria arose over "reefer madness," with wild stories about the alleged dangers of marijuana. A similar scare erupted in the 1980s over the so-called "crack babies."

Sensational news media stories appeared in 1988 about 375,000 crack babies born to addicted mothers. Reports claimed that these infants had severe physical and psychological damage, would never develop normally, and would be a permanent burden to society. One medical expert said, "It's as if the part of the brain that makes us human beings capable of discussion or reflection is wiped out."[2]

The truth turned out to be very different. The number of crack babies was grossly exaggerated. The original reports counted all babies who had been exposed to drugs during pregnancy, not just those who were genuinely addicted or even harmed. Some hospitals included mothers who had used marijuana. Later research found that the long-term damage even to addicted babies had been exaggerated. By age 4, those who received adequate care did rather well. It is true that drugs can harm a fetus, but tobacco and alcohol may do as much damage. The most serious problem with low-income babies is the lack of adequate prenatal care, especially good nutrition. Scare stories about reefer madness, crack babies, or drug gangs prevent us from thinking clearly about drug policy.

Myths and Realities about Drugs and Crime

To help sort our way through the debate over drug policy, we need to establish some basic facts about drugs and crime. As with most criminal justice issues, many myths about drugs and crime inhibit the development of sound and effective policies on this problem. Let us begin by exploring some of the facts about the extent of illegal drug use, drug use trends, and the relationship between drugs and crime.

The Extent of Illegal Drug Use The first question is: How extensive is illegal drug use? We currently have four different surveys. Two are general social surveys, while two survey specific subgroups of the population. There is much disagreement over what these four surveys say. There are problems with the methodology of each survey. In terms of the findings, it is important to distinguish between first-time use, continued use, and abuse (as indicated by some harm to the individual or society).[3]

The broadest general survey is the National Household Survey (NHS), which collects self-report data on a sample of the general population. The methodology is similar to that of the NCVS in its treatment of criminal victimization. The major limitations of the NHS are first, that respondents may not truthfully report their illegal drug use, and second, that it surveys households and misses many of the most serious drug abusers, who are transients, homeless, or in prison. The NHS data indicate that illegal substance use is fairly widespread. About 74 million Americans, or 36 percent of the adult population, have used an illegal drug at least once in their lifetime. An estimated 11.2 percent have used an illegal drug in the last year (1997 data), and 6.4 percent are "current users," meaning that they have used a drug in the past month. The good news from the NHS is that drug use has declined significantly. The number of current users dropped by more than half, from 14.1 percent in 1979 to 6.4 percent in 1997. Cocaine use has fallen more than 70 percent (see Chapter 1, Figure 1-2) and marijuana use more than 60 percent. This is a significant decrease and should be cause for celebration.

The Monitoring the Future (MTF) survey provides self-report data from about 45,000 students enrolled in grades 8, 10, and 12, in 433 public and private schools (1999 survey).[4] Students represent an important segment of the at-risk population. The major weakness is that it misses kids who have dropped out of school—precisely those who are most likely to be the heaviest drug abusers. The MTF data indicate that illegal drug use declined among young people between the late 1970s and about 1992, as it did for the general population, but then began increasing again. Use of any illegal drug by high school seniors in the past month, for example, increased from 14.4 percent in 1992 to 25.9 in 1999.[5]

A third survey, the Drug Abuse Warning Network (DAWN), uses a different methodology and tells a very different story. DAWN reports alcohol and drug-related *admissions* to emergency rooms and substance-related *deaths* from over 700 hospitals in 21 metropolitan areas and from 87 medical examiners (or coroners) in 27 metropolitan areas. While DAWN obviously does not estimate general patterns of illegal drug use, it does indicate trends in the most serious consequences of drug abuse. (One major limitation is that it reports *mentions* of drugs in a medical report, which does not necessarily mean that a drug *caused* the medical emergency.) DAWN presents a very grim picture. Cocaine and heroin-related emergency room admissions quadrupled between the early 1980s and 1989, declined in 1990, and then continued to rise significantly to the present. Deaths have also risen significantly since 1980 (Figure 13-1).[6]

The trends indicated by the DAWN survey are clearly at odds with those from the NHS. This divergence suggests that while illegal drug use declined

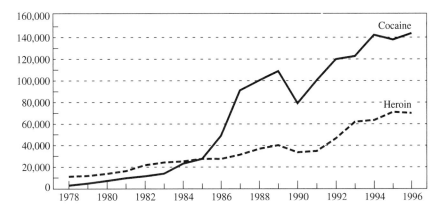

FIGURE 13-1 Cocaine and heroin hospital emergency room mentions, 1978–1996.

SOURCE: Office of National Drug Control Policy, *Data Snapshot: Drug Abuse in America, 1998* (Washington, DC: Government Printing Office, 1998), plate 76.

for the general population between the late 1970s and the 1990s, it became far more acute for one segment of the population. This supports our argument in Chapter 1, following on Elliott Currie's analysis, that we really have two separate drug problems, one related to the general population and another that affects the poorest minority communities.[7]

Finally, the ADAM (Arrestee Drug Abuse Monitoring) program (formerly known as DUF: Drug Use Forecasting) collects urine specimens and self-report data on drug use from arrestees. Steadily expanded since it was created in 1987, ADAM now collects data on adults in 35 cities and on juveniles in 10 sites. Although not a representative sample of the population, ADAM does provide useful data on drug use among criminal offenders. In New Orleans, for example, 46 percent of all male arrestees tested positive for cocaine in 1998, compared with only 25 percent in Omaha. In New York City, 67 percent of the female arrestees tested positive for cocaine, compared with 47 percent of the males. Moreover, cocaine use had declined significantly for males since 1994, but not for females.[8]

One of the most important contributions of the ADAM data has been to document the significant reduction in crack usage in many major cities in the 1990s.[9] Many criminologists believe that this reduction is closely associated with—and may be the major cause of—the drop in the crime rate. We will look at this issue in more detail later in this chapter.

The various measures of illegal drug use lead us to three general conclusions. First, illegal drug use has declined among the general population since the late 1970s (although it has increased among teenagers since 1992). Second, drug abuse increased sharply among a particular segment of the population between 1985 and the early 1990s. Third, crack use has declined significantly in many cities in recent years, and this reduction appears to be associated with the reduction in serious crime. As we pointed out in Chapter 1, the decline in crack usage and serious crime appears to be genuine and long-term. The important —and still unanswered—question is: What caused the decline in crack use?

The Drug-Crime Connection   A second important question involves the relationship between drugs and crime. Many people believe that drugs *cause* crime and that if we reduced illegal drug abuse, we would have much less crime. The myth persists of the "drug-crazed criminal" who robs and murders while high on drugs. This is similar to the old "reefer madness" view that women become sexually promiscuous because of marijuana. The federal Office of National Drug Control Policy publishes a frightening graphic purporting to show the direct and harmful "Consequences of Drug Use" on "family, crime, violence, health, economic [circumstances, and] community."[10] In short, drugs are commonly seen as the cause of almost all of our problems.

Drugs and crime are related, but the relationship is very complex.[11] Crime associated with drugs falls into three categories. First, there are *drug-defined crimes*: the possession and sale of illegal substances. Second, there are *drug-related* crimes, including violent behavior caused by the pharmacological effects of a drug or robberies committed to get money to buy drugs. Third, there are crimes *associated with drug usage,* meaning that an offender was using drugs around the time he or she committed an offense, but that the crime was not caused by drug use.[12]

The ADAM data confirm the fact that a large percentage of arrestees are involved with both drug and alcohol use. Merely testing positive for drugs, however, does not mean that the crime was *caused* by drugs. This is similar to the problem we discussed in Chapter 6: Just because a driver tests positive for alcohol does not mean that his or her driving was impaired by drinking. Only 13 percent of jail inmates and 17 percent of prison inmates say they committed their offense to get money to buy drugs.[13] A recent survey of offenders on probation found that half admitted to being under the influence of drugs or alcohol at the time they committed the offense for which they were convicted. Two-thirds reported they had used drugs in the past and about one-third admitted they had used drugs in the month before they committed the offense for which they were convicted.[14] This involvement with drugs does not, however, mean that the crimes these individuals committed were caused by drugs.

The federal government's national drug control strategy regards many substances—alcohol, tobacco, and "soft" drugs" such as marijuana—as "gateways" to more serious drug abuse and criminal behavior. The evidence does not support this view. Studies of high-rate offenders have found that many began their criminal activity before they began using drugs. For others, drug use preceded their criminal activity. Still others became involved in crime and drugs at about the same time. As a Justice Department report concludes, "For some individuals drug use is independent of their involvement in crime. These people may continue to commit crimes even if drugs were unavailable."[15] David Farrington argues that "violent youth have many other 'co-occurring problems.'" These problems include truancy, early sexual initiation and sexual promiscuity, unstable employment records, bad relations with parents, and many other factors.[16] It is impossible to say that any one (e.g., drug use) *caused* subsequent violent criminal behavior.

The NHS data provide further evidence that illegal drug use does not lead directly to criminal activity. Few of the estimated 74 million people who reported having used an illegal drug at least once in their life became either addicts or career criminals. Most drug use is casual and recreational and does not have serious antisocial consequences.

The lack of a direct causal link between drugs and crime has important implications for crime policy. It means that even if we succeeded in substantially reducing illegal drug use, we would not necessarily reduce crime to the same degree. Crimes related to drug trafficking would certainly be reduced, but the impact on crimes associated with deviant lifestyles, which include the vast majority of robberies and burglaries, would be very limited.

The Drug Policy Choices

What should we do about drugs and crime? Peter Reuter classifies policy advocates into three groups: Hawks, Doves, and Owls (these categories are borrowed from the debate over the Vietnam War in the 1960s and 1970s).[17] *Hawks* emphasize law enforcement to eradicate drug abuse, believing that we simply need to get tougher than we have been. Enforcement strategies include both supply reduction, designed to reduce the availability of drugs, and demand reduction, designed to decrease peoples' desire to use drugs.[18] American drug policy is dominated by the Hawk approach, with most of the emphasis on supply reduction.

Owls prefer prevention and treatment of drug abuse, which are essentially demand reduction strategies. Current drug policy includes prevention and treatment, but they have always received less emphasis than supply reduction–oriented law enforcement approaches.

Doves, meanwhile, believe that we should completely rethink our national drug policy. In general, they would prefer to define drug abuse as a public health problem. The National Council on Crime and Delinquency (NCCD) asserts that "it should be defined primarily as a health-related problem that should reside in the public health domain."[19]

The radical Dove approach is to legalize drugs. We discuss legalization later in this chapter. A more moderate approach is generally referred to as *harm reduction,* which generally means keeping the criminal penalties for drugs on the books, but not enforcing them as intensively. The title of Mark A. R. Kleiman's book, *Against Excess,* expresses this point of view. Both the war on drugs and legalization are excessively radical policies, and he argues in favor of a middle-range policy.[20] Harm reduction essentially represents the drug policies of many European countries, particularly the Netherlands.[21]

To a certain extent, the debate is over what causes the greatest harm: drugs or drug policy. Hawks believe that drugs are the problem. Doves believe that drug policy is the problem, causing more harm than good.

The Hawk/Owl/Dove categories do not conform to the conservative/liberal dichotomy we have used in this book. The Reagan and Bush administrations (1981–1993) put tremendous emphasis on tough law enforcement, while First Lady Nancy Reagan simultaneously led a highly publicized "Just say no" antidrug education campaign. The 1994 Violent Crime Bill supported by President Bill Clinton and many liberal Democrats includes both tough law enforcement measures (100,000 more police) and money for prevention programs.

THE WAR ON DRUGS:
POLICY AND CONSEQUENCES

Since the 1914 Harrison Act, the Hawks have dominated American drug policy. That is, we have defined certain substances as illegal and attempted to suppress their use though criminal law enforcement. Over the past 20 years, our policy has become increasingly hawkish, as a succession of presidents have declared "war" on drugs, and arrests and imprisonment for drug possession and sale have soared.[22]

National Drug Control Strategy—Five Goals

- I: Educate and enable America's youth to reject illegal drugs as well as the use of alcohol and tobacco.

- II: Increase the safety of America's citizens by substantially reducing drug-related crime and violence.

- III: Reduce health and social costs to the public of illegal drug use.

- IV: Shield America's air, land, and sea frontiers from the drug threat.

- V: Break foreign and domestic drug sources of supply.

FIGURE 13-2 The Office of National Drug Control Policy's mission statement.

SOURCE: Office of National Drug Control Policy, *Data Snapshot: Drug Abuse in America, 1998* (Washington, DC: Government Printing Office, 1998), plate 4.

The war on drugs intensified in the 1980s, placing even greater emphasis on enforcement. In his book *The Fix,* Michael Massing argues that national drug policy was far more moderate and more sensible under President Richard Nixon in the early 1970s. Despite a lot of "law and order" rhetoric, the administration's policy put a great deal of emphasis on treatment for drug users.[23] The really intensive enforcement effort did not begin until the mid-1970s, and it is at that point that the national prison population began to soar.

The five elements of current National Drug Control Strategy are indicated in Figure 13-2.

The Impact of the War on Drugs

As we argued in Chapter 1, the war on drugs has had an enormous impact on U.S. society, on the criminal justice system, and on racial minorities in particular. Federal expenditures for drug enforcement have soared, rising from $2.9 billion in 1976 to $17.1 billion in 1999. The number of persons arrested for drug offenses more than doubled, from 601,000 in 1975 to 1.5 million in 1996. Persons convicted of drug offenses are the primary factor in the spectacular increase in the prison population. By 1994, 60 percent of all adults in federal prison had been convicted of drug offenses, compared with only 25 percent in 1980. Convictions for drug offenses were responsible for half of the increase in the prison population between 1980 and the mid-1990s.[24]

Many critics argue that racial minorities are the primary victims of the war on drugs. The National Criminal Justice Commission argues that "we are on the verge of a social catastrophe because of the sheer number of African-Americans behind bars."[25] Some would argue that the catastrophe is already here. Data compiled by the Sentencing Project (see chapter 1, Figure 1-4) indicate that African Americans are treated more harshly at every stage of the criminal justice system. Yet the NHS indicates that this group is only somewhat more likely to use illegal drugs. Hispanics are even less likely than whites to use drugs. In 1995, 6.0 percent of whites were current users, compared with 5.1 percent of Hispanics and 7.9 percent of African Americans.[26]

The National Criminal Justice Commission argues that street-level drug enforcement "focus[es] almost exclusively on low-level dealers in minority neighborhoods."[27] The most blatant aspect of bias in the system, meanwhile, is the differential penalties for powdered and crack cocaine under the federal sentencing guidelines. Possession of 5 grams of crack nets a mandatory minimum sentence of five years, whereas possession of the same amount of powdered cocaine carries a maximum sentence of only one year. This has a grossly disparate racial impact, as crack is favored by African Americans and powdered cocaine is preferred by whites.[28] Yet, the Congress and the courts have refused to revise the guidelines.

Arrest and imprisonment have become extremely common experiences in underclass neighborhoods. And as we pointed out in Chapter 6, some deterrence theorists have suggested that it is possible that the deterrent threat loses its power.[29]

In short, the war on drugs has undoubtedly had a tremendous impact on U.S. society and on racial minorities in particular. Whether it has succeeded in reducing illegal drug use or serious crime associated with drug use is another question. Now let us take a look at some of the major components of the drug war.

Police Crackdowns

The streets are the front line in the war on drugs. As we learned in Chapter 5, simply adding more police patrol is not likely to reduce crime, including illegal drug activity. We have no reason to think that the 100,000 additional police officers promised by the 1994 Violent Crime Control Act, by themselves, will do anything to reduce drug abuse or drug-related crime.

The principal police strategy for reducing drug abuse is aggressive law enforcement. One variation is the *crackdown,* an intensive, short-term, geographically focused effort.[30] One well-known crackdown was Operation Pressure Point (OPP) in New York City's Lower East Side. Directed at an open drug market, OPP flooded the area with police officers, produced a high volume of arrests, and sought to scare away drug buyers. Evaluations of Operation Pressure Point claimed some short-term benefits: an end to open drug dealing and a reduction in crime. Many important questions remain unanswered, however. The enforcement effort may have displaced drug dealing to other areas. Even within the targeted area, drug dealers adapted their procedures to insulate themselves from the police. The evaluations made no serious attempt to assess the outcomes of the arrests. Improper police tactics may have been used, particularly the harassment of potential buyers who drove in from suburban areas. There was also no serious discussion of the long-term cost-effectiveness of a mass arrest policy.[31]

The most telling criticism of OPP is that the drug problem in New York City worsened dramatically over the next few years with the arrival of crack. Open drug markets spread to many neighborhoods. Even the New York City police department tacitly admitted that the crackdown strategy was futile, and in the early 1990s it reduced both the number of officers assigned to the tactical narcotics teams (TNTs) and the number of drug arrests.[32] Many street-level police officers candidly admitted that they could make all the arrests they wanted, but new dealers and buyers would just take the place of those arrested. Other crackdowns, such as Operation Hammer in Los Angeles, had little impact on drugs or gang activity and were done mainly for the short-term publicity effect.[33] The University of Maryland report concludes, "The evidence on drug crackdowns shows no consistent reductions in violent crime during or after the crackdown is in effect."[34] We agree.

PROPOSITION 43

Police crackdowns will not reduce illegal drug use or serious crime associated with drugs.

This does not mean that all police antidrug efforts do not work. As we found in Chapter 5, some problem-oriented policing programs have shown some signs of success. The SMART (Specialized Multi-Agency Response Team) program in Oakland, California, reduced drug-related activity without displacing it to neighboring areas. The difference is that SMART (and other problem-oriented policing programs) involves more than just the police. Taking a multiagency approach, it mobilizes other government agencies to attack a range of neighborhood problems, particularly housing. Instead of relying solely on arrest and prosecution, the traditional crackdown approach, it addresses underlying community problems using a combination of criminal and civil law strategies (e.g., housing code enforcement, cleaning up the physical appearance of neighborhoods, etc.). This is the approach recommended by the University of Maryland *Preventing Crime* report.[35]

Interdiction and Eradication

Two major supply reduction efforts by the federal government include *interdiction,* stopping the flow of drugs entering the country, and *eradication,* reducing the production of drug plants in the field. The conservative policy advocates William J. Bennett, John J. DiIulio, and John P. Walters argue that interdiction of drugs should be a "top national security priority" for the United States.[36] In fact, the federal government has made a huge and steadily increasing effort at interdiction. In 1997, federal agencies alone seized 108 metric tons of cocaine, 1,362 kilos of heroin, and 696 metric tons of cannabis.[37]

Major drug seizures by both federal and local officials are touted as evidence that enforcement is reducing the flow of illegal drugs. The truth is that interdiction efforts have been a failure. Many experts believe that the combined efforts of federal, state, and local law enforcement succeed in seizing only about 10 to 15 percent of the total supply.

The failure of interdiction is easy to understand. The 20,000-mile border of the United States is too great, the possible methods of smuggling drugs too many, and the number of people engaged in the trade too numerous. Increased enforcement, moreover, produces a variety of adaptations: new points of entry, new methods of smuggling, shifts in drug use as prices change, and so on.[38] Insofar as tougher enforcement raises the risks of drug trafficking, it drives the trade into the hands of those who are better organized, more heavily armed, and willing to take the risks—in short, the cartels that dominate the international cocaine market. Despite increased federal interdiction efforts, total worldwide production of drugs increased significantly between 1987 and 1991 alone. Production of marijuana rose from 13,000 to 23,000 metric tons, while coca leaf production increased from 291,000 to 337,000 metric tons.[39] A Rand report concludes, "Increased drug interdiction efforts are not likely to greatly affect the availability of cocaine in the United States."[40]

PROPOSITION 44

Drug interdiction and eradication efforts are doomed to fail

Tougher Sentencing

Tough sentencing policies for persons convicted of drug offenses has been another major strategy of the war on drugs. This represents the strategies of incapacitation and deterrence that we studied in Chapters 6 and 7. There is no need to cover that material again here.

Our conclusion was that neither strategy is effective in reducing crime. In the case of drugs, incapacitation is undermined by the *replacement effect*. Persons who are imprisoned for drug offenses are replaced by someone else who is willing to take the risks. The lack of legitimate opportunities (jobs, prospects for upward mobility) creates a substantial pool of potential new offenders.

It is important to note that drug use and crime associated with drugs has remained highest among the underclass, the very group that has been the primary target of the war on drugs. Arrest and imprisonment have obviously not had deterrent or incapacitative effects on that group.

PROPOSITION 45

Tougher sentencing is not likely to reduce illegal drug use
or serious crime associated with drugs.

LIMITS OF THE CRIMINAL LAW:
THE LESSONS OF HISTORY

Many critics of current drug policy argue that a war-on-drugs approach is doomed to fail. History provides valuable perspective on this issue by offering a number of examples of attempts to control products or services through the criminal law. Let us take a look at some of the more notable ones.

Prohibition. Between 1920 and 1933, the manufacture and sale of alcoholic beverages were illegal under the Eighteenth Amendment to the U.S. Constitution. Stories from Prohibition have entered the national folklore: speakeasies, Al Capone, gangland shootouts, and so on. Prohibition did reduce drinking and probably contributed to the decline in deaths from cirrhosis of the liver (from 13.3 per 100,000 in 1910 to 7.2 per 100,000 in 1930). Citing these figures, some historians argue that Prohibition was a success.[41] Other historians, however, argue that Prohibition clearly did not end all drinking and inflicted enormous collateral damage on the country.[42] By turning millions of casual drinkers into criminals, it undermined respect for the law. It created a vast illegal market that was filled by organized criminal syndicates. These syndicates corrupted police and politicians. Prohibition enforcement was accompanied by widespread abuses, particularly illegal searches and seizures.

Social gambling. Gambling policy in the United States has undergone a revolution in recent years, with the spread of state lotteries and casinos. Until recently, it was a heavily restricted activity, confined to a small number of racetracks, Las Vegas, and church-based bingo games. Nonetheless, millions of Americans routinely engaged in illegal betting—on athletic events, through the "numbers" game, and so on. The laws restricting gambling had many of the same collateral effects as Prohibition. Gambling has long been the primary source of revenue for organized crime and was the main cause of police corruption.[43]

Gun control. As we learned in Chapter 10, we have many laws barring certain people from owning guns, especially criminals. Yet active criminals have no trouble obtaining weapons through friends, the black market, or theft.

The old criminal abortion laws. Before the 1973 *Roe v. Wade* decision, abortion was a criminal offense in every state (several states did liberalize their laws between 1967 and 1973). Yet these laws did not eliminate abortions; in fact, as many as a million illegal abortions may have been performed a year. The harmful consequences included deaths and permanent injury to women from unsanitary back-alley abortions.

Sodomy, fornication, adultery, and prostitution laws. Various forms of sexual activity have traditionally been illegal in the United States: sex between members of the same sex (sodomy), sex between unmarried people of different sex (fornication), sex between a married person and someone other than his or her spouse (adultery), and sex for pay (prostitution). To put it mildly, these laws, which remain on the books in many states, have failed to stop people from engaging in these forms of sexual behavior. All of these behaviors have occurred since the beginning of recorded history.

The Lessons of History

These examples suggest the following conclusions about the limits of the criminal law in controlling products or services that a large number of people want.

- First, if a large number of people want a product or service, someone will try to supply it.

- Second, efforts to suppress that supply will result in massive evasion and the creation of criminal syndicates.

- Third, the enforcement effort itself will generate secondary crime (e.g., turf wars between gangs, corruption of law enforcement), abuse of individual rights (e.g., illegal searches and seizures), and loss of respect for the law.

- Fourth, intensifying the enforcement effort encourages adaptations, either substitution of products (as in the case of some drugs) or transfer of the service to people more willing to take the increased risks.

In short, criminal law enforcement is inherently weak in the face of a strong public demand for a product or service. This point helps explain the failure of the war on drugs. Shortly, we will look at some policies designed to reduce the demand for drugs.

When Social Control Does Work

It is not true that *all* efforts to prevent undesirable behavior fail. In principle, some prohibitions are good. The criminal law defines the basic standards of society. As children, we learn that stealing things and hitting people are wrong. To the extent that the criminal law shapes the values and habits of most people, it does work. The problem, of course, is that this process of socialization fails for a certain number of people.

The case of smoking offers an interesting example of an apparently successful attempt at curbing harmful behavior. Smoking among adults has declined significantly in recent years. Between 1965 and 1995, the percentage of American men who smoked fell from 52 to 27 percent. Among women it declined from 34 to 23 percent.[44] This is partly the result of formal restrictions on smoking in many buildings and public areas, along with a massive public education effort (including warning labels on cigarette packages).

It is important to recognize, however, that we have not completely eliminated smoking, and we have not tried to. The new restrictions only attempt to regulate and restrict smoking. In many respects, they have reinforced changing public attitudes about health. It is reasonable to speculate that a complete prohibition on smoking (similar to the one on alcohol in the 1920s) would produce a backlash that might only reinforce pro-smoking attitudes. We might speculate on what would happen if tobacco were out-lawed. Would prohibition succeed? Would the results be like those during Prohibition in the 1920s and like the current prohibition of drugs? Or would they be different?

It is also worth noting that smoking has recently increased among white teenagers, particularly females.[45] In other words, the national antismoking effort has not affected one major at-risk group, indicating that there are some limits as to what restrictions and education can accomplish. We will have more to say about this subject as we now turn to the question of drug education programs.

DEMAND REDUCTION:
DRUG EDUCATION

The Owl drug policy favored by most liberals includes demand reduction through education and treatment. Let us take a look at drug education programs.

"Just Say No"

The most widely used demand reduction programs involve public education efforts designed to persuade people not to use drugs. The most famous was Nancy Reagan's "Just say no" campaign in the 1980s. The first priority of a drug control policy proposed by conservatives William J. Bennett, John J. DiIulio, and John P. Walters is "Teach the young that drug use is wrong."[46] The relevant question, however, is whether drug education efforts actually work. Educational programs employ one or more of four different strategies.[47]

The most common strategy is *information dissemination.* This approach seeks to change behavior simply by providing information. Sex education programs, for example, discuss the basic facts about reproduction, while health education programs explain cholesterol.

A second strategy is *fear arousal,* which attempts to change behavior by frightening people. Safe-sex education programs emphasize the danger of getting AIDS from unprotected sex. In the "scared straight" program adult prisoners told juvenile offenders about the horrors of imprisonment.[48]

A third strategy is *moral appeal,* emphasizing the idea that certain behavior is wrong—that sex outside marriage is a sin or that gambling is immoral, for example.

A fourth strategy is known as *affective education.* This approach attempts to develop personal and social skills that will help people resist certain behavior. Sex education programs, for instance, try to teach teenagers how to say no to someone who is pressuring them to have sex.

Nancy Reagan's "Just say no" campaign combined fear arousal and moral appeal. The famous "This is your brain—this is your brain on drugs" ad campaign developed by the Partnership for a Drug-Free America also used fear arousal.

We have good reasons for questioning the effectiveness of antidrug educational programs. The problems are similar to the ones we discussed in Chapter 6 regarding deterrence theory: The message has to reach the intended audience, members of that audience have to perceive a real personal risk, and they have to make rational decisions to change their behavior.

First, many antidrug messages probably do not even reach their target audience. For example, the National Campaign for a Drug Free America runs expensive full-page ads in the *Wall Street Journal*. But how many teenagers or low-income people—those most at risk for illegal drug use—read the *Journal?* Second, many members of the target audience do not think that a real risk exists. Teenagers especially tend to believe that they are invulnerable—that they will not be caught by the police, that they are not too drunk to drive, that drugs will not hurt them, and so on. Also, as with deterrence theory, the risk has to be perceived in a cost-benefit context, as being worse than the alternative. But many people trapped in very poor neighborhoods do not perceive any realistic long-term hopes for economic advancement. Consequently, the short-term benefits of immediate gratification weigh much more heavily for them.

Some of the education program messengers, meanwhile, are not credible. Was Nancy Reagan, for example, an influential role model for low-income teenagers in the 1980s? Another problem is that some fear arousal programs backfire by glamorizing the forbidden behavior. They may heighten the allure of drinking, smoking, sex, and drugs by portraying them as adult-only activities. In fact, the famous "This is your brain on drugs" concept became the subject of many parodies that undermined the purpose of the original campaign.[49]

Third, we cannot assume that the members of the target audience will make rational decisions even if they hear the message. Teenagers, as we mentioned, are notoriously focused on short-term gratification rather than long-term consequences. An education program is only one small factor influencing behavior and is likely to be very weak in the face of peer group influence.

DARE: Success or Failure?

The most popular antidrug education program in recent years has been DARE (Drug Abuse Resistance Education). Created by the Los Angeles Police Department (LAPD) and the Los Angeles school system in 1983, the program consists of seventeen 45- to 60-minute classes, taught by sworn police officers, for fifth- and sixth-grade students. It relies primarily on affective education, attempting to provide the "skills for recognizing and resisting social pressures to experiment with tobacco, alcohol, and drugs" and "developing skills in risk assessment and decision making."[50]

DARE is extremely popular with parents, politicians, and the police. DARE bumper stickers can be seen everywhere. By 1997, the program was operating in 70 percent of all school districts, at a total cost of an estimated $750 million a year. Eighty percent of all local law enforcement agencies reported having a special unit for in-school drug education.[51]

Evaluations of DARE cast doubt on its effectiveness, however. Evaluations have measured students' knowledge about drugs, attitudes toward drug use, social skills in resisting pressure to use drugs, and actual drug usage. A meta-analysis of eighteen evaluations by the Research Triangle Institute (RTI) of North Carolina concludes that the program's effect on drug use is "slight, and except for tobacco use, not statistically significant."[52] Studies that have followed DARE and non-DARE students for up to five years after the program have consistently found that "DARE does not have long-term effects on drug use."[53] It is worth pointing out, too, that the recent increase in teenage drug use has occurred in spite of the massive DARE effort directed at precisely that audience.

There are several possible reasons why DARE does not affect drug use. The teaching method used, primarily classroom lectures, is inherently less effective than participative methods used in other kinds of programs. Some critics suggest that police officers may not be well trained for this activity and may not be effective role models. A more fundamental question is whether 17 hours of classroom lectures can overcome the other influences in a teenager's life—family (including a dysfunctional family), peer group, neighborhood, and so on. It is likely that the program works only where it supplements existing positive influences such as a strong family and peer group environment.

The evidence on DARE leads us to the following conclusion:

PROPOSITION 46
There is no evidence that DARE or other drug education programs reduce illegal drug use.

But *Some* Education Programs Do Work

Not all education programs are worthless. Some are effective, but it is important to examine why certain kinds of programs work for certain audiences.

AIDS education programs are a good example. Good evidence exists indicating that safe-sex education programs have changed behavior. In New York, the average number of unsafe sexual encounters per person dropped from eleven to only one per year between 1980 and 1991. As a result, the incidence of new AIDS cases among adult gay men also dropped. Nationally, the number of AIDS cases has dropped significantly since 1993.[54] Unfortunately, unsafe activity has continued among people in the underclass, including both unprotected sex and the use of unclean needles. As a result, AIDS has spread from male drug addicts to their female sexual partners and on to other men. Surveys of members of the underclass have found an incredible indifference to the known risks of using unclean needles and engaging in unprotected sex.[55]

Why the difference between the two groups? The adult gay community is a relatively successful group in U.S. society, with relatively high levels of education and professional careers. That segment of the gay community is also very cohesive, with a strong self-identity, networks of community institutions, and strong peer group support. Needle-drug users are at the other end of the social scale: They are unemployed, with little if any education, substantial criminal records, and no community identity or institutions. It is reasonable to conclude that successful educated people are more likely to respond to information dissemination programs: to receive the information, process it, and make a rational decision to change their behavior. This process reflects a sense of empowerment and capacity to control one's own life. That sense of power and control is precisely what people at the bottom of society do not have.

Despite the early success of safe-sex education programs, disturbing recent evidence indicates that they are not having the same degree of success with a younger generation of gay men. The reasons are not yet clear, but the situation does highlight the fact that people's behavior is influenced by a complex mix of personal and social factors. We cannot assume that education programs, by themselves, will have a dominant influence over behavior.[56]

Another example is the antismoking crusade, which we have already discussed. As we mentioned earlier, smoking has increased among teenagers recently, despite a significant decline among adults. Why the difference? We can argue that adults, especially successful, middle-class, and professional adults, are more likely to make rational choices about their behavior. Teenagers are far more likely to make reckless decisions, to consider themselves invulnerable, and to fail to think about either the immediate or the long-term consequences of their actions.

The response of different groups to education programs is closely related to the problems associated with deterrence theory, which we have already considered. Just as some people are more likely to be deterred by the threat of criminal sanction than others, so educational programs will be more effective with some groups than others. People with a stake in society are likely to respond very differently than people at the very bottom who feel they have nothing to lose.

DRUG TREATMENT

Along with education, drug treatment represents the prevention and demand reduction approach favored by most liberals. Treatment raises all of the issues related to rehabilitation that we discussed in Chapter 11. It is a planned intervention designed to change behavior.

One of the major issues related to drug treatment is the availability of treatment programs. Critics of current drug policy argue that programs are not adequately funded and that many people who want treatment cannot receive it. Their proposal calls for funding to provide "treatment on demand." Slightly more than 900,000 people have been enrolled in alcohol and drug treatment programs per year since the early 1990s. About 30 percent of them are receiving drug treatment only.[57] It has also been estimated, however, that about three or four times as many people need drug treatment as are currently receiving it.[58] One of the main arguments by the advocates of rehabilitation is that we have never adequately funded treatment programs to meet current needs.

Varieties of Treatment

As with drug education, several different kinds of drug treatment programs are available.[59]

Methadone maintenance. This treatment provides methadone as a substitute for heroin. A supervised medical treatment maintains the addiction at a steady level to prevent deeper dependency, eliminates the addict's need to turn to crime, and presumably reduces his or her association with drug addicts and criminals (and their peer influence). A supervised program of withdrawal can also be included. Because it involves providing an addictive drug, methadone maintenance is the most controversial of the three major forms of treatment.

Therapeutic communities. These are residential programs using intensive individual or group counseling techniques. Their primary goal is to temporarily remove the external influences that contribute to drug dependency and through counseling to restructure the client's personality. Some of the more famous therapeutic communities include Synanon and Phoenix House. The therapeutic community is the most expensive of the three major types of programs.

Outpatient drug-free programs. These programs provide counseling and other services to clients who remain in the community. Services include individual and group counseling on drug abuse and counseling or training for employment and family and other problems. Because they are the least expensive and least controversial type of program, outpatient programs are the most common.

Drug users can get into treatment in a variety of different ways. They can enter a program voluntarily. Many celebrities, for example, go to the Betty Ford Clinic, which is a therapeutic community. Others are compelled to enter treatment through the criminal justice system. Drug abuse counseling is often a condition of a diversion program, probation, or parole. Most of the new intensive probation supervision (IPS) and boot camp programs (see Chapter 11) include drug and alcohol counseling. Opponents of drug legalization argue that the coercive aspect of the criminal law is necessary to get most people into treatment.

Does Treatment Work?

The evidence on the effectiveness of treatment programs is very mixed. One review concludes that "all" the major types of programs "have been shown to be successful."[60] Another survey concludes optimistically that "research provides convincing evidence for the effectiveness of treatment for drug abuse."[61]

Evaluations of drug treatment programs generally show that clients who successfully complete the programs are less likely to use illegal drugs and to commit crimes than before treatment. An evaluation of one Philadelphia methadone maintenance program found that clients averaged nine "crime days" per month before treatment but only three after treatment; their average number of days per month employed went from three to eleven. Of 202 men who completed the Phoenix House therapeutic community program, 72 percent were arrested in the three years before entering the program, whereas 41 percent were arrested in the three years afterward. A Drug Abuse Reporting Program (DARP) outpatient treatment program reduced the arrest rate of clients from 87 percent beforehand to 22 percent after three years.[62]

Upon closer inspection, however, these claims are less impressive than they first appear to be. First, few if any programs claim to reduce completely illegal drug use or criminal activity. Especially disturbing are the high dropout rates in virtually all programs. Program evaluations that include only those who complete the program are artificially inflating their success rate.

Even more serious, treatment programs report high rates of relapse into drug use. The report that says treatment is effective also states that "relapse to drug use is the rule."[63] National data indicate that almost half of all heroin users in treatment have previously been in treatment three times or more. And almost 40 percent of cocaine users in treatment have previously been in treatment two or more times.[64] It is not exactly a ringing endorsement to say that failure is "the rule." Treatment programs seem to work for those clients who have made a personal commitment to get off drugs. Interviews with ex-addicts repeatedly reveal that they decided that the drug life was too much hassle, that they could not put up with it any more. In other words, treatment works for those who have decided to make it work. But treatment programs do not seem to be able to produce that change in personal commitment.[65]

The relapse problem arises with programs designed to treat alcoholism or smoking, reduce weight, or rehabilitate criminals. Millions of people try to give up smoking or lose weight every year. Most of them fail. In fact, most fail many times. We all know people who have made several efforts to quit smoking or lose weight. In some cases, however, they succeed. They finally quit smoking or lost the 20 pounds they always wanted to lose.

The challenge for effective treatment is to match the right program with the right client.[66] To a great extent, the "right" client is the person who has already made a commitment to change his or her life. But as one treatment expert puts it, "Little progress has been made in classifying drug users to identify what kinds of users will benefit most from particular kinds of programs."[67] If this sounds familiar, it is because it is another version of the prediction problem we have encountered several times before. As we have seen, bail decisions, selective incapacitation, probation, and parole all depend on identifying just the right people and only those people. Overpredicting produces false positives; underpredicting leads to false negatives. And as we have seen, the data and diagnostic tools are not available to us to make the precise predictions we want.

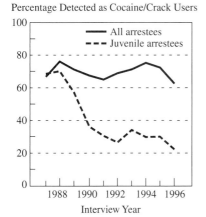
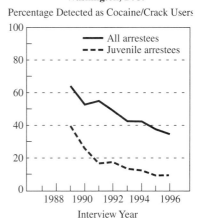

FIGURE 13-3 Cocaine use among arrestees, three cities, 1987–1996.

SOURCE: Andrew Lang Golub and Bruce D. Johnson, *Crack's Decline: Some Surprises across U.S. Cities* (Washington, DC: Government Printing Office, 1997).

This leads us to the following proposition:

PROPOSITION 47

Drug treatment can help individuals who have made a commitment to end their drug use. But there is no evidence that any treatment program consistently reduces drug use for all persons enrolled in the program.

But Something Positive *Has* Happened

Our review of drug policies so far has not turned up any policies that have demonstrated their effectiveness. But wait a minute: something positive *has* happened. Use of crack has declined substantially in many cities in the mid-1990s, and many criminologists believe that this is one of the factors—perhaps *the* factor—in the drop in the crime rate. In short, something has worked.

The ADAM program gives us very good data on illegal drug use among persons arrested. Figure 13-3 presents the findings on crack use among arrestees in Manhattan (New York City), and Washington, D.C.[68] Several points need to be emphasized. First, Manhattan is typical of many other cities in that the decline began first and was steepest among youthful (under age 18) offenders. This effect suggests that overall crack use in the city is likely to continue to drop as each cohort ages into adulthood. Second, crack use declined in Washington, D.C., despite the fact that its police department during these years was widely criticized for being disorganized and ineffective in dealing with crime. This effect suggests that the decline in crack usage is unrelated to police enforcement patterns. Third, crack use remained stable in Phoenix. In some other cities it rose during this period (Indianapolis, for example). This effect suggests that patterns in crack usage are highly sensitive to local factors, with very different trends in different cities.

What the ADAM data do *not* tell us is *why* crack usage has declined so significantly in so many cities. As we suggested in Chapter 1, several explanations are possible. New York City officials claim that it is because of their zero-tolerance crime policy. But as we have already suggested, this does not account for similar trends in other cities with very different enforcement patterns. The Clinton administration claims that the 100,000 new police officers are responsible. But the General Accounting Office and other critics point out that most of those officers have been hired in cities and towns that never had a serious drug or crime problem in the first place. Others claim that community policing is responsible. But there are very mixed reviews on the exact nature and impact of community policing programs across the country. Still others claim that our sentencing policies have reduced both drug use and crime through a combination of deterrence and incapacitation. But as we found in Chapters 6 and 7, there is no strong evidence to support that argument.

Another possible explanation is that crack simply went out of style—that it is no longer regarded as cool among those most likely to use it. A *New York Times* article suggested: "The crack epidemic behaved much like a fever: It came on strong, appearing to rise without hesitation, and then broke, just as the most dire warnings were being sounded."[69] This argument still does not answer the basic question, however. Why did the fever break? Why did crack go out of fashion? We cannot rule out the idea that a younger generation saw the damage it had done to the older kids in the neighborhood and decided not to let it happen to them. We cannot rule out the fact that enforcement played some part in that calculation: that they saw the effect of arrest and incarceration, in addition to the guns and the murders, and chose a different lifestyle.

LEGALIZE DRUGS?

By the 1980s, many thoughtful observers had concluded that the war on drugs was a disaster, particularly in terms of the impact on racial minority communities and the economic cost of the soaring prison population.[70]

These criticisms gave new life to the call to legalize drugs. Legalization is no longer something advocated by hippies left over from the 1960s. The advocates include prominent conservatives, such as the Nobel Prize–winning economist Milton Friedman and writer William F. Buckley. They are joined by civil libertarians, who agree with these conservatives on almost no other criminal justice issue.[71] The American Civil Liberties Union (ACLU) adopted a policy in 1994 calling for the "full and complete decriminalization of the use, possession, manufacture and distribution of drugs."[72]

The new debate over legalization was sparked by Ethan Nadelmann's 1989 article in *Science* magazine, "Drug Prohibition in the United States."[73] His case for legalization includes the following points: Criminal prohibition has not eliminated or even reduced drug use; we spend billions of dollars a year in this seemingly futile effort; the war on drugs produces numerous harmful side effects, including corruption and damage to poor and minority neighborhoods, prohibition of potentially beneficial medical uses of marijuana, and so on. The "logic of legalization," he argues, consists of two main points: that "most illegal drugs are not as dangerous as is commonly believed" and that abuse of the most dangerous drugs will not rise significantly under legalization.[74]

Public opinion on legalization is very mixed. Public opinion surveys have generally found that only about a quarter of the public support full legalization of marijuana, the softest of all drugs.[75] Yet nearly half approve of legalizing the medical use of marijuana. And in the 1996 elections, voters in California and Arizona approved referenda providing some legal use of medically prescribed marijuana.

Varieties of Legalization

The debate over legalization has been confused because the term means different things to different people. It is often used interchangeably with *decriminalization*. Both terms embrace a variety of specific proposals. The basic point of both is the removal of criminal penalties for the possession and sale of at least some currently illegal drugs. Beyond that, however, much disagreement prevails over four issues: (1) Are all drugs to be legalized, or only some? (2) Are possession *and* sale to be legalized, or only possession? (3) Will legalization apply to adults *and* juveniles, or just adults? (4) Will some kind of regulation replace criminal penalties, and if so, what kind?[76]

As Nadelmann points out, "There is no one legalization option."[77] Legalization *maximalists* take the extreme position, advocating legalization of both sale and possession of all drugs for juveniles as well as adults. Legalization *moderates* want to remove criminal penalties for the possession of many drugs, the sale of some drugs, but for adults only. Legalization *minimalists,* meanwhile, would eliminate penalties only for adult possession of marijuana and perhaps other less dangerous drugs. Finally, *agnostics* have not taken a final position on legalization but are convinced that current policy has failed and that we need a national debate on a new approach to drugs.[78]

Within this general framework are a number of different policy options. One approach is to give states the right to set their own drug policy, allowing them to experiment as they see fit. Doing this would abandon a national policy. Under a proposal drafted by Daniel K. Benjamin and Roger Leroy Miller, any conflict between federal and state laws would be resolved in favor of state law.[79] Another alternative would be to legalize particular drugs for medical use only. California and Arizona took a step in this direction in 1996. A more comprehensive option would have the government issue "user's licenses" to individuals who pass a required test.[80]

Except for radical libertarians, most legalization proposals would maintain some government regulation over drugs. The issue of regulation, however, is widely misunderstood. A wide range of "legal" products today are regulated (for example, tobacco and alcohol). Similarly, you cannot just buy a cow and sell milk from your front porch. These regulations are ultimately backed up by criminal penalties. It is illegal to sell cigarettes or beer to minors. Thus, legalization does not necessarily mean the complete elimination of all forms of government control or the threat of criminal punishment. But it does represent a shift in the basic direction of drug policy.

The Impact of Legalization

What would happen if we legalized drugs? Obviously, the answer depends on which form of legalization we are talking about. The effect of radical legalization would be very different from the moderate or conservative alternatives.

Whichever policy were adopted, these questions arise: (1) Would drug use increase or decrease? (2) Would predatory crime such as robbery and burglary increase or decrease? (3) How much money would in fact be saved? (4) What would happen to the drug-related criminal syndicates? (5) What would be the overall impact on the criminal justice system? (6) Would there be fewer violations of individual rights? (7) Finally, what would be the overall effect on the quality of life in the United States?

A Specific Proposal

To focus our discussion of these questions, let us examine a specific legalization proposal drafted by Richard B. Karel that appears in a collection of essays on the legalization debate.[81]

Karel proposes legalizing drugs only for adults and making distinctions among various drugs based on their toxicity and potential harm. He would completely legalize coca leaves, which could be sold in supermarkets "as tea is now sold." Granular cocaine would be illegal, but people could obtain cocaine gum similar to the nicotine gum currently available. Access would be rationed through an ATM-type system. You would have a card and you could "withdraw" so much per day or week. Crack cocaine would be completely illegal. Smokable and edible forms of opium would also be available through an ATM system. Heroin would be available to addicts, through either medical prescription or the ATM system, but PCP would remain illegal. Psychedelic drugs would be legally available to people who could demonstrate "knowledge as to their effects" through a written test and interview. The government would regulate the market by controlling distribution and ensuring product purity, much as the government now regulates alcohol and tobacco.

Karel's proposal falls somewhere in the moderate-to-conservative range of legalization alternatives. The most dangerous drugs—crack and PCP—would still be illegal. All drug use by and sale to juveniles would be illegal.

What would be the result? First, there would be an immediate and significant reduction in the number of arrests and persons sent to prison. This outcome would reduce the workload of the justice system and save a certain amount of money, particularly in terms of imprisonment costs. The dollar savings would be a lot less than many legalization advocates believe, however.

With cocaine still illegal for adults and all drugs illegal for juveniles, we would still maintain most of the present law enforcement apparatus. And we should not forget that police do a lot of other things besides investigate drug crimes. Criminal syndicates would probably not disappear, because they would still try to serve the demand for cocaine and other drugs that were still illegal. In short, many of the gains promised by legalization advocates—the dollar savings, the disappearance of the drug profits and the criminal syndicates—would not materialize.

Karel's proposal also makes some assumptions about drug users that are debatable. His scenario assumes that they are basically rational people, deciding to go to the clinic to get their ration of gum cocaine or methadone, much the way middle-class yuppies decide whether to buy domestic or imported beer. This scenario does not come to grips with the irrational and self-destructive nature of drug abuse. Among teenagers, drug and alcohol abuse are acts of rebellion. Among the underclass, heroin and cocaine abuse is a way of retreating from a brutal world with no apparent opportunities.

Would Karel's proposal reduce crime? In one limited sense, yes. By definition, it eliminates certain drug-defined crimes involving possession and sale. It is not likely to reduce drug-associated crimes such as robbery and burglary, however. As we already noted, most of this criminal behavior is part of a deviant lifestyle that is the product of many different factors. Relatively little predatory crime is directly caused by drugs, and legalization will not end that criminal behavior. Because crack would still be illegal, drug gangs would still engage in the same violent struggle for control of the market.

Let us move beyond Karel's proposal and discuss the legalization of all drugs. Would drug use increase? Much controversy exists over this question. Even Ethan Nadelmann, one of the leading legalization advocates, concedes, "It is thus impossible to predict whether or not legalization would lead to much greater levels of drug abuse."[82]

Opponents of legalization argue that a tremendous increase in drug use would result. They believe that existing criminal penalties curb drug use, both by the threat of arrest and punishment and because the criminal law represents a statement about society's values.[83] Some evidence, however, suggests that drug use would not increase. The National Household Survey clearly indicates that millions of Americans use illegal drugs every year without becoming heavy users, addicts, or criminals. They do not because the process of socialization operates somewhat effectively. They may engage in some minor deviance—casual drug use, vandalism, even some petty theft—but they do not cross over the line into addiction or criminality. Moreover, drug abuse is not rampant in those European countries that have relatively tolerant drug policies. These countries do not have the same level of crime the United States has, and their example may not be relevant in this context.

The danger, however, is that the mechanisms of socialization might be overwhelmed by legalization. In a suburban high school, for example, drug use could become so prevalent that peer pressure encourages pervasive cocaine use. As drug use increases, academic performance could decline, leading to a complete change in the culture of the school.

To a great extent, this is exactly what has already happened in many schools and neighborhoods. Drug use is so pervasive that it is extremely difficult for young people to resist the pressures to join. Drug-related crime contributes to the dreadful quality of neighborhood life. This is one of the main reasons that African-American leaders are some of the most vocal opponents of legalization. People such as Representative Charles Rangel, whose district includes Harlem, see a covert form of racism in the legalization idea.[84] They argue that it would abandon their communities to drugs.

The legalization issue is not completely polarized along racial lines. Kurt Schmoke, former mayor of Baltimore and an African American, is one of the leading advocates of an alternative to our current drug policy. In fact, his first-hand experience as a prosecutor convinced him of the futility of the war on drugs.[85] He and others argue that the war on drugs has already failed to protect poor neighborhoods. The calamity Rangel describes—of open drug trafficking and abuse, of rampant crime and violence—is already here.

One of the strongest arguments against the war on drugs is that it converts many otherwise law-abiding people into criminals. The Rand Corporation interviewed people arrested for drug offenses in Washington, D.C., and found that two-thirds held regular jobs. Drug dealing was essentially a part-time job. Their regular jobs paid an average of $11,000 to $14,000 a year, while they said they made an average of $24,000, tax free, from their drug dealing. The illegal drug markets represented a very tempting way to supplement their annual income. Looking at it another way, their $7-per-hour jobs were not adequate to support a decent lifestyle.[86] Legalizing drugs would eliminate this temptation to engage in criminal activity and save thousands of people from arrest and imprisonment and the subsequent problems associated with having a criminal record.

The full impact of legalization remains entirely a matter of speculation. This leads us to the following conclusion:

PROPOSITION 48

The impact of legalizing drugs on serious crime is not known at this time.

CONCLUSION

In the end, what can we recommend in the way of a sensible drug policy? The first step should be to face squarely the fact that we do not have any convincing evidence of a program or policy that has been proven effective in reducing drug abuse and crime associated with drugs. Politicians continually restate the same old policies ("longer prison terms," "more treatment") without any evidence regarding their effectiveness.

The starting point should be to recognize that we really do not have the answers at the moment. The major contribution of the advocates of legalization has been to force a wide-ranging discussion of our current drug policy. As Ronald Bayer argues, the advocates of legalization have "revitalized the public debate over the fundamental structure of American drug policy."[87] This is a major contribution. The Drug Policy Foundation's 1992 *National Drug Reform Strategy* calls for the creation of a national commission "to seriously examine alternatives to prohibition."[88]

The purpose of this book is to find policies that will reduce serious crime. As we have found, the drug-crime relationship is extremely complex. It does appear that most of the serious crime associated with drug use is not directly caused by drugs. Thus, even if we found a solution to the drug problem, we would probably still be faced with the crime problem.

NOTES

1. Elliott Currie, *Reckoning: Drugs, the Cities, and the American Future* (New York: Hill & Wang, 1992); Steven R. Donziger, ed., *The Real War on Crime: The Report of the National Criminal Justice Commission* (New York: HarperPerennial, 1996).

2. Dale Gieringer, "How Many Crack Babies?" in Arnold Trebach and Kevin B. Zeese, eds., *Drug Prohibition and the Conscience of Nations* (Washington, DC: Drug Policy Foundation, 1990), pp. 71–75.

3. Peter Reuter, "Drug Use Measures: What Are They Really Telling Us?," *National Institute of Justice Journal* (April 1999): 13. An extended discussion of methodologies and findings is in Thomas Mieczkowski, "The Prevalenceof Drug Use in the United States," in Michael Tonry, ed., *Crime and Justice: A Review of Research,* Vol. 20 (Chicago: University of Chicago Press, 1996), pp. 349–414.

4. Monitoring the Future, *Drug Trends in 1999 Among American Teens Mixed* 17 (December 1999).

5. Monitoring the Future, *Drug Trends in 1999 Among American Teens Mixed,* table 1b.

6. Reuter, "Drug Use Measures: What Are They Really Telling Us?"

7. Currie, *Reckoning.*

8. National Institute of Justice, *1998 Annual Report on Drug Use among Adult and Juvenile Arrestees* (Washington, DC: Government Printing Office, 1999).

9. Andrew Lang Golub and Bruce D. Johnson, *Crack's Decline: Some Surprises Across U.S. Cities* (Washington, DC: Government Printing Office, 1997).

10. Office of National Drug Control Policy, *Data Snapshot: Drug Abuse in America, 1998* (Washington, DC: Government Printing Office, 1998), plate 66.

11. David N. Nurco, Timothy W. Kinlock, and Thomas E. Hanlon, "The Drugs-Crime Connection," in James A. Inciardi, ed., *Handbook of Drug Control in the United States* (New York: Greenwood, 1990), pp. 71–90.

12. This typology is taken from Office of National Drug Control Policy, *Fact Sheet: Drug-Related Crime* (Washington, DC: Government Printing Office, 1994).

13. The data in this paragraph are summarized in Office of National Drug Control Policy, *Fact Sheet.*

14. Bureau of Justice Statistics, *Substance Abuse and Treatment of Adults on Probation, 1995* (Washington, DC: Government Printing Office, 1998).

15. Bureau of Justice Statistics, *Drugs, Crime, and the Justice System* (Washington, DC: Government Printing Office, 1992), p. 2.

16. David P. Farrington, "Predictors, Causes, and Correlates of Male Youth Violence," in Michael Tonry and Mark H. Moore, eds., *Youth Violence* (Chicago: University of Chicago Press, 1998), p. 431.

17. A good discussion of the different positions on drug policy is Peter Reuter, "Hawks Ascendant: The Punitive Trend of American Drug Policy," *Daedalus* 121 (Summer 1992): 15–52.

18. Mark H. Moore, "Controlling Criminogenic Commodities: Drugs, Guns, and Alcohol," in James Q. Wilson, ed., *Crime and Public Policy* (San Francisco: ICS Press, 1983), Chapter 8.

19. Marsha Rosenbaum, *Just Say What? An Alternative View on Solving America's Drug Problem* (San Francisco: National Council on Crime and Delinquency, 1989), p. 17.

20. Mark A. R. Kleiman, *Against Excess: Drug Policy for Results* (New York: Basic Books, 1992).

21. Ed Leuw, "Drugs and Drug Policy in the Netherlands," in Michael Tonry, ed., *Crime and Justice: A Review of Research,* vol. 14 (Chicago: University of Chicago Press, 1991), pp. 229–76.

22. Jerome G. Miller, *Search and Destroy: African American Males in the Criminal Justice System* (New York: Cambridge University Press, 1996); Donziger, ed., *The Real War on Crime.*

23. Michael Massing, *The Fix* (New York: Simon and Schuster, 1998).

24. Edna McConnell Clark Foundation, *Seeking Justice: Crime and Punishment in America* (New York: Edna McConnell Clark Foundation, 1995), p. 21.

25. Donziger, ed., *The Real War on Crime,* p. 99.

26. Department of Health and Human Services, *National Household Survey on Drug Abuse: Population Estimates 1995* (Washington, DC: Government Printing Office, 1996).

27. Donziger, *The Real War on Crime,* p. 115.

28. Michael Tonry, *Malign Neglect: Race, Crime, and Punishment in America* (New York: Oxford University Press, 1995), pp.

188–89; Bureau of Justice Statistics, *Sentencing in the Federal Courts: Does Race Matter?* (Washington, DC: Government Printing Office, 1993).

29. Daniel S. Nagin, "Criminal Deterrence Research at the Outset of the Twentieth Century," in Michael Tonry, ed., *Crime and Justice: A Review of Research,* V. 23 (Chicago: University of Chicago Press, 1998), pp. 1–37.

30. Lawrence W. Sherman, "Police Crackdowns: Initial and Residual Deterrence," in Michael Tonry and Norval Morris, eds., *Crime and Justice: A Review of Research,* vol. 12 (Chicago: University of Chicago Press, 1990), pp. 1–48.

31. Lynn Zimmer, "Proactive Policing Against Street-Level Drug Trafficking," *American Journal of Police* 9(1) (1990): 43–74.

32. "How Much Bang from TNT?" *Law Enforcement News* (31 December 1992).

33. Paul Hoffman, "The Feds, Lies, and Videotape," *Southern California Law Review* 66 (May 1993): 1453–532

34. University of Maryland, *Preventing Crime: What Works, What Doesn't, What's Promising* (Washington, DC: Government Printing Office, 1997), pp. 8–24.

35. Lorraine Greene, *Policing Places with Drug Problems* (Thousand Oaks, CA: Sage, 1996).

36. William J. Bennett, John J. DiIulio, and John P. Walters, *Body Count: Moral Poverty . . . And How to Win America's War Against Crime* (New York: Simon & Schuster, 1996), p. 189.

37. Office of National Drug Control Policy, *Drug Snapshot: Drug Abuse in America, 1998.*

38. Bureau of Justice Statistics, *Drugs, Crime, and the Justice System,* chap. 2.

39. Bureau of Justice Statistics, *Drugs, Crime, and the Justice System,* p. 36.

40. Peter Reuter, Gordon Crawford, and Jonathan Cave, *Sealing the Borders: The Effects of Increased Military Participation in Drug Interdiction* (Santa Monica, CA: Rand, 1988), p. xi.

41. Mark H. Moore, "Actually Prohibition Was a Success," in Rod L. Evans and Irwin M. Berent, eds., *Drug Legalization* (LaSalle, IL: Open Court, 1992), pp. 95–97.

42. Samuel Walker, *Popular Justice: A History of American Criminal Justice,* 2nd ed. (New York: Oxford University Press, 1998), pp. 158–59.

43. The Knapp Commission, *The Knapp Commission Report on Police Corruption* (New York: Braziller, 1973).

44. Bureau of the Census, *Statistical Abstract of the United States, 1998* (Washington, DC: Government Printing Office, 1998), p. 152.

45. See the Monitoring the Future data, which is partially reported in Office of National Drug Control Policy, *Data Snapshot: Drug Abuse in America, 1998.*

46. Bennett et al., *Body Count,* p. 187.

47. Gilbert J. Botvin, "Substance Abuse Prevention: Theory, Practice, and Effectiveness," in Michael Tonry and James Q. Wilson, eds., *Crime and Justice: An Annual Review of Research,* vol. 13 (Chicago: University of Chicago Press, 1990), pp. 474–77.

48. James O. Finckenauer, *Scared Straight and the Panacea Phenomenon* (Englewood Cliffs, NJ: Prentice Hall, 1982).

49. Jesse Greene, "Flirting with Suicide," *New York Times,* 15 September, 1996: p. 41.

50. Bureau of Justice Assistance, *An Introduction to DARE,* 2nd ed. (Washington, DC: Government Printing Office, 1991).

51. Bureau of Justice Statistics, *Law Enforcement Management and Administrative Statistics, 1997* (Washington, DC: Government Printing Office, 1999), p. xix.

52. Susan T. Emmett, Nancy Tobler, Christopher Ringwalt, and Robert L. Flewelling, "How Effective Is Drug Abuse Resistance Education? A Meta-Analysis of Project DARE Outcome Evaluations," *American Journal of Public Health* 84 (September 1994): 1394–401.

53. Richard R. Clayton, Carl G. Leukefeld, Nancy Grant Harrington, and Anne Cattarello, "DARE (Drug Abuse Resistance Education): Very Popular but Not Very Effective," in Clyde B. McCoy, Lisa R. Metsch, and James A. Inciardi, eds.,

Intervening with Drug-Involved Youth (Thousand Oaks, CA: Sage, 1996), p. 104.

54. Green, "Flirting with Suicide"; Bureau of the Census, *Statistical Abstract of the United States, 1998,* pp. 146–47.

55. Currie, *Reckoning,* pp. 247–51.

56. Greene, "Flirting with Suicide."

57. Office of National Drug Control Policy, *Data Snapshot: Drug Abuse in America, 1998,* plates 84, 86.

58. Bureau of Justice Statistics, *Drugs, Crime, and the Justice System,* p. 109.

59. George De Leon, "Treatment Strategies," in Inciardi, ed., *Handbook of Drug Control in the United States,* pp. 115–38; Bureau of Justice Statistics, *Drugs, Crime, and the Justice System,* pp. 107–11.

60. M. Douglas Anglin and Yih-Ing Hser, "Treatment of Drug Abuse," in Tonry and Wilson, eds., *Drugs and Crime* (Chicago: University of Chicago Press, 1990), p. 393.

61. De Leon, "Treatment Strategies," p. 120.

62. De Leon, "Treatment Strategies," p. 120.

63. De Leon, "Treatment Strategies," p. 127.

64. Office of National Drug Control Policy, *Data Snapshot: Drug Abuse in America, 1998,* panels 89, 90.

65. Currie, *Reckoning,* pp. 154–55.

66. Currie, *Reckoning,* pp. 132–33.

67. Anglin and Hser, "Treatment of Drug Abuse," p. 395.

68. Andrew Lang Golub and Bruce D. Johnson, *Crack's Decline: Some Surprises Across U.S. Cities* (Washington, DC: Government Printing Office, 1997).

69. Timothy Egan, "A Drug Ran Its Course, Then Hid With Its Users," *The New York Times,* 19 September 1999: 1.

70. Miller, *Search and Destroy.*

71. A history of the debate over decriminalization/legalization of drugs is in Ronald Bayer, "Introduction: The Great Drug Policy Debate—What Means This Thing Called Decriminalization?" in Ronald Bayer and Gerald M. Oppen-

heimer, eds., *Confronting Drug Policy: Illicit Drugs in a Free Society* (New York: Cambridge University Press, 1993), pp. 1–23.

72. American Civil Liberties Union, Board of Directors, "Minutes, April 9, 1994," ACLU Briefing Paper 19, *Against Drug Prohibition* (New York: ACLU, n.d.).

73. Ethan A. Nadelmann, "Drug Prohibition in the United States: Costs, Consequences, and Alternatives," *Science* 245 (September 1, 1989): 939–47.

74. Nadelmann, "Drug Prohibition in the United States," p. 943.

75. Bureau of Justice Statistics, *Sourcebook of Criminal Justice Statistics—1998,* p. 146

76. See the questions posed by James A. Inciardi, "The Case against Legalization," in Inciardi, ed., *The Drug Legalization Debate,* pp. 45–79.

77. Nadelmann, "Drug Prohibition in the United States," p. 939.

78. Drug Policy Foundation, *National Drug Reform Strategy* (Washington, DC: Drug Policy Foundation, 1992).

79. Cited in Arnold Trebach, "Thinking Through Models of Drug Legalization," in *The Drug Policy Newsletter* 23 (July/August 1994): 12.

80. These options are discussed by Trebach, "Thinking Through Models of Drug Legalization."

81. Richard B. Karel, "A Model Legalization Proposal," in Inciardi, ed., *The Drug Legalization Debate,* pp. 80–102.

82. Nadelmann, "Drug Prohibition in the United States," p. 944.

83. James Q. Wilson, "Against the Legalization of Drugs," *Commentary* 89 (February 1990): 21–28.

84. See the thoughtful discussion in William Kornblum, "Drug Legalization and the Minority Poor," in Bayer and Oppenheimer, eds., *Confronting Drug Policy,* pp. 115–35.

85. Kurt L. Schmoke, "Drugs: A Problem of Health and Economics," in David Boaz, ed., *The Crisis in Drug Prohibition* (Washington, DC: Cato Institute, 1990), pp. 9–12.

86. Peter Reuter, Robert MacCoun, and Patrick Murphy, *Money from Crime: A Study of the Economics of Drug Dealing in Washington, DC* (Santa Monica, CA: Rand, 1990).

87. Bayer, "The Great Drug Policy Debate," p. 20.

88. Drug Policy Foundation, *National Drug Reform Strategy.*

PART VI

❖

Conclusions

14

In the End:
What Works?

A s we enter the twenty-first century, we face an extraordinary paradox in crime policy. The crime rate has been falling steadily and dramatically since the early 1990s. In San Diego and New York City, the number of murders is the lowest it has been since the 1960s. Most other cities have experienced similar reductions in serious crime. This is a tremendous success story, one that we should all celebrate.

Events have contradicted the dire warnings of James Alan Fox about a "ticking time bomb" that would send violent crime rates even higher than their early-1990s peak. He and other criminologists predicted, on the basis of population trends, that a rising cohort of children would lead to soaring rates of juvenile gun violence.[1] Similarly, John J. DiIulio's frightening talk about "superpredators"—a group of utterly amoral and violent young criminals—now seems misguided.[2] Our streets have gotten safer rather than more dangerous.

And yet we cannot really explain why this has happened. To be sure, plenty of politicians and policy advocates with their own agenda claim to have answers, but we have precious little in the way of programs that have proven to be effective. Here it is useful to adopt the standard used by the University of Maryland *Preventing Crime* report: An effective program is one that has been independently evaluated, where the evaluation meets a high scientific standard, and where there are positive results that can be generalized to "similar settings in other times and places."[3] We have not found many programs that even begin to meet that test. The first proposition we offered in Chapter 1 still stands: "Most current crime control policies are nonsense." If that is true, how do we explain the dramatic decline in serious crime? Obviously, *something* is happening in American society. But what is it? What has caused crime rates, and violent crime rates in particular, to drop?

THE GREAT AMERICAN
PATERNITY FIGHT

As we argued in Chapter 1, we are witnessing a great paternity fight over falling crime rates. Everyone wants to take credit for the reduction in crime. President Bill Clinton claimed in 1997 that his administration's policies, particularly the 1994 Violent Crime Control Act, were responsible. Former New York City police commissioner William Bratton and his followers argue that the NYCPD's zero-tolerance policy toward minor quality-of-life offenses has sent a strong message that also helps reduce more serious crime.[4] Community policing advocates believe that their programs prevent crime. Conservatives across the country, meanwhile, argue that our massive imprisonment policy has successfully incapacitated repeat offenders. Death penalty advocates feel that the return of executions has deterred violent offenders. Supporters of DARE and other drug education programs believe that they have successfully discouraged illegal drug use.

There is an old cliché that says failure is an orphan but success has many parents. So it is with crime policy. Everyone wants to claim credit for our recent success. Our task is to sort our way through all of these claims, which are politically motivated on both sides, and try to develop a sensible explanation for the current crime trends.

A QUICK REVIEW
OF WHAT WE HAVE LEARNED

In response to the many claims of credit for reducing crime, let us review quickly some of what we have learned in this book.

Let us begin with policing, because that is the front line of the criminal justice system. The president of the United States claims that the funding for 100,000 additional police officers provided by the 1994 Violent Crime Control Act has played a major role in reducing crime. Yet we learned in Chapter 5 that simply adding more police does not prevent crime. Additionally, many of those new officers were hired in cities and towns that did not have serious crime problems to begin with. And, most important, we do not know what all the new officers are in fact doing out there on the street. We should be very skeptical about the claims made for the impact of the 100,000 officers.

Former police commissioner William Bratton, criminologist George Kelling, and others argue that the zero-tolerance policy adopted by Bratton in the NYCPD is responsible for reducing serious crime.[5] Several things are wrong with this argument, however. First, despite the claims of zero-tolerance advocates, the connection between minor offenses and murder is tenuous at best. Second, the reduction in crime began before Bratton was even appointed commissioner of the NYCPD. Third, a similar reduction in crime has occurred in San Diego, which added far fewer officers and has not adopted the aggressive zero-tolerance policy.[6] Crime is also down in Los Angeles, where, according to media reports, the police department is demoralized and making fewer arrests than in the past, and in Washington, D.C., where the police department has been very ineffective. The number of murders in Washington fell from 482 in 1991 to 260 in 1998. In short, we should be skeptical about the claims for zero-tolerance policing in New York City.

For decades, critics of the criminal justice system have been yelling that it is filled with "loopholes" that let dangerous criminals go free. Yet as we found in Chapter 8, the alleged loophole of plea bargaining is a myth. Similarly, the restrictions on police behavior imposed by the Supreme Court do not let thousands of dangerous criminals go free, as critics allege (Chapter 5).

Attempts to improve the effectiveness of criminal justice policy by improving our capacity to identify the truly dangerous criminals—those who are likely to go on to commit a high rate of serious crimes—have also failed. Our examination of the prediction problem, whether related to bail decisions or sentencing, found that our capacity to improve on decision making by officials is extremely limited. Human behavior is simply too complex and unpredictable to permit us to, for example, imprison only those criminals who are likely to become high-rate repeat offenders.

Since the early 1970s, we have had a virtual revolution in sentencing policy, marked primarily by the movement away from the highly discretionary indeterminate sentence and toward more tightly structured policies, particularly sentencing guidelines. Some of these reforms have included the abolition of discretionary parole release. Whatever the merits of these new sentencing policies for promoting more consistent sentences, there is no evidence that any of these changes are responsible for reducing serious crime.

Advocates of incapacitation believe that crime has fallen because so many repeat offenders are locked up in prison. Yet as we learned in Chapter 7, there is no solid persuasive evidence that incapacitation works as a crime reduction strategy. Even Zimring and Hawkins's study of imprisonment in California, which found some apparent incapacitative effect (but at a high social cost), could not clearly distinguish the precise causal relationship between imprisonment trends and crime rates.[7] Moreover, when you look at trends in incarceration rates, you find that the imprisonment binge began 20 years ago. If incapacitation works, the effects should have begun to appear at least by the early 1980s, not the mid-1990s.

The most extreme manifestation of our obsession with harsh sentencing was the appearance of so-called "three strikes" laws in the early 1990s. The evidence, however, indicates that most of these laws are not even used, mainly because they are so extreme, and where they have been used have no measurable impact on the crime rate.

Many of these policies have been a part of the "war on drugs." Yet there is no persuasive evidence that any reduce either illegal drug use or serious crime. And there is considerable evidence that the war on drugs has done serious damage to our society.

The DARE program is extremely popular with parents, police, and politicians. Yet as we learned in Chapter 13, evaluations of DARE have consistently failed to find any significant impact on illegal drug use.

Liberals continue to place their hopes in the traditional rehabilitation-oriented programs, including primarily probation and parole. Many continue to believe that they can be made to work effectively if they are simply improved in the right way. And yet there are no treatment programs that can demonstrate consistent effectiveness in reducing criminal behavior. Many clients fail to complete programs, and recidivism rates are high for those who do complete them. Treatment programs run afoul of another aspect of the prediction problem. In this case, it is a matter of matching particular offenders with programs that will effectively address their needs. Yet treatment programs generally deal with broad categories of offenders.

Intensive probation or parole supervision has long captured the hopes of many advocates of rehabilitation. Yet as we learned in Chapter 11, intensive supervision seems to be no more effective in producing rehabilitation. Even worse, intensive supervision and many of the other new intermediate punishments—boot camps, electronic monitoring—have become almost entirely control oriented, with little emphasis on rehabilitation.

In short, many claims are made for effective crime reduction programs, but the evidence to support these claims is weak at best. This conclusion, however, leaves the basic paradox unresolved. If crime control programs do not work, then why is crime down? The answer is that it may be difficult to specify a direct cause, at least in a way that would satisfy most social scientists. The fact is that human behavior changes in fundamental ways over the long term. Historians believe that serious crime and disorder in all industrial societies fell from the mid–nineteenth century until the post–World War II period.[8] Why? Police and prisons probably had little to do with it. A more general "civilizing" effect of the new urban society seems to have taken hold: pervasive patterns of work and daily life that disciplined behavior. Historians also agree that crime and disorder in all societies turned upward after World War II. Why? The answers are not clear, but it certainly was not any single cause, such as television (to name one popular villain).

It may be that we are at the onset of another broad change in behavior. Not only is crime down, but many other social indicators have been moving in a positive direction since the early 1990s. Teenage pregnancy is down. New AIDS cases are down. Infant mortality has fallen steadily since the early 1970s. The high school dropout rate has fallen, and the African-American dropout rate is half what it was 30 years ago. Unemployment is down.[9] We may not be able to identify a single cause of this generally positive picture, but it should give us pause about making claims for the effectiveness of any one crime policy, or even any combination of crime policies. Crime policy, for example, should have no direct impact on teenage pregnancy or AIDS. We need to look outside the criminal justice system for an explanation of this general social trend.

CRIME PREVENTION:
THE MARYLAND REPORT

The most comprehensive survey of the effectiveness of crime prevention programs is a 1997 report to Congress, *Preventing Crime,* by faculty from the University of Maryland.[10] As its subtitle indicates, it sought to identify what works, what does not, and what is promising. The primary purpose was to help Congress better understand the effectiveness of the nearly $4 billion a year that the U.S. Department of Justice spends on crime prevention. This figure is only one small part of the more than $100 billion (1992 data) that the country spends at all levels of government on criminal justice.

Preventing Crime identifies seven "institutional settings" in which crime prevention programs operate: communities, families, schools, labor markets, places (in the sense of "specific premises"), police, and criminal justice. The last setting includes a wide array of criminal justice system programs, including punishment-oriented programs such as imprisonment. The authors of the report properly note that the distinction between "prevention" and "punishment" is an artificial one. These terms represent different means to the same end: reduction in crime. Each of these institutional settings is the subject of a long chapter devoted to the relevant literature.

What did the Maryland team learn? Their systematic review of the literature found that some things work, a lot of programs do not, and, most important, there is a lot we do not know. Many crime prevention programs have not been studied at all, or have been studied imperfectly, or have been studied in ways that do not address larger questions of context (such that the impact of the program in question cannot be precisely determined). Many of the report's conclusions are similar to those in this book.

One clear pattern emerges from the *Preventing Crime* report, although the authors shy away from its political implications. Repeatedly, the report finds that the programs that do seem to work are most effective with the people and communities that need these programs the least. Consistently, their evidence points to solutions that lie outside the criminal justice system. Chapter 3, for example, concludes that "in study after study, evidence emerges that crime prevention programs are more likely to take root, and more likely to work, in communities that need them the least."[11] Moreover, "communities with the greatest crime problems are also the hardest to reach through innovative program efforts." The heart of the crime problem lies in the "underlying structural conditions" in high-crime areas.

Chapter 4 on family-oriented crime prevention programs points in the same direction. The Maryland team concludes that although some programs show promise, "whether these programs, by themselves, can overcome the effects of surrounding a family with a high-crime community is unclear."[12] A similar conclusion is reached in Chapter 5 about school-focused crime prevention programs. Some programs show promise of effectiveness, but "too many schools are overwhelmed by a criminogenic community context."[13] Common sense suggests that, as with communities, crime prevention programs are most likely to succeed with families and schools that are already basically stable and healthy. But the same interventions are much less likely to succeed in contexts that are swamped by crime and its related problems.

Chapter 6 on labor markets provides a context for the conclusions in other chapters and, at the same time reveals the major weakness of the entire report. The authors argue that "of all the dimensions of neighborhood life, this one [jobs, work] may have the most pervasive influence on crime."[14] This is hardly startling news. You do not need to be a criminologist to understand that having work and prospects for the future (as opposed to having neither) makes all the difference in your life and the life of your neighborhood. It is the lack of work, in the sense of the pervasive lack of employment opportunities (including jobs with prospects for advancements, not just dead-end jobs at the local fast-food restaurant), that defines our high-crime neighborhoods. Sociologist William Julius Wilson develops this argument in his book, *When Work Disappears.*[15] It is the lack of work that defines the "structural conditions" that limit the impact of the few successful community, family, and school-oriented programs that the report reviews. And it is entirely possible that the booming economy of the 1990s, which has produced record low unemployment rates, is ultimately responsible for the drop in serious crime.

Chapter 9 of *Preventing Crime* covers many of the same criminal justice programs examined in this book (although in a far more comprehensive fashion). It also finds "little evidence that increased incarceration has reduced crime" but is far more optimistic about the effectiveness of corrections-based drug treatment programs, prison-based rehabilitation programs, and the institutionalization of some juvenile offenders.[16]

The report's discussion of policing simultaneously contains some of the most hopeful news about crime policy and reveals a serious flaw in the overall report. It argues, as we did in Chapter 5, that simply adding more police will accomplish little but that clearly focused crime prevention programs appear to have genuine potential.[17] It does warn that too heavy-handed an approach (in the sense of overly aggressive policing, or abuse of citizens) can backfire, however, by undermining confidence in the police and respect for law.

Nonetheless, there is evidence of success in some problem-oriented programs. As we point out in Chapter 5, the key element of these programs is that they are multi-faceted, using a variety of different agencies and non-criminal justice remedies. The Oakland SMART program, for example, used aggressive housing code enforcement to clean up drug "hot spots" and included a program for training landlords. Similarly, the problem-oriented drug enforcement program in Jersey City, New Jersey, encouraged police officers to develop creative solutions to neighborhood quality of life issues. Many of the activities officers chose did not involve traditional criminal law enforcement but rather such things as seeing that garbage was picked up and that parks were maintained.[18]

The apparent lesson appears to be that some crime reduction programs can work, but they need to focus on particular places and simultaneously address a range of different problems, using more than just criminal justice strategies.

This is good news. But we should not ignore the larger context. The most serious flaw in the Maryland report is that it places virtually all of its hopes in police programs. The authors argue that once such programs achieve a certain "threshold level of public order and safety," other programs oriented toward families, community, schools, and labor markets might become more effective. The problem with this conclusion is that it ignores the clear message of other sections of the report. The authors make policing the linchpin for all other crime prevention efforts. Unfortunately, this emphasis asks too much of the police. They may be able to accomplish some good things, but it is unreasonable to expect them to save our society—and to save our poorest neighborhoods in particular.

Most important, in placing so much hope in the police, the authors of *Preventing Crime* ignore their earlier conclusions. After reviewing community, family, and school-based crime prevention programs, they repeatedly argue that even the successful programs are overwhelmed by the "structural conditions" of the neighborhoods in which they operate. They are very clear in their conclusion that programs are more likely to work in communities that need them least. It is equally reasonable to conclude what the authors refuse to: that police programs are more likely to be successful in the neighborhoods that need them least (that is, those with relatively less crime). Police crime prevention programs in neighborhoods that need them most are likely to be overwhelmed by the same "underlying structural conditions."

The report's refusal to address seriously these "underlying structural conditions" is clearly evident in the chapter on labor markets. Although the authors argue persuasively that work is the most important single factor relative to crime, they refuse to discuss policies designed to increase the availability of work. They cover various programs designed to fix people up to get jobs but not job creation programs.

There is a reason for this omission. To address the larger question of economic opportunity is to move the discussion of crime prevention out of the realm of criminal justice and into the world of social and economic policy. It would also point in the direction of some radical alternatives to current economic policy. The authors of *Preventing Crime* choose to focus on more limited issues.

But what if their conclusions in the sections on communities, families, and schools are right? What if the key to crime prevention really is the "underlying structural conditions"? What if William Julius Wilson is right in his closely related analysis that programs designed to help people and neighborhoods are doomed to fail "when work disappears"?

CONCLUSION

The purpose of this book has been to identify sensible policies to reduce serious crime. We found that most current crime policies and proposed alternatives are not effective. We found that both conservatives and liberals are guilty of peddling nonsense with respect to crime policy. And yet serious crime is down all across the country. The challenge now is just as great as it was when crime was at its worst. We still need to sort through the loud claims of success made by the advocates of different policies and look for solid evidence of what works.

Experts in criminal justice have a professional obligation to search for the truth and to speak the truth, even though most people would prefer not to hear it. The truth about crime policy seems to be that most criminal justice–related policies will not make any significant reduction in crime. If we have helped discover that truth in this book, we have fulfilled our professional responsibilities.

NOTES

1. James Alan Fox, *Trends in Juvenile Violence* (Washington, DC: Government Printing Office, 1996).

2. William J. Bennett, John J. DiIulio, Jr., and John P. Walters, *Body Count* (New York: Simon & Schuster, 1996), pp. 25–34.

3. University of Maryland, *Preventing Crime* (Washington, DC: Government Printing Office, 1997), p. 2–20.

4. William Bratton and Peter Knoblach, *Turnaround* (New York: Random House, 1998).

5. George Kelling and Catherine M. Coles, *Fixing Broken Windows* (New York: Kessler, 1996).

6. Gary Cordner, "Problem Oriented Policing vs Zero Tolerance," in Tara O'Connor and Anne C. Grant, eds., *Problem-Oriented Policing* (Washington, DC: Police Executive Research Forum, 1998), pp. 303–14.

7. Franklin E. Zimring and Gordon Hawkins, *Incapacitation: Penal Confinement and the Restraint of Crime* (New York: Oxford University Press, 1995).

8. Samuel Walker, *Popular Justice: A History of American Criminal Justice*, 2d ed. (New York: Oxford University Press, 1998).

9. Marc Miringoff and Marque-Luisa Miringoff, *The Social Health of the Nation: How America Is Really Doing* (New York: Oxford University Press, 1999).

10. University of Maryland, *Preventing Crime*.

11. University of Maryland, *Preventing Crime*, pp. 2–10.

12. University of Maryland, *Preventing Crime,* pp. 2–10.

13. University of Maryland, *Preventing Crime,* pp. 2–11.

14. University of Maryland, *Preventing Crime,* pp. 2–12.

15. William Julius Wilson, *When Work Disappears* (New York: Knopf, 1996).

16. University of Maryland, *Preventing Crime,* pp. 2–14.

17. University of Maryland, *Preventing Crime,* chap. 8.

18. Anthony A. Braga, David L. Weisburd, Elin J. Waring, Lorraine Green Mazerolle, William Spelman, and Francis Gajewski, "Problem-Oriented Policing in Violent Crime Places: A Randomized Controlled Experiment," *Criminology* 37.3 (1999): 541–80.

Index